All that I am,
praise the LORD;
everything in me,
praise his holy name.

PSALM 103:1 NCV

Introduction

God encourages us in his Word to give thanks in all things at all times. That's not a mistake. When we choose to focus on things we are grateful for, our satisfaction in life increases. Comparisons cease. Unnecessary pursuits pause. And we begin to notice the little things. The things that matter. Life. Breath. Connection. Kindness. Beauty. This is where we find deep intimacy with God.

As you reflect on these devotional entries, scriptures, and prayers, refocus your perspective and meditate on things that produce life and joy, that bring peace and comfort. Spend the beginning and end of your day with God, experiencing his goodness and being refreshed in his presence. Be encouraged as you take time to ponder how wonderfully unique and abundantly blessed you are.

Evaluate each day in the light of God's truth. Stand in awe of a God who gives beyond your wildest dreams. From the time you wake up, until the time you fall into bed at night, let your heart be filled with praise for his many blessings and wonders.

True Identity

Your eyes beheld my unformed substance.
In your book were written
all the days that were formed for me,
when none of them as yet existed.

PSALM 139:16 NRSV

You were created with intention, your being knit together with love and honor. You are not an accident! You are fearfully and wonderfully made, and there is no other like you. God saw your life unfolding before you even took your first breath. He is your life-source.

Will you come to him with all your questions and doubts and lay them out before him? He can handle each and every one. As you lay them down, line your lips with praise. You are his! You are a child of the Living God, and he is your faithful Father. Let your heart come alive as you let your imagination run wild with the truth that you were created in Love's image.

Creator, I am so thankful that you made me, not just to survive life but to thrive in it through a relationship with you. I won't stop praising you for the gift of life!

You saw who you created me to be before I became me!
Before I'd ever seen the light of day,
the number of days you planned for me
were already recorded in your book.

PSALM 139:16 TPT

Holy Father, as your child, I won't stop coming to you for my daily bread. You know my needs before they even reach my consciousness. Thank you for your provision today. Thank you for your persistent presence that illuminates the beauty of fellowship with you.

You walk with me, no matter what path I find myself on or the circumstances I face. I trust you to guide me in spirit and in truth all the days of my life. You have already seen every possibility, so I will rely on your loving leadership to direct me in wisdom. Your ways are embedded in faithfulness. Help me to be rooted in my identity as a child of God. Your Word is better than any other!

How does your identity as a child of God
affect how you live in the day-to-day?

My Sustainer

Preserve me, O God,
for in you I put my trust.

PSALM 16:1 NKJV

There is no amount of hardship or depth of pain that, when we look to God, he will not help us with. He is healer, sustainer, and restorer. He will not let us be taken out by the intensity of our circumstances when we put our trust in him. It doesn't matter how strong the storm that we are facing, his grace is more powerful. His mercy meets us in every season of the soul.

Let us put our hope in God, for he is our Savior. He will keep us safe in the refuge of his presence. He will restore our peace with his nearness, and our hearts will be continually filled with courage as we remember his power, as well as his goodness. Let us offer him our trust over and over again. He is faithful, he is worthy, and he is full of mighty power!

God, you are my strong shelter. I hide myself in your unchanging nature again today. You who are full of mercy, protect me from the schemes of the enemy. I trust in you!

Keep me safe, my God,
for in you I take refuge.

PSALM 16:1 NIV

My God, I have put all my hope in you. You are bigger and better than any grand plans I could come up with on my own. Your love is consistent and full of kindness. Your compassion runs deeper than any rebellion I have in my heart. Thank you for that! What wonderful news that I could never exhaust your mercy. I trust you to meet me with your love every time I turn toward you. You promise to never abandon me, and I rely on your nearness more than I can say.

There is no one else who is as persistently patient or as unfailingly caring as you. You are my safe place, and I can let down my guard in your presence. As I prepare myself for sleep, flood my being with your peace that passes all understanding. Give me rest as I take refuge in you. Keep me close and keep me secure. I am yours!

Do you trust God to take care of what you cannot control?

Abundance

*God is able to bless you abundantly,
so that in all things at all times,
having all that you need,
you will abound in every good work.*

2 CORINTHIANS 9:8 NIV

Are there times when you feel more able to trust God's goodness and provision than others? Though you may go through seasons of plenty and those of lack, God is always full of abundance. His resources never wane; the storehouses of his mercy are overflowing at all times. Whatever it is that you have need of today, God has more than enough to meet your need.

Meditate on the Word today: "so that in all things at all times, having all that you need." Remember, you have access to all that you require today, no matter the realities that you are facing. Put your trust in him, for he is your generous provider!

Great God, thank you for your generosity toward your children. I give you all my worries, because I know that you are more than enough for all that I need. Meet me with your abundance today!

God is more than ready to overwhelm you with every form of grace, so that you will have more than enough of everything— every moment and in every way. He will make you overflow with abundance in every good thing you do.

2 CORINTHIANS 9:8 TPT

God of abundance, you are the source of every good thing. I could never exhaust your mercy or reach the end of your love. It is more than I can comprehend! Thank you for the way that you met me today with your goodness. You are always full of kindness; I don't want to ever forget it. Your grace empowers me to do all that I need to do.

I am so grateful that when I fill up on your mercy, there is more than enough to overflow from my life to others. Thank you for the clear indicators of your generosity in my life. May I reflect the abundance of your kingdom on earth as it is in heaven.

How have you seen God's lavish grace show up in your life?

Never Abandoned

I had said in my alarm,
"I am cut off from your sight."
But you heard the voice of my pleas for mercy
when I cried to you for help.

PSALM 31:22 ESV

When the dark of night comes, and the shadows start messing with our minds, we may find that our beliefs begin to be dictated by our fears. But even the blackest night is as clear as the brightest day to the Lord. He is unchanging, and his love has not wavered for even a moment. He sees what we cannot.

Will we trust him to lead us? Will we give him our fear and press into the peace of his presence? He has not left us. He will never abandon us. As we turn our attentions to him, we will find that his comfort descends like a blanket over us. He is ever so close. May we see with eyes of faith, trusting that his purposes and plans have not changed even when our circumstances have.

God of mercy, I cry out to you when I feel anxiety rise within me. I trust that you have not changed a bit! You are good, you are present, and you are for me. Reveal your nearness to me again today.

In panic I cried out,
"I am cut off from the LORD!"
But you heard my cry for mercy
and answered my call for help.

PSALM 31:22 NLT

Lord, I'm so grateful that you answer my call for help every time I cry to you. You have not left me alone in the face of my trials or troubles. What a beautiful friendship this is! Thank you for always being available whenever I need you. Though panic may move me for a moment, your peace keeps me within your grip of grace forever. There is nowhere I could wander that your love would not reach me.

I am undone by the kindness of your affection toward me. You are consistent and kind, an ever-present help in times of trouble. You will never abandon me. Continue to rewrite my understanding of your love without conditions, which is so much better than any other love I've ever known. You are so worthy of my trust. Thank you for being with me, for extending your tangible mercy into my life, and for guiding me with tenderness. Fill my mind with your unmatched truths as I continue to meditate on you and give me greater glimpses into your glory.

How has God answered your cries for help?

Resurrection Life

If while we were still enemies, God fully reconciled us to himself through the death of his Son, then something greater than friendship is ours. Now that we are at peace with God, and because we share in his resurrection life, how much more we will be rescued from sin's dominion!

ROMANS 5:10 TPT

What does it mean to be fully reconciled to God? With nothing to get in the way of his wonderful love in our lives, he has done all that was required in order to restore the relationship we were always meant to have with him. This is more than friendship; it is freedom.

When Adam and Eve first walked with God in the garden, theirs was a perfect relationship. There was trust, honor, and love. There was unhindered fellowship. This is what we have through Christ. We share in his resurrection life and power, and we have been set free from the sin that entangled and kept us from walking in the liberty of love.

Jesus Christ, you are the way, the truth, and the life. I come to the Father through you, and I find my true belonging in fellowship with your Spirit. You have conquered the grave, and I am more than a conqueror in you!

Since our friendship with God was restored by the death of his Son while we were still his enemies, we will certainly be saved through the life of his Son.

ROMANS 5:10 NLT

Son of God, you are the one that liberates my soul. I dance in the freedom that you have given me! There is nothing I could offer you that would make you love me more, and there is nothing I could do that would make you love me less. I am loved by the God over all. What a wonderful truth! I am set free by the mercy of your heart. I am free to live, to love, and to grow.

Thank you for the overcoming power of your life, Lord. I don't rely on my own strength or resources to live an unhindered life; it is your resurrection power that has released me from the chains of sin and death. There is so much grace in you! I'm overwhelmed by the thought that your grace, mercy, and love never run dry. Thank you for restoration of life and purpose. Your ways are beautiful!

Are there any areas of your life
where freedom is still needed?

Come Close

Let us then with confidence draw near to the throne of grace,
that we may receive mercy and find grace to help in time of need.

HEBREWS 4:16 ESV

No matter what is going on in our lives, we can always approach God with the confidence of dearly loved children. He always makes space for us; he will never turn us away. Though our focus is limited, God's is not. He is not too busy to give us the consideration and care we need in every moment.

So then, whatever our worries, whatever our joys, we can come to him knowing that we have his attention. He is ready to pour out his mercy to strengthen us. He is ready with grace to empower us for every circumstance we face. May we never forget how fully loved and accepted we are. As his children, we need not linger at the periphery of his presence. Every time we draw near to him, he comes in even closer than we could imagine. Draw near today and be met by his overwhelming kindness.

Good Father, I approach your throne of grace with confidence today, knowing that you will receive me with delight. You are better than my expectations, and you always meet me with mercy. Come close as I draw near!

Let us come boldly to the throne of our gracious God.
There we will receive his mercy,
and we will find grace to help us when we need it most.

HEBREWS 4:16 NLT

Gracious God, your kindness is like anointing oil seeping into my pores. It both covers and fills me. I am grateful for your mercy that greets me every time my awareness is turned toward you. I am surprised by the abundance of your grace over and over again, though I should be used to it by now! Your goodness is immeasurable. If I could store up every evidence of your kindness toward me, it would just be a drop in the bottomless bucket of your love.

Whenever I feel shame's pull to hide from you, remind me that in you, all is made new. You are never surprised by me, and you won't ever turn me away. I won't stop coming to you. As our relationship builds, may the constancy of your affection keep me close to your heart. I don't ever want to forget how wonderful you are!

Where do you need God's grace in your life?

Shared Burden

If one part suffers, every part suffers with it;
if one part is honored, every part rejoices with it.

1 CORINTHIANS 12:26 NIV

Pain can be an isolating experience, but the burden of suffering was never meant to be carried alone. When we share our weighty problems with each other, it is easier to bear. Just as rejoicing is best done with others (who doesn't love a celebration?), our sorrows are also invitations for leaning on others.

God's love is not meant to just be experienced on an individual level. We get to know God's tangible mercy in the context of relationships with others. We are part of a family: a community of believers. When we fall, we do it as a unit. When we rise, we do it together. Do not hide your pain from those who would witness it today. Let them help, lightening the weight of your problems as you walk hand-in-hand toward healing. There is triumph in the overwhelming grace that God offers us, and all the more when we experience it in the context of community!

Faithful One, thank you for the reminder of the power of solidarity today. Help me to be vulnerable with trusted friends instead of trying to bear my pain alone.

Whatever happens to one member happens to all.
If one suffers, everyone suffers.
If one is honored, everyone rejoices.

1 CORINTHIANS 12:26 TPT

Lord, my constant companion, I have been leaning on your love to keep me afloat. I realize that I was not meant to bear the burden of my pain and suffering alone. Thank you for community. I ask that you continue to build it around me, and that I would know the safety of relationships with those who love you.

I have known the relief of comfort from loved ones, and I recognize the power of being able to offer the same to others. Keep me close in your kindness, that I may be moved with compassion whenever I recognize another's pain. Your love is made pure in my life when I offer it to others. There is always movement in it; it is not stagnant. May my heart stay soft and open in mercy. I don't want to miss out on what you're doing in your people because I am caught up in my own life. I lean on you, and I will lean on your people, as well as I help carry their loads.

When was the last time you asked a trusted person for help?

Test It Out

Do not believe every spirit, but test the spirits, whether they are of God; because many false prophets have gone out into the world.

1 JOHN 4:1 NKJV

We walk with wisdom as our guide. We are not helpless to the ways of the world or blown about by the winds of its ever-shifting expectations. We are secure on the foundation of God's Word. He has given us keys to his kingdom, and we are able to discern what aligns with him and what does not.

The fruit of the Spirit is a clear indicator of one who walks with the Lord. We should not blindly believe what one preaches as truth if their life does not align in God's love. God's standards are better than our own—full of mercy and kindness but also justice and truth. He is the only wise judge. He does not ask us to condemn others; rather, he instructs us to be wise about what we believe is from him. There is grace in the process, as with all things. May we press into the knowledge of the Lord more and more as we look for his likeness in others.

Lord, I recognize that I don't always test out the things I believe. Give me wisdom, that I may walk in the light of your truth and the power of your love in all things.

Do not believe every spirit,
but test the spirits to see whether they are from God,
because many false prophets have gone out into the world.

1 John 4:1 NIV

God, thank you for the reminder that I not only know your character, as displayed in your Word, but that I also can discern the spirits behind popular beliefs. Help me to be wise, so that I don't grab at the things that appease me in my humanity. Help me to be discerning, so that I do not judge others because I don't understand their life experiences. Their lives are marked by your love and mercy, too.

As I fellowship with you, teach me what it means to be like you in love. Give me your unparalleled perspective that takes into account what I don't consider. You are infinitely better than I'll ever be, and your motives are pure. I bind my heart to yours, and I will listen to your tender correction. As you break down the lies of misleading viewpoints that I have been holding onto, fill my mind with your peace and truth. Your ways lead to wholeness, life, and freedom. I will follow you!

How do you test the beliefs that you hold?

Capable

Using the Scriptures, the person who serves God will be capable,
having all that is needed to do every good work.

2 TIMOTHY 3:17 NCV

There is an abundance of wisdom for all who seek it. In God's Word, we are given the keys to his kingdom, and we are taught to recognize his unmistakable nature. No matter the problems we face, there are solutions to be found in God's living Word. He has not finished communicating with us; he is still speaking today. Whatever it is that we need, we will find encouragement in the Scriptures.

As we ask the Holy Spirit to illuminate the eyes of our hearts, we will understand with revelation-light what God is expressing to us now. His living and active Word is applicable to our lives in this moment in time. His unchanging character is timeless. We have all we need in our fellowship with God, and his Word is a beautiful reflection of his interaction with us.

Living Word, speak to me today. I know that you are alive and well, and that you are still moving in the same ways that you were in the Scriptures. Meet me with your love and truth!

*You will be God's servant, fully mature and perfectly prepared
to fulfill any assignment God gives you.*

2 TIMOTHY 3:17 TPT

Loving Lord, I have all I need in you. Your Word shows me all
that awaits me in a relationship with you. What a wonderful
gift! You are so very patient in love, and you are consistent in
mercy. I would not know what you were like if it weren't for
the Scriptures. Thank you for access to your nature through
Spirit and truth.

May my life continually align with your love as I discover
more of who you are. May I grow in wisdom and
understanding as I meditate on your Word. May I be perfectly
prepared to do all that you call me to do as I learn to be more
like you. I lack no good thing because I have access to you!
You are wonderful, and your Word is like sweet honey to
my soul. It satisfies what man's empty words cannot. Keep
teaching me as I look to you.

Can you recall a time when God's Word
pierced your heart with its relevance?

Come Again

My life's strength melts away with grief and sadness;
come strengthen me and encourage me with your words.

PSALM 119:28 TPT

In the depths of grief, when we cannot see past our sorrow, there is a friend who sticks closer than a sibling. The Spirit, our comforter, strengthens us with grace and encourages us with the honey of God's Word. He speaks what is true, filled with love and tenderness toward us. He lifts us up with the kindness of his truth; he never beats us down with shame. As our strength wanes, he comes and breathes his life into us.

There is no better comfort than the comfort that he gives. He knows just what to say when we are at a loss for words. He knows exactly what to do when we don't know what we need. He is everything we long for; in fact, he is the perfection of every longing. How could we not feel love brought to life in the communion of Spirit to spirit? The depth of his love overwhelms the depth of our loss—every single time. His presence is a balm that both soothes and heals us.

Comforter, come to me again with the tangible relief of your presence. Meet me with the peace and love that always accompanies you.

I weep with sorrow;
encourage me by your word.

PSALM 119:28 NLT

Holy Spirit, when my eyes are heavy with sorrow, wrap me into the embrace of your close comfort. I know that you are near. I have to believe that you have not changed even if everything around me feels like it has. Speak your words of life to my exhausted heart. Encourage me with your love that is close to the brokenhearted. Mend my wounded heart with the oil of your presence.

When I have no strength to stand on my own, let alone walk anywhere, will you draw near and carry me through? Though I am depleted, you are still abundant in love and mercy. I depend on you, God; there is no one else who can offer what you do. You are the one I rely on through every season of the soul; in the highs and the lows of this life, you are my daily bread. Let me catch a glimpse of your kindness for me. Let me know your nearness, Lord!

How have you known God's comfort in your life?

Rooted in Goodness

I certainly believed that I would see the goodness of the Lord
In the land of the living.

Psalm 27:13 NASB

When nothing good can be seen, and all the light of life turns to darkness in the deep valley of sorrow and suffering, there is still relief in the nearness of the Lord. He has not left us to be consumed by grief, and he won't let it be the end of our hope. Dark nights do not last forever. Winter seasons eventually give way to the dawn of new life. God will never stop restoring and redeeming that which is broken and seems lost. His power is marked by resurrection life.

We can be sure, as long as we live, that we will see the goodness of the Lord again. Suffering may last for a time, but joy will come in the morning. There is no lasting reason to despair when our lives are marked by the deliverance of our saving God. He won't stop working his redemption miracles.

Redeemer, I depend on your goodness in my life. I know that no matter what I am going through, I have not reached the end of your love. Show me your miracle-working power again!

I totally trust you to rescue me one more time,
so that I can see once again how good you are
while I'm still alive!

PSALM 27:13 TPT

Savior, I you are the one that I rely upon in life. Only you can rescue me from the pit of despair that threatens to swallow me up. Lift me into your comforting arms of love again tonight. Wrap me in the warmth of your affection. I long to know your present goodness with me. Give me eyes to see where you are, ears to hear what you are saying, and a heart that understands how marvelous your love is.

I want to taste your overwhelming kindness in a clear and tangible way. Will you meet me with the tenderness of your Spirit and soothe my wearied heart? I trust you, Lord, to rescue me from what I cannot outrun. I know that you will keep me safe. I know you will! I'm putting all my hope in you again, for you haven't failed me yet.

When was the last time you were overwhelmed
by the goodness of God?

Always Good

The LORD is good to those whose hope is in him,
to the one who seeks him.

LAMENTATIONS 3:25 NIV

It is a beautiful thing to spend our lives loving a God whose kindness is endless. When we look to him in all things, we will not be disappointed in his loyal and loving nature. He is good to those who put their trust in him. To those who seek him, God shows his compassion.

Look for him in the big and the little things. His ways are marked with the promotion of peace, mercy that covers our missteps, and miracles of restoration. His tangible goodness works out in our lives in a myriad of ways. Can you recognize the thread of his loving nature woven into the fabric of your life? Step back for a moment and look through a broader lens. Look over your history with him and see with fresh eyes how his faithfulness has met you.

Lord, I trust that you are not finished working things together for my good. Give me eyes to see where you have been weaving your mercy into my life and where you are doing it now.

The LORD is good to those who depend on him,
to those who search for him.

LAMENTATIONS 3:25 NLT

Good God, thank you for being a reliable help in times of trouble and a stable presence when all is going well. You are always there with a listening ear, and your words of life revive my weary soul. You send help just when I need it, and you never turn away. Whenever I look for you, I find you. I'm so grateful for your nearness, your comfort and your steadiness. Your love is like a firm foundation beneath my feet; I can stand upon you and not be moved. It doesn't matter what threats come; your mercy keeps me secure.

Let me see your goodness in my life in both little and big ways. Let me look through the lens of your perfect perspective so that I don't miss a thing! You have been so faithful to me; I know that I can count on you still. As I search for you throughout my days, let your revelation-light shine on the eyes of my heart, that I may understand your ways and follow them until the end.

Do you believe that God is always good?

New Life Coming

"To all who mourn in Israel,
he will give a crown of beauty for ashes,
a joyous blessing instead of mourning,
festive praise instead of despair.
In their righteousness, they will be like great oaks
that the LORD has planted for his own glory."

ISAIAH 61:3 NLT

This morning, as with every new day, is an opportunity to experience the fresh mercy of God meeting us right where we are. He is the God of new life, who trades our worn-out ways that bring us down for his overwhelming love that revives us. What he gives, no one can take away. What is weighing you down today? What heavy load have you been carrying? Give it to God today and take up his light load; it is full of joy, fresh perspective, kindness, and acceptance.

Will you dare trade your ashes for the crown of beauty he offers? Will you give him your disappointment and receive his festive praise in its place? If it sounds too good to be true, know that it is the gospel of his peace. He takes everything we give him, no matter how awful it seems, and offers us gifts from the riches of his glory.

Lord, I give you everything that weighs me down so that I can receive what you are offering. You are so glorious in kindness! Thank you for the freedom you give in abundance.

> *"To console those who mourn in Zion,*
> *To give them beauty for ashes,*
> *The oil of joy for mourning,*
> *The garment of praise for the spirit of heaviness;*
> *That they may be called trees of righteousness,*
> *The planting of the LORD, that He may be glorified."*

ISAIAH 61:3 NKJV

Righteous One, you are the one who comforts me in my mourning. You take the ashes of disappointed hopes in my life and offer me beauty in their place. You drench me in the oil of your joy, which seeps into the depths of my grief. You take the heaviness of sorrow and cover me in the garment of your praise. You have planted me in the garden of your kingdom, and the fruit borne of my life is a reflection of your tender care.

You are such an amazing counselor and a faithful friend. There is no one else who can coax life from destruction and defeat the way that you do. What you breathe on comes alive. You are the light of life itself. Where would I be without you? I have placed all my hope in you, and I won't take it back. Keep doing your restorative work in my life.

What have you been holding onto
that you can offer God today?

Everything I Need

"The LORD is my portion," says my soul,
"therefore I will hope in him."

LAMENTATIONS 3:24 ESV

It is a good practice to measure the resources we have available to us. When they are limited, a budget helps us live within our means, making sure that we can put the remainder toward our values and goals. We only have so much time on this earth, and how we spend our lives is as important as where we put our money. Take a quick inventory of your life; where do most of your time and resources go? Does this align with what you want your life to look like? If not, let this be an opportunity to reevaluate and realign.

Now, consider the areas of need that you have. Though your own resources are limited, God's are not. He is abundant in mercy, and the generosity of his heart never holds back from you. He will meet you with the provision you need because he is good. He is your abundant portion. As you align your life in the light of God's kingdom, know that you can put all your hope in him. He will never fail you.

Provider, I trust that you will meet the needs that I cannot. As I work to arrange my life in a way that glorifies you, I know that your mercy can cover everything.

> *"The LORD is my inheritance;*
> *therefore, I will hope in him!"*

LAMENTATIONS 3:24 NLT

Lord, thank you for the generosity of your love that meets me every day. You are my great inheritance, and the source of everything that I need each day. I won't take for granted the ways that you lavish your kindness in my life. I will remember how you answered every one of my desperate cries for help. You are a close and caring father, always providing for your children.

When my heart rests in the confidence of your faithful nature, I won't be afraid of what will come. You never stop working on my behalf, and I know that I can count on your goodness to lead me in wisdom. Continue to teach me what it means to be a child of the King of kings. You are so very lavish in love; I can't imagine the lengths of it! May my hope grow as your faithfulness continues to meet me in every area of my life. You are so good!

What is your first response to a need
that comes up in your life?

A Lamp

Your word is a lamp to my feet,
and a light to my path.

PSALM 119:105 NKJV

When we are making decisions in life, we often seek the advice of those we trust and admire. There is wisdom in looking to advisors for guidance. They often have different perspectives and nuggets of insight that can help us hone in on our choices.

How often do we look to God's Word to guide us in our decisions? The Scriptures say that his Word is like a lamp that lights our way. When we are confused about what to do or which direction to go, the Word can help us to see what we couldn't on our own. Remember, the Scriptures are meant to direct us in our relationship with the Lord. We have fellowship with the living Lord in Spirit and in truth. He is with us, and his voice leads us. Are we listening to what the Spirit is saying?

Wise God, I am so grateful for this relationship with you! You direct me by your Word and through your Spirit's life in me. Teach me to tune into your voice even more today.

Truth's shining light guides me in my choices and decisions;
the revelation of your word makes my pathway clear.

PSALM 119:105 TPT

Lord, you are the truth that I look to and that leads me. You guide me along the path of life, and I find everything I need along the way to overcome every obstacle I face. You are my constant companion and the gentle voice that redirects me when I am veering off course. The revelation that you give through your living Word is like a lamp illuminating the path in front of me. Your wisdom is better than the world's, and though it requires trust and obedience, it is unmatched in its fruitfulness.

May I always remember that your ways are better than any of my own. Your perspective is whole, taking in every detail. I will not stop seeking your perception over my own! Guide me in truth as I follow you all the days of my life. Your Word and ways are simple and clear; keep me from complicating it.

In what areas do you need God's wisdom to lead you?

Love Covers Everything

He has brought me to his banquet hall,
And his banner over me is love.

SONG OF SOLOMON 2:4, NASB

There is nothing in our lives that lies outside the realm of God's lavish love. His kindness reaches the depths of our shame and our greatest disappointments. He always leads in love—every single time. When we let shame lead us, we remain stuck in an unhealthy cycle of fear dictating our worthiness. But the truth is that we are not any more loveable on our best days than we are on our worst.

We cannot convince God out of his mercy. He leads us to the banqueting table of his goodness, and his banner over us never changes; it is always love. Will we let love lead us out of the shadows again today, into the light of his delight? There is nothing to fear in his presence. In him, we are made whole. We can trust him to always draw us in with kindness.

Great God, lead me into the fullness of your presence today—into the light of your love once again. It is almost too wonderful, and it is the overflow of your heart. I won't stay stuck today; I will follow your gentle leading!

He escorts me to the banquet hall;
it's obvious how much he loves me.

SONG OF SOLOMON 2:4 NLT

Loving Lord, may I never forget how fully you love me. Every one of my mistakes is covered by your marvelous mercy. You never hold my sins against me, and you don't keep track of my wrongdoings. Your love is fierce, burning up every shame and making me pure in the intensity of its consuming flames. There is nothing in my life that is outside the realms of your love.

Bring me into the feasting hall of your goodness again and shower your pure pleasure over me. I won't stay at the doorway of your delight any longer; I feel you drawing me in with the kindness of your affection. I want to be fully consumed by the flow of your mercy until my whole being is overflowing with the deep joy of your heart. Wash over every area of doubt and fill me with your unfettered compassion as I enter the courts of your presence. You are my joy, and I can feel you loving me to life again.

Where have you been hesitant
to receive God's love in your life?

He Sees Me

He will not ignore forever all the needs of the poor,
for those in need shall not always be crushed.
Their hopes shall be fulfilled, for God sees it all!

PSALM 9:18 TPT

When the winds of adversity pick up, what we once took for granted can seem like a luxury of the past. Though problems arise and crisis comes, we are not left on our own to pick up the pieces. God is an ever-present help for those who need him. He never, ever leaves. The light of his goodness shines on those who look to him.

It does not matter what circumstance we find ourselves in. No trial or tribulation can keep God's mercy from those who trust him. Do you believe that God sees you? He knows everything you are going through, and he already knows the way out. Let him lead you in love, for he has not changed!

Good God, I will follow your lead today. I know that you have not left me; you have not run out of mercy to sustain me. You are my hope; I know you will see me through every storm.

God will never forget the needy;
the hope of the afflicted will never perish.

PSALM 9:18 NIV

Merciful One, I am trusting that you still see everything as
clearly as you ever did. When you look upon my life, you don't
miss a detail. You see what is on the surface, but you also
recognize the currents underneath. I know I can trust you
in every season. I have watched you come through for me in
wonderful ways, and I believe that I haven't seen the end of
your miracle-working power in my life.

Now, Lord, come close with the comfort of your presence.
Fill me with the peace of your unworried heart. Even when
the world shakes around me, you are never moved. Your loyal
love will not be disturbed by bad reports or rumors of war.
You are the one I depend on, my only sure hope. As long as
I live, hold me close. Encourage my heart tonight in your
comforting care.

Is there something you feel that God has overlooked?

Never-ending Help

Do not worry about anything,
but pray and ask God for everything you need,
always giving thanks.

PHILIPPIANS 4:6 NCV

God is not being frivolous when he tells us not to worry. There is nothing that we can change by spending our time playing out the different possibilities of what could go wrong in our lives. Simply put, worry is wasted energy. What would it look like to let go of our ruminating apprehensions and instead offer them to God?

Though we have no influence over how most of life unfolds, there is one who is more powerful than the grip of death. There are no limits to God; we can trust him to do what we could never even dream of doing. Instead of spending time worrying about what we cannot control, let's cast every care on God each time one pops up. Let us practice what Paul instructs and see how it affects our well-being.

Constant Help, I offer you every overwhelming thought that comes to mind today. I will offer you the thanks that you are so deserving of. You are so worthy of my praise!

Don't be pulled in different directions or worried about a thing.
Be saturated in prayer throughout each day,
offering your faith-filled requests before God
with overflowing gratitude.
Tell him every detail of your life.

PHILIPPIANS 4:6 TPT

Great God, teach me to trust your heart of love as I offer you everything that I cannot control. I don't want to be pulled in different directions. Let my feet be rooted in the confidence of your loving nature that never changes. I will not stop giving you what I cannot carry on my own. I am so grateful that you always meant for the load to be shared; your present grace strengthens me for everything I face.

The more my mind meditates on your goodness, the more I see it around me. Knowing you and being known by you is the purest purpose I have in this life. I can love others well when I understand how extravagantly you love me. I won't stop telling you the details of my life because I know you care about every one.

What worries can you offer God today?

Everlasting Life

These things I have written to you who believe in the name of the Son of God, that you may know that you have eternal life, and that you may continue to believe in the name of the Son of God.

1 JOHN 5:13 NKJV

During his earthy life and ministry, Jesus clearly laid out the parameters for everlasting life. It is simple; believe that Jesus is the Son of God and profess that he is Lord. When our lives are aligned with his kingdom values, we realize that eternal life is a gift. We cannot earn our place in him. We receive it as a gift and submit our lives to his loyal love.

We can be confident that God is faithful, and he will do everything that he said he would. He will make every wrong thing right. May we keep our eyes fixed on the author of our faith, Jesus Christ. He is worthy, and he is God.

Son of God, you are my Savior and my God! You are my strong foundation, and the originator of my faith. It is through you that I know God and find my belonging. I believe in you.

I've written this letter to you who believe in the name of the Son of God so that you will be assured and know without a doubt that you have eternal life.

1 John 5:13 TPT

Jesus, thank you for the gift of eternal life. You are my saving grace, the one who lifts me from every pit of despair. It is through your resurrection life that I find my own. The firm foundation of my faith is you, not anything that I could do or offer to you. You are the one who qualifies me as a child of God. You have called me into your family, and you will never let go of me.

My confidence rests, not in my own faith, but in your faithfulness. You are better than anything I've experienced on this earth. Your love is purer than any other I've ever known. I have placed all my hope in you, and I trust that you won't let me down. Fill my heart with the peace and confidence that comes through knowing you. Put every worry to rest as I put my trust in you over and over again. You are so worthy.

Do you think that you have to earn your salvation?

Met by Mercy

Let us come boldly to the throne of our gracious God.
There we will receive his mercy,
and we will find grace to help us when we need it most.

HEBREWS 4:16 NLT

As a child of the King of kings, it is not too bold a thing to approach him confidently. In fact, it is those who are convinced of their parent's delight who walk best in the confidence of that love. They know that they will be received with open arms at every opportunity.

It is the same with the children of God. We need not shyly approach him. If we know that he is good and full of kindness toward us, we will not hesitate to come to him with every joy and every burden. We will always be met with the grace of his good nature, which strengthens and helps us. What is more, he is better than any love we've ever known. His love is purer, and his attention is never preoccupied. He sees us, welcomes us and lavishes his love over us whenever we turn to him. What a wonderful father he is!

Merciful Father, you are so good to me! I come boldly to you with all of my fears, with my excited hopes and everything in-between. I know that you meet me with love.

*Let us then approach God's throne of grace with confidence, so that
we may receive mercy and find grace to help us in our time of need.*

Hebrews 4:16 niv

Gracious God, what a caring father you are! Your goodness
is more than I can imagine, and you are so faithful with your
kind nature. I know that you meet me with the mercy of your
heart in every turn I make toward you. I don't want to get
caught up in my own head about things. When I am being
overwhelmed by the realities of my circumstances, may my
heart turn quickly toward you.

You always have more than enough grace to strengthen me.
The peace of your presence is plentiful, and it settles my
anxious heart. Every need I have is overwhelmed by the
generous provision that you pour out. You are more than
enough for everything that life will require of me. You are so
good, Lord! I can't help but love you more as the delight of
your affection pours over me.

Does your heart know the confidence
of being fully loved by God?

My Firm Hope

"Let not your heart be troubled;
you believe in God, believe also in Me.
In My Father's house are many mansions.
I go to prepare a place for you.
And if I go and prepare a place for you,
I will come again and receive you to Myself;
that where I am, there you may be also."

JOHN 14:1-3 NKJV

When your heart is troubled with the worries of this world, where do you turn? Do you check out by turning to your preferred coping mechanisms? Do you get lost in a TV series? Or do you escape by surrounding yourself with other diversions? These distraction techniques may help for a little while, but they do nothing to reach the actual roots of the issues that worries bring up in you.

Will you stop running from them today and offer them to God instead? Look into the Word and what Jesus promised. He has prepared a place for you, and it is a permanent place of belonging and hope. What he builds, no one can destroy. May you find your greatest confidence in the promised love, mercy, and eternal life that Jesus offers.

Jesus, let hope rise within my heart again today as I meditate on your promised return. I have placed all my bets on your faithfulness; I trust that you won't let me down.

"Don't let your hearts be troubled. Trust in God, and trust also in me. There is more than enough room in my Father's home. If this were not so, would I have told you that I am going to prepare a place for you? When everything is ready, I will come and get you, so that you will always be with me where I am."

JOHN 14:1-3 NLT

Savior, I trust in you. I trust that your Word is true, and your faithfulness will never let up. Your promises will be fulfilled, and you will not let your people down. I believe that you are the way, the truth, and the life. I have tethered my life to yours, and my heart belongs to you.

Would you fill my heart with hope again as I remember what you have said and what you have already done? I know that you are not finished working your miracles of restoration and redemption in this earth. You are with your people even as you prepare a permanent place for us in your kingdom realm. You are the firm foundation of my hope! You are the one I have built my life upon.

What is your greatest hope rooted in?

Home in Him

A father of the fatherless and a judge for the widows,
is God in His holy dwelling.
God makes a home for the lonely;
He leads out the prisoners into prosperity.
Only the rebellious live in parched lands.

PSALM 68:5-6 NASB

What areas of your life need love's liberation? Are there
places where you feel hemmed in and stuck? God's Word says
that he leads prisoners into prosperity. Where have you felt
imprisoned by lies, unhealthy compulsions, or dependence
on something other than his love? He leads us into freedom.
There is an invitation today to follow him into the wealth of
his mercy.

There is space to dance there. There is room to breathe.
The winds of his peace and joy blow off the dust of our
disappointment. He has made a home for the lonely. He is our
home. He makes us family. In him, we find our true belonging
and freedom.

Father, I follow your leading into the fields of freedom and
life! In you, there is room to run. Thank you for the joy of your
liberation. I never want to go back to living in the small cell
of my shame and the lies of never-enough. You are more than
enough for all I'll ever need.

To the fatherless he is a father.
To the widow he is a champion friend.
To the lonely he makes them part of a family.
To the prisoners he leads into prosperity until they sing for joy.
This is our Holy God in his Holy Place!
But for the rebels there is heartache and despair.

PSALM 68:5-6 TPT

Holy God, you are everything to everyone. You are the abundance and perfection of all I'll ever need or seek. You are the perfect parent, the most faithful friend, and the closest companion I will ever know. You are trustworthy and capable. You are kind and compassionate. You are full of mercy. You lead me into the liberty of your love over and over again.

I cannot begin to sing the depths of the wonder I feel, but I will try. You have saved me from every snare of the enemy. The traps that he laid are left empty because you freed me from every single one. I am overwhelmed with gratitude for all that you are and all that you've done. Thank you, thank you, thank you! I am so in love with you.

How has God met you in your need?

Holy Exchange

*"Blessed are the poor in spirit, for theirs is the kingdom of heaven.
Blessed are those who mourn, for they will be comforted."*

MATTHEW 5:3-4 NIV

On days when we feel completely depleted and we have very
little to offer anyone, including the Lord, may we remember
the words of Jesus. His kingdom is full of overflowing
mercy to meet us in the depth of our neediness. "Blessed
are the poor in spirit," says the Lord. He does not require
unending confidence and strength from us. What we have, we
surrender to him, and he gives us the abundance of his grace.
There is comfort for those who mourn, and there is strength
for those who are weak.

Lay down your mentality that says you have to earn God's
favor. That's not how the kingdom of heaven works. God's
favor is ours through Christ and only Christ. It is not based on
anything that we do. What a relief that is to the weary soul!

Christ, you are the fulfillment of the law of the Lord. You are
worthy of all my trust and every surrender of my will to yours.
I rely on your grace to strengthen me. You are better than any
other.

*"They are blessed who realize their spiritual poverty,
for the kingdom of heaven belongs to them.
They are blessed who grieve,
for God will comfort them."*

MATTHEW 5:3-4 NCV

Loving Lord, I give you everything I am, though it is not much. I need you more than I can express. Will you fill me with the strength of your Spirit in my weakness? When I am brought down by the sadness of my soul, I trust that you will lift me with the comfort of your love. Even on my best days, when the wind is at my back and I'm sailing along in life, let me remember that it is your grace that carries me still.

Whatever I encounter, I don't do it alone. You are with me wherever I go, and I lean on your understanding in every season and circumstance. You are the one who lovingly guides me through the brightest days of my deepest joys and the darkest nights of grief and sorrow. You are my God, and I depend on you through it all.

What can you give to God in exchange for his peace today?

Way of Peace

"Because of the tender mercy of our God,
With which the Sunrise from on high will visit us,
To shine on those who sit in darkness and the shadow of death,
To guide our feet into the way of peace."

LUKE 1:78–79 NASB

The peace of God is unmistakable. It runs deep and true. It puts every fear to rest and calms all anxiety. It is not rushed; it does not force your hand or make you feel as if time is running out. It is the atmosphere of God's very presence. It brings rest and space.

The pathway of peace is marked by the wisdom of God's ways. It seeks unity, promotes reconciliation and offers love in all things. It does not create chaos; rather, it untangles the confusion of conflicting views with the simplicity of truth. There is trust and confidence in the peace of God. There is hope and room for boundless joy. When we follow the path of peace, we will find that it leads to God's everlasting kingdom.

Merciful God, I want to dwell in the peace of your presence, no matter what circumstances I face. Your love leads me. Thank you for the promise of harmony with you in spirit and truth.

> *"Because of God's tender mercy, the morning light from heaven is about to break upon us, to give light to those who sit in darkness and in the shadow of death, and to guide us to the path of peace."*
>
> LUKE 1:78-79 NLT

Lord, it is your tender mercy that leads me into peace. I know that the darkness that accompanies nighttime will not last forever. When morning light breaks through the black of night, everything is illuminated. You reveal where you have always been. You show me what I could not sense that you were doing when my eyes could not see where you were. You never left me, not even for a moment.

You lead me with kindness, and your peace is the shroud that encompasses me. I will not fear with you as my loving guide and faithful friend. You are so much better than I realize in every single moment. You never stop moving in compassion, and your mercy has no limits. I am undone by the wonderful reality of your love!

Are you walking along the path of peace?

Greater Reality

Great is your mercy, O LORD;
give me life according to your justice.

PSALM 119:156 NRSV

What can compare to the endless mercy of God? If it feels like old news, then we need a fresh revelation of how truly endless and wonderful his love is. There is no end to the number of chances we have to start anew in him. He offers forgiveness for every wrongdoing. He offers us restored relationship when the connection is interrupted by fear, shame, or rebellion. He never turns us away; he always welcomes us home with open arms.

His love is not weak in its tendency toward compassion. It is stronger than the grave. Nothing can separate us from the unhindered affection of God in Christ Jesus. Nothing! Not death or life, not our biggest failures or our greatest achievements. Nothing can keep us from his love.

Lord, give me life according to your justice. Your love is so much bigger than I can imagine. May I never try to put limits on it. You never do! Today, show me how great your mercy is a new way.

*LORD, how great is your mercy;
let me be revived by following your regulations.*

PSALM 119:156 NLT

Merciful Father, you are the one I always come back to at the
end of the day. Your mercy is unmatched, and your love is
better than life itself. Just when I think that I know better,
my disappointed expectations in others and myself leads
me back to you. As I follow your path of love, may my heart
be revived in your kindness. Breathe your breath of life into
every crack and crevice in my soul. I want to come alive in the
light of your glory once again.

I know that you will never turn me away. You are just
that good! You are kinder, you are purer, and your heart
is brimming with generosity in every moment. I cannot
comprehend the lengths of your love, though I'll try. May joy
rise up within me at every new revelation of your goodness.
You are so very thoughtful in everything you do. You know just
what I need right when I need it. I am yours, Lord. I am yours.

How has God's mercy changed you?

Encounter with Goodness

"I will make all my goodness pass before you and will proclaim before you my name 'The Lord.' And I will be gracious to whom I will be gracious, and will show mercy on whom I will show mercy."

EXODUS 33:19 ESV

The verse that we are meditating on today is God's response to Moses after he asked that God show him his glory. What a bold request! Moses had been having a conversation with God in the tent of meeting, but he wanted more than just a discussion. He wanted an encounter. And God responded!

We can have the same boldness and the same expectation. We have the Spirit of the living God dwelling within us, which is an even greater reality than Moses and the Israelites had available to them. May we let our hunger drive us, and may we not be simply satisfied with what we have known up until now. There is more available. May we say, like Moses did, "show me your glory!"

Holy Lord, I want to know you more than I do now. I know that you respond to my desire for you. Show me your glory; I want an encounter, not simply a conversation.

"I will make all my goodness pass before you, and I will call out my name, Yahweh, before you. For I will show mercy to anyone I choose, and I will show compassion to anyone I choose."

EXODUS 33:19 NLT

Yahweh, you are so full of compassion and mercy to those who look to you. I know that I won't be denied by you. I long for more of your goodness in my life. I want to walk with you, hand in hand, all the days of my life. Show me your mercy and reveal your glory to me in a new way today.

With every new revelation, my heart grows in awe and understanding. As I walk in your wisdom, reach past the recesses of my mind and into the experience of my heart. Let me know your nearness, the breath of your life in mine. You are so full of beauty. I want to know you more and more and more! God, I will end this day how I started it, asking you to show me your glory.

How has God revealed his glory to you?

Drink Deep

*"I am the Alpha and the Omega—the Beginning and the End.
To all who are thirsty I will give freely from the springs
of the water of life."*

REVELATION 21:6 NLT

What we feed our souls affects how we process information,
what we grow a taste for, and what we have to give others.
What are you filling up on these days? Is it the wisdom of the
world that encourages self-promotion at all cost? Is it the
unending news cycle of world events that are overwhelming
your nervous system? It is good to be aware of what we use to
gratify ourselves.

Are you thirsty today? Drink from the wells of living water
that God offers. His waters satisfy the greatest thirst. Strength
will return as you are filled with his good news. His ways are
better and his solutions purer than any the world offers.

Alpha and Omega, in you, every being finds its fulfillment.
You are the source of all life, and you have not stopped
offering your living waters to all who thirst. I'm filling up on
you today! Satisfy me with the abundance of life in you.

"It is done! I am the Alpha and the Omega, the beginning and the end. To the thirsty I will give from the spring of the water of life without payment."

REVELATION 21:6 ESV

Great God, you have done all that was required for us to be reconciled to you. You give freely from your springs of life to all those who thirst, never requiring payment in return. There is no need to save up or put it off for another day. Salvation is here, now.

I will not hold back from you today. I come to you, with all my hunger and thirst, and I know that I will be met with the overflowing fountain of your love. This is where I am revived and refreshed. My soul knows encouragement in the presence of your Spirit flowing over me. In fellowship with you, my soul has found its home. I rest in your finished work. I am yours, and I won't stay away.

Where do you turn to satisfy the thirst of your soul?

Perfect Power

"My grace is sufficient for you, for power is perfected in weakness."
Most gladly, therefore, I will rather boast about my weaknesses,
so that the power of Christ may dwell in me.

2 CORINTHIANS 12:9 NASB

When your strengths become your weaknesses, and you are disappointed in yourself, what then? Do you despair in your inability to be perfect? Or do you recognize that perfection was never the goal? When it comes down to it, the most important things in life have to do with our relationships. How do we love—ourselves, others, and God? Do we have mercy for others and their mistakes, but little to spare for ourselves?

Compassion is a practice. Self-compassion is necessary. We cannot love others well if we do not first know how to offer and receive love within ourselves. God's power is made perfect in our weakness. Perhaps this is because his power is marked by mercy. We can boast in our weaknesses, for there we find that love meets us in overwhelming measure.

Gracious God, thank you for the perfect power of your love that fills the void of my weaknesses. May I learn how to extend the same mercy toward others and myself, just as you do.

"My grace is always more than enough for you, and my power finds its full expression through your weakness." So I will celebrate my weaknesses, for when I'm weak I sense more deeply the mighty power of Christ living in me.

2 Corinthians 12:9 TPT

Mighty God, your grace is everything I need to empower me to live in the light of your mercy. You fill me with strength when I have none of my own. Your love covers every lack I have. I lean on your mighty power when I have nothing to offer on my own accord. How could I do anything but celebrate the overcoming life I have within me through your Spirit? You do what I could never dream of. It doesn't matter how little I have; your abundance of grace meets me every single time I need it.

May I not take for granted the wonderful relationship I have with you. I never need to rely on my own strength because yours is unlimited, and you are my help in every moment. Show up and show off again as you make up for the shortage of my own dwindling resources. You are great, God!

How have you experienced God's power in your weakness?

Proven Character

We also have joy with our troubles,
because we know that these troubles produce patience.
And patience produces character,
and character produces hope.

ROMANS 5:3–4 NCV

When all is going right in our little worlds, and the joys
outweigh the sorrows, what a wonderful gift of ease we enjoy!
We know that life does not always go according to our plans,
and that suffering is bound to darken our doorsteps. This
is not a punishment or something that could be avoided. It
happens to us all. God never promised that this life would be
without sorrow or trouble. He did, however, promise that he
would be with us.

There is something to learn in every circumstance. In our
troubles, there is also an impenetrable joy that remains
in Christ. Trials produce patience, and patience produces
character. There is depth in the experience of one who has
suffered. And in that depth, God's faithfulness and love
meet us. There is hope in it all because we are never without
the loyal love of our ever-present God and help. He is our
companion. He is our defender. He is all that we need.

Faithful One, I know that you are with me in the good times
and the bad. Give me eyes to see what good you are producing
even during the hard circumstances of life. I know that you
won't let go of me.

Even in times of trouble we have a joyful confidence,
knowing that our pressures will develop in us patient endurance.
And patient endurance will refine our character,
and proven character leads us back to hope.

ROMANS 5:3–4 TPT

Loving Lord, in the cycles of this life, you are faithful. I will find your goodness in every circumstance and every trial. You never leave me; you are the hand that upholds me when my legs give way beneath me. You whisper your words of love to me and soothe my weary heart as I rest in you.

The confidence of your unchanging character is immovable. You will not stop extending your mercy toward me. You refine my character in the purifying fires of this life. You are for me, not against me. I will trust you to guide me through everything—every storm, every dark night, and every hopeful opportunity. You do not waver in your love toward me. I am filled with hope because of your unfailing love. I trust you more than any other.

How has your character grown through hard times?

Tapestry of Grace

*We are convinced that every detail of our lives is continually
woven together to fit into God's perfect plan of bringing good
into our lives, for we are his lovers who have been called
to fulfill his designed purpose.*

ROMANS 8:28 TPT

There is not a single detail of your life that is not woven into
the fabric of God's marvelous mercy. He has not missed a
thing! Do not worry about yesterday's mistakes or the lack
you have today. He is working in the details, and he won't
forget a single one. You can rest in the goodness of God's
perfect plans. He takes what looks like utter devastation and
somehow sows seeds of peace that grow into sweet Spirit fruit
in our lives. He is so good!

We have been called to fulfill his designed purpose, but the
great news is that we cannot miss the mark. It is his work
that we participate in, and it is full of mercy. It is full of fresh
starts and new beginnings. It is filled with restoration and
redemption. He is better than our most elaborate plans of
goodness.

Gracious One, you are so full of mercy. Your kindness is
revealed in every movement of your miracle-working love.
I know you will never fail.

We know that in all things God works for the good of those who love him, who have been called according to his purpose.

ROMANS 8:28 NIV

Good God, thank you for calling me in love. Your kindness
draws me in time and again. I can't stay away! I trust that
you are working all things out for my good even when I can't
understand what you are doing. I trust your nature more than
I trust my own perception of your goodness.

Broaden my grasp of your greatness as you reveal your
wonderful ways in my life over and over again. I have seen
the ways that you restore what I never believed you could.
I would love to never be surprised by you because I expect
your overwhelming goodness. Truth is, I cannot comprehend
how marvelous you truly are. I welcome the barrier-busting
wonders of your mercy in my life. May my wonder grow as
your faithfulness continues to work in this world.

How have you been surprised by the kindness of God?

Help Me

*It is good that one should hope
and wait quietly for the salvation of the Lord.*

LAMENTATIONS 3:26 NKJV

There is a season for everything under the sun, or so the
book of Ecclesiastes says. There is a time for weeping and a
time for rejoicing. There is a time to break down and a time
to build up. I would add, there is a time to cry out to the Lord
and a time to quietly wait.

The thing about seasons is that we intuitively know what is
right at the right time. We don't have to force it. In the same
way, when we truly hope in the Lord, and our confidence is
found in him, then we can wait quietly for his help. There's
no need to beg and shout because we already know that he has
heard us and that he is coming. His salvation is on the way!
We need only wait on him.

Faithful Father, I know that I can count on your faithful love
to help me. I listen to your Word and trust that you are my
saving grace for every trouble I face.

It is good that he waits silently
For the salvation of the LORD.

LAMENTATIONS 3:26 NASB

Lord, I wait upon you, knowing that you will meet me. You will not leave me to be destroyed by the fear that threatens my peace. I am confident in your kindness. You are faithful, and you have not changed a bit. I will rest in the expectation of your coming goodness. You won't let me down!

As I wait in hope for you to come through in my areas of need, I will not stop praising you for what you have already done. I will store up the remembrances of your faithfulness. May my heart burst at the seams for the love and gratitude I feel toward you. You are better than life itself, and you are always faithful to your Word. I will not be afraid, and I will not lose hope. I trust your love and that you always know what is best, including the right time to fulfill your promises. You are worthy of my faith.

How can you still hope in God in the waiting seasons?

A Higher Perspective

I pray that the eyes of your heart may be enlightened,
so that you will know what is the hope of His calling,
what are the riches of the glory of His inheritance in the saints.

EPHESIANS 1:18 NASB

When was the last time you considered that your perspective was not God's perspective? You see only in part: a very small fraction of what God perceives. Even so, there is so much opportunity to know the glory of our good God in the revelation-light of his love.

The eyes of your imagination, or as Paul says here, the eyes of your heart, can be enlightened to know God more. The screen of your mind is a place where you imagine what could be rather than what is right in front of you. It is a place of opportunity for encounter and understanding. Invite God to sanctify the eyes of your imagination and speak to you there, giving you a glimpse of his greater glory—the hope of his calling.

Holy God, I offer you the screen of my mind; wash over it with the cleansing of your mercy-tide. Illuminate the eyes of my imagination, that I may see you in a way that I have never seen you before and understand your love in a deeper, more meaningful way.

I pray that the light of God will illuminate the eyes of your imagination, flooding you with light, until you experience the full revelation of the hope of his calling—that is, the wealth of God's glorious inheritances that he finds in us, his holy ones!

EPHESIANS 1:18 TPT

Holy One, as I lay down to sleep tonight, would you fill my mind with revelations of your goodness through dreams? Meet me in the place of my imagination; bring light and effortless understanding to that which I could not understand with logic. You are so much more creative than I give you credit for; I will not stand in the way of your love, no matter how it wants to meet me.

Give me eyes to see what I could not comprehend on my own. I want to know the full revelation of the hope of your calling. Peel back the layers of your mercy, revealing another aspect of your wonderful character with each one. I long to know you more! Thank you for the knowledge of you in every sense of my being—even in my imagination.

Do you believe that God can meet you in your imagination?

Revelation's Light

Your faith and love rise within you as you access all the treasures of your inheritance stored up in the heavenly realm. For the revelation of the true gospel is as real today as the day you first heard of our glorious hope, now that you have believed in the truth of the gospel.

COLOSSIANS 1:5 TPT

Can you remember the way you felt when you first believed the glorious hope of the gospel? Were you filled with joy and gratitude? Awe and wonder? Were you humbled by the greatness of God's mercy meeting you in your great need? Whatever you have known up until now is but a foretaste of the generous goodness of God. His glory has not diminished one bit. His love is overflowing without measure in every single moment.

If the truth of God's kindness feels stale today, there is a new revelation waiting for you in fellowship with God. The Spirit illuminates the eyes of our understanding so that we can see what we could not perceive before. Simply ask, and you will receive.

Great God, enlighten me today to see you in a way that I have not before. Remind me of the overwhelming goodness of your love, so that faith and love will rise in my heart in response. You are wonderful!

We have heard from your faith in Christ Jesus and your love for all of God's people which come from your confident hope of what God has reserved for you in heaven. You have had this expectation ever since you first heard the truth of the Good News.

COLOSSIANS 1:4-5 NLT

Jesus, you are the hope of my heart. You are the source of any love that I feel or express. You are full of kindness, and I am a humble and willing recipient of your marvelous compassion. Help me not to forget the great mercy you have shown me over and over again. With the same manner of kindness, may I offer the benefit of the doubt to those around me. And when I am hurt and offended, may I extend the forgiveness you so generously show me.

I know that the perfection I am looking for is only found in you. You are the fulfillment of every longing, and my confidence will never be let down when it is rooted in your unfailing nature. I am in awe of the ways you move. You are so patient with your people. Thank you for the gift of knowing you as I am fully known by you. I will not stop seeking you, for you are my faithful friend, the confidant and lover of my soul.

How has the Good News of the gospel affected your life?

Forever Faithful

The Lord always keeps his promises;
he is gracious in all he does.

PSALM 145:13 NLT

God is loyal to his Word. He fulfills every promise and faithfully draws close to all those who look to him. He is the sustainer of the weak and lifter of those who are burdened by shame. He is provider, and he is the one who satisfies the hungry.

Today, look to the testimonies of other lovers of God, and be encouraged by his faithfulness in their lives! He is the same caring father toward you as he is to any other. He has not abandoned some of his children and chosen to spoil others. He is full of lovingkindness toward you. Draw near, learn to hear his voice, and trust his unfailing character. He is gracious in all he does; you will not escape his goodness.

Faithful Father, you are full of more kindness than I can even recognize. Thank you for calling me your own; I am honored to be your child. Let faith and hope rise in my heart as I remember the greatness of who you are.

*You are the Lord who reigns over your never-ending kingdom
through all the ages of time and eternity!
You are faithful to fulfill every promise you've made.
You manifest yourself as kindness in all you do.*

PSALM 145:13 TPT

Kind God, I can barely comprehend how truly wonderful
you are. I am amazed by the thought of the generosity of your
love. Lead me deeper into uninterrupted fellowship with
you, that you would be my closest friend and my greatest
confidence. You are faithful and true, and there is no one else
like you. You are bigger than my faith, perseverant in mercy
in everything you do. Your kingdom is never-ending, and you
have invited me to take part in it. What a wonder!

Continue to work out your wise and beautiful plans of
restoration and redemption as I follow your lead. I know that
you won't let a single promise go unsatisfied. What looks
to the naked eye like a wasteland will turn to gardens of
grandeur in your hands. What you do, no one can undo. You
are wonderful in all of your ways.

How has God been faithful to you?

Passionate Love

Christ proved God's passionate love for us by dying in our place while we were still lost and ungodly!

ROMANS 5:8 TPT

It can be a difficult task to define what love looks like. There are some loves that are fleeting and others that last our whole lives. There is the love of deep friendship, the love of family, romantic love, and the love of life and all that it's made of. There are many examples and expressions. Some are purer than others. However, there is one love that outshines them all: the passionate love of God.

It is not self-seeking or looking for a return. It took Christ to the cross, enduring shame, torture and death when he deserved none of it. God's love counted this cost and considered us worthy of it. God went to the ultimate end to show us that he would do everything it took to restore the connection that was always meant for us: unhindered relationship with him. What a wonderful love!

Wonderful One, how can I begin to thank you for the incomparable love that you have poured out? You stand alone in the purity of your purposes. I cannot help but love you in return.

*God shows his love for us in that while we were still sinners,
Christ died for us.*

ROMANS 5:8 ESV

Lord, you are so generous in mercy. You humbled yourself,
left your throne in heaven and put on flesh and bones to show
us what perfect love looks like. You didn't count your life as
more important than ours; you died for us even when most
did not recognize who you were. You defeated death and rose
from the grave, ensuring that not even death could separate
us from you. You didn't let anything stop you; your love
propelled you when in your humanity you did not want to die.
No one wants to suffer, but you did it anyway. You did it for us.

Let me understand the depths of your love in a more acute
way today. Shower me with the revelations of your kindness.
You are more wonderful than I've known. You are better
than I ever imagined you could be! Your love is sweeter than
life and more powerful than the grave. You are worthy of my
pursuit both now and forever.

How does God's love stand apart from others you've known?

Even More

God gives us even more grace, as the Scripture says,
"God is against the proud, but he gives grace to the humble."

JAMES 4:6 NCV

Where there is weakness, there is an opportunity for God to meet us with the overwhelming strength of his grace. There is no disgrace in the hunger we have, and there is no shame in our need. There is no reason to act like we've got it all together when we don't. Pride convinces us that we can handle things on our own, while modesty recognizes that there is strength in the giving and receiving of help.

There is power in support. God is an ever-ready help in times of need, no matter what the need is. Why would we strive to go it alone when there are unending resources found in God's grace? May we lay down our need to prove ourselves in favor of resting in the peace of God and allowing him to assist us in every trial. He is with us through it all. May we share our joys and our troubles, knowing that he is always ready in love.

Gracious One, I will not resist your support today. I rely on you in my weakness and in my strength, for even my greatest gifts are nothing compared with yours. I submit myself to you, for you are always leading in love and so very worthy of my trust.

He continues to pour out more and more grace upon us.
For it says, "God resists you when you are proud
but continually pours out grace when you are humble."

JAMES 4:6 TPT

Great God, whenever resistance rises within my heart against you, will you remind me of your great love that melts all my defenses? Your ways are better than my own: better than the noblest pursuits I could dedicate myself to in this life. You are endless in kindness, offering your support whenever your children cry out to you. I need your wisdom to guide me, and your tender care to keep me on the path of righteousness. Keep me close to your heartbeat of mercy as I live and love those around me.

I'm so grateful for your unending measure of grace that empowers me to live in the light of your life. You are my hope, you are my song, and you are the keeper of my heart. I trust you to do what no one else can. I bind my life to yours in trust because you are wonderful to me.

Where do you need God's grace to empower you today?

Ask Again

Oh that I might have my request,
and that God would fulfill my hope.

JOB 6:8 ESV

There is a proverb that reflects the tension of the process of the long-awaited desire: "Hope deferred makes the heart sick, but a desire fulfilled is a tree of life" (Proverbs 13:12). In the waiting period, when we are feeling the heartsickness of not having our longings satisfied, let us not lose hope. God is faithful to meet us with overwhelming love as we surrender the timing of our great hopes.

May we yield our hearts to him, trusting him to hold us closer than that which we long to hold with our own hands. And yet, may we not let discouragement keep us from asking, for he cares for us! Will we open these vulnerable places up to the Lord and trust him to meet us in them? He is gentle with us, and he always knows exactly what we need right when we need it. He is so much better than we could ever give him credit for. Lean into his love again today.

Loving Father, I will not hold back from you today. I know that you see what I cannot, and I trust that you will work all things together for my good. I place my hope again in you, and I let you into every part of my heart.

Oh, that my request might come to pass,
And that God would grant my hope!

JOB 6:8 NASB

Gracious One, I will not stop asking you to come through
for me. Your reputation is bigger than my little life; your
faithfulness is world-renowned! I am not willing to let
disappointment dictate my hope in you. I know that you see
everything as it is, and you always have a plan for redemption.
I stand on the firm foundation of your loyal love. Even when
storms rage and darkness keeps me from seeing what is
around me, I know that you never change. You are victorious
in power, and you are mighty in mercy. I rest in the peace of
your uncompromising character.

I am baring my heart before you again; let the oil of your
love penetrate every crack and crevice, leaving nothing
untouched. Here are all my longings and my questions, Lord.
They are yours to answer and fulfill. I give you full access to
every part of me. You are not just my savior and my God; you
are the perfect counselor, the ultimate healer, and the source
of every longing I have.

Is there something that you've stopped asking God for
due to disappointment?

Marvelous Mercy

Magnify the marvels of your mercy to all who seek you.
Make your Pure One wonderful to me,
like you do for all those who turn aside to hide themselves in you.

<small>PSALM 17:7 TPT</small>

When we look for God's fingerprints in this world, including in our own lives, we will find him. His Word is living and active, and it is working even now. God's wonderful love touches our lives; we cannot escape it! As we come to know the ways in which God moves, we will see where he meets us.

May we be quick to see and acknowledge the power of his mercy in our lives. His miracles are not reserved for the mountaintop experiences alone. They are in the flooding of his peace in our minds when we would be overtaken by anxiety. His love is present in the offering of support to our loved ones. His joy is there in the unbridled laughter of a child. He is with us in the mundane and in the extraordinary. He is with us in love through it all.

Pure One, may I never forget how present you are. Your mercy is marvelous, and it is ever flowing toward me. As I receive it, I have so much to offer others. How great you are!

Show me your unfailing love in wonderful ways.
By your mighty power you rescue
those who seek refuge from their enemies.

PSALM 17:7 NLT

Magnificent Lord, you are so incredibly generous with your
love. I cannot count the ways that you meaningfully meet
me with the kiss of your mercy in my life. You are beyond
comprehension, so much bigger and better than I could
ever think to tell. And yet, you care for me! I'm undone at
the thought of your mindfulness toward man. You give me
confidence to pray big prayers and make bold requests. You
are able to do much more than I could imagine.

In light of that, I will dream as big as I dare, knowing that you
will meet me. Let my faith rise as your Spirit fills the sails of
my heart. You are full of power to save, but you do so much
more than a simple rescue. You are a constant help. You are
a faithful father. You are a loyal friend. You love me to life in
your living waters of mercy, and you do it over and over again.
I can't help but love you; you are so incredible!

In what wonderful ways have you experienced God's love?

Calmed by Comfort

When anxiety was great within me,
your consolation brought me joy.

PSALM 94:19 NIV

There is a real and close comfort in the presence of God. He wraps around us with the nearness of His Spirit, enfolding us in the embrace of his peace. Where there is chaos, it is calmed. Though the pressures of life may cause anxieties to rise within us, God's comfort eases the tensions. We can trust him. He knows every possibility, and he sees exactly how it will play out. He won't suddenly decide to abandon us. He is with us in the bending, the breaking, and the building.

If we will give God our worries, there is more room to receive his abundant kindness. Take a moment now and slow down. Focus on the present moment—on the breath moving in and out of your lungs. With every breath, remember that the Spirit of God is as close as the air, both within and around you. He is so very near!

Holy Spirit, thank you for ministering your comfort to me. I am grateful for your presence in my life. Come even closer today and wrap around me with the peace that you bring.

*Whenever my busy thoughts were out of control,
the soothing comfort of your presence calmed me down
and overwhelmed me with delight.*

PSALM 94:19 TPT

Loving Lord, you are the calming balm to my wearied soul.
You breathe your life into me, and I am refreshed. Whenever
you draw near with your presence, I cannot help but be
overcome with gratitude. You are the strength I depend upon
in my weakest moments. You are the rock of my salvation,
and my only sure hope. When my thoughts are racing, you are
the one that settles them. You are my confidence.

Though I come to the end of my own limits time and time
again, you are infinite in wisdom and power. You always
know exactly what I need, and you provide for me every time.
You are dependable in peace, with none of the quick fixes or
superficial bandages that the world offers. Your peace is deep,
surpassing the logic of this world. It calms and revives me.
I am so thankful for your supernatural ways that lead me in
love and lift the burdens of my temporary troubles.

Is there something overwhelming you today?
How can you invite God into it?

Led by Love

"I will bring the blind by a way they did not know;
I will lead them in paths they have not known.
I will make darkness light before them,
and crooked places straight.
These things will I do for them and not forsake them."

ISAIAH 42:16 NKJV

There are no challenges that we meet in life that cannot be experienced with the overwhelming love of God as our steady guide. God himself leads us. When we are turned around by the storms of life and we cannot discern left from right, God directs our steps. We can trust him to do it; we need not rely on our limited and skewed understanding. His wisdom sees everything as it is.

He doesn't miss a single detail. He sees every bump in the road and every sharp turn ahead. He will not let us fall off the path that leads to life. He tucks us into the crook of his arm and holds us close, hiding us beneath the shelter of his cloak when the path becomes treacherous. Sometimes, it is easier to follow him when he is all we can sense, not distracted by what is going on around us. We have such a faithful and kind shepherd.

Good Shepherd, I trust you to guide me along the paths you have prepared. I don't want to stick to my safe route when you know a better way. I lean into your love, for you are always leading me in mercy.

> "I will walk the blind by an unknown way
> and guide them on paths they've never traveled.
> I will smooth their difficult road
> and make their dark mysteries bright with light.
> These are things I will do for them,
> for I will never abandon my beloved ones."
>
> ISAIAH 42:16 TPT

Constant Companion, you are full of wisdom for every problem I face. Whenever there is a fork in the road, you advise me in the way to go. I know that I can trust you to guide me in truth and in love. The best part about all of this is that you go with me. I am never alone to figure out what to do. You know how limited in perspective I am, and yet, you are teaching me to trust your voice.

As I do, I find that I grow in the confidence of intuition. Your love sets me free as I walk along unknown paths. You are full of tenderness in your leading. I trust in your steadfast love that covers me. I will never be without it, for I am walking in the light of your revelation. I am so grateful to know you and be led by you!

Do you trust that God will always guide you in his goodness?

Perfect Father

You did not receive a spirit of slavery to fall back into fear,
but you have received a spirit of adoption.
When we cry, "Abba! Father!" it is that very Spirit
bearing witness with our spirit that we are children of God.

ROMANS 8:15-16 NRSV

God has so much love to give us. He did not ever intend for us to relate to him as a worker reporting to their boss. From the day he created Adam and Eve, relationship between God and humankind was always meant to be familial.

Have you gotten caught up in the need to prove your worth to God in what you have to offer him? There is no fear in the love that he gives, including the fear of disappointing him. As his beloved child, you cannot make him love you any more or any less. He loves you because you are his. You don't need to prove a thing to him. Lay down the fear of making a mistake, and let his kindness refine you.

Father, I come to you as I am today. Let all of my fears fall away as your perfect love awakens me to my true belonging in you. I am so grateful to be your child!

You have not received a spirit that makes you fearful slaves. Instead, you received God's Spirit when he adopted you as his own children. Now we call him, "Abba, Father." For his Spirit joins with our spirit to affirm that we are God's children.

ROMANS 8:15-16 NLT

Abba, you are the only perfect father. May I understand the lengths of your abundant love and mercy, not assigning my own earthly father's imperfections to you. You are so much better than we, in our humanity, could ever dream of being. Your parenting is perfect. So, I trust you to lead me well in love.

As I grow and mature in my faith, I understand that my identity as a child of the King of kings is all that truly matters. Any confidence I have is from knowing that I am yours. When everything else fades, you remain. Teach me to be like you. I won't stop looking to your incredible nature, learning how you relate to others. May I mirror you in the way that I love those around me, reflecting the belonging that I have found in you.

Do you relate to God as a loving father?

Sustained by Peace

*You will keep in perfect peace those whose minds are steadfast,
because they trust in you.*

ISAIAH 26:3 NIV

There is a peace that covers those who trust in God. When
the winds of the world shift and storms come raging in, the
foundation of their faith will not be upset. When worries
come knocking on the door of your heart, do you let them take
over? Or do you turn them over to the Prince of Peace who
resides within you? There are no mysteries to God; therefore,
he can never be surprised.

Will you turn every anxiety over to the one who calms the
storms of this life with just a word? Take your cues from him;
he is trustworthy and reliable in every single situation. His
nature is unchanging even when life takes a turn. Cling to
him, for he is steadfast, and his ways are true. Let your hopes
be rooted in the confidence that he is a good God, and that he
is for you.

Prince of Peace, I give you all the worries I have been
carrying. I know that you are bigger than every one! I trust
in your dependable love; keep me close in the confidence of
your kindness!

*You will keep in perfect peace
all who trust in you,
all whose thoughts are fixed on you!*

Isaiah 26:3 NLT

Faithful One, I put all my trust in you, for you are unchanging in wondrous love. Your wisdom is more astute than the most compelling knowledge of the sages and seers. You never fail to move in the mercy of your generous heart of affection. Whenever I begin to waver in worry, remind me of your faithfulness. I will turn my thoughts toward you as often as it takes for my views to align with your ways. Your clarity brings peace and settles the confusion that opposing views bring up in me. You are able to hold the weight of the world and be unaltered by it all because you are the source of every living thing.

This world is your creation, and I am included in this. You know me better than I know myself, and you will not hold back your goodness. No matter what is happening around me, I can rest assured that you will get me through it with the peace of your presence as my faithful companion and covering!

Has there been something disturbing
God's promised peace in you?

Constant and True

Jesus Christ is the same
yesterday and today, and forever.

HEBREWS 13:8 NASB

It is difficult to imagine one who is perfect in love, though we can look at the life of Jesus as Son of Man and Son of God and find that he is the standard. He is the fulfillment of the law—the need for a Messiah. He is the Redeemer that was promised, and he is the resurrected King. He is the same yesterday, today and forever. He has not changed in loyal love since the beginning of time.

When we question what God is like, we have a great place to look. The Word of God reveals the nature of God through the life of Jesus. He came to destroy the bondage of sin and death and to overcome everything that kept us from God the Father. We have been reconciled to God because of the love and blood of Jesus. It is as powerful today as it was when Jesus gave his life for ours. Jesus is resurrected, and it is in the power of his life that we come boldly to the throne of grace, where we are met with God's overflowing love.

Jesus, thank you for the gift of life that you have given. I am overwhelmed by the incredible kindness and mercy of your heart. You are so worthy of my affection. You're worthy of my life!

Jesus, the Anointed One, is always the same—
yesterday, today, and forever.

HEBREWS 13:8 TPT

Anointed One, you are the ultimate representation of God's love. I cannot begin to adequately thank you for all that you have been for me—my source of joy and life, the sustainer of my heart through seasons of darkness and hardship, and the hope that constantly flows under the surface of my life. I could attempt to explain you with words, but they all fall short. They cannot contain the great lengths of your majesty. You are so much more than I can comprehend, and so much sweeter than I have even tasted. Your affection is purer than any other.

You are the beginning and the end; and you sustain everything in between. You are present in every moment. Your love overwhelms my fears every time I turn my attention toward you. There is nothing you cannot do. You are beautiful, Lord, and for as long as I live, I want to know you more. Unchanging Lord, overwhelm my senses with your glory!

How have you recognized God's consistency in your life?

Wait on Him

As I thought of you I moaned, "God, where are you?"
I'm overwhelmed with despair as I wait for your help to arrive.

PSALM 77:3 TPT

The psalms are filled with the emotional responses of humanity. The psalmists did not hold back their very real feelings and fears from God, trusting that he could handle each one. Often, we see that they went from being in deep despair to remembering the nature and faithfulness of God.

It is okay for us to approach God in the same way; there is no need for pretense. God already knows the state of our hearts, and he wants us as we are. We do not need to embellish our faith, for God can meet us where we are at all times. He is more patient than we acknowledge. Until we are honest with ourselves, how can we invite God into these places? May we have the courage to be as real with God today as the psalmists were in their time.

God, I won't hold back the reality of my feelings and thoughts today. I recognize that you don't need me to manage them for your sake. I invite you into my fears and worries. As I confess them, will you settle them with your peace?

I think of God, and I moan,
overwhelmed with longing for his help.

PSALM 77:3 NLT

Holy One, you have not changed in your loyal love. I know that
you don't require perfection from me, and I'm so thankful
for it. Settle my heart with your peace as I turn to you. I will
continue to practice turning every thought and every emotion
over to you, just as I would offer them to a trusted friend. You
are more reliable, and a much wiser counselor than any other
I have in this life. Though I trust them, I trust you more!

Will you meet me in the waiting? As soon as I look to you,
come rushing to me with your words of life. Your love is better
than anything I've ever known, and I know that you won't let
me down. Even in my darkest days, I am not overcome by
my despair because I am already overwhelmed by your love.
Come again, Lord, and help me. I trust that you will.

When was the last time you offered
the reality of your heart to God?

My Constant Companion

Surely your goodness and love will be with me all my life,
and I will live in the house of the LORD forever.

PSALM 23:6 NCV

There is a confidence in the companionship of the Lord that we can carry throughout our lives. It runs deep and is unmoved by shifts in the world around us. He is the same loving, trustworthy advocate throughout the ages. We cannot outrun the tremendous goodness of his mercy. It is present in every circumstance—every trial and every victory.

Our forever-home is found in the kingdom of God. It is not in the temporary dwellings we inhabit on this earth. This life is but a blink, but the steadfast love of the Lord is our ever-present companion through it all. His presence both sustains and strengthens us. We can rest in his fellowship, knowing that he is leading us through every situation until we stand face-to-face with him on eternity's shores. When that day comes, everything else will dim in comparison to the overwhelming glory of his presence.

Constant One, I am so grateful for your loyal friendship. What a wonderful and blessed hope you have put in my heart—that you are leading me into life through every circumstance. I cannot escape your kindness!

Why would I fear the future?
For your goodness and love pursue me all the days of my life.
Then afterward, when my life is through,
I'll return to your glorious presence to be forever with you!

PSALM 23:6 TPT

Loving Lord, you are the pursuer of my heart in every season of the soul. You never walk away from me, no matter where I find myself. How thankful I am for your fierce love that sticks closer than any other! With the confidence of your faithful love leading me, I will not fear the future or anything in my path. As long as I have you, I have everything I need.

Sustain my life with your grace and mercy and kiss my life with the kindness of your pure pursuit. I cannot lose, even in death, for there I will find your full and glorious presence, leaving behind all pain, shame, and sorrow. How my heart longs to know the fullness of your glory! Will you give me a glimpse of your unsurpassable grandeur today to revive my heart in hope? I know that I only see in part, and when this life is over one day, I will see you fully. Draw me close in your love and broaden my expectations with the revelations of your goodness.

How does the constant companionship of God
encourage and embolden you?

Spilled Out

I spill out my heart to you
and tell you all my troubles.

PSALM 142:2 TPT

Do you offer God the transparency of your reality, or are you giving him what you think he wants? Perhaps you try to convince yourself that your worry is wasted and therefore is not worth bringing to him. But even when you brush it aside, it does not leave you. Perhaps you think that God can only receive the parts of you that you offer with confident faith. The truth is that God sees you clearly, including every thought and motivation. This shouldn't disturb you; rather, it should be a comfort. You are fully seen and known by the Creator, and he loves and accepts you as you are.

Give him every part; there is nothing that you need hide from him. Spill out your heart before him. Tell him each and every trouble: every trial, every question, every worry. His love reaches for you at all times. In every turn of your heart—in every opening of it—you will be met with the healing balm of his affection and delight. Oh, how he loves you!

God, what I can I say to a father that loves me so completely? Your pure devotion is unmatched; I can barely fathom it. Thank you for loving me and accepting me just as I am. I won't hide myself from you.

I pour out my complaint before Him;
I declare before Him my trouble.

PSALM 142:2 NKJV

Father, I will not hold back even an iota of the worry that
weighs on my chest. I do not want to bear the burden of my
anxiety alone, and I know that I don't have to. Here is the
reality of my situation; here is what I see. Will you give me
eyes to see from your perspective? Will you open my ears to
hear your voice of clarity and wisdom when it speaks? I must
know what you see when you look at my life and the troubles
I face.

Speak tenderly to me, and do not hold back. I have known
your kindness; it has led me back to you over and over again.
Draw near and speak your words of life over the troubles of
my heart. You are my peace, and the confidence of my life.
I have built my life upon you. Will you let what needs to be
shaken fall away and reveal the firm foundation of your love
to me once again? I know you won't turn me away when I look
for you, and you will not ignore my cries of help. Ease my
worries in the waterfall of your mercy-kindness. I trust you.

Do you trust God with the vulnerable places of your heart?

Still Hope

For You are my hope;
Lord God, You are my confidence from my youth.

PSALM 71:5 NASB

In the innocence of our youth, it can be so easy to believe things that seem impossible. The opportunities of life are like an open book before us. When our stories are in the beginning stages, there is an ease and rhythm to everything. The thought of the future is exciting to most, not intimidating. The more life we live, the more experience we get, and the more unknown variables insert themselves into our stories. What once seemed simplistic is complicated by matters that challenge our belief systems.

But this is where our stories deepen, and the faithfulness of the Lord shines through the testing of our faith. Through it all, God is unchanging. His loyal love never leaves us. As our understanding of his kindness deepens along with the pain we inevitably experience, our capacity for extending his mercy also grows. Still hope, for there is always more available through fellowship with the Spirit.

Lord God, you have faithfully walked with me through my life. Though my understanding has broadened and changed, you remain the same. I see your love in a deeper way when I allow your truth to challenge my assumptions. Your ways are so much better than my own.

You are my only hope, Lord!
I've hung on to you,
trusting in you all my life.

PSALM 71:5 TPT

Lord, you are the hope of my heart, no matter what I am walking through in the moment. Though the seasons of life shift and change and bring unexpected troubles and heartache, you remain the same in loyal love. You are so worthy of my trust through it all. You never leave me, staying as close as the air in my lungs. You are always just a turn of my attention away; in fact, you are even closer than that.

Though I may not always recognize your nearness, you have promised that you are with me. I know that it is true even when I cannot sense you. You are the truth I cling to, the overwhelming goodness that gets me through the dark nights of the soul. You have never abandoned me, and I know that you will not do it now. Show off your marvelous mercy in my life and restore what is impossible for any other. You are better than life itself!

How has hope in the Lord sustained you in hard seasons?

Never Forgotten

God will never forget the needy;
the hope of the afflicted will never perish.

PSALM 9:18 NIV

How often do we feel isolated in our suffering, struggling to share the intensity of our pain with others? No matter what we go through, we do not do it alone. God is close to the brokenhearted, and he is near to those who are crushed in spirit. That is what his Word says. When we are brought low in our neediness, not knowing where to turn for help or how we will meet the overwhelming requirements of what is before us, God is near.

He sees every need, and he will provide for us. He is the same God who clothes the lilies of the field and who provides food for the animals. He will also provide for us, and not just the minimum. He is aware of our hardships, and he has solutions for each one even when we don't understand what he is doing. May we bind our hearts to him in trust whenever we feel adrift at sea, for he is faithful.

God, you are my strong deliverer. You are so rich in love even when I cannot discern what you are up to. I know that you will not let me drown in my circumstances. Your faithfulness keeps me; you are my mighty tower of refuge.

The needy will not be ignored forever;
the hopes of the poor will not always be crushed.

PSALM 9:18 NLT

Faithful Father, keep me close to your heart of love when I am overwhelmed by the hardships of life. Draw me near in your kindness and strengthen my heart in your mercy. I know that you don't abandon your children, and so I take hope in your Word that assures me of your overcoming victory in every situation. I do not trust in my own strength or resources, for they are limited in their scope. But you, oh Lord, are abundant in every good thing.

Do not withhold your love from me today, but rush into my heart, soul, and mind with the rivers of your living waters. Purify my life with the refining fire of your mercy. Lift me up when I fall under the weight of my worries; I don't want to carry them any longer. Give me the peace of your pure presence that wraps around me like a winter coat. Calm my racing thoughts and bring my attention back to the greatness and the goodness of who you are.

Do you believe that God will never leave you?

Clothed in Love

In addition to all these things put on love, which is the perfect bond of unity. Let the peace of Christ, to which you were indeed called in one body, rule in your hearts; and be thankful.

COLOSSIANS 3:14-15 NASB

The greatest call we have in life, beyond any other purpose, is to love. Does this seem too humble a pursuit? Though simple, it is far from easy. Jesus summed up the whole of the Old Testament law in this: that we should love God with all our hearts, souls and minds, and that we should love others as we do ourselves. Love covers over a multitude of wrongs. When we truly offer others the consideration that we expect from them, we will find that our hearts open up with compassion, able to hold the space for their experiences, as well as our own.

We are called to unify with our brothers and sisters in Christ. Is this true of us? Are we seeking peace and reconciliation instead of digging our heels into the places of difference? Let us follow the lead of Jesus, who did not consider his own life (though he is God!) as more important than the lives of those he served. His humility was not his weakness, for it moved him with compassion. May we also live with kindness propelling us toward loving action.

Humble Lord, what a worthy pursuit it is to follow you in your ways of love. Thank you for the reminder of what truly matters in this life. You are worthy of every sacrifice of my pride.

Over all these virtues put on love, which binds them all together in perfect unity. Let the peace of Christ rule in your hearts, since as members of one body you were called to peace. And be thankful.

COLOSSIANS 3:14–15 NIV

Christ Jesus, you are the perfect expression of God's pure love. You are the one I look toward to ground me in mercy and kindness. When offense settles in and I am tempted to erect walls around my heart, I look to you and see a better way. You never let the misunderstanding of others, or their accusations and ridicule, keep you from extending mercy and kindness. You were strong in dismantling the pride of the religious elite, rebuking them for their misplaced fervor, but you never turned away an open and searching heart. You were friend of sinners and outcasts, and you spent your time revealing the love of the Father through humble acts of service.

May I echo your love in my own life as I lay down my own preferences for the good of others. May I not let apathy keep me from the hard and rewarding work of letting your mercy-kindness infiltrate every piece of my heart and life. Your ways are pure, and I will choose to follow you on the path of laid-down love, no matter what it costs me.

How is God's love revealed in your choices?

Beyond the Pain

This light momentary affliction is preparing for us an eternal weight of glory beyond all comparison, as we look not to the things that are seen but to the things that are unseen. For the things that are seen are transient, but the things that are unseen are eternal.

2 Corinthians 4:17-18 ESV

When our eyes are fixed on our circumstances, it is easy to become overwhelmed by the unknowns of tomorrow. Sure, when things are going well, we may feel settled. But what about when the unexpected knocks the wind out of our sails? As long as we are focused solely on what we can see and understand on our own, the accompanying emotions will rise and fall with our shifting realities.

Let us lift our eyes to the one who sees and understands the whole of our circumstances, as well as the broader scope of humanity. God's perspective is broad and doesn't miss a thing. He is full of wisdom to bring us clarity, peace to settle our anxious hearts, and love to subdue the fear that floods our minds. His kingdom is eternal, and his ways supersede the ways of this world. We can trust his mercy-kindness to keep us through every storm. Let us look to him and find fresh courage to face the day!

Holy One, you are unchanging in power and glory. Your love hasn't let up for a moment. As I look to you today, lift the weight of the burdens I face. I know that there is eternal joy, hope, and love accessible in you right now.

We view our slight, short-lived troubles in the light of eternity.
We see our difficulties as the substance that produces for us an
eternal, weighty glory far beyond all comparison, because we don't
focus our attention on what is seen but on what is unseen. For
what is seen is temporary, but the unseen realm is eternal.

2 Corinthians 4:17-18 TPT

Unseen One, I know that you are with me. Your Spirit is my confidant and my companion through every trial and every circumstance. I trust your loyal love to guide me through it all. When I am caught up in the demands of my troubles, will you remind me to shift my gaze to yours? I know that if I catch a glimpse of you that you will settle my heart with your peace. You are strong in mercy, and you won't turn away from me. I look to you, Lord, for you are unchanging in your plans for redemption. You always bring something beautiful out of the rubble of my life. You will do it again.

Keep my heart in perfect peace as I set my face toward the future with your faithfulness as my confidence. You have not abandoned me yet, and I know that you never will. When all temporary trials give way to your eternal goodness, may I be able to say with a full heart that I trusted you even when I could not see you.

> When was the last time you asked God
> for his perspective on your life?

Holy Help

The LORD will fight for you,
and you shall hold your peace.

EXODUS 14:14 NKJV

God is defender of the helpless and advocate of the weak. It doesn't matter how big or small your challenge is—the Lord will fight for you! He will defend you when your reputation is at stake. He holds the scales of justice in his hand. He will not let you be ashamed, for he is your present and strong help. He will come through for you.

Let the generous portion of his presence with you be your peace. No one can take it away. His abundant mercy covers you at all times. Instead of wearying yourself trying to defend your good name, let the Lord be the one who advocates on your behalf. He is more than capable. Rest in the confidence of his faithfulness, for he will not let you down.

God, my mighty defender, I depend on you to uphold your truth in my life. I know that you will not let slander take me out; you won't let me be overcome by the schemes of those looking for my downfall. You are a wise and mighty defender, and I trust you!

The LORD himself will fight for you.
Just stay calm.

EXODUS 14:14 NLT

Lord God, be the one to fight my battles. I have no strength of my own, and even if I did, it would not last long. You have wisdom to see to the bottom of every matter. You take into account what everyone else misses, for you see everything as it is. Your clarity is clearer than my most astute understanding, so I will rest in your ways.

Take over the causes that I have poured myself out upon; I have little left to offer. More than anything, may I rest in the peace of your calming presence that soothes every anxiety and fear. As I remember how you faithfully delivered your people out of Egypt and led them to the promised land, it gives my heart hope to know that your miracle-working power is the same today as it was then. Be my defense, Lord. I depend on you.

What areas can you give to God
and rest in his advocacy for you?

He Knows

He was despised and rejected by men,
a man of sorrows and acquainted with grief;
and as one from whom men hide their faces he was despised,
and we esteemed him not.

ISAIAH 53:3 ESV

It is easy to overlook the humanity of Jesus though the lens of hindsight. We see his God nature more clearly when we see how everything tied together—the prophecies that led up to his life and death, the confirmation of his resurrection, and his ascension to the Father. However, we miss out on the depth of Christ's compassion when we fail to fully consider the depth of his human experience.

In this passage in Isaiah, the prophecy spoke of the Messiah as a "man of sorrows...acquainted with grief." Jesus knew suffering in his life, and not just the suffering of his crucifixion. He knew the pain of betrayal, the sorrow of loss, and the general limits of his human form. He grew up, as any do, not only physically, but in wisdom and knowledge. There is so much solidarity to be found in the God who understands our trials, because he also experienced them in the boundaries of flesh and bones.

Son of Man, may I never forget that you experienced rejection, sorrow, and grief. When I am walking through suffering, I know that your presence is more than a balm; you understand me. Thank you for this revelation truth.

He was despised and rejected by men
a man of deep sorrows
who was no stranger to suffering and grief.
We hid our faces from him in disgust
and considered him a nobody, not worthy of respect.

Isaiah 53:3 TPT

Wonderful Savior, may I not overlook your humanity when I am grappling with my own sorrow. You experienced deep sorrows in your life, and you understand my plight. Instead of pulling away from you in my distress, I will press closer. Your comfort is unlike any other; it reaches to the depths of my soul and soothes my aching heart.

Though every grief experience is unique, you know me well—better than any other. I recognize that you learned the limitations of your flesh and blood life, but you remained perfect in love through it all. As I surrender my will to yours through the twists and turns of this life, I trust you to guide me in empathy. Your kindness is wonderful and humbling. I am awed by you, man of sorrows and savior of all.

Is there something in your life
that you think God can't understand?

Pure Motives

The LORD wants to show his mercy to you.
He wants to rise and comfort you.
The LORD is a fair God,
and everyone who waits for his help will be happy.

ISAIAH 30:18 NCV

Have you gotten caught up in the trap of relying on yourself to get through any and everything that comes your way? We seem to idolize self-reliance in our society, believing that we are the only ones that we can truly count on. But that is not God's way, and it doesn't have to be yours, either. The Lord is just, and he is faithful to help all those who wait for him to move. He is full of compassion and understanding. He will always extend his mercy toward you.

Will you trust that he can do a far better job of leading you in wisdom than you can with the limitations of your understanding and resources? He will show up, and he will astound you with his provision. He is better than you can imagine.

Merciful One, instead of trying to fix the problems that arise in my life with what I have, I trust that your wisdom and ways are better. Put your hand to the messes in my life and do what only you can do. I will wait on you to guide me.

*The Lord is still waiting to show his favor to you
so he can show you his marvelous love.
He waits to be gracious to you.
He sits on his throne ready to show mercy to you.
For Yahweh is the Lord of justice,
faithful to keep his promises.
Overwhelmed with bliss are all
who will entwine their hearts in him,
waiting for him to help them.*

ISAIAH 30:18 TPT

Gracious God, it astounds me that you are always ready to show mercy to those who look to you. I want to know the wonderful depths of your love, always expecting the abundance of your affection to meet me every time I turn toward you. I have entwined my heart with yours, and your delight fills me up to the very brim of my being.

How can I not come alive in the living waters of your marvelous love? You are my joy, my strength, and my song! I wait on you, knowing that you will help me whenever I need it. I have placed all my bets on you. There is no greater hope than you, and I trust that you will come through for me in wonderful ways when I have run out of solutions.

Are you rushing forward in your own strength
or waiting on God's help?

Surrender Is Worship

Let us be thankful, because we have a kingdom that cannot be shaken. We should worship God in a way that pleases him with respect and fear.

HEBREWS 12:28 NCV

The kingdom of God is eternal. It cannot be swayed by the winds of this world that are always shifting. Popular opinions change with the times, and they cannot be counted on as truth. There is not a kingdom of the earth that operates in the purity of God's truth, so God's government stands above them all.

Let us worship him in spirit and truth, yielding our lives to him above any other. While we could give our lives to a noble cause on the earth, there is nothing greater than aligning our lives with God's kingdom ways. His law of love will stand as the eternal standard. May we labor for unity and break down the offenses that seek to divide us from one another in mercy. In that way, we live with worship as our lifestyle, respecting God's ways and his nature.

Mighty God, I know that your ways are higher than mine. I will trust that when I live according to your mercy-love, that I am offering the purest form of worship I can. You are worthy of it!

Since we are receiving our rights to an unshakeable kingdom we should be extremely thankful and offer God the purest worship that delights his heart as we lay down our lives in absolute surrender, filled with awe.

HEBREWS 12:28 TPT

Wonderful Lord, I am so thankful for the kingdom of your loyal love that I call my forever home. I look forward to the day when I walk through the physical gates of your kingdom straight into the fullness of your glory. Until then, I will offer you what I have to give—my life.

I surrender to you, knowing that you always lead in kindness. You are not a demanding master, but a loving and faithful father. I come alive in the truth of your mercy that sets me free! I will not hold back any part of my life from you knowing that you deserve it all. When I stand before you in the age to come, all of this will be a memory. Your incomparable glory will be worth every sacrifice and submission. You are worthy.

Does your life reflect your trust in God?

Wonderful News

"The blind see again, the crippled walk, lepers are cured, the deaf hear, the dead are raised back to life, and the poor and broken now hear of the hope of salvation!"

MATTHEW 11:5 TPT

The verse we are reading is what Jesus tells John the Baptist's disciples to report back to him when they ask if he is the awaited Christ. Signs and wonders were the testimony of God's power in Jesus' ministry. He opened blind eyes, made the crippled walk, cured incurable diseases, opened deaf ears and even raised the dead back to life.

All of this was the seal and signature of the Spirit's power in Christ's life. He walked in power and in authority. Even more, he exuded compassion to those that society, especially the religious elite, overlooked. He empowered women, he spoke to and touched those who were untouchables in the community. He healed their diseases and pointed them all toward the kingdom of heaven. What a wonderfully compassionate Savior he was and is!

Savior, what you did in your ministry on this earth, you are still doing today. You are still healing, delivering and saving. May I witness the miracles of your power in my life as I follow in your ways.

*"The blind see, the lame walk, those with leprosy are cured,
the deaf hear, the dead are raised to life,
and the Good News is being preached to the poor."*

MATTHEW 11:5 NLT

Christ, you are the bringer of good news to all those who look
to you. Your mercy is always reaching out, covering those who
call on your name. I don't want to just know about you, Lord.
I want to witness your power in my life. You assured your
disciples that everything they watched you do they would do
in their own ministries—and even more.

As your follower, I know that this is a promise to me, too. As
I walk in the authority of your name, may I release the power
of your kingdom that confirms the reality of your love that
breaks every chain that holds us back. You are quick to save!
Give me bold faith to pray big prayers, knowing that it is not
presumptuous, but actually what you have called me to. I will
follow your lead, Jesus, and rely on your miracle-working
power to break through.

Have you witnessed God's power first-hand?

Lifted Up

*Be humble under God's powerful hand
so he will lift you up when the right time comes.*

1 PETER 5:6 NCV

In the upside-down kingdom of God that names the humble as leaders and the proud as fools, will you trust God to lead you in his better way? There is no need to promote yourself at all costs, calling attention to your strengths and wit. There is a time and a place to advocate for yourself, but a lifestyle of self-promotion will only take you so far.

No matter what your job, your place in life, or your gifts, be sure to keep an attitude of modesty before God. Be humble before him, for he knows you through and through. Trust in him, and he will lift you up when the time comes, and he will open doors that no man can shut. Rely on his timing, for he knows precisely what he is doing. Though you may strive and be able to get your foot in the crack of a door, God will bring you to where you need to be. You may just find yourself in a space where you wonder how you got there at all! Trust him, he will do it.

Faithful One, I submit myself to you again today. I trust that your ways and your timing are better than my own. I will keep living with a heart of surrender to you, for you are faithful.

*Humble yourselves under the mighty hand of God,
so that He may exalt you at the proper time.*

1 PETER 5:6 NASB

Mighty God, I humble myself in your presence. You are the leader of my life, and I trust you to guide me into spaces that I could never get myself into. What you call me to, you will provide a way for. I need only follow you. I will walk in the wisdom of your ways and put away the temptation of both insecurity and pride that demands I promote myself to get ahead. You are my promoter, and I trust you to do it in your perfect timing.

I recognize that this life is a journey and that I will never reach the end of looking for more until I reach eternity's crossing. Keep me close to your side, that my life may reflect the heartbeat of your love. I am covered by your kindness, and I won't forget what you have already done for me. I will walk hand in hand with you, letting peace guide me.

Do you trust God to take you where you need to go?

Dwelling Place

"God's dwelling place is now among the people, and he will dwell with them. 'He will wipe every tear from their eyes. There will be no more death' or mourning or crying or pain, for the old order of things has passed away."

REVELATION 21:3-4 NIV

In the eternal kingdom of heaven, all ends will cease and the pain of earthly separation will be but a memory. There will be fullness of joy, for the King of heaven will dwell with his people without anything to separate them. In the new order of God's eternal kingdom, there will be no fear, no pain, and no mourning.

Even in this in-between space, God is with us through his Spirit. He dwells within, and we have fellowship with the comforter here and now. We currently have a glimpse into the wonders of this heavenly realm with the fruit of the Spirit deposited in our lives. But what we see dimly through a dark glass now, will be clear as day then!

Emmanuel, I know that you are with me now, but how I long for the day when I will dwell physically with you. You are light, life, and everything I long for.

> *"God's tabernacle is with human beings.*
> *And from now on he will tabernacle with them as their God.*
> *Now God himself will have his home with them*
> *'God-with-them' will be their God!*
> *He will wipe away every tear from their eyes*
> *and eliminate death entirely.*
> *No one will mourn or weep any longer.*
> *The pain of wounds will no longer exist,*
> *for the old order has ceased."*
>
> REVELATION 21:3-4 TPT

God, you are my God! You are the one I take hope in both now and forever. I look forward to the age to come, where we dwell together in perfect unity. I can only imagine a day when the pain of my current wounds and heartache is just a memory. I look forward to death being a thing of the past.

Until then, be with me in every turn and twist of the road I travel. Be my steady guide and the one who catches me every time my foot slips. You have been so faithful to me, and I know that you will continue to be. Come close, Spirit, and continue to reveal what 'God with us' looks like.

What does the thought of dwelling with God evoke in you?

Steady Steps

The LORD makes firm the steps
of the one who delights in him.

PSALM 37:23 NIV

God leads those who follow him in light and truth. He will not lead us into destruction. Even when we walk through suffering, he makes our steps firm and smooths out the path before us. His merciful nature marks every bit of our stories, for we are covered by his compassion in every season and circumstance.

We need not fear what tomorrow will bring; let us put all our trust in the one who is faithful to lead us. May our hearts come alive in the purity of his love for us, and may we respond with the delight of dearly loved children! He is so very good to us. He takes joy in every movement of our lives that follow his loving lead. He is a proud father! How could we not adore him?

Faithful Father, I am grateful for the tender leading of your mercy in my life. I will not stop following you because your ways are true and right. May hope and joy rise within my heart again today as I look to you!

The steps of the God-pursuing ones
follow firmly in the footsteps of the Lord,
and God delights in every step they take to follow him.

PSALM 37:23 TPT

God, you are my guiding light in this life. Every question I have, every problem I encounter, is met with the wisdom of your eternal Word. Your truth is beyond human logic, and it extends beyond our reasoning. I will not stop following your ways, which are so much better than my own even when I don't understand why you require what you do. May all of my choices be covered in your mercy, that I may extend the same mercy toward others in my life.

You have been the goal I have set my life upon, and that continues to be true. Even through the unexpected trials of this life, you have proven faithful. Everything else pales in comparison to the glory of your goodness. You turn deserts into gardens with your redemption power. I will continue to pursue you, for you are better than anything else I've ever known.

How are you following God's lead?

A Thousand Generations

Know that the LORD your God, He is God, the faithful God who keeps covenant and mercy for a thousand generations with those who love Him and keep His commandments.

DEUTERONOMY 7:9 NKJV

Everything God does is with eternity in view. He is not short-sighted. When he leads us, he always sees where he is taking us, and he considers the effects it will have on future generations. Will we trust that his ways really are higher than our own? We see a very small part, but he sees the whole—from the beginning to the end and everything in between. He is faithful to do all that he said he would. Though his timing may be different than our preferences, he will never let his words return to him void.

As we follow him, obeying his commands, may we consider that our choices not only affect our lives, but also those around us—including the ones that will follow us. When we follow in his merciful ways, future generations will also reap the benefits of his kindness.

Faithful God, you bless the lives of those who choose to love and follow you, and you don't stop there. The blessings will be poured out on the generations that follow. You never stop moving in mercy; how wonderful you are!

*Understand, therefore, that the LORD your God is indeed God.
He is the faithful God who keeps his covenant for a thousand
generations and lavishes his unfailing love on those who love him
and obey his commands.*

DEUTERONOMY 7:9 NLT

Lord God, reveal to me again the surpassing wonders of your ways. You are faithful in every vow you make, and every word that comes from you is fulfilled. It does not simply affect a single life, but it spreads through generations. Your promises are reaped by all those who love and look to you.

Keep my heart woven into the fabric of your love, that I may be quick to obey your voice when you speak. I know that your wisdom is far above my own understanding, so I won't try to get my own way when you offer a better one. I know that my choices will also affect the generations coming after me, and I don't want to be short-sighted. Keep my eyes on your eternal kingdom and give me eyes to see from the broad perspective of your insight.

Do you believe that God is who he says he is?

Yes You Are

Once you were not a people, but now you are God's people; once you had not received mercy, but now you have received mercy.

1 PETER 2:10 ESV

God gives families to the lonely ones, and he is close to those who call on him. If you are feeling isolated in your experience, know that your God is a good father, and he has made you for community and fellowship. If you follow God, and you love those around you as he has commanded you to—with mercy, peace, and kindness—then you are his.

Jesus said that whoever comes to him, he will receive as his own. He draws us with lovingkindness and covers the mistakes of our past with his compassion. He is quick to forgive, and he is extremely patient in returning because he wants as many who would choose him to do so. Nothing can disqualify you from going after and knowing God, if that is what you want. He is waiting with open arms of mercy to receive you, every time you call on him.

My God, I am thankful that you have accepted me as your own. My identity as your child marks me more than anything else in this life. I won't stop running to you!

At one time you were not God's people, but now you are.
At one time you knew nothing of God's mercy,
because you hadn't received it yet,
but now you are drenched with it!

1 PETER 2:10 TPT

Merciful Father, you are so patient with me. I cannot begin to comprehend the grand scope of your love, though I am captivated by it again and again. Every time you reveal a new facet of your nature, I am undone with awe. You move, and I am fascinated with wonder. Though I haven't always known your great kindness, it has changed my life. I could not imagine living without the covering of your mercy, and I never want to! You are better than my wildest dreams could depict you to be, and I want to know you more and more and more.

There is nothing in my life that lies outside the power of your love. Will you open my eyes to see where you are weaving the thread of restoration in my life? Your resurrection life is still raising the dead, both figuratively and physically. In my life, I want to see how you are bringing new life out of the ashes of shattered dreams. Don't stop your wonderful work!

How have you seen God's patient mercy in your life?

Miracles of Mercy

*Lift your hands and give thanks to God for his marvelous kindness
and for his miracles of mercy for those he loves!*

PSALM 107:8 TPT

When was the last time you took the time to thank God
for what he is doing in your life? He is always working, no
matter what your circumstances look like in the moment.
With a heart of gratitude, look for the blessings—the people,
provisions, and fulfilled promises—that are present in your
life. Look past the obvious, big things. Search for the nuggets
of God's faithfulness in your life. If you look for them, you
will find them!

Will you offer thanks for those things that you find, and keep
your eyes open, looking for more deposits of his kindness
that are already within and around you?

Marvelous Lord, you are kinder than the most thoughtful
person I know. You see past the surface into the depths, and
you work in the small details as you do in the bigger picture.
I am so thankful for who you are and for what you have done.
Thank you for what you are doing.

*Oh, that men would give thanks to the L*ORD *for His goodness,*
And for His wonderful works to the children of men!

PSALM 107:8 NKJV

Good God, your goodness is unmatched by any other. What you give, no man can take away, and what you take, no one can grab back. I trust your faithful character that knows what I need right when I need it. I know that you will not leave me even when I cannot sense you. You have been so wonderful to me.

When I think back to how you have faithfully provided for me, in more ways than I can count, I am undone by gratitude. I could not exaggerate your goodness; no one could! You give grace away, knowing there is an endless supply. May I not be stingy with my thanks, instead stirring it up with every remembrance of who you have always been. Give me eyes to see where you are moving in mercy. You are so very good to your children, and I am grateful to be yours.

What can you give thanks for today?

He Is Better

To the LORD our God belong mercy and forgiveness,
though we have rebelled against Him.

DANIEL 9:9 NKJV

God is full of mercy toward us. He does not ration it, only allotting a certain amount to each person. No, his compassion is limitless. As long as it is called 'today,' it is an opportunity to receive the kindness of his love that covers over a multitude of sins. You have not tapped out the resources of his love, though you may question how much is too much. The answer to that is: there is always more.

There is no such thing as "too much" in the kingdom of heaven. However great your rebellion, God's mercy is greater. He can cover every one of your mistakes with the oil of his forgiveness. Do not delay today. Receive the love that he is offering and be restored in freedom again. He will not turn you away.

Great God, your ways are so much better than any I've ever known. I come to you with all my errors in judgment and the rebellion of selfish choices. Wash me in the cleansing tide of your love, and I will live in the liberty of your mercy.

To the Lord our God belong compassion and forgiveness,
because we have rebelled against Him.

DANIEL 9:9 NASB

Merciful One, I cannot begin to thank you for the compassion
of your forgiveness. You not only pardon me when I
repent, but you throw every one of my sins into the sea of
forgetfulness. You don't hold a thing against your children
when they are reconciled to you.

Oh, that I would be more like you, that I would forgive the
way that you do. As I receive your mercy in great measure,
may I also extend it to those that hurt me. In doing so, I will
reflect the kindness of your love that leads me to life. Every
time I rebel against your law of love, would you draw me back
to you so that I can be realigned in your mercy? A life lived
in rebellion, thinking I know what is better than you do, is
a wasted one. I don't want to reach the end of my days and
regret the choices I made. Lord, keep me close to your heart.
Let your love burn true and bright in my life.

How has God surprised you with his love?

So Much Grace

From his fullness we have all received,
grace upon grace.

JOHN 1:16 NRSV

Are you living life with a poverty mentality? This doesn't just apply to your finances. When we approach any area of our lives as if we are always working from a deficit, we are bound to the limitations we perceive even if they are not reality. When it comes to God's grace, we need to understand that it is not finite. There is no lack in God, and we are his children. He freely gives to us out of the abundant storehouses of his goodness. From his fullness we have received grace upon grace. That will always be true!

May we recognize areas where we are operating in the mentality of scarcity instead of abundance and allow God's overflowing love to enlarge our understanding. He is so much bigger and better than anything we could try to equate him with on this earth.

Gracious God, as I meditate on the abundance of your love, will you broaden my comprehension of your grace? It is always enough to meet me where I'm at, to strengthen, uphold, and empower me. You are so good, God!

Out of his fullness we are fulfilled!
And from him we receive grace heaped upon more grace!

JOHN 1:16 TPT

Wondrous One, I can barely comprehend your goodness, and yet what I have tasted is sweeter than the richest delicacies this world has to offer. Your love is unending! You fill me up whenever I am poured out, and you do it for all of your loyal lovers, as many times as it takes. Your grace never runs dry; what a wonderful thing to meditate on.

I don't want to live with the tension of feeling that I am always at risk of running on empty. With you, that never need be my reality. You fill me to overflow with the fullness of your very nature. I cannot get enough! The more I rest in your love, the more I am able to offer others, and the more I offer others, the more it sends me back to you to be filled again. What a wonderfully dependent cycle this is. I don't ever want to rely on my own strength when yours is available in abundance.

Do you put a limit on God's grace in your life or others?

No Need to Despair

"Don't worry, because I am with you.
Don't be afraid, because I am your God.
I will make you strong and will help you;
I will support you with my right hand that saves you."

ISAIAH 41:10 NCV

There is no situation you encounter that God is not with you. He is your God, and he will always help you when you rely on him. He will give you the strength you need for every moment, and he will support you when you cannot stand on your own.

Trust him, for he is faithful. Give him every worry. There's no need to play out endless possibilities when he already knows the outcome. When fear is clawing at your insides for control, know that you can let go and stand on your faith in God. He always comes through. He knows what he is doing, and he will not let you go!

Faithful One, I bind my heart to yours in trust, remembering that you never abandon me. Thank you for your presence that surrounds me, no matter what is going on around me. I trust you. Deliver me from fear and keep me close in love.

"Do not yield to fear, for I am always near.
Never turn your gaze from me, for I am your faithful God.
I will infuse you with my strength
and help you in every situation.
I will hold you firmly with my victorious right hand."

ISAIAH 41:10 TPT

Loving Father, I look to you this evening. I know that you are the same faithful God who has walked with me through storms and through pleasant days. You have kept me this far, and I trust you to continue to guide me. Fill me with your strength when my own is depleted. Help me when fear threatens to overcome the peace of your presence. I know that your love is stronger. Hold me firmly with your hand and do not let me go.

I remember that you are near. You are so very near! May my heart grow bold in faith as you continue to prove your faithfulness in my life. I say to my soul, 'trust in God! For he is my liberator and my faithful God.'

What worries can you give to God today?

Victory

Every child of God defeats this evil world,
and we achieve this victory through our faith.

1 John 5:4 NLT

What does it mean for a child of God to defeat the world? Through the confidence we have in Jesus, we are conquerors over the systems of this world. We live according to God's ways and laws, and they supersede the laws of the land. Though we may know that murder is against the law, God will not only express justice, but also mercy. They go hand in hand.

In this world, justice usually looks like the dropping of a hammer, or at the very least, a fair judgment for the crime. As children of God, we don't put our hope in the world's systems, but in our greater God's ways. He is our confidence, and in him all things will find their fulfillment. This includes our hopes!

God of Justice, I believe that you have the final word over everything that happens in the earth. You will rule in justice and mercy, and what you declare, no one will be able to argue. Thank you!

Everyone who has been born of God overcomes the world.
And this is the victory that has overcome the world—our faith.

1 JOHN 5:4 ESV

Victorious One, it is by your blood that I have been set free to live in the light of your life. You have liberated me in your love, and I am able to know the Father in the reconciliation of restored relationship. What a wondrous thing, that I can know the Creator of the universe without separation or anxiety! It is almost too incredible to grasp.

In your victory, Jesus, I have also overcome the ways of this world. You have opened a new reality to me—the reality of your kingdom. Where love is the law, and the fruit of the Spirit is the food that we feast upon. Where there is no competition or need for proving oneself. My confidence is in you, Lord, and not in my own abilities. What a relief! I rely on you to lead me through every problem with the wisdom of your Word. You are my greatest assurance.

Is your confidence rooted in God?

Immeasurable Goodness

To him who is able to do immeasurably more than all we ask or imagine, according to his power that is at work within us, to him be glory in the church and in Christ Jesus throughout all generations, for ever and ever! Amen.

EPHESIANS 3:20-21 NIV

God is able to do so much more than we can dream of. His power is at work within us because we have aligned our lives with him. We have unhindered relationship with the King of kings and Lord of lords. Can you imagine? The truth of his love is so much grander than we can think of.

May our faith rise with the levels of our understanding all the days of our lives. May our perceptions of him expand with our knowledge of his goodness in our lives. It is not just a believing with our minds, but an experience within our very existence. He is so much better than we can envision. Will we let the goodness of his love increase the possibilities of his greatness in our expectations? Let's dream bigger and ask bolder!

Great God, my heart is growing in expectation of your goodness in my life. You are indescribable; yet, my heart hungers to know you more. Fill my experience with the fruit of your presence.

*With God's power working in us, God can do much, much more
than anything we can ask or imagine. To him be glory in the
church and in Christ Jesus for all time, forever and ever. Amen.*

EPHESIANS 3:20-21 NCV

God, I know that your power is at work in my life. I have
chosen to follow you, and my heart turns to you again and
again. When I wander for a while following my own whims,
I turn and find that you are closer than I imagined you could
be. You are so faithful to me in love, and you are always ready
to restore the connection of our relationship when I come
to you. I cannot begin to imagine how large your mercy is,
though I try.

If I get lost in anything, may it be in how limitless your love
is. Stir my heart to pray big, bold prayers that reflect your
own heart. I want to see your kingdom come and your will be
done, on earth as it is in heaven.

What is the most grandiose thing you've asked God to do?

Safe Space

The LORD also will be a refuge for the oppressed,
a refuge in times of trouble.

PSALM 9:9 NKJV

When the winds of adversity pick up, there is a safe place that we can run to—the refuge of our God. He is a firm foundation that can never be shaken. Though our lives will feel the effects of the storms of this world, there is an undercurrent of love that runs steady.

With our roots firmly planted in the Lord, we will produce the fruit that comes from feeding on his mercy-kindness in our lives, no matter the climate of our present circumstances. He is a sure place of shelter in every season. We can always come to him with our burdens and find relief for our souls. As we turn to him, his peace surrounds us and his love rushes to meet the deep caverns of our needs. He is always more than enough.

Father, you are my strong shelter. I run to you whenever I need respite from the world's wearying ways. Keep me safe in the refuge of your peace and calm my anxious thoughts with your tender and reliable truth.

All who are oppressed may come to you
as a shelter in the time of trouble,
a perfect hiding place.

PSALM 9:9 TPT

Lord, you are my hiding place. When I cannot bear the
burden of other's expectations, I turn to you for guidance and
perspective. When I am crushed by the weight of the state
of this world, I enter your presence and receive rest. There
is no fear or lie that can stand in your presence. Your truth
outshines them all.

Will you light up the shadows of my life with the revelation-
light of your Word? Encourage my soul as I follow your lead.
I will rest in your love, and there I will be refreshed and
restored. As I lay my head down to sleep tonight, flood my
body, soul, and mind with your Spirit's peace. May I be lulled
to sleep in the safety of your loving embrace that holds me
close. You are my trustworthy help at all times. I rest in you.

When you are overwhelmed by life's storms,
where do you turn?

Wisdom's Path

Know that wisdom is the same for your soul;
If you find it, then there will be a future,
And your hope will not be cut off.

PROVERBS 24:14 NASB

The wisdom of the Lord is full of clarity to guide us in this life. He does not hide his insight from those who long to follow him in spirit and truth. He reveals his wonderful nature to those who look for him. As we dig through the Word, there is so much treasure to be found. He gives us eyes to see his goodness as we acquaint ourselves with his character and the ways in which he moves in the world.

His truth doesn't appease the ego, but it does encourage the spirit. God's ways are full of mercy. The fruit of the Spirit indicates a life rooted in God's great love. May our lives be established in the soil of God's nature through fellowship with him. There is so much more life to discover in him!

Lord, you are the anchor of my soul. Lead me in your wisdom all the days of my life. I trust that you always know better than I do. I submit my heart to yours in love again today.

Then you will perceive what is true wisdom,
your future will be bright,
and this hope living within will never disappoint you.

PROVERBS 24:14 TPT

Wise God, I want to know the wonders of your insight and how it applies to my life. I know that you see everything clearly; nothing surprises you. When I am overwhelmed by the choices I must make, will you guide me into peace and clarity by your Spirit?

As I look to your Word for direction, speak directly to my heart. Enlighten the eyes of my heart to see what you are doing and open the ears of my spirit to hear what you are saying. Do not stay hidden from me. I know that when I look for you, I will find you, every single time. You are the hope living inside of me. As I align my life with your love, flood my path with the light of your glory. Your ways are better than any other. I won't stop going after you!

How do you look for wisdom when you need it?

Not the End

Surely there is a future,
and your hope will not be cut off.

PROVERBS 23:18 ESV

It can be discouraging when life takes an unforeseen turn and our plans derail. Have you ever been disheartened by a change in your life? Perhaps that is a silly question; it is part of the human experience, after all. Whatever disappointments you have experienced, there is a greater hope that awaits you. It cannot be disturbed, for it is the promise of eternal life with the King of kings.

Align your life with the Lord, and you will always have something to look forward to. Surely God is not done working his miracles of restoration in your life. But every single one will pale in comparison to the fullness of God's beauty that we will one day encounter when this finite existence passes away, and we are ushered into his forever-kingdom.

Wonderful Lord, when I try to imagine the fullness of your glory, I cannot! But my heart rises with the hope and expectation of your exceptional goodness. Reveal more of yourself to me today that it may stir my heart in wonder at how incredibly marvelous you are!

*Your future is bright and filled with a living hope
that will never fade away.*

PROVERBS 23:18 TPT

All-knowing One, as I look to the future, may I see it from
your eternal perspective. I can make my plans, and I can
dream up big ideals for my life, but you are the one who
leads me through the unexpected twists and turns that
would otherwise trip me up. You always guide me in your
lovingkindness. I know that no matter what the details of my
life look like, I am looking to a greater glory in the coming age
of your kingdom reign.

In eternity, I will dwell with you in the fullness of your
splendor. Your light will never dim, and every moment of
suffering on this earth will fade. There will be no more
mourning and no more pain of separation. What a hope! It is
alive inside of me, and I feel the confidence of your joy rising
within me. I am so thankful for the promised fullness that
awaits me in your presence.

What does your ultimate hope lie in?

Celebrations

They celebrate your abundant goodness
and joyfully sing of your righteousness.

PSALM 145:7 NIV

There is a time for weeping and a time for celebration; this is what King Solomon says in Ecclesiastes. In a busy world, where we can always be looking to the next thing or what we may have missed in the shuffle, we can easily skip past the moments that should be celebrated. Whether big or small, there is so much opportunity to honor the goodness of God in our lives.

Think over the last few weeks and see if you can't pinpoint something that was significant to you or to a loved one. Did someone do well on a test? Was there something special that happened at work? There are so many things that can be celebrated, if we will look for them. Let's build a lifestyle of rejoicing in both the little and big victories. We become more like God when we learn to revel in the goodness he gives. He is full of delight toward us! Let us joyfully offer the same pleasure back to him.

Joyful King, I know that you are good. As I recognize your wonders in my life, I will take the time to celebrate! You are full of joy, and I want to be just like you.

Our hearts bubble over as we celebrate the fame
of your marvelous beauty, bringing bliss to our hearts.
We shout with ecstatic joy over your breakthrough for us.

PSALM 145:7 TPT

Marvelous One, you are so full of beauty to behold. I know as I look for reasons to celebrate that I will find them. May I resist the urge to skip over opportunities to embrace joy in favor of striving for more. There is a kingdom element to resting and enjoying what is right in front of us. Teach me to harness the delight of each day and to model joy well to others.

I want to celebrate those I love in the same way that you delight over us—with wild dancing and unrestrained joy! I know there is something powerful in the bubbling up of bliss and not trying to manage it. May my heart come alive in your gladness! You, Lord, are more wonderful that I can contain. In promises fulfilled, longings met and in the great joy of your companionship, I have so much to thank you for. You are so, so good!

What can you celebrate today?

Living Hope

Blessed be the God and Father of our Lord Jesus Christ, who according to His great mercy has caused us to be born again to a living hope through the resurrection of Jesus Christ from the dead.

1 PETER 1:3 NASB

When Jesus rose from the grave three days after he was laid there, his resurrection power broke the sentence of death once and for all. Our hopes are not rooted in a school of thought; they are rooted in the living God-man, Jesus Christ. It is through his resurrection power that we are able to overcome everything we face, for there is nothing that can nullify his victory. In his mercy, we have been born again.

Our life in him is vibrant and full of the confident expectation of his goodness at every turn. He will never leave us—not even for a moment. We have real relationship with him here and now, with nothing to separate us from his great love. He has chosen us, and it is our joy to choose him in return.

Lord Jesus, my hope is found in you, and it cannot be moved. It doesn't matter what I face, because you are with me. You are so very loyal in love, and you have broken every chain of sin and death that would keep me from you. I am so thankful to be yours!

*Celebrate with praises the God and Father of our Lord Jesus Christ,
who has shown us his extravagant mercy. For his fountain of
mercy has given us a new life—we are reborn to experience a living,
energetic hope through the resurrection of Jesus Christ from the dead.*

1 PETER 1:3 TPT

Holy One, you have covered all my shame with your
overwhelming mercy. You cancelled all my debts, everything
I could not repay you, and you have given me the freedom
to live a life of liberty in you. How could I not celebrate your
incredible kindness toward me?

I am blessed to be a child of God. May I never take for granted
the belonging I have found in relationship to you. Lead me
in your love as I continue to build my life upon the firm
foundation of your truth. What a hope I have found in you! It's
unlike anything else I've ever known. Refresh my mind, heart,
and body as I meditate on your nearness. Thank you, Lord.

How has hope in God affected your outlook on life?

Unwavering Love

The Lord takes pleasure in those who fear him,
in those who hope in his steadfast love.

PSALM 147:11 NRSV

God is full of untiring love that flows freely from his throne of grace into our lives. When we look at the different areas of our lives, can we see where we have aligned ourselves to God's ways? We have to build our hopes on something. Is it based on ourselves and our own capabilities? Or are our lives built on the foundation of God's unwavering mercy?

He is faithful and trustworthy, so let us live with that kind of confidence. He takes so much pleasure when his children follow in his footsteps and heed his wisdom. We don't need to go looking for a better way to live; God has already offered us all the knowledge we could ever need through fellowship with him. His love is strong enough to cover every misstep and mistake; don't be discouraged. Just keep returning to him!

Lord, I believe that you are full of love that breaks every barrier. I know that your wisdom supersedes the scholars of this world. As long as I live, I will place my hope in you, for you are faithful, just, and true.

The Lord shows favor to those who fear him,
to his godly lovers who wait for his tender embrace.
Jerusalem, praise the Lord! Zion, worship your God!
For he has strengthened the authority of your gates.
He even blesses you with more children.

PSALM 147:11 TPT

God over all, I wait on you when I don't know what else to do. I know that you will meet me with your tender affection. You are such a kind father, and I will not relegate you to my human experience of flawed relationships. I am grateful for how I see your love reflected in healthy family, but I recognize that you are so much greater than any of us could ever be.

I worship you, because you made me. I praise you because I am the work of your hands. Not only that, but you have drawn me to yourself with kindness and given me the freedom of choice. How could I not choose you when you are perfect in love? I am your beloved child, and you are everything I could ever hope for, and more.

What is your greatest confidence based in?

All-access Pass

This hope we have as an anchor of the soul, both sure and
steadfast, and which enters the Presence behind the veil.

HEBREWS 6:19 NKJV

When Jesus took his last breath on the cross and died, we are
told through the accounts of Scripture that the earth shook
and the veil in the Jewish temple that separated the holy of
holies, or the place where God's presence resided, from the
rest of the temple, tore in two.

This is significant! The holy of holies was the most sacred
part of the temple, and only the high priest could enter it once
a year. When he did, he tied a rope around himself so that if
he died, others could pull him out. When Jesus died, the need
for separation between God and man passed away. Through
Jesus, we are free to enter the presence of God. What is more,
the presence of God dwells with us through his Spirit.

Holy One, what a wonderful reality to know that there is no
more separation between you and us. Thank you, Jesus, for
dying so that we could be reconciled to the Father. Thank you
for your presence that is with me. I am undone!

We have this certain hope like a strong,
unbreakable anchor holding our souls to God himself.
Our anchor of hope is fastened to the mercy seat
which sits in the heavenly realm beyond the sacred threshold.

HEBREWS 6:19 TPT

God, my hope is tethered to your mercy. I'm so thankful that it is not a far-off thing that I could only dream about. Your mercy is with me right where I am. You are the living expression of my longings. You are all that I need, and much more than that. I cannot comprehend your majesty, but oh how I will try!

Spirit, reveal the nature of God to me in a fresh way. I want to dream of the wonders of your glory as I drift off tonight. Fill my mind with the awe-inspiring beauty of who you are. I don't want to live off of old encounters and understandings. I know that there is always more to discover in you, and I want more! More revelation, more knowledge, more experience. More of you! Come near and do what only you can do. Let your astonishing love ignite the hope in my heart, so that I might burn for you.

Is there anything that keeps you from going to God?

Satisfied Hope

I wait for You, LORD;
You will answer, Lord my God.

PSALM 38:15 NASB

In waiting seasons, when all we can do is hope that God is moving on our behalf, how do we bide the time? There are promises that are quickly fulfilled and yet others that delay for what seems a lifetime. When we cannot control the outcomes and we must surrender our timing, let us look at how our hearts respond. Self-protection may seek to shut down the desire at all, and self-doubt may question whether the hope was a worthy one in the first place.

There is a perseverance in learning to wait that produces godly character. God is faithful; we have not missed the boat on that truth. He is reliable. So, then, in the meantime, will our hearts choose to trust him, or will we waver in the uncertainty of our humanity? No matter the journey of our faith, every moment is a new opportunity to turn toward him. He is wise, and he is loving. Let us open up to him today.

Loving Lord, you are the one I have put my hope in. More than any wish for this life, it is your unchanging nature that is the anchor for my soul. I trust you.

Lord, the only thing I can do is wait and put my hope in you.
I wait for your help, my God.

PSALM 38:15 TPT

My God, it is you I wait for. May my heart remember that any promise you make is a vow that you will keep. When I consider past longings that were fulfilled, I recognize how quickly I can move onto another, newer hope. But you never change, and you are always abundant in love. When I put my hope in you, it will never be dissatisfied.

In the waiting, all I can do is trust you. I know that you will come through for me when I need it. You do not ever abandon your children. I am desperate for you, Lord. Know that I need you more than I can express. In this in-between space, lean in with the power of your presence and sustain me with your grace that strengthens me. With you as my help, I lack nothing. You are my God, and I rely on you!

What has waiting produced in you?

Boundaries

Happy are those whom you discipline, O Lord,
and whom you teach out of your law.

PSALM 94:12 NRSV

There is wonderful freedom in the love of God. We get
to choose how we will live, but this also means we make
mistakes along the way. God's expectation is never our
perfection. He knows that we are dust. Don't let shame
convince you that when you mess up, you have somehow
fallen out of favor with God. Instead, when he corrects you,
see it as the teaching moment it is. He disciplines those he
loves, but do not think that his discipline is like that of our
flawed fathers.

God is perfect in all of his ways. Even his correction is laced
with kindness. Will you choose to lay down the old ways that
don't work in his kingdom-likeness and follow him on the
path of surrendered love? There is joy in submission to him—
such great joy!

Good Father, I am so thankful for your correction in my life.
You don't let me go astray in my own way for too long without
calling me back with your strong yet tender voice. Thank you
for your mercy that covers my mistakes. Your forgiveness is
sweet, and your instruction full of life.

*Lord, there's such a blessing that comes
when you teach us your word and your ways.
Even the sting of your correction can be sweet.*

PSALM 94:12 TPT

Wonderful Lord, you are the ultimate teacher. Whenever I think I have it right, but I'm actually missing the point, will you guide me back to your perfect ways? I am your student, and I want to become like you. I am your child, and I know that you are raising me up to be a representation of your goodness on earth. Keep my ears tuned to your voice and open my eyes to see you clearly.

Even in correction, I will find the light of life. May I always adjust to your kingdom ways, and not look for how I can fit you into my life. When I model your ways instead of expecting you to be like me, I find that there is an expansion, not only of my understanding, but of your mercy in my life. You are wonderful in all you do. Teach me, and I will learn. Correct me, and I will lay down my pride and reconcile to you. You are so worth it!

How have you experienced the sweetness of God's correction?

Eagerly Waiting

*If we hope for what we do not see,
we eagerly wait for it with perseverance.*

ROMANS 8:25 NKJV

There is blessing in the development of our faith. When we cannot see the physical representation of our hope, but we eagerly await its coming, gritty persistence keeps us expectant. May we be tenacious in faith, not letting go of the anticipation of our fulfilled longing. Whenever we grow a bit tired in believing, let us look to him who is steadfast in marvelous mercy. He will infuse us with strength.

What a glorious hope we have in him! The fulfillment of his promises is not dependent on our own reliability, but on his. We can be persistent in belief because it is based on his unchanging nature, not what we're waiting for. He is so much better than we can fully comprehend, so let's place our attention on his overwhelming goodness.

Jesus, you are the one I look to today. You are my hope, my firm foundation, and the basis of my faith. I believe that you are who the Bible says you are, and that you will be faithful to your Word.

Because our hope is set on what is yet to be seen,
we patiently keep on waiting for its fulfillment.

ROMANS 8:25 TPT

Faithful One, you are the hope that I have set my confidence upon. I know that you are faithful, so I am certain of the fulfillment of every promise you make. I am so thankful to have a living relationship with you, the Creator of the universe. You hold all the wisdom of the world and exceed the knowledge and power that any human being can wield in this life.

Your ways are so much better than the ways of this world, so I choose to follow you. I believe that you are as wonderful as I've heard; in fact, I believe that you are even greater. Fill my heart with joy and confidence as I set my faith on you. Keep my heart woven into your present mercy as time goes on. I know that I will eat of your goodness along the way. You are faithful and true, and there is no one else like you.

What fuels your faith in times of uncertainty?

Sing Praises

Sing praises to God, sing praises!
Sing praises to our King, sing praises!

PSALM 47:6 NKJV

There is always a reason to sing praises to our King! No matter what we are walking through, the glorious reality that Jesus is the same yesterday, today, and forever remains. He is always steadfast in love. He is the Beginning and the End, and he is faithfully present with us at all times through his Spirit. He will be with us until the end of life as we know it, and he will faithfully remain beyond that.

May we stir up the adoration of our hearts today as we consider his beauty. And if we need even more inspiration, let's look at his wonderful and consistent character. We are filled up by his love, and the response of our hearts is a natural overflow of affection right back to him. So, sing praises today to our King! He is so very worthy.

King of all, I offer you the praise you are due. I will sing songs of joy that overflow from my heart. I won't hold back from you, for you are worthy of all the honor I could ever give you.

Sing and celebrate! Sing some more, celebrate some more!
Sing your highest song of praise to our King!

PSALM 47:6 TPT

Glorious King, I offer you the sacrifice of my praise even when
I have to dig deep to get the song from my heart to my lips. As
I consider the kindness of your mercy in my life, and how you
have met me time and again with the provision of your hand, I
can't help but feel gratitude swell within my heart.

I won't hold back from singing a melody of thanksgiving! You
have been so faithful to me. You are my deliverer, my healer,
and my savior. You rescued me from the pit of my despair and
put my feet on the solid rock of your compassion. I see now
that you have never left me alone, and I trust that you never
will. You are my constant support and my exceedingly good
friend and father. May the song I offer you be like a sweet,
fragrant offering to you tonight!

What is your favorite song to sing to the Lord?

Generations of Mercy

*"His mercy is for those who fear him
from generation to generation."*

LUKE 1:50 NRSV

The Lord's mercy is so much larger than our little lives can contain. When we are overly concentrated on the magnifying lens of our own lives, we miss out on what is happening around us. Let us look through history for the miracles of God's love and how he faithfully met with and led his people out of captivity into their liberation. In doing so, may our hearts grow in capacity to understand how expansive he is.

Scripture is a great place to observe God's faithfulness from generation to generation. When we look through a larger lens, we are able to recognize the theme of loyal mercy throughout the ages. In our own histories with God, can we not identify the mark of his devoted love that has led us through the hills and valleys of life? He does the same for all his people. He is so very faithful!

Merciful One, help me to see your vast love through the broader perspective of the generations. I can get so distracted by my own life, but I know that you are so much bigger. Encourage my heart as you reveal the wonders of your goodness throughout the ages.

> *"He shows mercy from generation to generation
> to all who fear him."*
>
> LUKE 1:50 NLT

Holy God, you are the same yesterday, today and always. You don't ever withhold your mercy from those who look for you. You are a kind and gracious father. You are a loyal and ever-present help in times of trouble. You are all-powerful, and you cannot be defeated. You are faithful and true.

Your Spirit reveals your wonders time and time again. You are a miracle-working, mountain-moving, all-consuming fire of a God! What you overwhelm, no one can take over. What you claim for your own, no one can steal from your hand. You are better than the best and purer than the most refined. You are incomparable and beyond comprehension. You are too wonderful for words! Thank you for the perspective of time that reveals your nature as consistent. I join with those who have gone before and walked with you and trust you with my life. There is no one greater.

When was the last time you looked
at the history of God's mercy?

Steady Support

*If I say, "My foot slips,"
Your mercy, O LORD, will hold me up.*

PSALM 94:18 NKJV

When something unexpected jolts you, or a surprising trial in life knocks you to the ground, do not be dismayed. Even in your falling, you are not outside of God's gracious grip. He is not astonished or alarmed by what shocks you. He sees everything clearly, and his kindness will keep you close.

Lean on him, especially when you don't understand what is going on. He will be your hiding place, if you let him. He will keep your heart covered in peace even in the unknown, for nothing is a secret to him. Trust him; he is still faithful. Rely on him; he will not let you be crushed. Let your confidence be found in him, and not in the control you feel in life because that will never last. He is faithful throughout all generations.

Merciful Father, I rely on you to catch me when I fall. Be the one to uplift and uphold me when I have nothing else to lean on. You are the one I trust more than any other.

I cried out, "I am slipping!"
but your unfailing love, O LORD, supported me.

PSALM 94:18 NLT

Lord, on my hardest days, when I feel my grip is slipping,
I trust that you will hold me steady. When I don't have
the strength to stand on my own, let your mercy be the
ground that rises up to meet me. Keep me covered in your
compassion and don't let me go. Breathe your peace into my
fretful heart, and I will not be afraid. Remind me how very
close you are, and I won't tremble with anxiety.

You are my safe place and my security. Even when I can't
sense you, I know that you will never leave or forsake me. As
I rest tonight, flood my being with the peace of your Spirit. In
your great love, draw even closer with your tangible presence,
and enfold me in the embrace of your comfort. You are my
hope still, and I trust that you won't ever let me go!

Where can you see the support of God's love in your life?

How Much More

I am weary with my sighing;
Every night I make my bed swim,
I flood my couch with my tears.
My eye has wasted away with grief;
It has grown old because of all my enemies.

PSALM 6:6-8 NASB

When grief sweeps into our lives without warning and we cannot escape the sorrow stretching the boundaries of our souls, how does our faith respond? The wonderful news of the Savior is that he is our help in every trial and trouble. He is also our comforter. He comes in close with the solace of his presence. We are never alone—not in our joy, and certainly not in our suffering. He is near to the brokenhearted and the protector of the weak.

When we are bombarded by the harsh realities of humanity, he is our close and faithful friend. He is not discouraged by our discouragement. He is full of loyal love at all times. There is no need to superficially bolster our hopes when we are wearied by the crushing weight of grief. Let's allow him into the reality of our weakness, and he will strengthen us there.

Comforter, I trust that you will meet me where I am and deliver me with your love and peace. Though I cannot escape the suffering of my grief, will you make the burden lighter with your deep and lasting joy? I don't grieve without hope, but oh, how I grieve!

I'm exhausted and worn out with my weeping.
I endure weary, sleepless nights filled with moaning,
soaking my pillow with my tears.
My eyes of faith won't focus anymore, for sorrow fills my heart.
There are so many enemies who come against me!
Go away! Leave me, all you troublemakers!
For the Lord has turned to listen to my thunderous cry.

PSALM 6:6-8 TPT

Faithful Lord, turn to me and listen to my cries for help. I know that you do, but I long for the reassurance of your presence to remind me that you are ever so near. When sorrow takes over my heart, I will not wish it away. I will welcome you into it, knowing that you do not require of me what I am unable to offer. You lead me in healing and you restore my soul.

I know that suffering does not mean that I have somehow gone off course; you never promised ease in life to those who follow you and your ways. Oh Lord, you are the lifter of my head, so pick my chin up, that I may meet your tender gaze once again. Calm my anxious heart with your comfort and be my strong defender to the forces that are working against me. I trust you, faithful Father!

Do you trust that God will take care of you?

Unifying Love

*If there is any encouragement in Christ, any comfort from love,
any participation in the Spirit, any affection and sympathy,
complete my joy by being of the same mind, having the same love,
being in full accord and of one mind.*

PHILIPPIANS 2:1-2 ESV

God's love does not hold back or have requirements, but our
heart responses are evaluated by the Lord. Ultimately, we are
held accountable to God in all we do. We cannot control the
actions or reactions of others, but we can choose our own. We
must not get caught up in putting qualifiers on the mercy we
offer others, for that is not true love. God's compassion does
not depend on our response to it. He loves because he loves.

We will emulate the grandeur of his kindness if we offer love
and kindness without condition. This is the kind of love that
recognizes differences but does not get caught up in them.
This kind of love is humble, it is pure, it is generous. It
forgives offenses. This is unifying love.

Lord of all, as I walk in the ways of your compassion, help
me to lay down my offenses and offer the same mercy to
others that I receive so freely from you. You are worthy of the
sacrifice of my pride, and so I humble myself before you and
others.

Look at how much encouragement you've found in your relationship with the Anointed One! You are filled to overflowing with his comforting love. You have experienced a deepening friendship with the Holy Spirit and have felt his tender affection and mercy. So I'm asking you, my friends, that you be joined together in perfect unity—with one heart, one passion, and united in one love. Walk together with one harmonious purpose and you will fill my heart with unbounded joy.

PHILIPPIANS 2:1-2 TPT

Holy Spirit, I long to know you more, and not just in the limits of relationship with you. As I receive your tender mercy, I know that I cannot hoard it to myself. Teach me to walk in your generous ways, that I may reflect your love in every area of my life. There is unity in your love. I know that the most important quest in my life is to live a life that is so consumed by your mercy that I offer it to everyone I meet.

I recognize that this is not an easy road to walk, but it will be worth it. Help me to make space for others lived experiences and not hold them to my stringent standard of what I think is most important. Instead, let your focus be my main one: to love, accept, encourage, and celebrate others in their God-given identity. I want to do the work of unity that does not just shout loud praises to you but makes room for seeing and serving others.

What would unity in love look like
in relationships in your life?

You See It All

You do see!
Indeed you note trouble and grief,
that you may take it into your hands;
the helpless commit themselves to you;
you have been the helper of the orphan.

PSALM 10:14 NRSV

The Lord does not turn a blind eye to the evil that is working in the world. He notices the wicked and their true motivations. He sees everything done in secret, and he will hold them to account for every immoral act. Though we observe in part, he perceives the full picture. Though we may question God's timing, his purposes are pure.

Even in suffering, God is close to the helpless; he has not abandoned the vulnerable. When we see others who are suffering, it is right to be moved by compassion and to rise up on their behalf. We should not wait idly by when there is something that we can do to make a difference. But even in our action, let us not for a minute lose sight that God is the only perfect, righteous Judge.

Righteous One, I am so grateful for your mercy that meets me in my trouble, and I know you are the same to all who call on you. When I can help another suffering soul, may I never hesitate to do so. May I be moved by your compassion today!

Lord, I know you see all that they're doing,
noting their each and every deed.
You know the trouble and turmoil they've caused.
Now punish them thoroughly for all that they've done!
The poor and helpless ones trust in you, Lord,
for you are famous for being the helper of the fatherless.
I know you won't let them down.

PSALM 10:14 TPT

Wise Lord, meet me right here and now in my questioning.
When I wrestle with your truth, I know that you will guide
me in your wisdom. I believe that you will come through for
the poor and helpless, though I need help to see things from
your perspective. You are so very patient in your mercy, but
I confess that I struggle sometimes to understand why you
would wait to deliver those in the captivity of other's evil plans.

I am looking to you for clarity, for I cannot find it on my own.
I know that your ways are higher than my own, and I trust
you. Give me revelations of your goodness, past the logic that
I use to reason everything. Surely you won't let down those
who look to you for help. Surely you are as faithful today as
you ever were or will be. Give me eyes to see you more clearly.

Do you believe that God sees everything?

It Is Time

Sow for yourselves righteousness;
Reap in mercy;
Break up your fallow ground,
For it is time to seek the LORD,
Till He comes and rains righteousness on you.

HOSEA 10:12 NKJV

Today is the day that the Lord has given us. Let us not get caught up in the regrets of yesterday or in the far-off dreams of tomorrow. Let us slow down and dig into the present moment. Right now, wherever you are, notice the way your body meets the surface beneath you. Take a deep breath and note the rise and fall of your belly. This is the day we have to engage in. This very moment is all we have.

How will we spend it? Distracted by something that does not matter right here and now? Or fully recognizing and receiving the gift of life as it is? It is time to seek the Lord. Now is the time. Let us turn our attention to him; he will surely meet us.

Ever-present One, you are closer than the air in my lungs. You are more real than the ground beneath my feet. You are all that matters, and I focus my mind on you. Meet me with your presence and speak your immediate word to my soul.

Sow righteousness for yourselves,
reap the fruit of unfailing love,
and break up your unplowed ground;
for it is time to seek the LORD,
until he comes
and showers his righteousness on you.

HOSEA 10:12 NIV

Lord, I am grateful for the gift of your presence in every moment. I am never without you! It is almost too glorious a truth to comprehend. Whenever I start moving on autopilot, will you do something that redirects my attention to your constant love, which is always doing something new?

I'm looking for you, Lord. I'm watching for your telltale fruit in my life. May my eyes quickly discern where you are moving, and may my heart stay soft to your guidance. I know that waiting on you is an active thing; help me to keep first things first in my walk with you. Your love, oh Lord, is better than life! I can consume it every day, and it always satiates my hunger. Keep me close in your mercy and reveal yourself in wonderful ways in my current reality.

How can you ground yourself in the present?

No Fear

Even though I walk through the darkest valley,
I will fear no evil, for you are with me;
your rod and your staff, they comfort me.

PSALM 23:4 NIV

Whatever dreadful circumstances we face, there is a truth that supersedes every one: God's perfect love drives out all fear. His love is ever-present, for God is with us at all times. He never abandons his children. Even in the darkest night, he is closer than we can comprehend. He has not left us alone—not ever!

When our anxieties rise and worry creeps into our consciousness, may we turn our attention to the reality that God is Emmanuel. He is "God with us." He is our present comfort, our help in time of need, and our joyful companion. We can never escape the intense mercy of our God; he leads in kindness and keeps us close in tender friendship. This is what he does for those who love him!

Good Shepherd, you keep me tucked close to your tender heart with the gentle and firm voice of truth. There is no reason to fear when you are near. I confidently follow you, no matter the uncertainty I face.

Even though I walk through the valley of the shadow of death,
I will fear no evil, for you are with me;
your rod and your staff, they comfort me.

PSALM 23:4 ESV

Loving Lord, I follow the lead of your loyal love that guides me. You are so close in comfort. Every time I need reassurance, you are there. I will not be overcome with fear, because you are the Good Shepherd. You lead me along the path of life. I am confident that your kindness is near. Even when I walk through the darkest valleys of life, you see everything clearly.

I trust your Word to guide me, for you perceive the best route. It is your wisdom that I long for, and when I ask for clarity, you give it. I trust your constant character to deliver me from every trouble I face. I lean closer to hear your heartbeat. You are so steady in love. Whenever fear begins to unsettle my nerves and doubts crop up, let the oil of your love cover my mind, so that I may recall that you have not changed. You are wonderful, Lord!

How has God's presence settled your fear?

He Still Heals

"I have seen what they have done,
but I will heal them.
I will guide them and comfort them
and those who felt sad for them.
They will all praise me."

ISAIAH 57:18 NCV

God's ways are so much better than ours. Though we are inclined to love those who love us, how many of us would, of our own accord, offer unhindered kindness to those who treat us poorly? God sees everything as clear as day, and he chooses to extend generous mercy time and again.

He does not hold our rebellion against us. He does not keep a record of wrongs. In fact, the Scriptures say that "he has taken our sins away from us as far as the east is from west" (Psalm 103:12). Micah 7:19 also says, "You will have mercy on us again…you will throw away all our sins into the deepest part of the sea." He is so very rich in love—a love that heals, liberates and revives. He will guide, comfort, and restore us. He is faithful in meeting us with kindness.

Savior, you are wonderful in mercy! I cannot begin to thank you for the endless kindness you show me. I offer you all of my life—the broken parts, as well as the thriving. Heal me, and I will be healed.

"Even though I've seen their ways, I will heal them.
I will guide them forward and repay them with comfort,
giving mourners the language of praise."

ISAIAH 57:18 TPT

Faithful One, you are the one who offers joy for mourning and the spirit of praise for heaviness. Your love reaches me in my sadness and restores my soul in hope. There is so much joy in your wonderful mercy! Keep guiding me and refresh me with the living waters of your Spirit's presence along the way.

I know that you do not ignore my cries for help, no matter what led to my needing it. I rely on your love to keep me on the path of life. I have submitted my life to yours, so you are my guiding light and my strength. You see the areas that need healing, and those that need reviving. I trust you to do what I cannot. Meet me in my weakness and infuse me with your power that heals all of my diseases. Bring into alignment all ideologies that are out of line with your kingdom ways. You are so lavish in abundant kindness!

Where do you need God's healing in your life?

His Work

The LORD will fulfill his purpose for me;
your steadfast love, O LORD, endures forever.
Do not forsake the work of your hands.

PSALM 138:8 ESV

God is faithful to his promises. We can never be over-reminded of this truth. Let this be encouragement for our hearts today: God is working out his steadfast love in our lives. The purposes that he has set forth, he will complete. His faithfulness is not dependent on our faith, for his love knows no bounds—certainly not the limits of our beliefs. He cannot be relegated to the small boxes of our understanding. He is so much larger than we can ever imagine!

Instead of simply looking for how God fits into our little lives, may we open to the infinite possibilities of finding him in the greater world around us. His love reaches to the heavens, and his mercy cannot be contained by this universe. He is so much better, so much brighter and so much more than we can ever comprehend.

Lord, thank you for the wonderful revelation of your overwhelming love. I am grateful that you are so much larger than the limitations of my understanding. Keep doing your wonderful work in my life and in the world.

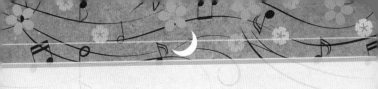

You keep every promise you've ever made to me!
Since your love for me is constant and endless,
I ask you, Lord, to finish every good thing that you've begun in me!

PSALM 138:8 TPT

Wondrous One, I want to know your constant and endless love in a new way. Reveal the wonders of your mercy to my mind, that my comprehension of you may expand just a little more tonight. Whether through your Word, through conversation with loved ones, or through a supernatural experience or dream, I want to know you more. I want to have eyes to see the fingerprints of your kindness all around me.

I know that you are so much greater than my understanding. Open up my thoughts to the insights of your kingdom. I want to know your wise ways more than I rely on my flesh and blood senses. As I consider how you have faithfully fulfilled previous promises in my life, how can my heart but overflow in gratitude toward you? You are so very good! Keep doing your perfect work in me, for I am clay in the Potter's hand.

Do you trust that God is working things out
even when you can't see how?

All Things with Love

Love bears all things,
believes all things,
hopes all things,
endures all things.

1 CORINTHIANS 13:7 ESV

How has God's loyal love kept you afloat in the storms of life? We know that God is endless in compassion, and he never gives up. When was the last time you reached the end of your rope, and threw your hands up in surrender? These are inevitable and pivotal moments. What happened next? Where did your heart turn?

In this passage of Scripture, popularly known as "the love chapter," we find a beautiful record of ways in which God's love is revealed in our lives. This is the same kind of love that we are called to extend to others. His love is beyond comprehension and yet extremely practical. May we emulate this endlessly hopeful and faithful love as we continuously receive it from our Good Father.

Loving Father, I am so thankful for the wonderful love that does not stop flowing from your heart of compassion. As I receive from you, may I offer the same merciful kindness to those around me. Your love is my life-source!

Love is a safe place of shelter,
for it never stops believing the best for others.
Love never takes failure as defeat,
for it never gives up.

1 CORINTHIANS 13:7 TPT

Merciful God, you have shown me what it means to love others. Jesus, your life is the perfect example of laid-down love. Soften my heart tonight as I meditate on what your compassion looks like. Where I have put limitations on it, I surrender my pride and self-protection. Your love asks for nothing in return, but it elicits a response, nonetheless.

Where your love never stops believing the best for others, I admit that I often fall short in my estimation of the people around me. Keep my heart pliable as I humbly submit my ideas of mercy to your greater example. Even in the face of failure, your love does not stop believing for better. It perseveres, never giving up. I am grateful for how your mercy never gives up on me. I don't want to give up on others, either. Your ways are best—this, I know for certain. So, I will follow you on your path of loyal love, learning along the way.

How does this definition of love reflect in your life?

Strong and Brave

On the day I called you, you answered me.
You made me strong and brave.

PSALM 138:3 NCV

God is the faithful leader of his lovers. He does not hesitate in answering the cries of his beloved ones. He always breaks through for those who are hemmed in by their circumstances. He is the Mighty Deliverer, after all! How has he met you with his dedicated love? How has his presence given you courage to keep going when you would otherwise have given up hope?

Feast on his faithfulness today as you recall how his loyal love has already met you. Let the courage of a reassured heart lead you into boldness this very day. Remembrance is a powerful tool, for it stirs our hearts with the promise of God's tangible goodness. Be inspired today to walk in the confidence of God's constant and loving nature!

All-powerful God, you are the strength that keeps me moving and my overwhelmingly great reward. Whenever I think about how you meet me with your mercy in my life, I am encouraged in faith to keep believing you for more. You are so very good to me!

At the very moment I called out to you, you answered me!
You strengthened me deep within my soul
and breathed fresh courage into me.

PSALM 138:3 TPT

Faithful One, I know that you always meet me when I cry
out to you. You know just what I need in every moment, and
you provide it. You are the strength of my soul, the one who
gives me courage, and I am so thankful for you. Through
relationship with you, I find everything my heart longs for.

There is nothing that can be truly satisfied outside of your
love. Keep my heart vibrant with the shining light of your
mercy. In your hands, I am loved to life over and over again!
You show me the way to go, and I follow. I have bound my life
to yours, for you are wise, the only one who can lead me to
everlasting life. I rest in the goodness of your presence, and
your peace washes over me. You make me brave, so I can walk
on the waters of uncertainty. I won't sink, because my eyes
are fixed on you.

What was the last brave thing you did?

Fighting for Me

The LORD your God is the one who goes with you to fight for you against your enemies to give you victory.

DEUTERONOMY 20:4 NIV

Do you feel alone in your battles? Take heart today, for the Lord your God is with you. He fights for you! He is your strong and mighty defense, and he will overcome the tactics of the enemy with his powerful love. Just watch him do it! You can rest in the assurance of his help, for he will not leave you to be overtaken by wicked schemes.

He will deliver you! Do not be afraid, for the Savior of all is your companion and your advocate. Trust him with your whole heart, and you will know the confidence of his peace and joy. As a child of God, you are taken care of through every trial. Can you recognize his power at work in your life?

Lord God, I put all my hopes in you again. I remind myself of your faithfulness, and I turn my attention toward your overwhelming love that flows freely from your presence. I trust in you!

The LORD your God goes with you,
to fight for you against your enemies and to save you.

DEUTERONOMY 20:4 NCV

Victorious One, I lean on you, both in times of ease and times of trouble. You are the one who advocates for me, my Mighty Defender. I know that you will save me from peril. You are strong and mighty to save. You keep me safe in the refuge of your mercy-kindness. My life is tethered to your unbreakable love, and I will not be moved from the foundation of your kingdom.

I am so grateful that I never need worry about how I will survive on my own, for you are always with me. You never leave me alone—never, ever! I trust in your power to deliver me all the days of my life. Whenever I am in trouble, you are my present help. I lay down every anxiety at your feet and welcome the peace of your presence to usher me into rest. Fill my mind with your wonderful Word that brings revelation and comfort.

How can you rest in God's advocacy today?

Entwined

Here's what I've learned through it all:
Don't give up; don't be impatient;
be entwined as one with the Lord.
Be brave and courageous, and never lose hope.
Yes, keep on waiting—for he will never disappoint you!

PSALM 27:14 TPT

What a wonderful gift we have in the Spirit of God who dwells with us. We have unhindered relationship with God, thanks to Jesus. He paved the way to the Father, and we have been restored in love, without need for fear or separation. Whatever our understanding of the love of God, it is so much greater than our comprehension. There is always more goodness to be found in his glory. There is always more revelation to broaden our knowledge of who he is.

The Spirit breathes on us, and we are loved to life. There is redemption, healing, and the joy of liberation in fellowship with him. Let us be entwined with the Lord, as those who are woven into the fabric of his love. Let us never grow tired in getting to know him more. He is always better than we can fully imagine him to be.

Righteous One, I invite you into the deeper parts of my heart that have been kept hidden in the shadows of my subconscious. I trust your love to faithfully peel back the layers of my brokenness and make me whole in the light of your glorious life.

Wait patiently for the LORD.
Be brave and courageous.
Yes, wait patiently for the LORD.

PSALM 27:14 NLT

Lord, I wait patiently for you now. I set aside my agenda and give you the space to move as you will. Meet me with the refreshing waters of your presence. You bring life to my soul! I will not let discouragement keep me from seeking you, for you are faithful and true. I have to believe that you will continue to operate in your marvelous mercy in my life.

Redeemer, restore what no one else ever could, and bring life to that which appears desolate to man's eyes. I will press into this liminal space—where my deep calls to your deep, and Spirit ministers to spirit. I know that you won't let me down, for you are loyal. You are dependable. You are endlessly kind. You always come through, and you are not about to stop now. Draw near, Lord. Come close and revive my hope in your perfect love once again.

How can you keep hope alive in your waiting?

Promises Kept

Sustain me according to Your word, that I may live;
And do not let me be ashamed of my hope.

PSALM 119:116 NASB

How have you seen God fulfill his Word in your life and in the lives of those who also follow him? What testimonies of his goodness have caused your heart to swell with hope? He is full of lovingkindness to all who look to him.

If you are in a time in life where you struggle to see what he is doing, draw on the experience of others for encouragement. What seems like the end to you is an opportunity for God's restorative power to break through for you. He is not limited by human restrictions, so do not hamper your faith in his wonderful mercy by trying to fit him into the confines of your limited logic. Take time reading or listening to testimonies of his faithfulness in the lives of others and see how that affects your own expectation.

Constant One, thank you for the experience of community and the encouragement that comes with it. I will not get lost in my circumstances today, but I will look for you both within and outside of myself.

Strengthen my inner being by the promises of your word
so that I may live faithful and unashamed for you.

PSALM 119:116 TPT

Faithful Father, strengthen my inner being tonight as you remind me of how your miracles of mercy have played out in my life already. I cannot help but be encouraged when I see the ways that you have woven your loyal love through my story. Surely, you who have been faithful will continue to be.

I have submitted my life to you, and that is no small thing. I have given you everything; don't let me be ashamed or brought down by disappointment. I recognize that the way you do things takes more into consideration than I can perceive. But you are good; I know this to be true. You have been good to me. Speak to me now and revive the hope within my heart once again. You always know just what to say. I wait on you now. Spirit, speak your words of life and my joy will overflow.

What promises has God already fulfilled in your life?

Healing for My Heart

For you who fear my name,
the sun of righteousness shall rise with healing in its wings.

MALACHI 4:2 ESV

No matter what is happening in your life at this moment, you have the comfort and counsel of the Living God available to you right now. He is full of the clarity you long for, as well as the peace you crave. He is the God who sees past the movement of our lives to the motives of our hearts.

Welcome him into the questions that you are grappling with, for he is full of wisdom to calm the chaos of the unknown. His understanding brings with it the peace of his presence. In his wonderful kindness, he heals what we don't even know is broken. He will give you eyes to see as he heals your broken mindsets and aligns the attitudes of your heart with his overwhelming love. Open up and let him do his miracle work today!

Righteous One, you are infinitely kind in manner, and I am so grateful to have fellowship with you. You change my heart with your mercy. Please, heal me again.

For you who honor me,
goodness will shine on you like the sun,
with healing in its rays.

MALACHI 4:2 NCV

Good God, you are so very rich in mercy! Let your goodness
shine upon my life. You know how I long to honor you with
the submission of my life to yours. Heal me, Lord, and I will
be healed. You are the one who revives my weary soul time
and again with the refreshing waters of your living Word.
Flood my awareness with the peace of your Spirit's presence,
and minister to my broken parts with the healing touch of
your mercy.

I offer you all that I am and all that I have, for you are worthy
of it all. You have been good to me, and I know that you
are not finished working your miracles of restoration and
redemption in my life. Shine on me with your love's light.
Let its rays mend what needs repairing and restore my soul.
I trust you with my whole life, Comforter and Friend.

How has God's goodness brought healing to your heart?

Rock of Salvation

My God is my rock. I can run to him for safety.
He is my shield and my saving strength,
my defender and my place of safety.
The LORD saves me from those who want to harm me.

2 SAMUEL 22:3 NCV

God is a firm foundation to stand upon in every battle and storm that comes our way. He is not just the rock of our eternal salvation; he is also the rock that keeps us steady in the times of unrest and chaos that we encounter in life. He is a safe place to rest, no matter what is happening around us.

Can you access the peace of God even in the turbulence of the unknowns in life? Can you recognize God's steady hand holding you when everything feels as if it is falling apart? He has got you, and he will not let you go! Trust him and find your security in his faithful love today.

Savior God, you are safe place I hide myself when it all gets to be too much. You are strong and able to save; there is nothing you cannot do. I rely on you to keep me safe because you are my help.

The God of my strength, in whom I will trust;
My shield and the horn of my salvation,
My stronghold and my refuge;
My Savior, You save me from violence.

2 Samuel 22:3 NKJV

God of my strength, I call on you in my time of need! I am
so grateful that you do not ration your love based on the
measure of my need; you always give out of the abundance of
your limitless source of love. Teach me to lean on you and to
rely on your power in the little as well as the large things in
life. You keep my heart in perfect peace when my attention is
solely focused on you.

Would you broaden my awareness so that anxiety would
subside more swiftly in your presence? I realize that you are
as close as the air on my skin, and you don't ever turn your
children away. Meet me with your great grace as I look to you,
for you are my only salvation.

Do you trust God to save you
or do you feel the need to prove yourself?

Always with Me

"Those who love me, I will deliver;
I will protect those who know my name.
When they call to me, I will answer them;
I will be with them in trouble,
I will rescue them and honor them."

PSALM 91:14-15 NRSV

There is no need to worry when God is our help and deliverer. According to his Word, he delivers those who love him. He protects those who know his name. When they call on him, he will surely answer. He promises to be with them in trouble and to rescue and honor them.

Why, then, would we let anxiety rule in our hearts? Why would we allow fear to displace God's peace? God will not abandon us. Look at the wonderful ways of his faithful nature. There is no need to plead our own case with God, for he already accepts us. He is our defender and our mighty deliverer! With God on our side, we will not fall under the assault of weapons moving against us.

Mighty One, I turn my attention toward you again today, remembering that your mighty power to save is at work in my life. Every worry that pops up in my mind, I will turn over to you, for you will not let me be overcome. You are faithful.

> *"Because he holds fast to me in love, I will deliver him;*
> *I will protect him, because he knows my name.*
> *When he calls to me, I will answer him;*
> *I will be with him in trouble;*
> *I will rescue him and honor him."*

PSALM 91:14-15 ESV

Faithful Father, here I am again, calling on your name. I know that you draw me in with your tender affection, and in kindness you cover me with compassion. Why would I stay away when your love is better than life? You are my constant help whenever I need it, and you are my faithful friend through the highs and lows of this life. I love you more than I can express. I am so grateful for the ways you have delivered me from evil time and time again.

Be with me, Lord, through it all. Draw close to me as I draw close to you. I know that you always will, for you are more responsive than the most attentive friend. I lean on you and your wisdom. Refresh me in your living presence again as I cast all my cares upon you.

What worries can you give God today?

A Gentle Reminder

"Are you weary, carrying a heavy burden? Then come to me. I will refresh your life, for I am your oasis. Simply join your life with mine. Learn my ways and you'll discover that I'm gentle, humble, easy to please. You will find refreshment and rest in me."

MATTHEW 11:28-29 TPT

In life, we cannot escape the inevitable losses that cause pain. There will be disappointment, but God is greater. There will be grief, but God is still full of love. There will be questions, but God is faithful. Whatever we walk through, he is our loyal companion. He will not let us be crushed by the weightiness of the world's ways.

There is no need to carry the burdens—any of them—alone. It doesn't matter where we picked them up or who passed them to us. He is willing and able to do the heavy lifting. As we offer them to him and learn how brilliant he truly is, we will discover how wonderfully easy he is to please! He offers rest and constant refreshment for our souls.

Wondrous God, would you lift the heaviness that I have been carrying as I come to you again today? I know that your ways are better than my own, and I long for the refreshment your presence brings.

> *"Come to me, all you who are weary and burdened, and I will give you rest. Take my yoke upon you and learn from me, for I am gentle and humble in heart, and you will find rest for your souls."*
>
> MATTHEW 11:28-29 NIV

Refuge of my soul, I bring you all the worn hopes of my heart, along with the weighty worries that slowly bring me down. I am so grateful for the renewal you offer every time I come to you! It doesn't matter how many times a day I turn toward you; you meet me with the same generous grace every time.

Thank you for the kindness of your tender love that consistently mends my broken ideas of love. You are better than any other, and you always will be. I will keep my heart tethered to yours in the partnership you offer, for I will never find a better one. You are my holy help, my joyful hope, and my resting place. Communion with you is the best fellowship there is.

Is there a heavy burden that you have been bearing alone?

Never Left Alone

Those who know the LORD trust him,
because he will not leave those who come to him.

PSALM 9:10 NCV

We have access to an incomparable confidence in the faithful love of our God, no matter how we may feel about it in the moment. He will not leave those who come to him, so we can be fully convinced of all that he says he will do. He is faithful and true, and he will not change.

Even when we cannot perceive what he is doing in the details of our lives, we have his steady presence to soothe us. We have his unwavering mercy to cover every single one of our failures and weaknesses. He is greater than we could ever give him credit for, and he is always so rich in love. May we spend our lives learning how to submit to him in all things, for he is wiser, truer, and purer than we could ever dream of becoming.

Trustworthy One, I won't stop coming to you with everything in my life. You are the faithful God who sees me through it all; how could I but trust you?

Those who know your name trust in you,
for you, O LORD, do not abandon those who search for you.

PSALM 9:10 NLT

Loving Lord, your nearness is my strength. To know that you are with me is courage to my soul. I have heard the fame of your faithfulness, and I will not stop searching for the fingerprints of your mercy in my life and in the world around me. When I catch glimpses of your mercy, I am astounded by your thoughtfulness! You even care about the little things that others would overlook. Nothing is too small a detail for you to consider.

When I look at my life, I remember what you have done for me, and I won't stop thanking you for it. My expectation for your continued faithfulness rises when I meditate on your tangible goodness. Never stop meeting me where I'm at and weaving the wonderful thread of your mercy through every part of my story. Give me eyes to see your wonder-working power right here and now, as you are moving in my present circumstances. Thank you!

How have you recognized God's presence in your life?

Source of Healing

Do not be wise in your own eyes;
Fear the LORD and turn away from evil.
It will be healing to your body
And refreshment to your bones.

PROVERBS 3:7-8 NASB

Isn't it refreshing when you realize that you don't have to know all the answers? When our will and ways are set upon Christ, and not on the world's expectations or ourselves, what freedom we find! The action of humility is refreshing. When we recognize that we don't know it all, nor do we need to, there is then the space to move in the direction of curiosity toward wisdom.

Will we align our lives in the mercy of God, turning away from pride? If we do, we will find the healing that we didn't even realize we needed. There is beautiful mercy in beginning anew in God as we lay down our worn-out ways that don't reflect his love. Let his law of love be the standard we set our lives to; there we will find submission supersedes perfection every single time.

Wise God, I lay down my limited logic before you and look instead to your perfection. I know that I will always fall short, but you never hold that against me. You only want my humble heart. Here it is, Lord!

Do not be wise in your own eyes;
Fear the Lord and depart from evil.
It will be health to your flesh,
And strength to your bones.

PROVERBS 3:7-8 NKJV

Perfect Lord, you are the standard of love that underlies my life. I will not let pride keep me puffed up in my own mind, thinking that I know best. I know that's not true. I see such a small part of the whole, while you see everything clearly. I want to lean into your wisdom and trust your leadership, no matter what it costs me.

If it means that I lay down my offenses, or it leads me to a different option than I had originally planned for, it doesn't matter. What matters is that you are the strength of my soul, and there is no one else like you. When I surrender my ways to you, I find relief in your love, as well as peace that passes understanding. You hold the keys to life-thriving, fruit-bearing life! My life is yours.

How has pride kept you from submitting to God?

Shining Star

Do everything without grumbling or arguing, so that you may become blameless and pure, "children of God without fault in a warped and crooked generation." Then you will shine among them like stars in the sky as you hold firmly to the word of life.

PHILIPPIANS 2:14-16 NIV

God's love covers over a multitude of sins. It makes space for different experiences and different expectations, for it meets us in overwhelming measure where each of us are in our walks with him. There is no need to get caught up in petty grievances, or to nurse our offenses, unless we want to trivialize God's love. He has called us to unity in him, and we must lay down our shiny ideals in favor of mercy and kindness.

We are all in this together, and to sharpen each other without hurting one another, we must always wear love. There will be nothing to hinder the radiance of God's light in our lives when we remain submitted in love to God and to each other.

Pure One, in the light of your love, I come alive. May I not hinder that life with unnecessary complaining. I know that you take account of all of my days, and nothing I do for you is wasted. Forgive my pride and teach me how to love like you do.

Do everything without complaining and arguing, so that no one can criticize you. Live clean, innocent lives as children of God, shining like bright lights in a world full of crooked and perverse people. Hold firmly to the word of life; then, on the day of Christ's return, I will be proud that I did not run the race in vain and that my work was not useless.

PHILIPPIANS 2:14-16 NLT

Holy God, you are the shining sun, and I reflect your light like the moon in the night sky. I do not have to produce the light on my own; it is your glory shining in my life that radiates. May I continually submit to you, laying down my preferences and pride in favor of your better ways. Keep my heart pure in you, as I continually offer the same mercy to others that you so freely give to me.

I will not let go of your Word of life that refreshes and refocuses me. Instead of looking out for myself and my own selfish desires, I submit them all to you, knowing that you are pure in compassion. As I look to your love, keep me from getting distracted by petty arguments that don't matter. You are so abundant in kindness. May my life reflect your wonderful nature.

What complaints can you give up on
in order to make room for compassion?

Rejoicing in Comfort

Sing for joy, O heavens, and exult, O earth;
break forth, O mountains, into singing!
For the LORD has comforted his people,
and will have compassion on his suffering one.

ISAIAH 49:13 NRSV

God is close to the brokenhearted, no matter what it was that caused the pain. He does not limit his compassion based on how we got to the point of our breaking. In fact, he doesn't limit his compassion ever. He is full of loyal love to all who look to him! He is our gentle shepherd and our strong and sure deliverer. He is more than we could ever imagine, and the fullness of his glory eclipses all of our possible pain.

When he draws near in support, may we recognize his touch. What a wonderful God he is! There is so much to be thankful for, because we are his children, and he is for us.

Extravagant God, you are so rich in love and mercy. Your compassion is overflowing in my life; how could I but thank you? I am overwhelmed with gratitude toward you!

Sing for joy, you heavens!
Shout, you earth, and rejoice with dancing, shouting, and glee!
Burst into joyous songs, you mountains,
for Yahweh has comforted his beloved people.
He will show tenderness and compassion to his suffering ones.

ISAIAH 49:13 TPT

Wonderful One, I offer you the gratitude and praise of a thankful child. I see how you have marked my life with your mercy, and you're nowhere near done. How amazing is your compassion! Your tenderness is without guile, and you never hold a thing against me. Your motives are pure, and your heart is full of overwhelming affection.

I can't help but be in awe of the wonder of your love. It is strong enough to conquer death and to set every captive free. It is my freedom, my teacher, and my joyful confidence. Thank you for always being with me, that I never need worry about how I will face any trial or problem on my own. I lean on you, for you are my wisdom and my great source of strength in every season.

How has God's comfort shown up in your life?

No More Walls

He himself is our peace, who has made us both one and has broken down in his flesh the dividing wall of hostility.

EPHESIANS 2:14, ESV

We can be sure of this truth: nothing can ever separate us from the love of God in Christ Jesus our Lord. With the power of his love, he broke down every wall that kept us separated from God's presence. His blood was shed, his body broken, and his life laid down. And then, his body rose from the grave. He is alive! Jesus did all that was necessary to reconcile us to the Father.

When we submit our lives in love to him, living as he instructs us to, he becomes our peace. Our response to him is our portion of this process. We can do nothing to add or to take away from what Christ has already done. May we live in the freedom of this unhindered relationship, as we are meant to.

Jesus Christ, you are my living hope and the very reason I can have confidence before you. Thank you for peace with God, so that I can know you in spirit and in truth. I will worship you with my life, because you are worthy!

Christ himself is our peace. He made both Jewish people and those who are not Jews one people. They were separated as if there were a wall between them, but Christ broke down that wall of hate by giving his own body.

EPHESIANS 2:14 NCV

Lord Jesus, I recognize that without you, I would not have peace with God. But through you, I have living relationship with the Living God. You are better than I could ever ask for, and your love renews my hope. I am so grateful that nothing can separate me from your abundant mercy.

You meet me with kindness at all times even when you correct me. There is no one else like you in all the world! What a wonderful life I have found in you. You don't keep me from pain, but you comfort me with your peace in it. There is solace in your presence and overwhelming joy in your love. May I be like you in the way I live my life submitted to your love. You are worth the discomfort of transformation.

If there is nothing that separates you from Christ's love, how can you live more freely?

Led by Truth

Guide me in your truth and teach me,
for you are God my Savior,
and my hope is in you all day long.

PSALM 25:5 NIV

When you are faced with making big decisions, how do you go about making those choices? How about the smaller, daily ones? There is so much room in the will of God to move around. His plans are not a tightrope; they are more like the flow of a rushing river.

Will you trust God to guide you even if you cannot sense a clear direction from him? There is liberty in his love, and it more than covers every choice we make. Even if we were to go completely off-course from his best, he would never leave us. He always leads us in love. If you knew that you could never risk disappointing him, what would you do? By all means, seek the truth and God's great wisdom. But also, don't let fear keep you from the liberty of his generous mercy.

Righteous Father, in living a submitted life, I trust you to guide me even in the nuances of my day. This journey of life is much more about relationship and less about rigid rule following, so I won't put on myself what you never intended. Thank you for the freedom that your truth leads me to.

Lead me in Your truth and teach me,
For You are the God of my salvation;
On You I wait all the day.

PSALM 25:5 NKJV

God of my salvation, I wait on you when I don't know what to do. You are my loving leader, and I will not ignore your tender voice of truth. Speak to me tonight, and let my heart know the clarity of your wisdom. With revelation lighting the way, open my eyes to see what you are doing. I know that there is no need to fear making wrong choices; you are not a demanding and stern father. You advise me when I seek you, and you lovingly lead me in your gracious knowledge.

Why would I look anywhere else for answers when you hold the words of life that I'm looking for? You have been my teacher, and you will continue to be. Show me the way to walk, and I will follow you. When there is freedom to choose between my own preferences, help me to be in touch with my own God-given desires, gifts and leanings. You created me with intention, and I can know you in the freedom of my own unique expression.

How has God's truth guided your decision-making?

Good Gifts

Grace, mercy, and peace will be with us,
from God the Father and from Jesus Christ,
the Son of the Father, in truth and love.

2 JOHN 1:3 NASB

In the gracious tide of God's mercy, there is so much strength to be found. The peace of God is our plentiful portion in every moment. There is no reason to live without it! Whenever we recognize fear and anxiety taking over the peace of God's presence, may we quickly turn to him again.

There is always an abundance of grace to empower us to live merciful lives, in reflection of the generous kindness that we have been shown. Where we are running low on love, there is an overflowing fountain that we can fill up on at any time. He is our source and our sustenance; there is no need to strive in vain, because he never runs out or runs dry.

Father God, I receive from your plentiful love today the grace, mercy and peace of your presence. Fill me with to overflow, that my life would spill over with your kindness to everyone I come across.

*God our Father and Jesus Christ, his Son, will release to us
overflowing grace, mercy, and peace, filled with true love.*

2 JOHN 1:3 TPT

Wonderful God, you are so far beyond what my limited
understanding can comprehend. May I be filled with the
awe of your greatness as I meditate on your large love this
evening. In all ways, at all times, in all circumstances, you
are overflowing with grace, mercy and peace. May my life be
lined with your pure love that conquers every fear and puts all
anxiety to rest.

Enlarge my capacity to know you; I must know you more!
I have seen glimpses of your goodness, but I am longing for
greater comprehension. Your insights are like nuggets of
pure gold-treasure that enriches my life. Reveal more of your
beauty as I look to you. What I have known is sweeter than
anything else I have tasted, and I yearn for a fresh portion.
I know that you won't ignore me; I wait on you, Lord.

Have you filled up on the good gifts
of God's abundant love lately?

Keep Me Close

I have tried hard to find you—
don't let me wander from your commands.

PSALM 119:10 NLT

In the reliable leadership of our Good Shepherd, we will find that he is tender toward us and always reaching out when we need a firm hand to steady us. He will not hide himself from us when we seek him. He is easier to find than we may realize, for he is always closer than we expect. When we seek God, longing to follow in the footsteps of his mercy-law, he will not leave us to find our own way. There is a wealth of God-knowledge to be found in his Word.

Let us not throw up our hands when we cannot sense his presence. He is faithful, whether we can discern what he is doing or not. When we align our lives with his law of love and follow on the pathway of his peace, we will not be lost. He does not confuse us; he clears things up! Do we trust his simple gospel for guidance?

Constant One, you never change, and for that I am grateful. You keep me close to the heartbeat of your love as I follow after you. You amaze me with your faithfulness, time after time!

With my whole heart I have sought You;
Oh, let me not wander from Your commandments!

PSALM 119:10 NKJV

Father, I have submitted my whole heart to you, and I know that is no small thing to you. You do not expect me to perfectly perform everything that I want to offer you. What a gift that is! When I fall short, you fill the gap. I promise you my submission, and every time there is a disconnection, I turn right back to you. Repair the connection of relationship whenever I repent and lead me in the freedom of your truth.

Shame has no power over your children, unless we let it. But I know that you do not barter in it. You forgive me, and I am clean. There is nothing that could ever stop your marvelous love's overflow in my life, and I am so grateful for that. Spirit, flood my heart with your glory-light as I open to you again. You are too wonderful for words, and I am undone in your presence!

How does the gospel inform your life?

Into His Heart

It is impossible for God to lie for we know that his promise and his vow will never change! And now we have run into his heart to hide ourselves in his faithfulness. This is where we find his strength and comfort, for he empowers us to seize what has already been established ahead of time—an unshakeable hope.

HEBREWS 6:18 TPT

In this passage of Scripture, we hear an echo of a truth spoken to God's people in the Old Testament. In Numbers, it states that "God is not a man, that he should lie." His promises stand firm throughout the ages, and each one will find its fulfillment at the proper time. The vow that God made with his people still holds its weight.

Whenever we are discouraged by the goings-on of the world around us, may we find encouragement by submerging ourselves in his faithfulness. Let's meditate on his truth that never changes. God is not a liar. The hope that we have found in his living Word is immoveable. It can never be overpowered! So, let's trust him today with what we can see and what we can't. He is still God, and he will do all that he said he would.

Faithful God, I run into your heart again today, knowing that I will find strength and courage there. Refresh my own heart as I dwell on yours. You are so, so good!

By two unchangeable things, in which it is impossible for God to lie, we who have fled for refuge might have strong encouragement to hold fast to the hope set before us.

HEBREWS 6:18 ESV

Righteous One, your great faithfulness fulfills the vows of generations past and those still to come. You never go back on your promises, for you could never tell a lie. I'm so relieved by that! There is no hidden motivation to uncover in your heart; you are pure in love and generous in kindness. You are not waiting to drop a hidden hammer.

You are goodness. You are the source of all compassion, empathy and mercy. There is no one greater than you. You are my refuge, and your constant character is balm to my weary soul. You are not flippant with your vows, and you do not forget anything that you speak. Your love is incomparable, and I am immersed in it. Thank you, Lord!

What does it mean for your life that God does not lie?

Something that Lasts

*"All flesh is like grass and all its glory like the flower of grass.
The grass withers, and the flower falls,
but the word of the LORD remains forever."*

1 PETER 1:24-25 ESV

In the shifting of seasons, we are reminded of the cycles of death and rebirth in life. In the springing up of new blooms, hope awakens within our hearts that there is abundant beauty to still be found around us. The barrenness of winter does not last forever, and the lush greens of summer are also fleeting. Just as the shifting seasons display the altering seasons of life, and how brief it can be, there is wisdom in knowing the signs of the times.

Though our experience in this life is finite, the Lord is eternal. His kingdom never ends, and when we submit our hearts and lives to God in love, we can rest assured that we will dwell with him forever. Though lives fade around us, his forever-Word promises that there is more life to be found in the coming age of his rule and reign.

Holy God, your Word stands forever as truth. I know that you will be faithful to every promise you have made. Though this life does not slow down, I trust you to guide me into eternity as I follow your ways.

> *"All people are like grass,*
> *and all their glory is like the flowers of the field;*
> *the grass withers and the flowers fall,*
> *but the word of the LORD endures forever."*
>
> 1 PETER 1:24-25 NIV

Lord, you are the Creator of all that we see in the universe around us. The moon and the stars were set in motion by a single word from you. You spoke, and there was light. You said it, and up sprang mountains, seas and lush gardens. You took the time to mold man in your image and breathe your Spirit-breath into his lungs. You fashioned woman out of man's side, and you said that they were good.

Though this short life is but a blink, there is an eternity more, without end in sight, to discover your great goodness face-to-face. Your Word is courage to my soul, and it fuels my faith because I have seen how your faithfulness plays out. You are wonderful, God! What a glorious reality I have to look forward to in your kingdom.

How does the eternal endurance of God's Word encourage you?

Come Again

You who are my Comforter in sorrow,
my heart is faint within me.

JEREMIAH 8:18 NIV

Oh, that we could escape the deep pain of grief in this life!
When loss comes sweeping into our lives, there is no evading
the heartbreak that accompanies it. But God has not changed.
He is as loyal in love as he ever has been or will be. He never
promised that walking with him would allow us to escape
the pain of humanity; he did, however, promise to be with
us through it all. He comforts us, heals us, and restores our
souls.

He is the constant help that we long for, and he will do what
no one else ever could. He supports us in our heartbreak,
mending us and leading us into deeper knowledge of his
ever-present kindness. He meets us where we are with
gentleness. Will we trust that he is still more than enough?

Lifter of my head, come close with the purity of your presence
and surround me with your peace. You are the one I lean on.
When my heart is breaking, hold me together.

My grief is beyond healing;
my heart is broken.

JEREMIAH 8:18 NLT

Comforter, when I cannot make sense of my pain, and my world has come crashing down around me, I trust that the truth of your Word still stands. Come close and wrap around me the relief of your love's embrace. I don't want to simply know that you are near with my mind; I want to feel the tangible warmth of your presence wrapping around me like a blanket. Cover me in your compassion, and tuck around me with the peace of your Spirit.

I do not need questions answered when the pain is great. I just need to know that you will hold me closer than anyone else ever could. You are my relief, my strong support, and my confidant. You read my thoughts so well; I don't need to say a single word for you to already know what is going on. Lift the weight that I cannot on my own. I depend on you, my God; don't let me down!

How has God comforted you in your grief?

It's Certain

Certainly God has heard me;
He has attended to the voice of my prayer.

PSALM 66:19 NKJV

There is no need to waver in wondering whether God hears our prayers or not. His Word says over and over again that God hears the prayers of those who love him. He listens to those who cry out to him. Whether it's a shout or a whisper, God does not miss a word you say even if it's written deeply within your heart.

Will you trust him with your prayers and requests? Do you have confidence that he will answer you? He is faithful, merciful, and fiercely kind. He is more attentive to you than your most trusted confidant and friend. He will not let you down. You can approach him with confidence at every turn, for you are his dearly loved child.

Faithful One, you lift every burden of my heart when I offer it to you. You are so faithful to me. I will not hold back a thing from you, because I know that you care for me.

Truly God has listened;
he has given heed to the words of my prayer.

PSALM 66:19 NRSV

God my friend, I offer you every part of my heart tonight. I know that you care about the details that I obsess over, and you take care of them in ways that are better than I could have known. I will not worry, because you don't miss a thing. You answer the cries of my heart with your abundant love every time. It is powerful, breaking the chains of shame and despair. You wash me in the living waters of your presence, and I feel light as air; I know that you have made me clean.

You provide for every need I have, and you don't do it grudgingly. You are full of generosity every single time I ask. Who else is there like you? I've never known one so kind as you. Thank you, Lord, for your amazing friendship. I cannot begin to convey the depths of my gratitude toward you.

Do you believe that God hears what you say to him?

Face like Flint

The Lord God helps Me,
Therefore, I am not disgraced;
Therefore, I have made My face like flint,
And I know that I will not be ashamed.

ISAIAH 50:7 NASB

When our confidence is based on our own reserves and capabilities, it will eventually falter. But when our confidence is in the God who never changes and who always comes through in faithfulness, it need never be shaken. Let us remember who he is and what he has done. He is an ever-present help in time of trouble, and he won't ever abandon his loyal lovers.

May we keep our lives in line with his love, remembering that his mercies are new every morning, and stay attuned to his presence with us. When we place all our bets on him, he will not let us be humiliated. There is tremendous grace in his constant presence that teaches, guides and delivers. What a confident hope we have!

Lord God, I have put all my trust in you and your faithful love to help me. You are better than the most dependable parent. I know I can have confident expectation in your unwavering love.

The Lord Yahweh empowers me, so I am not humiliated.
For that reason, with holy determination,
I will do his will and not be ashamed.

ISAIAH 50:7 TPT

Yahweh, I set my life according to your ways, and I will follow you. It doesn't matter what comes or goes, you are faithful, guiding me with your constant love every day of my life. You never lift your hand of mercy from me, not even for a moment, because I am yours. I won't be ashamed in the end; your Word will prove true. Your kindness graciously pulls me whenever I start to go down the path of fear about the unknown.

I never need fear, for you, my God, are with me! You don't abandon me at any point. What a wonderful gift it is that your loyal nature keeps me close. You are the one I trust. I will not give up on you because you never give up on me. Give me strength to believe that your goodness is mine even in the waiting.

How has God come through for you?

Light of Wisdom

The teaching of your word gives light,
so even the simple can understand.

PSALM 119:130 NLT

Do not worry. When you seek the Lord, you will find him. He teaches those who look for knowledge with his pure truth. God's wisdom is not confusing! To those who would seek him, he illuminates the simplicity of his ways. When you follow the light of his truth, you will not fall. And when life is as dark as a moonless night, press into the nature of his heart and trust his gentle whispers. He will not steer you wrong.

We were not created simply to obey; we were created for vibrant relationship. It is not a one-way connection where God dictates what we do and we fall in line. He has always wanted us to know his heart the way that he knows ours. Let's not stop at obedience; let's develop our connection with him because he is so very good to us!

Wise God, your ways are purer than the ways of man. You always know just what to do. I look to your Word to instruct me and your Spirit to guide me in truth.

Learning your words gives wisdom
and understanding for the foolish.

PSALM 119:130 NCV

All-knowing One, I submit my ways to yours. You are full of revelation-light to instruct me in life. Above all, I want to know you. I don't want to simply know what you are like; I seek to grow my relationship with you. You are faithful friend, constant comforter, wonderful lord and savior. You are more than I can imagine—so much more!

In you is found the perfection of every relationship and role. You are a perfect father, the most loyal lover, the most tender friend, my most constant and reliable help. You are more than my mind can contain, and much more than I have tasted. But what I have tasted is so good! I will not let doubts about your goodness keep me from you, for you are bigger than each one. I will build my life upon your truth, counting on your wonderful mercy to rush to meet me every time I look for understanding.

What do you need wisdom for?

Always Reliable

The Lord is faithful, who will establish you
and guard you from the evil one.

2 THESSALONIANS 3:3 NKJV

Do you trust that God will protect you even when you cannot see a way out of your current trouble? He is faithful to follow through on his promises to be with us because his Word is dependent on his character, not ours! What a relief it is to know that God is better than we expect at every turn and more reliable than we could put our greatest hopes in. He really is that wonderful!

Cast all your concerns on him today because he cares so deeply for you. You can rely on his dependable nature to come through in mercy. In fact, if you were to keep count of his help in your life, you may be surprised to see how much he does for you. Trust him! He is always reliable.

Loving Lord, your faithfulness stretches beyond the skies; who can measure it? May my worries be put to rest as I remember your unchanging love, Lord. Keep showing your loyalty for your name's sake. You are wonderful!

Lord Yahweh is always faithful to place you on a firm foundation and guard you from the Evil One.

2 THESSALONIANS 3:3 TPT

Lord Yahweh, your loyal love is the firm foundation beneath my feet. I will not be moved from the rock of your salvation, because you are the one who set me upon it. You are faithful through the ages, and you haven't changed one bit. Keep me close and guard me from the schemes of the evil one. Keep me safe in the shelter of your presence, and don't let the wicked destroy my reputation. You are the unshakeable groundwork that my life is built upon, so don't let me be knocked down.

I know that you are more faithful than any other, no matter the circumstances of my current season of life. I trust you to guide me through because your mercy is greater than my biggest strength and deeper than my greatest weakness. You are able, and you will do it! For your name and for your glory, you will always be faithful to your Word.

Do you depend on God to keep you safe?

All Seen

In hope we have been saved,
but hope that is seen is not hope;
for who hopes for what he already sees.

ROMANS 8:24 NASB

What is your confidence based upon? Is it solely rooted in what you can tangibly see, feel, or experience? Or does it run deeper than that? God is gracious to us; he gives us glimpses of his glory through moments of mercy that manifest in our lives. But we still only see a very small part! He sees the whole; the complete story of humankind from beginning to end. He knows what is happening in every heart, and he is never surprised by anything he finds.

As you build your relationship with God, can you trust that his Word will come to pass in his timing? Rapport is built through fellowship with the Spirit. As you come to know God more and more through communion and submission, your hope will grow in response.

Wise God, you are the hope that my life is built upon. May it grow ever firmer and more expectant as I watch you faithfully move in my life and in the world. I know that you are working. You are my saving grace.

This is the hope of our salvation. But hope means that we must trust and wait for what is still unseen. For why would we need to hope for something we already have?

ROMANS 8:24 TPT

Faithful One, you are more reliable than the rising of the sun in the morning. You are more consistent than the shifting seasons. You are Alpha and Omega, and you are the source of every living thing. As I meditate on your nature, and the power of your great name, the roots of my hope grow deeper in your love.

I long for the day when I see you face-to-face and every mystery is made clear. I cannot wait until hope is not necessary because every promise you have made is fulfilled. But until that day, I build the practice of hoping in you. I look to your Word for encouragement and wisdom. I lean on the presence of your Spirit to empower me with grace to face any and all things in this life. I will not stop praying and seeking you. In you is the fullness of everything I long for!

How does hope keep you expectant on God?

Great Acceptance

"The Spirit of the Lord is upon me,
and he has anointed me to be hope for the poor,
freedom for the brokenhearted, and new eyes for the blind,
and to preach to prisoners, 'You are set free!'
I have come to share the message of Jubilee,
for the time of God's great acceptance has begun."

LUKE 4:18-19 TPT

What a beautiful God we serve! He offers what every heart and body is longing for. He freely gives to all, and he is so personal in how he meets us. For those locked in the bondage of shame, he offers liberty. For those broken down under the world's systems, he offers hope for a better life. For those who are crushed by heartbreak, he offers the freedom of wholeness in him. For those who cannot see, he offers sight.

And these are just examples of his merciful power at work in our lives. Above all, he has welcomed us in as sons and daughters. He has ushered us into his family. We find our ultimate belonging as children of the Mighty God. What a wonderful gift!

Father, I am beyond grateful to be yours. Raise me up in the wisdom of your ways and teach me, so that I may know to the core of my being how fully loved and accepted I am. It is more than good news; it is the best news, and it continually changes me.

*"The Spirit of the Lord is upon me,
for he has anointed me to bring Good News to the poor.
He has sent me to proclaim that captives will be released,
that the blind will see, that the oppressed will be set free,
and that the time of the Lord's favor has come."*

LUKE 4:18-19 NLT

Lord over all, the good news of your gospel is full of light and life to all who partake of it. I want to know deeper freedom in you, and I know that you are not finished peeling back the layers of old, worn-out ways and mindsets in my life. Would you meet me right now with the overwhelming affection of your heart? May I receive a greater portion of your love as I open up my heart to you again?

You set the oppressed free. Where I am living under the oppression of lies, liberate me with your life. I don't want to spend my life telling others about something that I don't experience on a regular basis, and that's not what you require! Your Spirit administers healing, freedom, and acceptance, to me as well as to others. Spirit, come and do what only you can do tonight.

Are there any areas of your life that have felt off-limits to freedom in God?

Worth My Trust

The LORD is for me; he will help me.
I will look in triumph at those who hate me.
It is better to take refuge in the LORD
than to trust in people.

PSALM 118:7-8 NLT

When discouragement sets in, who are the people you look to for inspiration? Is there a practice that you have to help turn your disappointments into hope? We all have coping mechanisms, but they don't all serve us well. Without shame or condemnation, consider what you go to when the worries of life begin to overwhelm you. How does this help?

For those of us who need the reminder, God is an ever-present help whenever we are in need. He meets us with the overwhelming grace of his compassionate heart in every moment. He has strength to spare; in fact, his Word says that his strength is made perfect in our weakness. When we are let down by those around us, let us remember that there is one who is perfect in all he does. We can run into the shelter of his love every chance we get.

Lord, you are worthy of my trust today and forever. Instead of mindlessly checking out when I am overwhelmed today, I will practice turning my attention to you. Lift the weight of my burdens as I rest in the confidence of your help.

You stand beside me as my hero who rescues me.
I've seen with my own eyes the defeat of my enemies.
I've triumphed over them all!
Lord, it is so much better to trust in you to save me
than to put my confidence in someone else.

PSALM 118:7-8 TPT

Savior, you are the one I turn to both in good times and in bad. You are the one who lifts me up when I fall, who redirects me when I wander, and who saves me when I have no other hope. What a wonderful advocate and defender you are. You fight my battles for me! You know that I would easily be crushed under the enemy's schemes on my own, but you have promised that I am never alone. What a comfort it is to know that you are always my willing and able help.

I have bound my life to yours, and I have seen your deliverance in my life more than once. I trust you more than any other, for you are the only wise God and my holy help at every turn. You won't ever abandon me or let me down when I need you. Why would I put my full confidence in another when no one else compares to you?

Who do you turn to the most in trouble?

Comforting Words

The precepts of the LORD are right,
giving joy to the heart.
The commands of the LORD are radiant,
giving light to the eyes.

PSALM 19:8 NIV

God's Word offers us keys to his kingdom life. When we search the Scriptures and meditate on his ways, how can we help but be encouraged by what he offers? His comfort is close, as we hear over and over again in the book of Psalms. He is a strong and mighty tower. There are poems about God's powerful deliverance and his tender mercies toward those who look to him for help.

He gives renewed joy to those who are crushed in spirit. He restores what the world destroys and gives hope to the hopeless. Whatever we need, he has it in abundance. May we tether our lives to his, trusting that his ways lead us into the abundance of his goodness over and over again.

Yahweh, you always lead those who look to you with the clarity of your wisdom. My heart is filled with joy when I recognize your wonderful love at work in the details of my life. You fill me with expectation. You are my radiant and life-giving hope!

His teachings make us joyful and radiate his light;
his precepts are so pure!
His commands, how they challenge us to keep close to his heart!
The revelation-light of his word makes my spirit shine radiant.

PSALM 19:8 TPT

Pure One, I know that you do not require anything of me that you would not offer freely yourself. In fact, when I look at the life of Jesus, I can clearly see what your laid-down love looks like. I will not hold onto the reins of control, seeking to get my own way any longer. I know that your ways are better than my plans, so I submit my heart to yours. I surrender my own ideas of what should and shouldn't be, and I follow the leading of your mercy-kindness that breaks down the walls I have erected around my hopes.

Your love is so much more expansive than my small opinions can account for. I want to walk in the radiance of your life-giving light all the days of my life. Lead me on in your wonderful ways, and I will follow.

When was the last time you felt delight at God's teachings?

Feet of Jesus

Come, let us bow down in worship,
let us kneel before the LORD our Maker.

PSALM 95:6 NIV

The Lord is so very worthy of our trust and our submission. When we struggle to offer him what we have dreamt up in our hearts, why is it that we question his goodness? He can be trusted with our hopes, dreams and longings. He is not a dismissive or cruel father. He is a marvelously good and faithful parent. He knows us better than we know ourselves, and yet he never forces our hand. He wants us to share our lives with him!

He has so much wisdom to offer us, and it produces wonderful Spirit fruit when we live by his insights. He is always worthy of honor and respect, for he is endlessly pure and good. Let's give him our attention today; he is worthy of our adoration.

Lord and Maker, I offer you the attention of my heart right now. Spirit, as I look to the wonder of your nature, come close with your trademark fruit. I want to know your unhindered joy as I offer my heart to you again. You are so worthy of all that I could ever offer you.

Come and kneel before this Creator-God;
come and bow before the mighty God,
our majestic maker!

<small>PSALM 95:6 TPT</small>

Creator God, you are majestic in all of your ways. The fact that you would humbly come to seek and serve those who were lost in this world—including me—reveals the unsurpassable beauty of your love. I won't hold back from you today. You are awe-inspiring! Your mercy is more freeing than any other love I've known. You do not ask me to be anything that I am not; you just want me to invite you into my life. It's there that transformation happens, from the inside-out.

I humble myself in your presence, welcoming you to meet me with the purity of your affection that loves me to life. I am so grateful that my relationship with you is safe. I hide myself in your nature, for you are unchanging in your marvelous kindness. As I gaze on the wonders of your creation, I cannot help but be awed by your creativity. I want to know you more with each passing moment and through every season of the soul.

What can you humbly present to God in worship today?

Always Learning

Wise people can also listen and learn;
even they can find good advice in these words.

PROVERBS 1:5 NCV

We never reach the end of the impact of God's wisdom in our lives. As long as we are journeying through this life, we will always be learning and unlearning. Let us intentionally look to God's Word and his faithful nature as we wrestle with the big questions in life. Let us lay down the old ways of thinking and doing as we discover their limitations, in favor of God's more expansive love.

It is a part of life, when we mature, to realize that what we once thought was set in stone was actually never meant to be a platform to build our lives upon. There are truths that never change, and we discover their magnitude unfolds in new ways and revelations as God leads us in his love. May we never get so caught up in being right about something that we refuse to learn from the Lord and grow. Pride has no place in his kingdom. It is the humble heart that garners understanding.

Wise God, I recognize that there are questions I have that don't have clear answers. But you have given your Word as a guidepost to help us. More than that, in relationship with you, I find that it is your character and the fruit of your Spirit that separate your ways from the ways of this world. Teach me!

For the wise, these proverbs will make you even wiser,
and for those with discernment,
you will be able to acquire brilliant strategies for leadership.

PROVERBS 1:5 TPT

Mighty God, you give discernment to the seeking heart,
and you give strategies to those who listen for your wisdom.
There are so many keys to your kingdom life that are found
in the wisdom of your Word. I won't stop seeking out your
perspective on my life. I know that when I am stumped by a
problem, you always have a solution. Instead of looking to
solve it on my own, with my limited understanding, I depend
on your revelation-light to open my eyes to your insights.
I lean not on my own comprehension, but on your more
trustworthy truth that doesn't miss a detail.

You are brilliant, Lord, so I look to you! Whatever wisdom I
have is only through the wonderful grace of your Spirit's work
in my life. I want to know what you see when you look at my
life. I want to know your greater perspective. Lead me, and I
will follow. Teach me, and I will learn. Keep doing it, Lord!

Are you actively growing in the wisdom of the Lord?

Great Expectation

All praise to God, the Father of our Lord Jesus Christ. It is by his great mercy that we have been born again, because God raised Jesus Christ from the dead. Now we live with great expectation.

1 PETER 1:3 NLT

Have you had pivotal moments in your life that you can point to where something changed the trajectory of your life? In Christ, we are being continuously transformed to his likeness as we submit our days and ways to him. But there was also a rebirth, or a renewal, that happened when we first gave him our lives.

In his mercy, he washed us clean from all our sins. Every stain or blemish that could be held against us was removed by the power of his blood. That is not to say that there isn't more refining that can happen, but God has freed us from the power of sin and death through his victorious resurrection from the grave. We are free in him to live with great expectation!

God, thank you for your liberating love at work in my life. You have broken every chain that kept me in cycles of sin and shame. You are the overcoming one, and I am fully alive in you.

Celebrate with praises the God and Father of our Lord Jesus Christ,
who has shown us his extravagant mercy. For his fountain of
mercy has given us a new life—we are reborn to experience a living,
energetic hope through the resurrection of Jesus Christ from the dead.

1 PETER 1:3 TPT

Merciful Father, I am undone at the wonder of living in the freedom of your love. Though I look for my guilt, you have washed it away. You have declared me free, so I am truly free. Your mercy has revived my soul and given me hope to look forward to your endless goodness.

You are constantly working in my life, and I am so grateful! I offer you the unhindered adoration and praise of my thankful heart. You are worthy of all that I could ever offer you, and so much more. All I have is yours, for you are the source of my life. I will trust your kind and faithful character to continue to work in me, producing the living fruit of your Spirit. You are my joy, Lord! And what an incomparably deep joy it is.

What is your great expectation in life?

Good Father

*"Don't worry. For your Father cares deeply
about even the smallest detail of your life."*

MATTHEW 10:30-31 TPT

It may be a given to trust God with the big things in life;
we expect him to take care of those things. But what about
the smaller details? Do we look for him in those? He is as
concerned with the little things as he is with the large ones.
He is not limited in his attention; his capacity is far greater
than we could ever imagine for ourselves.

If it is true that he not only notices, but deeply cares, about
the details of our lives, why would we not trust him with
them? What worries have been cropping up in our thoughts?
What is weighing on our minds? Whether big or small, God is
invested. He sees it all. Let's cast every little care upon him,
for he tenderly cares for us.

Father, lift the weight of my worries as I offer you the trust of
my heart. I believe that you are as concerned with the little
things that preoccupy me as you are with the big things that
are completely out of my control. Fill me with your peace and
give me eyes to see your faithfulness in the everyday details of
my life.

*"Even the very hairs of your head are all numbered.
So don't be afraid; you are worth more than many sparrows."*

MATTHEW 10:30-31 NIV

Attentive One, you are so thoughtful in your notice of the
details of my life. You see every little part that makes me who
I am, and you delight in it. You don't miss a single feature.
Why would I worry about provision when you faithfully
provide for things that I constantly overlook?

As I look at the overview of my life and the details, would
you give me eyes to see where you take care of me? I know
that you do. I want to love you rightly, and part of that is
understanding how wonderful you truly are. I press into
your perfect love this evening. As I do, will you drive the fear
and doubt from my mind? You are a kind and caring father,
and I'm so very grateful to be your child. Meet me in the
seemingly insignificant things and broaden my awareness of
your nurture in my life.

Do you invite God into the details of your life?

Carried by Grace

In all their distress He was distressed,
And the angel of His presence saved them;
In His love and in His mercy He redeemed them,
And He lifted them and carried them all the days of old.

ISAIAH 63:9 NASB

When we look at God's leadership of his people throughout the Scriptures, we get an idea of his leadership through his Spirit to us today. He is full of mercy, entering into our circumstances with us and extending the kindness and care of a gentle shepherd.

He is full of truth, but he is not demanding. He teaches us through the wisdom of his Word and asks that we would trust his unfailing nature. He reminds us to not fear and instead to walk in boldness and courage, because he is with us. He is a mighty deliverer, faithful provider, and our Redeemer. Let us follow his lead, with submitted and expectant hearts. And when we are brought to a standstill because of suffering, he will carry us through with his grace.

Good Shepherd, I will follow your lead in my life. I see how you have faithfully met your people throughout the ages, carrying them along when they could not press forward on their own. I trust you to do the same for me.

When they suffered, he suffered with them.
The Angel of His Presence saved them.
Out of his enduring love and compassion
he redeemed them.
He lifted them up, carried them in his arms,
and cared for them all the days of old.

Isaiah 63:9 TPT

Close Comforter, you are always present with your love and mercy. May I never forget how deeply your compassion runs in my life. Your miracles of mercy have done more for me than any self-help could. You are incomparably wise, and so very attentive to your people. Though you are all-powerful, you do not wield your might with arrogance. You are full of kindness; it is hard to comprehend how wonderfully tender you are.

You redeemed your people with the sacrifice of your own blood and did not count it too great a cost. In their suffering, you suffered. In your suffering, we are set free. There is no other help like you. In you, there is fullness of life, and salvation for our souls. Who else could offer such a thing?

How has Jesus' suffering affected the way that you relate to God in your own suffering?

In Perfect Faithfulness

LORD, you are my God;
I will exalt you and praise your name,
for in perfect faithfulness you have done wonderful things,
things planned long ago.

ISAIAH 25:1 NIV

We see a small part, but God's scope is so much larger than we can comprehend. He is not limited by time or space, for they were created by him in the first place. When our lives are submitted to his leadership, we benefit from the grandness of his wisdom and perfect plans. Though our own ideas about our lives may change, his intentions never do.

Let us live with open hands of surrender and hearts that trust his leadership, no matter where it takes us in this life. He is worthy of our confidence because he never fails. He never wavers in faithfulness, so he can hold the weight of all our hopes. Let's give him the praise he's due.

Perfect One, you are faithful in all your ways. I put all my hopes in you even, and especially, in the face of great uncertainty. No matter what, I know that you will be loyal to your Word.

Lord Yahweh, you are my glorious God!
I will exalt you and praise your name forever,
for you have done so many wonderful things.
Well-thought-out plans you formed in ages past;
you've been faithful and true to fulfill them all!

ISAIAH 25:1 TPT

Yahweh, you are worthy of all my praise! I will lift your name up, for there is none other like you. When I count the wonderful things you have done in my life, my heart swells with gratitude and joy. Don't stop pouring your love into my life, Lord, for it keeps me going in hope. You don't need to scramble when my plans go awry, because you already know just what to do.

I'm so grateful that you are not worried about my life. I put all my confidence in you, letting go of the need to dictate how and when your promises are fulfilled. You always know best. I will rest in the assurance of your great love that leads me in every single situation. You are great and greatly to be praised!

Can you spot God's faithfulness
in specific moments in your life?

Kindness Given

The Lord God is like a sun and shield;
the Lord gives us kindness and honor.
He does not hold back anything good
from those whose lives are innocent.

PSALM 84:11 NCV

Our innocence is based on our position in Christ, not in our past mistakes or sins that have already been washed in his blood. If we have trouble believing that God's love has covered and qualified us, let us be reminded today that his finished work on the cross is the basis for our salvation.

The apostle Paul is clear in his letter to the Ephesians that we are saved by grace, through faith. It is the gift of God, and it never needs to be earned. He gives us kindness and honor out of the abundance of his love for us. He will not withhold anything good from those who are hidden in him. Don't hold back from receiving what he is offering!

Kind God, thank you for the reminder of your grace that flows freely from your compassionate heart into my life. I receive the gift of your love and its many expressions. You are so wonderful! Thank you.

The Lord God is brighter than the brilliance of a sunrise!
Wrapping himself around me like a shield,
he is so generous with his gifts of grace and glory.
Those who walk along his paths with integrity
will never lack one thing they need, for he provides it all!

PSALM 84:11 TPT

Lord God, I walk along the path that you lead me upon. You know my heart; even when I mess up, I want to do what is right. I'm grateful that you don't hold my sins against me. You are lavish in lovingkindness, and I am never without it. Let me never forget that you are the one who qualifies me. You have chosen me and called me your own.

I will follow you, for you are full of grace and your ways lead me to vibrant life. You are the peace that transcends all my circumstances and the hope that holds me together. I trust in you, God! I know you will always provide everything I need, for you already have done it countless times over. You are so faithful!

Do you put conditions on receiving God's love?

He Calms My Soul

He awoke and rebuked the wind and said to the sea,
"Peace! Be still!" And the wind ceased,
and there was a great calm.

MARK 4:39 ESV

When we are overcome with worry, let us remember that God is not. Jesus was not worried about the storm when his disciples woke him up in the boat. Clearly, this was no small storm; it was a raging squall. They were worried for their very lives. But Jesus, commanding the winds and waves to be still, was not for a moment concerned. In fact, if we continue in this passage, we see that Jesus was instead perplexed at the lack of his disciples' faith.

What areas of our lives feel so threatened and exposed that we question the very nature of our God? Let us align our hearts with his and trust through faith that we will not be destroyed. What's more, in our helplessness, we are not actually powerless. He who is able to calm the fiercest storm has given us authority to calm the storms around us with his peace, as well.

Jesus, my peace giver, forgive me for my lack of faith and how easily distracted I am by the threat of disaster. I know that you are not just powerful to save, but you are also the one who stills the chaos. Speak stillness to the thought storms that rage in my mind, so that there would be rest in the peace of your presence.

He got up, rebuked the wind and said to the waves,
"Quiet! Be still!" Then the wind died down
and it was completely calm.

MARK 4:39 NIV

Jesus, you are still the one who calms the raging seas with
just a word. You speak, and creation responds. My heart also
responds to your voice. Will you release the peace of your
made-up mind over my heart now? I see more clearly when
the fog of confusion is lifted. I understand more fully when
the clarity of your revelation-light shines on my mind. I know
that you are always full of love to pour out on your people. I
want to drink deeply of the waters of your mercy.

Refresh me in the cool breeze of your breath of life. When
you move, the earth reacts. And you have not stopped your
work in this world. I stand in the waterfall of your living love,
and I am filled with peace, joy and love once again. Increase
my faith that as I walk with you, my confidence would grow
stronger with each step.

What storms in your life have been calmed by God's peace?

Truth that Remains

The very essence of your words is truth;
all your just regulations will stand forever.

PSALM 119:160 NLT

There is no reason to go searching the ends of the earth for truth that lasts. God has freely given us access to his life-changing wisdom. There is none better to be found. In relationship with him, we get to know what he is like through his Word and through his faithfulness in our lives.

His love is like no other, without condition or restraint. If he senses our withdrawal, he does not pull back. He will never force us to receive his kindness, but it is there for the taking, nonetheless. How does the essence of his loving truth show up in our lives? We can look into his Word and find clues and keys to Spirit life. He is the way, and he is not hiding from us!

Good God, you are truth. Your words are life-giving and life-altering. You speak, and the earth trembles. My heart responds in kind. You are too wonderful for words. Thank you for revealing yourself to me through your Word.

The sum total of all your words adds up to absolute truth,
and every one of your righteous decrees is everlasting.

PSALM 119:160 TPT

Righteous One, the words you speak are truth, and each one
is fulfilled by the faithfulness of your nature. What you do
lasts forever, and what you speak is eternally significant.
May I not get sidetracked by ideologies that reject the truth
of your living love. Only you know the true significance of
your mercy, and I won't rely on my own limited capacity to
understand. You are the one who gives revelation and makes
your Word come alive.

Keep my heart entwined with yours as I meditate on your
Word, seeing how it so beautifully plays out in real ways in my
life. You are better than the most well-intentioned pursuer.
Your ways are purer than the humblest servant. You are
perfect in all of your ways, and I trust your Word more than
any other. You are the way, the truth and the life, and I won't
stop following after you, Lord.

What is your life aligned with?

Champion Defender

He alone is my safe place;
his wrap-around presence always protects me.
For he is my champion defender;
there's no risk of failure with God.
So why would I let worry paralyze me,
even when troubles multiply around me?

PSALM 62:2 TPT

If you knew that you could not fail, what would you do? Whether in life, love, or endeavors, how would the confidence of freedom change your life? Surely, we know that in life we will have troubles.

But let's be clear: with God, there is no risk of failure. When we live our lives for him, we cannot disappoint him. He leads in love, extends mercy in love, redirects us in love, and so on. He loves it when we take big risks for him! Why should we worry about the troubles around us when God is our safe place and our champion defender? He will continue to be our refuge and our place of refreshment.

Mighty God, when I consider your nearness and the ways that you take care of me, I can feel the confidence of my trust growing stronger. You won't stop wrapping me in your loving presence. You are the one I run to for refuge, and I trust you to keep me safe.

Truly he is my rock and my salvation;
he is my fortress, I will never be shaken.

PSALM 62:2 NIV

Strong Deliverer, you are the foundation that my life is built upon. I will not be shaken! You surround me with the unbreakable power of your love, and I am kept safe. Continue to pour out your mercy in my life, just as you have been doing. I have experienced your hand of protection, and I know that it won't be the last time. I'm grateful for your careful watch over me, so that I am never left alone. I find rest in the shelter of your presence.

Soothe my worries with the peace that you bring. I know that you are always close, but I'm longing for a fresh revelation of your nearness with me here and now. Open my understanding to see you as you are, and my heart will respond with awe and thanksgiving. Revive my hope with your loving presence. You are my fortress, my strength, and my sustainer; in you I will trust.

How has God protected you?

Restored by Peace

The LORD is my shepherd, I shall not want.
He makes me lie down in green pastures;
he leads me beside still waters;
he restores my soul.

PSALM 23:1-3 NRSV

The kingdom of God works in a different way than the systems of this world. Though we are pushed to do more with what we have, pursue more interests, and produce in ever-increasing measures according to the world's standards, God encourages us to rest. We can only do so much before we are too tired to keep going. And God never requires us to be "on" all the time. Busyness does not equate to godliness.

Again, filling our schedules with endless to-dos does not make us holy. After God created the world and everything in it, he chose to rest. He built rest into the rhythms of his people's lives by setting apart the Sabbath for a day of rest. Let's follow his example and his lead by building space without agenda into our schedules.

Shepherd of my soul, I lay down my need to prove myself with my time. I recognize that rest is a ritual that you created. Lead me beside the still waters of your mercy and cover me with your peace, so that I can rest without guilt. Restore my soul.

The Lord is my best friend and my shepherd.
I always have more than enough.
He offers a resting place for me in his luxurious love.
His tracks take me to an oasis of peace, the quiet brook of bliss.
That's where he restores and revives my life.

PSALM 23:1-3 TPT

God, in the resting place of your love, I find that my soul comes alive. With your peace as my portion, my mind quiets and my heart dreams again. There is so much delight to be found in your presence! I would not miss drinking in your goodness in the quiet of communion with you for all the world.

I give up my striving and rest in the confidence of your love. There is nothing to prove here. There are no hoops to jump through. You never misunderstand me, for you know me better than I know myself. Your kindness leads me to the brook of your bliss, and I rejoice in it. In rest, I find that you have always been easy to please. Help me to follow your rhythms of rest as you designed. I was not made to burn out, but to be continually filled up by you. You are the oil in my lamp. Your love is the fuel for my very life. I honor you!

How has God's presence restored your peace?

Not Far Away

*The LORD is near to the brokenhearted
and saves the crushed in spirit.*

PSALM 34:18 ESV

When you are suffering, how do you cope? Do you withdraw, or do you seek out the comfort of friends? Do you mentally check out, or do you overthink? No matter your reaction, God is the same toward you in every circumstance. He is closer than a trusted companion, and he is more knowledgeable than an attentive parent. He is near in your heartbreak and in your pain. He is not overwhelmed by what overwhelms you.

Lean into his comfort, for he offers you peace and rest. His requirements are few, and his love is always without condition. Turn your attention to him, and you will find that he already has his eye on you. He is full of compassion and tenderness. He wraps the blanket of his love around you and pulls you close to his heart. Lean in and let him hold you.

Spirit, move in a way that I can recognize today. Comfort me in my pain and soothe me in my discomfort. You are always near, so I know that this isn't a big request of you. Thank you for hearing me.

The Lord is close to all whose hearts are crushed by pain,
and he is always ready to restore the repentant one.

PSALM 34:18 TPT

Loving Lord, I know that you are with me at all times. In my joys, you celebrate with me. In my victories, you rejoice with me. In my sorrows, you sit with me. In my heartbreak, you comfort me. In every season, you are present. Your love restores me over and over. You never stop loving me to life.

Though pain may rip my heart in two, you hold me together with your unfailing mercy. You mend what was broken, and you make me whole again. There is restoration, redemption and abundant new life to be found in your presence. You never stop working. Your Word says that you are close to all whose hearts are crushed, and I will take you at your Word every time. Draw even nearer with the tangible goodness of your presence. Restore me, Lord, for I long for unhindered connection with you at all times. You are my hope.

Have you known God's nearness in heartbreak?

Not to Worry

Do not throw away your confidence,
which has a great reward.

HEBREWS 10:35 NCV

When life gets tough, we can tell a lot about our inner worlds by how we react. Do we automatically go to the worst-case scenario? Do we throw our hands up in surrender? Do we push through on our own strength? Do we try to manage the outcome?

The questions could go on, but we know our go-to reactions. Whether or not they are healthy has no bearing on God's faithfulness. No matter the trials or troubles, he is with us. He is our great confidence. Instead of mindlessly responding to our circumstances, what if we intentionally turned our thoughts toward the Lord? He is able and willing to help us, and he never fails. Whatever comes our way, may our confidence be rooted in the unfailing love of Jesus, our Savior.

Enduring One, your love is more than enough to sustain me. Your grace empowers me to endure whatever may come with confidence. I know that your mercy never, ever fails. You have not changed, and with my feet on the rock of your salvation, I will not be moved.

Don't lose your bold, courageous faith,
for you are destined for a great reward.

HEBREWS 10:35 TPT

Faithful God, my hopes are not built upon the stability of my circumstances. They are built upon the firm foundation of your heart of mercy. You, who never change in love, will be faithful to finish every work that you have started. Your Word will be accomplished, your promises fulfilled. I will not fear when the winds of adversity pick up in my life, for I know that is part of the human experience. Let my faith rise along with the winds that come, so that I may boldly stand on your unchanging character through it all.

I know that you note every submission of my heart to yours, and you will not leave me to be overtaken by fear. I will be strong and courageous, just as you instructed your people to be. Because you are with me, I have nothing to be afraid of. You are the Victorious King over all! One day, every knee will bow before you, and every tongue will confess that you are Lord.

What doubts can you give to God today?

Overflowing Affection

*We were all baptized by one Spirit so as to form one body—
whether Jews or Gentiles, slave or free—
and we were all given the one Spirit to drink.*

1 CORINTHIANS 12:13 NIV

Where there are dividing lines between God's people, there are indications of a lack of love. We are all a part of God's family, though we have many expressions of his goodness among us. Let us lay down the walls of offense and get rid of the grudges we hold. As children of the Most High, we are not called to criticize each other, but to love one another deeply and without prejudice.

The Spirit of God is not divided against himself, and neither should the family of God be. Let's follow the generous example of our merciful Father and offer compassion instead of condemnation, kindness instead of derision. Let us be promoters of peace among the people of God, for that is what he offers us.

Spirit of God, I humbly repent for how I have upheld divisions in my heart toward my brothers and sisters instead of the unity of your love that breaks down walls. I recognize that love promotes peace and picking needless fights doesn't help. Keep me in check with your mercy, that I may freely offer what I have received from you.

Some of us are Jews, and some are Greeks. Some of us are slaves, and some are free. But we were all baptized into one body through one Spirit. And we were all made to share in the one Spirit.

1 CORINTHIANS 12:13 NCV

Perfect Father, in your presence is fullness of joy, for we are fully accepted by you. You hospitably welcome the refugee to your table and treat them as warmly as any other. You do not judge the way that we are prone to judge. You are not distracted by the outer layers of a person; you see straight to the heart.

I want to be like you! Give me eyes to see past the differences that distract from loving a person well. Difference in personality, culture, and preferences means nothing to your love. You made us each unique and in your image. May I see others through the lens of your tender compassion. Keep me from the poison of offenses as I continually submit my heart to yours. There is so much beauty in the diversity of the people you have created and a richness to be found in how we can spur each other on in love.

How has God's love pushed you out of your comfort zone?

He Hears

Blessed be the LORD!
For he has heard the voice of my pleas for mercy.
PSALM 28:6 ESV

Whatever you are dealing with today, God is in it with you. Offer him every worry and trust in his unfailing wisdom. Do you lack patience today? Then ask him. Are you tired and dreading the day ahead? Ask God for his grace that strengthens you. Are you lacking focus for the tasks at hand? Turn your attention to him and let his Word bring the clarity you need. Are you full of joy? Then praise him!

In everything, turn to God and know his fellowship. Build the relationship that is available here and now; there is no better time. He is full of love for you, and he delights in your friendship. As you know him more, you will trust him more. He will not let you down.

Lord, I want to know your impact in every area of my life. I don't want to be in the habit of simply asking you for things. I want to know your presence with me and the tone of your voice. Come close now and reveal yourself to me!

May your name be blessed and built up!
For you have answered my passionate cry for mercy.

Psalm 28:6 TPT

Merciful God, you always answer when I call on you. I see how you responded so lovingly to my prayers earlier today. You meet me with your mercy, and I am changed. Thank you for fellowship with your Spirit, that I may know you and not just know about you. You have called me as your own, and as such, my life is covered by your constant compassion. May your name be glorified in the earth! May all people know the tremendous lengths of your love and the almighty power of your salvation.

I have tasted and seen your goodness in my life, and I know that it is just a glimpse of your glory. Thank you for your consistent kindness toward me. I will never be able to repay you, but that's not what you are after, anyhow. You are persistent in this relationship, that I would know you as you know me. What a pursuit! I'm coming after you, God, just as you press into my life with your tangible presence. Where we meet, there is unceasing joy.

How has knowing God hears you influenced your prayer life?

It Belongs to Him

*Yours, LORD, is the greatness and the power and the glory
and the majesty and the splendor,
for everything in heaven and earth is yours.*

1 CHRONICLES 29:11 NIV

If everything in heaven and earth belongs to the Lord, then
we can rest assured that they will respond to his voice. He is
full of power, his glory greater than we can imagine. Do we
trust him today to take care of the things in our lives that we
cannot control? He knows that we are weak, and he does not
expect us to fix the messes we end up in on our own. He is a
better help than that!

That is not to say that we don't take responsibility for
anything. If we refused to do that, it would be pride. But we
know that God is close to the humble. Who could help a proud
person? Let us offer back everything that God has given us
with open hearts and hands, never holding too tightly to the
gifts and thus missing the greater beauty of the giver of those
gifts. He is trustworthy, and his plans for us are better than
our own.

Glorious Lord, I loosen the grip of my own narrow ideas
about what my life should look like and let you do what you
will. I recognize that you are better than my greatest hopes. I
trust you, for you are great and greatly to be praised.

Yours, O LORD, is the greatness,
The power and the glory,
The victory and the majesty;
For all that is in heaven and in earth is Yours;
Yours is the kingdom, O LORD,
And You are exalted as head over all.

1 CHRONICLES 29:11 NKJV

Lord, everything I see and all that I cannot belongs to you. You don't miss even the smallest change in your creation. You are attentive to all that you have made. Why should I fear how you would move in my life? You see how everything connects, and you are much more astute than the wisest scholars.

I trust you, God! I surrender my own will to yours—the ideas that I have held to like truth—and trust that you will do a better work in me than I could ever dream up on my own. You are powerful to save. You are our Redeemer and restorer. There is nothing too far-gone from your grip of grace. You can restore everything to its intended purpose. I let go of the need to monitor what is not mine to know. I press on in relationship with you, knowing that you will guide me to where I need to go, no matter how long it takes to get there. You are faithful!

Is there something that you have been trying to control that you can entrust to God today?

Peace at Every Turn

The Messiah has come to preach this sweet message of peace to you, the ones who were distant, and to those who are near.

EPHESIANS 2:17 TPT

Through Jesus' sacrifice, we all have been offered peace with God. This wasn't just reserved for those who already followed God, but for those who were far from his ways. This is still true; salvation is the gift of God for all who would receive it. There is peace for the chaos in our lives, and there is peace for those of us already at rest. There is serenity of spirit for all those who mourn, as well as for those who are rejoicing.

The message of God's peace knows no bounds. It is not reserved for some, though all who hear his message can choose to reject it. The peace of God leads us into relationship with God, and the peace of God keeps us there.

Messiah, thank you for the gift of unhindered companionship with God through the peace offering of your sacrifice. Calm the chaotic thoughts of my mind with your powerful Word and settle every anxious feeling in your presence. Keep me here, wrapped up in your peace.

*He brought this Good News of peace to you Gentiles who were far
away from him, and peace to the Jews who were near.*

EPHESIANS 2:17 NLT

Savior, you are the good news that every heart is longing
for. There is no lasting peace outside of you. You have
brought us into the courts of God's presence with the seal of
your powerful love. Nothing could stand in the way of your
sacrifice; what you have done, no one can nullify. You have
already qualified us as children of the Most High because you
chose us as your own. We choose you as a response, but that is
not where the power lies. It is in your overwhelming affection
and mercy that covers every sin and shame.

There is nothing that can separate us from this love. All
who come to you are led by peace. All who look to you are
satisfied. There is nothing we could ever need that does not
find its perfect fulfillment in you. I look to you, God, and I am
washed in the peace of your presence. Thank you!

Does your heart know the confidence of God's peace?

Holy Union

"I am the Way, I am the Truth, and I am the Life.
No one comes next to the Father except through union with me.
To know me is to know my Father too."

JOHN 14:6 TPT

Jesus' life and ministry reveals the heart of the Father. He was not just a good man; he was and is the Son of God. Through wonder-working miracles and supernatural wisdom, Jesus demonstrated the power of God in human form. Do we live with the assurance that Jesus' ways are God's ways?

When we look at the gospels, Jesus did not flaunt his identity. He came to seek and save the lost. He was humble and barrier-busting in his ways. He rebuked the pride of the religious elite and offered compassion to those that society overlooked. He is still the way, the truth, and the life. When we come to him, we are brought to the Father. When we know Jesus, we know God.

Redeemer, you are the perfect example of God's living love. When I start to get sidetracked by needless distractions, pull me back on your path of love, which is lined with mercy and peace.

> *"I am the way and the truth and the life.*
> *No one comes to the Father except through me."*
>
> JOHN 14:6 NIV

Jesus Christ, I believe that you are the way, you are the truth, and you are the life. You are my great and high priest—the one who brings me to the throne of the Father. Through you, I am purified, and I am able to fellowship with Father, Son, and Spirit without fear of rejection. You welcome me in with open arms of love that overcome every shadow and offense. You remove the stain of my sins, and you make me whole in you.

I come alive in the living waters of your affection, and my heart brims with the joy of belonging. You are better than any other love! Keep me close to your heart as I grow to know you more. Your ways are truer than the wisest strategies in the earth. I will follow you, for you are faithful. You are so worthy of my love, my surrender, and my trust.

How well do you know God?

Help at Hand

Every time they cried out to you in their despair,
you were faithful to deliver them;
you didn't disappoint them.

PSALM 22:5 TPT

When troubles arise and you are not sure what to do about them, what is your expectation of God? Do you trust that he will come through for you, faithfully providing and guiding you through the unknown? Or is there a mistrust there that subtly expects disappointment? If the latter is the case, it may be a good time to get curious about your heart reaction. It is not a sin to doubt or to worry; God is faithful to deliver his people even when they are desperate and in despair. But there is also a greater peace when we take God at his Word.

Consider what could be driving doubt in you and offer it to God. Ask him to give you discernment and show you what it was that caused you to expect disappointment. The answer may surprise you. But let this be something that drives you into deeper relationship with God. He can handle whatever you give him. He will still be faithful, regardless.

Faithful One, give me clarity in your presence to trust you more fully. I want to confidently expect your goodness. Show me false narratives that stand in the way. Lead me to your abundant peace and life again.

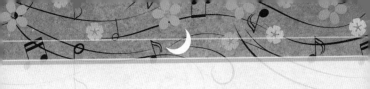

To you they cried and were rescued;
in you they trusted and were not put to shame.

PSALM 22:5 ESV

Savior, you are my help at all times. I will not stop crying out
to you, whether in messy and desperate need of you, or in
the more succinct matters in life. I am so grateful that your
faithfulness is not dependent on my faith but upon your
Word. What you promise to do, you follow through on.

But I do want the confidence of my heart to also grow as
I know you more. You so clearly tell your people to not be
afraid. I don't want to let fear cripple me. I look to you when
I am feeling strong in faith, as well as when I am feeling weak
and doubtful. You are the same through it all. As I look over
the history of my walk with you, I can't help but remember
how you faithfully provided for me along the way. And where
I cannot understand why you didn't do what I expected, I
submit my heart to yours in trust. I still believe that you are
good and that someday all will be made clear. I love you!

How has God been your help?

Called by Divine Love

His divine power has granted to us everything pertaining to life and godliness, through the true knowledge of Him who called us by His own glory and excellence. Through these He has granted to us His precious and magnificent promises, so that by them you may become partakers of the divine nature, having escaped the corruption that is in the world on account of lust.

2 PETER 1:3-4 NASB

There is nothing that we need look for outside of what God has already offered us. His divine power has given us access to all we need to live an abundant and holy life. We have been called by the him, and he does not withhold any good thing from us.

When we need wisdom, we can find it in his living Word. When we need strength, he fills us with his grace. When we need perseverance, he infuses us with hope. When we need comfort, he is already closely pulling us into his love. What is that you need today? Whatever it is, ask God for it. He is generous in love, and he will give it freely.

Wonderful One, here I am with open arms to receive from your abundant heart of mercy again today. Fill me with everything I need to live for you, and let your Spirit unveil what is already available. Thank you!

Everything we could ever need for life and complete devotion to God has already been deposited in us by his divine power. For all this was lavished upon us through the rich experience of knowing him who has called us by name and invited us to come to him through a glorious manifestation of his goodness. As a result of this, he has given you magnificent promises that are beyond all price, so that through the power of these tremendous promises you can experience partnership with the divine nature, by which you have escaped the corrupt desires that are of the world.

2 Peter 1:3-4 tpt

God, my promise keeper, your gifts are full of your presence, and I am filled with joy! Thank you for living partnership with you, that I need never depend on my own limited resources and strength. You have so much more available, and I've barely tasted a morsel of your goodness.

What a feast I find in your presence; it contains everything I need to live a godly life in line with your powerful kindness. You overshadow my weakness with your marvelous mercy, and I can run in the light of your life. Shine on me with the radiance of your glory. You are so wonderful!

Has feeling ill-equipped kept you from living fully for God?

Empowered to Hope

May the God of hope fill you with all joy and peace in believing, so that you may abound in hope by the power of the Holy Spirit.

ROMANS 15:13 NRSV

What is your greatest hope in this life? Where does it stem from? Do not judge this hope, for it is there for a reason. How does fellowship with the King of kings affect it? Today, may you find that joy and peace rise within your heart as you meditate on God being with you.

He knows the longings of your heart, and he sees the true desire behind each one. You can trust him with it all! He is your advocate, so you don't have to make things happen in your own strength. He offers grace that empowers you to believe. Will you let the Spirit fan the flames of your hope today?

God of my hope, I trust you with the deepest longings of my heart. I know that you are good and that you are faithful. Breathe your breath of life into my soul, and I will come alive in your joy and peace.

May God, the inspiration and fountain of hope, fill you to overflowing with uncontainable joy and perfect peace as you trust in him. And may the power of the Holy Spirit continually surround your life with his super-abundance until you radiate with hope!

ROMANS 15:13 TPT

Holy Spirit, surround me with the generosity of God's kingdom, so that my hope may radiate through my very life. You are the greatest reward; knowing you is its own generous return. As I get to know you more in this life and I see your wonderful nature at work in the details, I cannot help but trust you more.

Keep my mind in perfect peace as I follow along the pathway of your loyal love. Fill my being to overflow with your unrestrained joy, that I would be free to delight in you the way that you delight in me. You are the inspiration I need, for any and everything in life. You feed my creativity more than anything else, and you fill my heart with hope. I am so grateful to be yours and to know you. Lead me deeper into your uncontained kindness today, and the passion of my heart will be fired up even more. I want to know you more!

Have you been striving to hope,
or have you been living in the overflow
of God's peace and joy?

Not Done Yet

*Rejoice in hope,
be patient in tribulation,
be constant in prayer.*

ROMANS 12:12 ESV

As long as we are drawing breath into our lungs, God is not finished working his mercy-miracles in our lives. No matter what our circumstances, our confidence can remain unshaken because God is unchanging. Though our lives will not be untouched by trials or troubles, his character never changes. He is full of kindness, compassion, peace, power and strength. When our hope is set on God, we always have a reason to rejoice!

Let us lift our eyes above our temporary troubles and look to him who is above it all. He is faithful and still loyally working both within us and around us. He will never fail! Let our hearts remain open and continually communicating with him through the fellowship of his Spirit with our spirits. We are never alone.

Faithful One, my heart rejoices in hope today, for you are the one that my expectations are set upon. Give me strength to press on in confidence, through patience, while always in conversation with you.

Let this hope burst forth within you,
releasing a continual joy.
Don't give up in a time of trouble,
but commune with God at all times.

ROMANS 12:12 TPT

God of my joy, no one else compares with you. You are my help in times of need, my support in weakness, and my faithful deliverer. You don't ever leave me alone, and you have promised that abandonment is not an option. I am so grateful to know you and be known by you.

May the hope of my heart swell as I look to your glorious character. You are so loyal in love! You never disregard my pain, and you don't overlook the seemingly insignificant things that I find myself longing for. You are bigger and better than any gift you could ever give, and yet you never hold back your generosity. I will not stop pouring out my heart to you, for you are the sustainer of my soul. Let joy be my strength today as you fill me with wonder.

Do you trust that God is not finished working in your life?

Real Rest

*All who have entered into God's rest have rested from their labors,
just as God did after creating the world.*

HEBREWS 4:10 NLT

Rest should not be a reward for reaching a certain goal, but rather a rhythm and practice that we set into our schedules. Overworking is not godly. Burnout is not our goal. God has given us guidance so that we can live lives that reflect his values. In this modern age, we tend to uphold the idea that more production equals more value offered to the world. However, in God's kingdom, we see that there is a different ideal. We work, and that is good, but then we rest.

It is important to know what brings you real rest. This may look different for each person. How can you begin, or continue, to give yourself the space for Sabbath? Make room in your life to step away from the demands of work and see what practicing rest does for the other areas of your life.

God, I confess that I often get caught up in my to do list, not giving myself the space for even a day without needing to be productive. Teach me what real rest looks like. I want to build a space where I can be refreshed in you.

Whoever has entered God's rest has also rested from his works as God did from his.

HEBREWS 4:10 ESV

Creator, I know that everything you do is with intention. You did not take the seventh day to rest for no reason. Help me to build this same kind of space into my schedule. Your ways are better than my own. My personal preferences, though helpful at times, do not reflect the higher wisdom of your kingdom ways.

I recognize that rest is holy. I lay down my need to prove myself through the work of my hands. I know that I need never prove myself to you, anyway. You have welcomed me into your family with open arms. You accept me as I am, and I have found true belonging here. Though I may find joy in my work, I realize that you don't love me for what I offer you. You love me because I am your child. You delight in me, and I will find more freedom as I delight in you while I rest.

What does it look like for you to really rest?

Sought and Found

"You will seek me and find me
when you seek me with all your heart."

JEREMIAH 29:13 NIV

Are you in touch with your heart? Can you tune into your motivations and your emotions? Whether it is natural for you or a continued learning experience, you can trust God to meet you where you are. Your conscious decision to seek God is a reflection of a desire to know him. Look for him, and you will find him. He is not far away.

How do you tune into God's presence? What is your go-to way of meeting with him? Is it spending time in his Word? Is it worshiping with praise songs? Is it in prayer? There are many expressions of relationship, and they all matter. Know this— God is easily found by those who look for him. Reach out, and you will discover he is within your grasp.

Ever-present One, thank you for your ready communion. I find that you are eager to speak to me when I look for you. As I discover more of you, I realize that I was first found by you. What a wonderful God you are!

*"If you look for me wholeheartedly,
you will find me."*

JEREMIAH 29:13 NLT

God, thank you for the promises of your Word. You do not hide yourself or avoid those who search for you. You are always closer than I expect. Thank you for love that reaches me, no matter where I am. I could never escape your mercy! If I climbed to the highest mountain, it would be there. In the deepest caverns, there you are also.

Would you open the eyes of my understanding to know you more this evening? I want a fresh revelation. I know that there is always more to discover about you. Meet me in my longing and reveal what only you can—the glory of your radiant presence. You are beyond anything that I could ever ask for and so beautiful in all your ways. I trust your character even when I cannot understand the happenings around me. I know that you are good. Here's my whole heart, looking to be filled by the overflow of affection from yours. You are life to me. Fill me anew in the light of your living presence.

How do you practice seeking God?

My Praise

Heal me, LORD, and I will be healed;
Save me and I will be saved,
For You are my praise.

JEREMIAH 17:14 NASB

What areas of your life need God's intervening power? He is healer, he is savior, and he is our Redeemer. There is nothing that he cannot do. Lay it all on him! Stir up the remembrance of what he has already done. Remember the fame of his faithfulness and miracle-working power as you look to the Word and to the lives of his loyal lovers. He never abandons his children; he is present through every harsh storm and every field of opportunity.

Press into his close presence and find the peace that your heart longs for. Meditate on his Word and find the encouragement you need for today. Never stop praying, for he is always listening. He is your plentiful portion, both now and forevermore.

Great God, I praise you for what you have done and for what you are doing. You are so worthy of my honor, and I will not hold it back from you. Please, meet me in the depth of my need. I know you will!

LORD, heal me, and I will truly be healed.
Save me, and I will truly be saved.
You are the one I praise.

JEREMIAH 17:14 NCV

Lord, your healing is lasting, your salvation eternal. When you rescue me, no one can stop your help. You are my hope and the one in whom I trust. When I think about your faithfulness, I can't help but praise you! Meet me in the reality of my circumstances and move in miracle-working ways.

Your power is unmatched, and I know that you will not let me waste away. You are my hope, you are my help, you are my strong and mighty tower of refuge. In you, I am loved to life again and again. Your mercy makes a way where there was none before. Your kindness leads me back to you, and I am restored. I could never wander so far from your path of truth that your love would not meet me. Even so, keep me close! I honor your redemption work in my life, and the kindnesses you have shown me. I will not stop looking for you, for you are where I find true belonging, joy, and peace.

How does your admiration of God affect your prayers?

If You Would

*I begged the Lord three times
to take this problem away from me.*

2 CORINTHIANS 12:8 NCV

Is there some sort of suffering that you are overwhelmed by? Or an annoyance that you wish would just quit? When Paul said that he begged the Lord to take his problem away, he was speaking of a "thorn in [his] flesh." This was something that humbled him and perhaps tormented him a bit. We do not know exactly what this 'thorn' was, but it is possible that it was the constant harassment he endured because of his ministry.

Whatever it was, God's response is important to look at. He spoke to Paul and said, "My grace is enough for you. When you are weak, my power is made perfect in you" (verse 9). We need never repress our emotions when communicating with God, but we also must make room for his response. His grace will always be enough for us.

Lord, when I am feeling deflated and defeated, I will not hold back my honest prayers from you. I also recognize that this is not a one-way relationship. Respond to me, and I will listen.

Three times I pleaded with the Lord
to relieve me of this.

2 Corinthians 12:8 tpt

Father, I'm so grateful that I need never withhold what I am feeling in the moment from you. You can always handle me just as I am. I'm never too much for you, and you welcome my emotions even when I do not understand them. When I am overcome, I will pour out my heart to you. When I am overjoyed, my heart will spill out with gratitude for you.

Speak to me, for you always know the right thing to say. Illuminate your Word to me, that I may be filled by the fruit of your living wisdom. Teach me, and I will follow your ways. Guide me, and I will be led to life. Relationship with you is the best thing I have, for you have all that I desire and all that I need. I lean into your love and let go of my rights to be comfortable. I need your grace more than I need my preferences to be met. Let your strength be made perfect in my weakness.

Do you censor your prayers, or are you authentic with God?

Secret Strength

I know what it is to be in need, and I know what it is to have plenty. I have learned the secret of being content in any and every situation, whether well fed or hungry, whether living in plenty or in want. I can do all this through him who gives me strength.

PHILIPPIANS 4:12-13 NIV

Do your circumstances dictate the state of your inner world? Does your heart feel strong on days when everything is going your way, but desperate when a problem arises? Or have you learned what Paul speaks of in this passage?

He went from being a well-respected Jewish leader and theologian, even persecuting the early Church, to a humble follower of Jesus, preaching his message wherever the Lord led him. He learned that contentment had little to do with his circumstances in life and much more to do with his connection to the source of life. Let us remember, along with Paul, that we can do all things through Christ who gives us strength.

God, you are the source of life. You give me the same strength to live in overcoming victory in times of plenty or in just enough. No matter my current situation, your grace remains the same.

I know what it means to lack, and I know what it means to experience overwhelming abundance. For I'm trained in the secret of overcoming all things, whether in fullness or in hunger. And I find that the strength of Christ's explosive power infuses me to conquer every difficulty.

PHILIPPIANS 4:12-13 TPT

Powerful God, you are my source of strength. I depend on you to fill me with the grace that empowers me to continue walking in the way of your love and truth. No matter what comes my way, you are the same faithful provider. You are the same help in times of trouble. You are my constant companion in the joys and in the pain. You are unchanging, and you are with me.

It is your life in mine that makes a difference. I give up trying to prove myself, for you have already accepted me. I will not rely on my own understanding to make it through the shifting seasons of life, but instead on your unmatched wisdom to guide me through. Train me in the secret of overcoming all things in all circumstances. I am your willing student. Teach me, Lord!

Have you learned to depend on God's strength, no matter the circumstance?

Spirit Satisfaction

The kingdom of God is not eating and drinking,
but righteousness and peace and joy in the Holy Spirit.

ROMANS 14:17 NASB

The kingdom of God is not about following a rigid set of restrictions to be holy. We have already been made holy by the life of God in us. Let us not get distracted by details and differences that do not matter. When it comes down to it, is the Holy Spirit producing righteousness, peace and joy in our hearts? Is relationship with God transforming our mindsets and attitudes? Are we moved by compassion, or the need to be right?

The unique expression of God in each of us can look vastly different, but the core fruit is the same. The important things of God's kingdom are not in what we consume, but in how we live. When others look at our lives, they will know we are his by the way we love.

God Most High, keep my eyes on the eternal things of your kingdom and not on the temporal things of this life. Keep my heart in tune with yours, that I may always make room for your love to move. It will lead me to your peace, joy, and a right life.

The kingdom of God is not a matter of rules about food and drink,
but is in the realm of the Holy Spirit,
filled with righteousness, peace, and joy.

ROMANS 14:17 TPT

Lord, show me the ways that I am getting distracted by superficial differences that don't matter in your kingdom. I want my heart to be aligned in your large love, so that I have room to know you in the various expressions of the people around me. May I stay tuned to your mercy that covers over offenses and offers the benefit of the doubt. In living a right life with you, keeping my heart tethered to yours, I will find your peace and joy fill me.

Let your love be the lens I see through. Give me your true understanding in place of my limited and proud knowledge. I confess that I know very little, but I want to learn your ways. Break the bonds of religious thinking that put extra requirements on your ways. I know that the gospel is simple, and I want to live according to your truth all the days of my life.

How does the fruit of the Spirit show up in your inner world?

Look No Further

Since we have been justified by faith,
we have peace with God through our Lord Jesus Christ.

ROMANS 5:1 ESV

Let us be reminded, right here and now, that peace with God is not unattainable. It is ours through faith in Jesus. Faith is not simply a set of beliefs; it spills over into how we live our lives. We can rest assured that peace with God is ours, letting everything else flow from that place. We do not strive to be made righteous, for we are covered in the mercy-love of God that has made us right with him.

As we journey through this life in relationship with God, submitting our hearts to him regularly, he teaches and guides us in the ways of his laid-down love. The love offering of our lives is a natural response to the one who laid down his own for us. He has everything we need—and even more than that, all that we long for.

Lord Jesus, thank you for ushering me into the kingdom of God through relationship with you. I stand covered in the mercy of your love, and you have made me clean. There is nothing I could ever add or take away from your finished work on the cross. Thank you, Lord!

Our faith in Jesus transfers God's righteousness to us and he now declares us flawless in his eyes. This means we can now enjoy true and lasting peace with God, all because of what our Lord Jesus, the Anointed One, has done for us.

ROMANS 5:1 TPT

Anointed One, may I rest in the confidence of your sacrifice being my righteousness. I can never prove my worth to you, and I know that is not at all what you require. Be Lord over my mind, as well as my life, and fill me with the truth of your revelation-light.

You who are perfect in love have perfected me in it. I can freely live my life for you, not worrying about how every action could risk a break in our relationship. You are better than that! Your mercy-kindness receives me whenever I turn to you. You cover my mistakes with your love and give me grace that empowers me to rise above the limitations of my own ways. In you, I find satisfaction for my soul. Meet with me now with the overwhelming kindness of your presence.

Are you still looking for fulfillment outside of God?

Unchanging One

Answer me, O LORD, for your steadfast love is good;
according to your abundant mercy, turn to me.

PSALM 69:16 NRSV

God is full of love that never changes in intensity or in power. It is strong enough to break every chain and get past any defense. This love raises the dead and heals incurable diseases. It forgives the most heinous acts of wickedness. It is so much larger than we can imagine, and the force of it more powerful than we can give it credit for.

When we call on the Lord, we can expect his help in return. His help may not always look exactly the way we expect, but if we know his character, then we can easily recognize his presence among us. Let us not grow weary in relating to God, whether in our need or in our abundance. He is always the same loving father and friend.

Lord over all, I praise you for your constant mercy in my life. Thank you for answering me when I cry out to you, and for lovingly meeting me whenever I call on your name. You are so incredibly good!

Oh, Lord God, answer my prayers!
I need to see your tender kindness, your grace,
your compassion, and your constant love.
Just let me see your face, and turn your heart toward me.
Come running quickly to your servant.
In this deep distress, come and answer my prayer.

PSALM 69:16 TPT

Lord God, you are my tender and attentive Father. I look to you more than any other, for you have the words of life that revive my weary heart. You are the sustainer of my faith, the one who lifts me when I fall, and the steady ground that I stand upon. Without you, I don't know what I would do!

Answer the prayers of my heart as I pour them out to you. I won't hold back from you. Meet me with the compassion of your overflowing love and lift me from the ashes of disappointment. Give me your perspective, that I may see what you do when you look at my life. Just a glimpse of your glory is enough to refresh my waning hope. I know that there is always more to discover in you. Please, reveal yourself to me tonight.

What do you need from God right now?

Refreshed

He saved us, not on the basis of deeds which we did in righteousness, but in accordance with His mercy, by the washing of regeneration and renewing by the Holy Spirit.

TITUS 3:5 NASB

The Holy Spirit is not a bonus of walking with the Lord. The Holy Spirit is the Lord God himself. Father, Son, and Spirit are one, and in them, we are made whole.

Do you know the fellowship of the Spirit in your life? The tangible presence of your great God and King? As you submit your life to God, the Spirit is transforming you into the likeness of your Good Father. It is through communion with the Spirit that we are empowered by mercy, renewed in spirit, and receive all that we need. The power of God is made manifest through the work of the Holy Spirit in this earth. How do you know if the Spirit is living and active in your life? Look for the fruit of his Spirit, as laid out in the Scripture.

Spirit, thank you for your presence with me. I want to know your tangible goodness in my life more and more. Show me how you are already moving, right here and now.

He came to save us. Not because of any virtuous deed that we have done but only because of his extravagant mercy.

TITUS 3:5 TPT

Holy Father, my helper, I am so grateful that your mercy is not dependent on me or what I could ever offer you. You do not wash me in the cleansing flow of your compassion because of anything I did or do, but because of the extravagance of your pure affection for your people. You offer forgiveness freely, without hidden motive or agenda. Who else loves like that? You restore me in your perfect peace because you have chosen to do so.

I gladly receive what you offer and continue to yield my heart to you as I walk the path of your love. You are so kind to me, and I know that you won't stop. Even your justice and righteousness do not change the weighty force of your mercy. You are wonderful in all of your ways. Keep drawing me in love as I offer you my moments. You are worthy of every single one.

What Spirit fruits are present in your life?

Watched Over

The LORD keeps you from all harm and watches over your life.
The LORD keeps watch over you as you come and go,
both now and forever.

PSALM 121:7-8 NLT

The Creator of the heavens and the earth is the one who guides us in life. He keeps watch over our lives and lovingly leads those who submit to him. He never forgets us or misses a detail. He does not grow sleepy and he does not get distracted. He is able to see everything as it is and focus in on the particulars of our lives all at the same time. He is not limited in his scope as we are, in our humanity.

Let us take comfort and courage in the fact that God is always with us. He is the lifter of our heads and the protector of our very lives. Let us stop putting criteria on ourselves that he never puts on us. He will always be faithful, and he is with us.

Yahweh, my heart takes courage in the overwhelming revelation of your steadfast love as my constant companion and guard. Thank you for always being with me. I can face anything with you by my side.

He will keep you from every form of evil or calamity
as he continually watches over you.
You will be guarded by God himself.
You will be safe when you leave your home
and safely you will return.
He will protect you now,
and he'll protect you forevermore!

PSALM 121:7-8 TPT

Faithful God, you keep me safe with your resolute love. You never waver in your intentions toward me. You are fixed in purpose, and your mercy moves on my behalf. What a wonderful truth! I offer you every worry and anxiety about the unknown, and I make room to receive more of your peace this evening.

I don't need to control a single thing; I simply need trust in you and your faithful love. You are the one who protects me, so please, keep on doing it. As I look to you now, will you meet me with the presence of your living Word? Speak to me, Lord, for I am listening. You are the courage to my soul and the hope in my heart. Keep showing me more of you, and I will know pure joy.

How have you experienced God's protection in your life?

I Look to You

To you I lift up my eyes,
O you who are enthroned in the heavens!

PSALM 123:1 NRSV

When we look expectantly to the Lord, our hearts reach out to his. What do we long for? What do we need? How do we need his mercy and grace to meet us? It is good to recognize where we're at, and it is also necessary to look to God to encounter us with the abundance of his kingdom resources. There is so much more available to us than we realize!

May we offer him the attention of our hearts and get lost in the wonder and beauty of his incomparably good nature. There is no one else like him. Let us lift our eyes from our temporary troubles and fix them on our unchanging Lord, who is glorious in all his ways.

Creator God, you are far above any trial or trouble I face, your power overwhelmingly capable of saving me. I will not get lost in the fear of what could come; rather, I fix my eyes on you, Lord. You already see the end from the beginning. I know you will lead me in love all the days of my life.

O God-Enthroned in heaven,
I lift my eyes toward you in worship.

PSALM 123:1 TPT

Heavenly Father, I offer you the weight of everything that happened today. Meet me in my weariness and infuse me with your gracious strength. I look to you now and give you my full attention. Encounter my thoughts with your truth and overpower the lies that fear produces in my mind. Your wisdom brings clarity to the fog of confusion. When you speak, the light of your revelation-wisdom shines into my inner being. I know your peace when I am aware of your nearness.

I honor you, Lord, and worship you because you are worthy. My heart is eager to know you more in this moment. Breathe your breath of life in me again, and I will be refreshed. Sing your songs of deliverance over me, and I will be free to dance before you. You are the one I look to over and over again, and I won't stop! You have been, and will be, incomparably good.

What does lifting your eyes to the Lord do for your heart?

Focused Attention

We don't focus our attention on what is seen
but on what is unseen.
For what is seen is temporary,
but the unseen realm is eternal.

2 CORINTHIANS 4:18 TPT

When we focus our attention on God's will and ways, we will be continually built up and renewed within. No matter what is going on around us, our inner worlds can thrive at all times! God's presence is the lifeblood to our systems. Our hearts will grow strong as we draw from his strength that is always available.

With the root systems of our minds, hearts, and souls planted in the soil of God's mercy, we develop courage and tenacity. No storms can take us out, for the persistence of God's love keeps the growth of our root systems expanding and going ever deeper. Let us keep our focus on the eternal realm of God's kingdom, remembering that what lasts can never be shaken.

Everlasting God, you are the source of my life and the reason that I am here. I will not stop looking to you, for in worship and reverence, I remember what lasts and what will not. Keep my heart tethered to your unfailing love and remind me of your overwhelming goodness when I begin to forget.

We don't look at the troubles we can see now;
rather, we fix our gaze on things that cannot be seen.
For the things we see now will soon be gone,
but the things we cannot see will last forever.

2 CORINTHIANS 4:18 NIV

Eternal One, instead of focusing on the problems in life, I readjust my perspective and look to you. You are the one who was, who is, and who is to come. You are full of mercy, truth, and love. Your grace is sufficient for every soul in every moment. Your justice is unmatched, and what you declare, no one can undo! You are faithful to your Word. You are merciful in your ways. You are with me.

I look ahead to what you have promised, and my heart takes hope in your living Word. You will do everything that you have set out to do. My hopes are set on you, the one who is faithful and true. Refresh my heart in the overwhelming beauty of your love again. You are worthy of my attention!

What is your attention focused on these days?

Keep Going

I have fought the good fight,
I have finished the race,
I have kept the faith.

2 Timothy 4:7 NCV

How do we persevere through trials when all we want to do is give up? Firstly, let's remember that God never requires us to strive for his love. It is always a free gift, overflowing from his heart into our lives. Secondly, it is important to be compassionate with ourselves, just as we would be with those in our lives who are overwhelmed.

Also, support is a huge part of what it means to be in the family of God. We can lean on others to help encourage us and spur us on in faith. And let us not forget the importance of rest! Rest can be a wonderful way to reset. Life is not an all-or-nothing battle; it is a journey of faith through the nuances of life. We are not meant to burn out, but to burn bright. In order to do that, we need to keep looking to the light of our lives.

Great God, I am thankful for the keys of your kingdom that you reveal to us in your Word. Instead of beating myself down when I want to give up, may I instead lean back into the rest of your loving embrace and recalibrate to your mercy. With you as my anchor, I will keep my faith, for you are its object and its very source.

I have fought an excellent fight.
I have finished my full course
and I've kept my heart full of faith.

2 TIMOTHY 4:7 TPT

Good Shepherd, continue to guide me in grace as I follow along the path of your mercy-love. There is no better way to journey through this life than to do it hand in hand with you. Thank you for the solidarity of your people, who help to push and encourage me. You are so wise in the way that you've set us up for community, not isolation. In my relationship with you, I have everything I need, and in my relationship with others, I get to know you more.

When discouragement weighs me down, would you lift the heaviness with your truth? You are faithful, and you are near. What a wonderful reminder to my soul. Keep me close to your heartbeat of love and may the lure of the world's ways lose their luster. You are so much better! Following you is, and always will be, worth it.

When you feel like giving up, how do you persevere?

Choose Forgiveness

*Be kind to each other, tenderhearted, forgiving one another,
just as God through Christ has forgiven you.*

EPHESIANS 4:32 NLT

In showing kindness to one another, we reveal the same kind of mercy that we have been shown through Christ. When we choose to forgive, we show that we understand that what we have received from God is what we are to offer others. It is difficult to extend what we do not already have. Are we lacking in love and understanding?

Let us first receive it from God, who gives in abundance. Then we will have an endless supply of compassion to give. In the kingdom of heaven, the more you are filled, the more you have to give. And if you run out, you can be filled once again! This is a constant cycle of dependence that allows us to thrive, not just to survive. Leaning on the Lord is always the answer.

Merciful God, thank you for your love that has swallowed up my sin. Fill me again today, and I will have more than enough to offer others in compassion, understanding, and forgiveness. I choose to be like you in kindness, for you are wonderful.

Be kind and affectionate toward one another.
Has God graciously forgiven you?
Then graciously forgive one another in the depths of Christ's love.

EPHESIANS 4:32 TPT

Loving Lord, I cannot hoard your goodness to myself. The kindness and affection you pour out on me will mean little if I don't let it change my life. I want to be like you in mercy, Lord, so search my heart this evening and reveal if there is something or someone that I have been resistant to forgiving. You have been so incredibly gracious with me, and you continue to be. In the same way, help me to also offer this same kind of grace to others.

When I have been hurt by others, especially unintentionally, help me to let go and offer the kindness of compassion. When I have been legitimately wronged, help me to work through forgiveness and to choose it even when it requires healing and choosing it more than once. I know that you will help me. I won't keep your mercy from changing my heart.

Is there someone you need to forgive today?

A Better Way

The word of the LORD is upright,
and all his work is done in faithfulness.

PSALM 33:4 ESV

Though we may think we know the right way to live, unless we are submitted to the Lord in humility and aligned with his Word, we may actually miss the point. His faithful love cannot be overstated, and he will fulfill his Word. When we live our lives with his mercy guiding us into his truth, we will find that we have all we need for a godly life.

God's ways are different than the world's ways. Instead of forcible promotion of self and our preferences onto others, God's ways are much more subtle. Though the preaching of his Word should be clear, the response to it is completely out of our hands. He calls us to obedience, to faith, and to humility. He calls us to love, offer mercy, and to be kind. Let's leave our judgments behind and let God be the judge. Instead, let's follow his example of laid-down love through submission of our lives to his ways.

Lord, I know that you are full of wisdom and truth, and I know that I understand only a small part. Forgive me where pride has kept me from loving well and fill me with your compassion. You are the Righteous Judge, and I leave that job to you.

God's Word is something to sing about!
He is true to his promises, his word can be trusted,
and everything he does is reliable and right.

PSALM 33:4 TPT

Wonderful God, your Word is filled with life-giving truth.
The light of your revelation-knowledge shines, and I am
filled with the radiance of understanding. When a revelation
hits deep, I am filled with deep wonder and awe at your
glory. Thank you for the life and hope that you bring to those
you show yourself to. I know that I can trust your Word, for
everything you do is just and true. You will always be faithful
to your promises.

I present my heart to you again as an open vessel to your love.
My life is a living sacrifice. Continue to guide me into your
overwhelming goodness as I follow you and your ways. I submit
my own plans and ideas to you, trusting that whatever my life
looks like, you are the same merciful and present God through
it all. Your love is better than life, so fill me up once again.

Do you trust that God's ways are better than your own?

God's Goodness

Do you despise the riches of His goodness, forbearance, and longsuffering, not knowing that the goodness of God leads you to repentance?

ROMANS 2:4 NKJV

When we are actively resisting God's leading in our lives, do we realize the strain in our hearts? What do we do with our hurt, our pride, and our guilt? God is infinitely greater than we could ever give him credit for. He does not run out of kindness to show us—not ever! Resistance and scorn toward God are indicators that we need a fresh reminder of the lengths of his immeasurable love.

Instead of getting more obstinate in our own ideas, let us turn toward him with open hearts once more. Will we allow his extravagant kindness to meet us where we are and lead us back to restoration of relationship with him? No offense is worth refusing his love.

Wonderful One, thank you for the gift of repentance. When I am caught up in my own offenses and lack of understanding, help me to lay them down and let you in. Only you can love me to life!

*Do the riches of his extraordinary kindness make you take him
for granted and despise him? Haven't you experienced how
kind and understanding he has been to you? Don't mistake his
tolerance for acceptance. Do you realize that all the wealth of his
extravagant kindness is meant to melt your heart and lead you
into repentance?*

ROMANS 2:4 TPT

Lord, may I never take for granted your wonderfully
extravagant kindness. I know that your mercy excludes no
one. May that knowledge not lead me to pride and offense,
but instead to humility and compassion. You have restored
me over and over again with your extraordinary mercy. I
have been forgiven much, so why would I seek to control this
mercy that you have to others, as well?

It is in knowing you that the capacity of my understanding
grows. Much more than theory, I see how righteous, faithful,
and loving you are. Whenever pride begins to harden my
heart, melt me with the sweetness of your kindness that I may
come right back to your heart of affection and be restored
again. Thank you for forgiving me, teaching me, and never
giving up on me.

How has God's goodness restored your heart?

Compassion for All

*"I will have mercy on whom I have mercy,
and I will have compassion on whom I have compassion."*

ROMANS 9:15 NRSV

Are there people in your life that you just cannot seem to show mercy to? Do you have trouble showing compassion to certain types of people? It may be worthwhile to get curious about this lack of love. Why do you react this way? Can you pinpoint someone who was like this or a mindset that was passed down from family members?

In any case, it is not our place to pick and choose who gets to receive love. God offers mercy and compassion to all, though not all will receive it. If we are picky about it, that should indicate areas where we need to submit to the Lord and grow in understanding of his kindness. Let's remember that love is a lifestyle, and not simply an ideal. He who has mercy will also have mercy on us for the journey of growing up in his ways.

Merciful Father, I admit that I am nowhere near as merciful as you. But on this submitted journey of life, thank you for leading me in your mercy. Fill my heart with your love, so that compassion may flow more freely from me.

> *"I will be merciful to whomever I choose
> and I will show compassion to whomever I wish."*
>
> ROMANS 9:15 TPT

Compassionate God, I honor your love in my life. It is more consistent than I can consciously understand, and it is more powerful than any other force in my life. You are motivated by your love, and in your righteousness, your standard of mercy cannot be outdone. I am so grateful to live in right relationship with you because of your mighty mercy.

Align my heart with yours as I submit my ways to you again. Where I have been resistant in love, give me revelation to see the greatness of choosing it. Though it is your prerogative as God to be merciful to whomever you choose, it is not mine. Obedience to your loyal love is the goal. May I choose mercy instead of judgment every time. And when I mess up, there is mercy to be found there. I trust your heart and your ways more than I do my own understanding. Lead me, and I will follow.

How does God's mercy affect your relationships?

Strength for Today

"Be strong and courageous.
Do not be afraid or terrified because of them,
for the LORD your God goes with you;
he will never leave you nor forsake you."

DEUTERONOMY 31:6 NIV

The Lord reminds his people over and over again in the Scriptures that he will be with them wherever they go. He never abandons his children. Not only this, but the very fact that he had to tell them to not be terrified and to take courage meant that what they were facing was not easy. In hard times, when the proverbial rug gets pulled out from beneath us, that is when God says, "be strong and courageous...do not be afraid."

Do we trust that God's Word to his people throughout the ages is the same Word he speaks to us today? When we would otherwise be overrun by anxiety and fear, God reminds us that he is with us and that he will never leave. So, take courage today; the Lord is your strength!

Lord my God, thank you for the reminder of your presence with me in trouble and in the face of the unknown. I praise you, for you are right here, guiding me through the storms of uncertainty. I will be strong, and I will be courageous, for you, Lord, are my confidence.

> *"Be strong and of good courage,*
> *do not fear nor be afraid of them;*
> *for the LORD your God,*
> *He is the One who goes with you.*
> *He will not leave you nor forsake you."*

DEUTERONOMY 31:6 NKJV

Ever-present One, you are with me as I lift this prayer from my heart to yours. You see me right where I am, and you are not worried about a single thing. Speak to me now and fill me with the courage of your presence. Remind me of your wisdom that sees clearly in every circumstance. You are not swayed by the shifting winds of the storms of life, and I am so very thankful for that!

Fill my heart with the peace that passes all understanding, and I will be comforted and at rest. I am seen and I am known, right here and now in this moment. You love me fully and accept me as your own. What a wonderful Father you are! I am overcome and undone in the glory of your presence.

What are you needing courage to face today?

Called His Own

"The LORD will not abandon His people on account of His great name, because the LORD has been pleased to make you a people for Himself."

1 SAMUEL 12:22 NASB

God was not satisfied to simply create humanity, and it wasn't enough for him to restore relationship through salvation. He has called us his own, making us part of his family. His love is larger than the borders of culture, and it goes beyond the boundaries of tribes and nations.

It is clear in Scripture that God set Israel apart as a nation for himself; this we cannot overlook. However, when Jesus came in flesh and blood, he made it clear that, as the Messiah, his salvation message was for all who would hear and receive. This includes us! May we know the beauty of belonging, having been chosen by the King of kings.

Lord God, you are the Savior of all the world! What a beautiful home I have found in you. I have never known such honest love and such true belonging. Thank you for saving me, and for welcoming me into your family.

"The Lord will not reject his people,
because the Lord was pleased to make you his own."

1 Samuel 12:22 NIV

Lord of lords, it is almost too much to take in that the Creator of the heavens and the earth would choose me as his own. I have been grafted into the family of God through the sacrifice of Jesus on the cross. In his resurrection, new life was made possible. I am beyond grateful for the gift of belonging. I am undone that you know me through and through and have made me your own. I am a child of the Living God!

With the King of kings as my Father in heaven, I have peace that passes understanding as my portion. I have mercy that meets me in every situation. I have been made new, and I am consistently being transformed to your likeness as I align my life with your values. What a wonderful God you are! In your delight, I have found my freedom.

Do you know the peace of belonging to God's family?

Unload the Burdens

"Come to me, all you who are weary and burdened, and I will give you rest. Take my yoke upon you and learn from me, for I am gentle and humble in heart, and you will find rest for your souls."

MATTHEW 11:28-29 NIV

God is not a demanding taskmaster. Do we know this to be true in our relationship with him? He is a tender father, patient in love and understanding. He is compassionate toward us and knows that we are but dust. He is merciful and kind, lifting every burden that we bring to him.

Are you weighed down by the worries of this world? Are you tired and broken down by the burdens of life? Come to Jesus, and he will lift the load you bear. Offer him your heavy burden, and he will give you the rest of his light yoke. Partner with him, for he will always do the heavy lifting when you are connected to him. Find your rest in him; this offer won't ever expire!

Jesus, you are the lifter of my burdens and the one who teaches me how to love with gentleness and humility. My soul longs for the peace that only you can offer. Thank you for rest in you.

"Are you weary, carrying a heavy burden? Then come to me. I will refresh your life, for I am your oasis. Simply join your life with mine. Learn my ways and you'll discover that I'm gentle, humble, easy to please. You will find refreshment and rest in me."

MATTHEW 11:28-29 TPT

Faithful One, thank you for always lifting the heavy weight of the burdens I bear. You always bring refreshing with the peace of your presence. I come to you this evening with open hands, an open heart, and a submitted life. Speak to me and teach me your ways. I want to know you more.

What a beautiful reminder I have been given in your Word, which says that you are easy to please. You do not make it hard to know you or to love you. You are better than any other lover I have ever known. No one comes close to your pure and extravagant affection. Restore my hope this evening as I meditate on your incomparable goodness. I am yours, Lord—forever yours!

Have you learned to rest in God's presence?

Positioned for Rescue

I'm exhausted! My life is spent with sorrow,
my years with sighing and sadness.
Because of all these troubles, I have no more strength.
My inner being is so weak and frail.

PSALM 31:10 TPT

In life, we cannot avoid suffering. Grief is inevitable, for in this short life we will experience loss many times over. It is not a sin to suffer. We are not being punished when we are brought low by the overwhelming pain of sorrow. It is the anguish of being human. But even in this, we can know the present love of our Comforter. He gives us grace that sustains us, and in his mercy, he carries us when we cannot move an inch on our own.

In these times, let us remember that God is our Savior and our helper. He will rescue us again! He will bring life out of the ashes of disappointment and despair. He will do it! Let us lean into his love at all times, especially when we cannot stand.

Jesus, my saving grace, you are the one I lean on in every season of the soul. When I encounter the pain of grief, will you hold me close in your loyal love? Surround me with your comfort and lead me through the dark night of suffering with your steady guidance. You are my hope!

I am dying from grief;
my years are shortened by sadness.
Sin has drained my strength;
I am wasting away from within.

PSALM 31:10 NLT

Merciful God, meet me in the depth of my pain and sorrow. When I have nothing left to give, and all my hope feels like a luxury of the past, remind me of your steadfast love that never leaves me. Wrap me up in the comfort of your presence and strengthen my heart in your ever-present grace. I know that you will not let me waste away in my pain. You won't let me be ashamed of the hope of my calling, for you are it.

Revive me in your mercy-kindness today and love me to life once again! I need to know the tangible relief of your nearness when I am overwhelmed by the suffering of life. Though grief can feel unbearable, I know that you are the all-consuming fire. Purify me in the pain, but also relieve the intensity of it, if it is your will. Help me, for I have no better hope.

When you are at the end of your emotional rope,
how has God met you there?

Confident Hope

*Faith is confidence in what we hope for
and assurance about what we do not see.*

HEBREWS 11:1 NIV

Faith, as an ideology, can be a difficult thing to quantify. What does it look like to be a person of faith? To believe for what we cannot see and be completely confident that it is real and true? In Scripture, faith is illustrated as a conviction that leads to action. James 2:26 says, "As the body without the spirit is dead, so faith without deeds is dead."

If we think about it in terms of our relationships, those in our lives who follow through with what they say are seen as trustworthy and reliable. We know that God is. But even beyond this, we can tell a lot about what a person believes by how they live their life. In fact, the fruit of their actions speaks to the underlying values present. When we live with our values aligned with God's kingdom, the fruit of our lives will show it.

Faithful One, may my values reflect your own. Help me to see where my actions don't line up with my beliefs, revealing that which is out of sync with you. I humbly submit myself to you as your child, your disciple, and your willing student. Refine my faith, Lord!

Faith is the substance of things hoped for,
the evidence of things not seen.

HEBREWS 11:1 NKJV

Great God, thank you, first off, that your faithfulness is not dependent on my faith. You are so much larger than my limitations, and you do not regulate your own nature according to them. I am grateful for your guidance that reveals where I still fall short in trusting you fully. I want to trust you more as I continue to submit myself to you.

I know that as long as I keep walking in the ways of your wisdom, looking to you in every season of my soul, you will continue to purify me in the refining fires of your presence. I can never make so many mistakes that you will give up on me. What a relief! I persevere in believing because I know I have not reached the end of knowing you. There is so much more to uncover in your love. Will you show me where in my life faith is producing fruit that will last? Speak, Lord; I am listening.

Can you see the evidence of faith in your life?

More Mercy

Do not, O Lord, withhold your mercy from me;
let your steadfast love and your faithfulness keep me safe forever.

PSALM 40:11 NRSV

The mercy of God is like an ocean and we are like grains of sand. It is so much more abundant than we can imagine, and yet each time our understanding is stretched, waves of wonder wash over us. We can never outrun the love of God, and we cannot upset God's faithfulness. He is full of loyal love that propels promises into action.

We need never stop asking God to reveal more of himself to us. It is not a lack of faith to ask God to pour out his mercy in our lives. He is gracious and patient with us, and he will never stop fulfilling our needs with his abundant generosity. May our prayers today be bold ones.

Merciful God, you are full of powerful, life-changing kindness. Flood my awareness with your presence and pour out your tangible mercy in my life. I expect you to meet me with your goodness once again.

*Lord, don't hold back your love or withhold
your tender mercies from me.
Keep me in your truth and let your compassion overflow to me
no matter what I face.*

PSALM 40:11 TPT

Lord, may I echo the psalmists' prayers by not being afraid to ask you for the same things over and over again. It is your mercy I need, and your love is the only thing that will truly satisfy me. No matter the worries of my mind, I know that your faithfulness outshines them all. I offer you every doubt and disappointment, and I ask you to cover me with your compassion.

Don't ever withhold your kindness from me, for you are what I've built my life upon. Your Word is encouragement to my soul, and your presence is the sustaining hope of my heart. Blow me away with your wonderful goodness that reveals the shining glory of your countenance. Your ways are beautiful. As long as I live, may your wisdom be my guide. You are my salvation, and you are my great reward.

How has desperation affected your prayer life?

Satisfied

Even lions may get weak and hungry,
but those who look to the LORD will have every good thing.

PSALM 34:10 NCV

Have you ever looked at a need in your life and been
completely overwhelmed by it? Perhaps it was an unexpected
bill or a health diagnosis. Or it could have been a sudden loss
or tragedy. There are many times over in this life that we will
see a lack and have no idea how it will be met.

How has God's faithfulness played into these moments? God
is a provider, and he always presents a way for those who
look to him. Though outcomes may not be exactly what you
originally hoped, how has God's provision and restoration
worked out? He is trustworthy. Can you find your satisfaction
in him and trust him to deal with the details you cannot
control?

Provider, you are creative in the ways that you meet me with
your mercy. Fill my heart with your peace as I look to you
in uncertainty. Fill my mind with your Words of life that
embolden my faith. I trust you.

Even the strong and the wealthy grow weak and hungry,
but those who passionately pursue the Lord
will never lack any good thing.

PSALM 34:10 TPT

Lord, you are the one who provides for everything I need. You are rich in love, and you are attentive in affection. I look to you today. Settle the fears that have been creeping into my consciousness with your perfect peace and may the overwhelming power of your love calm my nervous system. I trust you to do what only you can do. You will not leave me to waste away in hunger.

I have been pursuing your heart, Lord, and I will not stop. I know that you satisfy everyone who looks to you. Do it again this evening, and surprise me with the wonderful ways that you come through for me. I will not be dismayed, for you are the same yesterday, today, and forever. You are always the Good Father, and I depend on your watchful care to sustain me in ways that I cannot even know to ask for.

What are the good things that the Lord has satisfied you with?

Constant Comfort

Your words have comforted those who fell,
and you have strengthened those who could not stand.

JOB 4:4 NCV

In relationship to those we love, we may run out of comfort to offer. Though we can love sacrificially, we will never do it perfectly. But God is perfect in love. He never runs out of mercy. He also sees beyond what we can—into the heart of a person.

What we see in part, he sees the whole. He sees every detail. He knows every thought, every intention, and the hidden hope of every heart. He offers infinite grace to strengthen those who are weak. He comforts those who mourn with the overwhelming peace of his presence. He never pulls back in love. He always presses in closer to those who look to him. Do we trust that he will always flood our scarcity with his generosity?

Comforter, thank you for lovingly closing in around me with your tender presence. You are the lifter of my head and the hope of my heart. Please, meet me today with the abundance of your mercy.

Your words have upheld him who was stumbling,
And you have strengthened the feeble knees.

JOB 4:4 NKJV

Holy God, speak to me with the comfort of your living Word.
I long to know your refreshing encouragement this evening.
Revive my spirit in the calming presence of your Spirit. Let
your peace wash over the screen of my mind, clearing away
the accumulation of the world's worries and cares. I know
that you are faithful and true. You are the strength that carries
me when I cannot stand. You are the one who lifts me when
I fall. You are the way, the truth, and the life. And you will
always be.

I'm so grateful that you never grow weary. It is almost
too much to comprehend that you don't tire of offering
compassion and mercy. I receive from the abundance of your
heart with a grateful heart of my own tonight. Thank you for
loving me so completely, so consistently, and so willingly. I
cannot help but love you in return.

How has God's Word upheld you in times of trouble?

Alive in Christ

God, being rich in mercy, because of His great love with which He loved us, even when we were dead in our wrongdoings, made us alive together with Christ (by grace you have been saved).

EPHESIANS 2:4-5 NASB

Let us never forget that God's mercy is ours because of his great love, not because of anything we could ever do or earn on our own. Even when we were cycling in our shame and lost in the confusing patterns of the world, Christ died for us. It is by his grace that we have been saved from sin and death, and nothing else.

No matter how long we have been following the Lord, let us remember that our righteousness comes from Christ himself. Are there things in our lives that do not reflect the freedom of God's living love? Let us, then, offer them to Jesus. His power is enough to break every chain and limitation!

Jesus Christ, thank you for your wonderful saving grace. I have nothing to boast in but your love, and it is so powerful! Shine on me with the light of your glory and bring liberty to parts that have been hidden in shadows.

God still loved us with such great love. He is so rich in compassion and mercy. Even when we were dead and doomed in our many sins, he united us into the very life of Christ and saved us by his wonderful grace!

EPHESIANS 2:4-5 TPT

Wonderful God, your love is so much better than I can grasp. It is higher than the highest heavens and deeper than the deepest seas. It is full of power that raises the dead to life and sets prisoners free. Your love is the foundation my life is built upon. It is abundant enough to cover every weakness and turn it into strength. It is the through-line of my story, and it keeps my life tethered to the life of your kingdom.

I will never be without it. And yet, I want to know it in ways that I have yet to comprehend. Show me how great you are! You set my heart free to hope as I recognize your love's signature restoration and redemption power in my life. You are wonderful.

Are you living in the freedom of God's saving grace?

Tender Mercy

*His unforgettable works of surpassing wonder
reveal his grace and tender mercy.*

PSALM 111:4 TPT

When God reaches down into our lives in tangible ways, how can we help but be awed by the enormity of his mercy? He has not forgotten a single promise he has made, and he will do so much more than we could think to ask him. He consistently meets us in the details of our lives with his love. He knows the deepest secrets of our hearts, and we can trust him to fulfill our greatest longings. He is better than we could anticipate at every turn.

Let us remember his wonderful works of grace and mercy in our lives. Stir up the memories of his goodness. Look into his Word and see his faithfulness so clearly written throughout the pages. He is endlessly good!

Merciful Father, when I begin to wonder where you are, will you reveal yourself again? I know that you are near because you said that you never abandon your lovers. I love you, Lord, and you are my hope.

He causes us to remember his wonderful works.
How gracious and merciful is our LORD!

PSALM 111:4 NLT

Lord, as I think back on my journey with you, I can see your hand of mercy on my life. Remind me of moments that have slipped my mind, and my heart will swell with gratitude once again. You are gracious, God, and I offer you my open hands of surrender. I hold onto you, and not onto my own understanding, for stability. You are better than my own plans, and your ways are infinitely more fruitful.

You consistently call me out of the shadows into your glorious light and life, and I come alive in your wonderful presence. When I remember how gracious you have been to me, how could I but praise you? You are my living hope and my overwhelming peace. I pour out my love on you again, Worthy One. Your close and tender leadership is much more than I deserve, and yet such a pure reflection of your affection. Thank you!

What wonderful works has God done in your life?

What Matters Most

*Three things will last forever—faith, hope, and love—
and the greatest of these is love.*

1 CORINTHIANS 13:13 NLT

What is the foundation of your life? What is the guiding principle that leads you? If it is anything other than the love of God, it will not last forever. It is good to have justice as a cause, and it is a worthwhile pursuit to advocate for the defenseless. There is nothing wrong with building a legacy for your family and in being excellent in your career. But as Paul asserted in 1 Corinthians 13, anything done without love is meaningless.

Let us remember that if we do anything, even what we claim to be for God, but we do not do it with love, we gain nothing. Let us not grow weary in love, but instead be refreshed and strengthened in it today. There is more for us to discover in him; if we lack, let us ask God who gives freely from his heart of mercy.

Loving God, whenever I think I have a grasp of your compassion, you show me that it is so much better. Fill me with a fresh revelation of the purity of your love today. I must be filled up first if I am to have anything to give away. Thank you!

There are three things that remain:
faith, hope, and love—yet love surpasses them all.
So above all else, let love be the beautiful prize for which you run.

1 Corinthians 13:13 TPT

Faithful One, your love is deeper, wider, longer and higher than I can ever imagine. What a worthwhile pursuit it is to know your love! When I am filled with the awe of your mercy, I have so much more grace to offer others in my life. I know that your love is patient, it is kind, and it is humble and not self-seeking. It does not boast in what it can offer even though it is the source of all life.

Let your overwhelming love flood my very being as I meditate on your exceeding goodness. Your love rejoices with the truth, it keeps no record of wrongs; it trusts, hopes, and perseveres. It is the lifeblood to my spirit, and it is everything I need. May I never grow tired of leaning into your love. May I never lose the wonder that it evokes in my heart! It is so much better than any words could convey. Thank you for your overcoming love.

Is there a lack of love in any area of your life?

Coming Back Home

Let the wicked forsake their way,
and the unrighteous their thoughts;
let them return to the LORD,
that he may have mercy on them,
and to our God, for he will abundantly pardon.

ISAIAH 55:7 NRSV

One of the most beautiful pictures of God's abundant love and mercy is the parable of the prodigal son (you can find it in Luke 15, if you would like a refresher). Jesus tells the story of a loving father who gives his sons their inheritance when the younger asks for it. This son goes off on his own and travels the world, squandering away his wealth on things that don't last. He loses it all.

In the end, in the midst of a famine, he found himself hungry and homeless. Destitute and humiliated, he decided to return to his father's house to beg a position as a servant in his household. His father recognized it was his son returning even though he was dressed like a beggar and ran out to meet him. He was so overcome with love that he embraced him with tender affection even though the son felt awful. He welcomed him back with open arms and a celebration.

Father, may I always return to you when I feel the guilt of sin weighing me down. I want to be safe in the shelter of your loving embrace and home in you.

The wicked need to abandon their ways,
and sinful ones need to banish every evil thought.
Let them return to Yahweh,
and they will experience his compassionate mercy.
Yes, let them return to God,
for he will lavish forgiveness upon them.

ISAIAH 55:7 TPT

Loving God, may I never stay away from your presence longer than I need to because of pride or fear. I leave behind the foolish ways of my youth and make my home in your abundant mercy. You are the one who welcomes me with open arms each time I turn to you. I am undone by the tender affection of your heart toward me every time. You are better than I've known in any other relationship, and no one will ever outdo your compassion.

May I become more like you as I dwell in the safety of your life-giving love. You take my dirty rags and give me a beautiful robe in their place. I am completely covered by your abundant kindness. Thank you seems insufficient, but I will say it nonetheless; thank you!

Is there a thought pattern or habit
that has led you away from the Lord?

Can't Stay Away

Those who go to him for help are happy,
and they are never disgraced.

PSALM 34:5 NCV

When was the last time you can recall God's help in your life? Was there something that you were desperately asking him for, and now it is present in your life? Take a moment to recall both the big and the little answers to prayer. Can you recognize the thread of God's faithful love through it all?

Instead of being distracted by the answers you are still waiting on, purposefully look for the areas that he has already come through for you. How has his provision met you? Do you trust that he will continue to be faithful to you? He will never leave his children to fend for themselves. You are not a beggar in his kingdom; you are a beloved child. Come to him again, and you will see what your Father does.

Faithful Father, I cannot stay away from you. When I remember how you have met me with your abundant provision time after time, how could I be but encouraged in hope? I trust you with it all, Lord, and I submit my heart to yours once again.

Those who look to him for help will be radiant with joy;
no shadow of shame will darken their faces.

PSALM 34:5 NLT

Radiant One, you are my joy and my strength. Your faithful love displayed in your acts of mercy in my life builds courage and hope within my heart. I know that you are trustworthy. What I have been wasting time worrying about is but a minor detail to you. You already know how you are going to work it all out. I bind my heart to yours in trust, and I look to your glory-filled presence this evening for empowering hope that exceeds my wildest dreams.

You are so wonderful in love! You refresh me in the peace of your nearness. Your friendship is richer than any I've ever known. Thank you for consistently meeting me with your overwhelming love. You breathe on me, and the dust of disappointment blows away. You are my constant help and my reliable support. How grateful I am for your incomparable affection! May I never take it for granted.

How has God's help affected your well-being?

Hopeful in the Spirit

This is no empty hope, for God himself is the one who has prepared us for this wonderful destiny. And to confirm this promise, he has given us the Holy Spirit, like an engagement ring, as a guarantee.

2 CORINTHIANS 5:5 TPT

If God is the one who has prepared us for eternal life and salvation, then he is the one that it all depends on. If we have surrendered our lives to Christ, believing that Jesus was the Son of God and confessing him as Lord of our lives, then we have this firm assurance. Hope of eternal life is ours, and this is no vain hope. It is God's promise.

The Holy Spirit, as our present help in all circumstances, is the kiss of God's promise in our lives. The Holy Spirit's work is tangible. This is important for us to realize. The actual working-out of God's love in our lives and in the earth is the work of the Spirit. What we taste and see now is but a glimpse of the greater glory of God's fulfilled promise. Let us take hope, for God himself is our living hope.

Spirit, fill me with the fruit of your presence as I continually submit my life to yours. You lead, and I follow. You teach me, and I learn. I lean on your wisdom instead of my own limited understanding. You are my hope and my assurance in all things.

The one who has fashioned us for this very purpose is God, who has given us the Spirit as a deposit, guaranteeing what is to come.

2 CORINTHIANS 5:5 NIV

Lord, as I experience the tensions of this short life, my longing for the glory of your eternal life and peace grows. The pangs of pain in this human experience send me further into your heart, looking for the hope that you have promised. I know that this temporal experience will pale in comparison to the incomparable lengths of your glorious love that lasts from eternity to eternity. There is no end in your love.

Come close, Spirit, as I offer my heart to you like an open book. Write your living Word upon my heart; fill me with the confident expectation of your goodness through the fulfillment of your promises. You are wonderful, Lord! You would not settle for anything less than what you know that you offer freely. My guarantee is nothing less than you. Your Spirit, who dwells within me and gives me strength for my weakness and comfort for my mourning, is the deposit of your greatest promise. I am undone, and yet so incredibly filled with your loving presence. Thank you.

Are you sure of your hope in Christ?

Greater Love

Don't set the affections of your heart on this world or in loving the things of the world. The love of the Father and the love of the world are incompatible.

1 JOHN 2:15 TPT

Love is a wonderful thing, and true love, a worthy pursuit. When we think of true love, we may be tempted to imagine a great romance, full of knights in shining armor and helpless damsels in need of saving. And while this may meet some fantasy of our hearts, this is an incomplete reflection of perfect love.

Consider the life of Jesus. The Word says that he was humble, and nothing about his appearance made him attractive to us (Isaiah 53). He was overwhelmingly ordinary until he started his ministry. He demonstrated his love through acts of mercy. Real, pure love is love that lays itself down for another. It is not self-seeking. It does not look for a reward. Love that lasts does not change with the shifting winds of worldviews and preferences. The love of the world will never satisfy, but the love of God lasts forever.

Jesus, when I look at your ministry, I cannot help but hunger for the love that you spoke of. Even more, I long for the love you demonstrated in the laying down of your life for humanity. It is more beautiful than the most extravagant fairy tale. I want to know your love more today.

Do not love the world or the things in the world.
The love of the Father is not in those who love the world.

1 JOHN 2:15 NRSV

Father, may my heart remain tethered to yours, not moved around by the shifting values of the world. Though I value comfort, you are constantly pushing me outside of my comfort zone. And I am always better for it! Keep my heart pure as I live for you. Whenever I get too caught up in chasing after the whims of the world, will you redirect me in your kindness?

I know that even when I get what I had set out to obtain, it only satisfies for a moment. But your love, oh Lord, there is always more of. I can be satisfied and yet know that there is so much more yet to discover in you. I know that when I live my life for your love even when it looks like sacrifice and hardship, it will be worth it. You never said it would be easy, but I do believe that your way is the better way. And there will be abundant fruit! Your love, Father, is lasting love. And it will bear good fruit in my life.

What kind of love are you living for?

Love Meets Me

Fill us with your love every morning.
Then we will sing and rejoice all our lives.

PSALM 90:14 NCV

There is no reason for us to live off of the stale bread of yesterday's portion. There is always a fresh portion of mercy, love, and goodness to meet us. Do we want to rejoice in praise? Then let's spend time every morning connecting with the source of life and love.

God never withholds from those who seek him. His love is like an ever-flowing fountain over our lives. When we are filled to the brim with God's love, we pour out a reaction of love and gratitude right back to him. Worship is a response, a natural one, when we are filled with God's goodness. Just as we need food to sustain our bodies, we need spiritual food to sustain our spirits and give us energy. There is no need to ration it because he always has an abundance.

Generous Father, fill me with your love today and speak to my heart. I long to know more of your wonderful mercy as it meets me in this moment. Then I will sing and rejoice, for you are my plentiful portion.

Let the sunrise of your love end our dark night.
Break through our clouded dawn again!
Only you can satisfy our hearts,
filling us with songs of joy to the end of our days.

PSALM 90:14 TPT

Faithful One, shine on me with your glorious light of love. Reveal the treasures hidden in darkness as you light up every shadow. You are the one I hope in, and you are my saving grace. Whenever I need your help, here you are with your generous mercy. You are the only one who can satisfy my heart, and you reveal that there is always more.

I don't need to gorge on your love, for it is always accessible. I don't need to ration it, for you always have plenty more to give. I receive the portion you offer and fill up on your truth as I look to you. What a wise and wonderful counselor you are to me! Thank you for your ever-present goodness in my life. You are my joy, and I will sing your praise all my days.

How often do you fill up on God's love?

He Is Powerful

"Let us praise the Lord, the God of Israel, because he has come to help his people and has given them freedom. He has given us a powerful Savior."

LUKE 1:68-69 NCV

God's powerful love breaks the chains of those bound by fear, sin, and shame. It breaks open prison doors, that the captives may be free. In this journey of life, there are big moments of breakthrough, and there are also ordinary moments of breakthrough. In fact, it is in those simple, overlooked areas that we have the opportunity to know God's mercy in marvelous ways.

In love, he breaks the power of cycles we don't even realize are keeping us held back. He is our freedom in every area where we are bound by limitations. Instead of being discouraged by feeling pressed down, let's look at these areas as places of opportunity for breakthrough and God's powerful liberty.

Savior, I praise you today, for you are my help and my Redeemer. You never stop working your love in my life, and I have not reached the end of its power that breaks unhealthy cycles in my life. Thank you for hope and a better future in you.

"Praise the Lord, the God of Israel, because he has visited and redeemed his people. He has sent us a mighty Savior from the royal line of his servant David."

LUKE 1:68-69 NLT

Lord God, you never stop leading your people in your love. You have poured out your presence with your Spirit, and you empower us to live in the liberty of your great affection. Your mercy has been my source of strength for as long as I have been walking, hand in hand, with you. You are wonderful in your ways, and I am overcome with gratitude!

Lord, you see my life more clearly than I can. I want to live in your freedom. Will you set me free from limiting beliefs that do not align with your kingdom values? Let your hope flood my heart and fill me with courage to keep pressing on in faith. You have not let me down, and I trust that you never will. I am yours, Lord; do what you will in me.

Is there an area of your life that has yet to experience God's freedom?

Don't Turn Away

O LORD; give ear to my pleas for mercy!
In your faithfulness answer me,
in your righteousness!

PSALM 143:1 ESV

When our lives are in turmoil, it can be difficult not to feel the desperation of our circumstances. When we are afraid, let us turn to God. When we are worried, let's look to him. When we are tired, he is our place of rest. When we have nothing to give, he fills us up with his grace.

There is no problem too big for him. God is not worried! He sees the end from the beginning and every moment and detail in between. He is endlessly faithful, and he will hold us secure in his steadfast love. He is our overwhelming joy, and he is our portion of plentiful peace. Whatever we lack, he has in abundance. Instead of trying to scrape by on our own strength, let us depend on God for all that we need. He will gladly provide for us.

Faithful Father, I look to you today. You are the source of all that I need, so I will not worry. Meet my needs and fill my heart with courage as I fill up on your love and faithfulness. You are so incredibly good, and I trust you.

*Lord, you must hear my prayer,
for you are faithful to your promises.
Answer my cry, O righteous God!*

PSALM 143:1 TPT

Righteous God, as the sun sets and the moon rises, I give you my attention again. You are still the place of my hope and strength. I know that you are faithful. In areas where I have yet to see your promises fulfilled, I rest in the confidence of your unfailing nature. I remind myself of the overwhelming reliability of your love.

Meet me here and now with the liquid kindness of your presence. Fill me with the tangible peace of your Spirit's life. I hide myself in you tonight. I lay aside every worry and the weightiness of the unknown. I lay it all down. Wrap me now in your comfort. Remind me of your plans. Rekindle the joy that I have known in communing with your pure presence. You are wonderful—too wonderful for me to comprehend! I know that you will answer all that is still a question. For now, I focus on you and rest in your faithful love.

Do you believe that God listens to every prayer you pray?

Steady Hand of Mercy

*"You in Your mercy have led forth the people
whom You have redeemed;
You have guided them in Your strength
to Your holy habitation."*

EXODUS 15:13 NKJV

When God led his people out of their captivity in Egypt, he provided for them in miraculous ways. His steady hand of mercy was always with them. From the parting of the Red Sea, so they could escape Pharaoh's army, to the provision of daily bread in the wilderness, he never left them.

In the same way, God leads our lives with mercy. Will we trust that his ways are good and that he will always provide what we need? Or will we be enchanted by the empty promises of this world that demand that there is better outside of him? Let us consider whether we are trusting his mercy or our own ideas of what is good and true. The God of the ages is our portion; will we still insist that there is a better way?

Merciful God, forgive me for the ways I have trusted in my own ideas and plans rather than in your wonderful provision. You have given me your Spirit and made me your holy habitation. There is nothing better than that!

> *"In your unfailing love you will lead*
> *the people you have redeemed.*
> *In your strength you will guide them*
> *to your holy dwelling."*

EXODUS 15:13 NIV

Holy Lord, you lead me in your unfailing love, just as you did with your people all throughout history. You have redeemed me out of the captivity of the world's systems and into your glorious life. You guide me in strength—not my own, but yours. I lean on your wisdom, recognizing that my own understanding will change many times over in this life.

I want to learn and grow in you as I trust your loving leadership to guide me through the wild places. You won't stop guiding me until we have reached the ultimate destination—eternal life in you. In the coming age of your kingdom reign, I will know your great and faithful love fully, not just in part. Until then, keep me on the path of your righteousness. You know best, so I will follow you all the days of my life.

Do you trust that God's mercy leads you?

Nothing Expected

*What can I ever give back to God
to repay him for the blessings he's poured out on me?*

PSALM 116:12 TPT

As we walk the path of this life, surrendered to God's leadership, we will not miss out on his goodness. His blessings store up in our lives like a treasure trove. We can build altars of remembrance so that we honor his mercy in our lives, as his people did in the Old Testament.

What God gives, he does out of the abundance of his love. He does not bless us with hidden motive or agenda. He does not require anything in return, and yet, it is a natural response to pour back out gratitude and love. His gifts are good—so much more than we could ever earn. But a gift earned is not a gift at all. Let us receive with open and willing hearts from the Father. And though any return may feel inadequate, let us offer the gratitude of full hearts.

Generous Father, I am learning that you don't want me to repay you for what you give me. But I am also learning that you delight in my offerings. What a wonderful God you are! Here is my grateful heart, Lord.

What shall I return to the LORD
for all his goodness to me?

PSALM 116:12 NIV

Lord, this evening, I offer you this space and time. Speak to my heart as I pour myself out to you again. I am so grateful for this relationship with you. Though I could never deserve your love, you are always overflowing with it. You are the most generous Father. You are the kindest friend. You are the holiest God. You are the most sufficient provider. All that I could ever need, I already have in you!

I could never repay you. I could never even dream of it! And yet, you take this humble heart and life as if it were the most treasured gift you could receive. I will not hold back from you—not in any way. You have my attention, you have my submission, and you have my trust. You are more wonderful than I can express, and my heart overflows with thankfulness. Thank you for always being better than I expect. You are glorious, and you are full of all light and life. I am yours!

When you feel the inadequacy of your offering,
will you still give God gratitude?

Peace Is My Portion

"My people will live free from worry in secure, quiet homes of peace."

ISAIAH 32:18 TPT

There is no worry that God cannot take care of. There is no dilemma that his wisdom cannot solve. In all things, in all ways, we can know his all-surpassing peace. This kind of peace brings calm to the chaos of our lives. It quiets the anxieties of our hearts. It soothes the fears of our egos. His peace is our plentiful portion in every season.

Are there areas of our lives that don't know his peace? Let us offer every bit of our need to control the outcome, and let God be God. He can take care of us better than we know to do for ourselves. He will not let our families go hungry or leave his people destitute. His presence is ours, and in his presence, there is peace.

God, I invite the peace of your presence to saturate every area of my being. Fill my life with your perfect peace that is not dependent on logic or reason. You are so much better than I can express. Thank you!

*"My people will live in peaceful dwelling places,
in secure homes,
in undisturbed places of rest."*

ISAIAH 32:18 NIV

Comforter, you have prepared a home for me in your dwelling place. Until I live in the fullness of your kingdom in the eternal age to come, I have your Spirit with me here and now. Your presence brings calm to the anxious thoughts that jump ahead into the unknown. Your peace fills my heart with a confident stillness. I know that every expectation of your faithfulness to work out in my life will come to pass. You will fulfill every promise that you have made, and your Word will be satisfied!

Though I do not know the details of how you will work everything out, I trust you. You are reliable in love and mercy, and there is no need to fear. Bring rest to my body as I lay down to sleep tonight. May my sleep be undisturbed, and may I awake refreshed in body and in spirit. I value the peace that you give more than I can say. Thank you, Lord.

Where has peace penetrated your life?

Heard

Hear the voice of my pleas for mercy,
when I cry to you for help,
when I lift up my hands toward your most holy sanctuary.

PSALM 28:2 ESV

No matter how many times we come up against troubles and trials in this life, God will never stop answering our cries for help. Every single time we turn to him, he rises up on our behalf. He is God our defense, God our stronghold, and God our rescuer.

There is no need to hold back from him. It is not our shame to ask him for help; it is our strength. He is full of power that sets us free, peace that keeps us settled, and joy that overflows the flood banks of our souls. He is always good, and we can count on our Savior's ready help whenever we need it. He is with us, and he is for us.

Mighty God, I won't stop crying out to you. When life beats me down, I will call on you. When trials keep coming, I will call on your name. I know you haven't abandoned me. You are with me.

Hear the sound of my prayer,
when I cry out to you for help.
I raise my hands toward your Most Holy Place.

PSALM 28:2 NCV

Holy One, I lift my hands toward you this evening as I surrender the cares of my day over to you again. Lift the weight of my heavy burdens and flood me with your peace. Your love is still the sustaining force of my life; that has not changed. I trust you to work miracles of mercy in every impossible situation I face. I know that I am not alone, and that you are for me. Everything you do is laced with your kindness.

Set in place the things that need to be in order for your restorative work to happen. You are better than my best intentions, and your ways are merciful enough to cover my greatest mistakes. Do what only you can do, Lord. In the meantime, I will rest in you. You are my confidence, and there is no one more trustworthy than you.

How does the confidence of being heard affect your prayers?

Endless Kindness

May God himself, the God of peace, make you pure, belonging only to him. May your whole self—spirit, soul, and body—be kept safe and without fault when our Lord Jesus Christ comes.

1 THESSALONIANS 5:23 NCV

We are made pure in the lifeblood of Jesus. It is his sacrifice of love that has brought us into unhindered relationship with God the Father. His mercy keeps us safe, and not just our mortal bodies. He is the keeper of our souls, and our spirits know true union with him.

Let us not go off on our own way, trying to earn what we have received freely. May we remember that it is grace alone, through faith in him, that has saved us. We have nothing to boast about but God's mercy. When we belong to him, that identity—as his—is the only one that truly matters. It is what lasts. He has cleansed us in the flow of his mercy poured out in living love. The power of his resurrection life is our hope and our strength.

Holy One, thank you for endless kindness in your love. You are so good to me. Thank you that I have been made pure in you; there is absolutely nothing that separates us now.

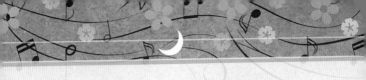

May the God of peace and harmony set you apart, making you completely holy. And may your entire being—spirit, soul, and body—be kept completely flawless in the appearing of our Lord Jesus, the Anointed One.

1 THESSALONIANS 5:23 TPT

God of peace, may my entire being be kept pure in you until you come again in flesh and blood. I rely on your goodness to keep me steady in your love. Through continual submission and surrender, I find new life rising within me because of your great mercy. You are producing fruit in my life through your Spirit's work in me. It is nothing that I can do on my own, and yet I am not worried about falling outside of your grace. I know that I never can.

You are the one who peels back the layers of hurt that a lifetime in this world builds up. You reach to the depths of my soul and shine your loving light of life on me. In your radiance, I come alive! Thank you for setting me apart. Keep me close to your chest, where I can hear your heartbeat. When I start to wander on my own way, lead me back to you in love every time, and call me back in kindness.

Do you rely on your own goodness to be like God, or do you trust that it is his work in you?

Treasure

Your laws are my treasure;
they are my heart's delight.

PSALM 119:111 NLT

When was the last time that God's Word encouraged your heart so profoundly, it changed the way you approached a situation or relationship? There is so much goodness to be found in the wisdom of the Scriptures. We see over and over again how the ways of the Lord lead his followers to life.

In our humanity, we will struggle. That is not a question of if it will happen, but rather what we will do when it happens. Will we give up when the going gets tough, or will we go to the Lord and rely on his help? We will find a rich trove of treasure when we align our lives in the law of God's love. Let's not give up hope, but instead keep pressing on in the mercy of our great King. We will not regret it, in the end. If we let it, his Word will change our lives for the better.

Great God, your Word is better than the greatest wisdom of this world. I align my heart, my life, and my mind with your living Word. As I meditate on your truth, lead me deeper into the ways of your kingdom, where mercy reigns.

I will follow your rules forever,
because they make me happy.

PSALM 119:111 NCV

Loving Lord, I know that true joy is found in following you. You don't lead at a distance, but closely. You hold my very hand, staying with me in the darkness of deep valleys of pain, and you faithfully lead me out of my despair. You are a much kinder leader than any other I've ever known! I will follow your kingdom ways for as long as I live, for there is abundance of life to be found there.

Even when I am disappointed in your people, may my heart never waver in confidence of your goodness. You never err in judgment, and you don't turn away when things are hard. You always make space for those who need to be seen and heard, and you heal all our wounds and diseases. You are better than any other, and you always will be—infinitely better! Reveal more of your heavenly wisdom to me as I spend time meditating on your Scriptures. Your Word brings me joy and courage.

How has God's Word enriched your life?

Better than Life

Because Your favor is better than life,
My lips will praise You.

PSALM 63:3 NASB

On our best days, God's love is even better. And yet, our most joyous celebrations pale in comparison to the glory of God's great mercy. Let's never stop praising God, for he is always worthy. Has it been awhile since you tasted the joy of God's presence? Ask him for a fresh encounter with his living love! His Spirit dwells with us, always ministering out of the generosity of his mercy-heart.

It is hard to imagine unending joy, and a forever-season of fullness of peace, love, and hope. But that is what awaits us in God's everlasting kingdom. His love is better than life! One day, we will truly know the enormity of God's kindness. For now, let's thank him for the glimpses we get of his goodness, and let's ask for more. He is a generous father.

God my joy, there is an endless ocean of joy in you! Though I have only tasted a small portion of your goodness, it leaves me longing for more. Reveal yourself to me in a new way today.

Your unfailing love is better than life itself;
how I praise you!

Psalm 63:3 NLT

Lord, your unfailing love is better than anything I've tasted
in this short life. It is better than life's uncertainty, its ups
and downs. You never waver in love, and you are always full of
kindness whenever I look to you. It doesn't make sense to my
mind, for in this world there is no love that compares. You are
pure in motive, and never-ending in second chances. What a
wonderfully kind father you are!

As I seek your kingdom and pray for your will to be done on
earth as it is in heaven, I am always met by your overwhelming
love. Thank you! I will not stop praising you. I know that
there's so much more I have yet to discover in you, and I'm so
very grateful for the chance to know you. Will you break the
molds that I have put you in with my small thinking? I want
to see from your perspective this evening. Give me a fresh
glimpse at your wonderful love.

How have you tasted the overwhelming goodness
of God's love in your life?

Made Complete

*Rejoice, mend your ways, be comforted, be like-minded,
live in peace; and the God of love and peace will be with you.*

2 CORINTHIANS 13:11 NASB

God has created us to live, learn, and grow in the context of community. We are not isolated in our faith. Ultimately, we are responsible for our own actions and motivations. We should not seek to control others, but to offer the love that we have been shown. Everything we do—everything God has called us to—is in the context of relationships. We do not love others simply to fulfill something inside of ourselves.

As we are made complete as a unified body of believers, being like-minded in love, living in God's peace, there is heavenly joy in this kind of fellowship. May we not be easily offended or divided against one another. God's love unifies; it does not segregate. Let us consider how we can love others and lay down the superfluous things that come between us.

Holy One, thank you for the reminder of the importance of unity in you. I lay down my preference to be right in favor of your love that covers a multitude of wrongs. Keep me humble in your mercy.

Beloved friends, be cheerful! Repair whatever is broken among you, as your hearts are being knit together in perfect unity. Live continually in peace, and God, the source of love and peace, will mingle with you.

2 CORINTHIANS 13:11 TPT

God of peace, forgive me for the offenses that I have held against your people. I humbly ask for your help to show mercy. I have been shown so much. Will you flood my heart with compassion, so that I am able to see others through your lens of living love? I choose to extend kindness instead of judgment. I will let love lead me even when pride wants to pull me away. May joy be the product of restored relationship.

Where I know that I have held things against my brothers and sisters, I lay them down at your feet. Help me to be humble, to do what I can to restore those relationships, and to leave the rest to you. I know that you have called your people to unity even as you are one. Help me to be a promoter of peace, and to lovingly reach out whenever it is in my ability to do so.

Are there any broken relationships
that are in your ability to repair?

Practicing Patience

Be still in the presence of the LORD,
and wait patiently for him to act.
Don't worry about evil people
who prosper or fret about their wicked schemes.

PSALM 37:7 NLT

Comparison is a trap. It can convince us that where we are and what we're doing is not enough. What is God doing in your life? What has he called you to? Keep your eyes in your own lane, doing what you know is right for you to do. Wait on the Lord and be patient. He is not slow in keeping his promises, as the Scriptures remind us.

Let the peace of God tend to your heart and keep looking to him. He will not withhold from you. When you need wisdom, he will give it. When you are weak, he will make you strong as you rely on his grace. In a world where we can get almost anything we want in moments, it will take practice to be patient. But the wait is not in vain. It will be worth it, for he knows what he is doing.

Lord, thank you for your patience with me. Teach me how to persist and endure in peace, rather than rushing on in my own strength. I wait on you now, making space for stillness in my heart and mind.

Quiet your heart in his presence and pray;
keep hope alive as you long for God to come through for you.
And don't think for a moment that the wicked in their prosperity
are better off than you.

PSALM 37:7 TPT

Holy One, I quiet my heart in your presence this evening.
I rely on your faithfulness to fulfill every promise you have
made. Awaken hope as I wait on you. I don't rely on my own
resources; they have run out, anyway. I need you to come
through for me. When I am distracted by others who have
gone their own way and seem to be prospering in their
wickedness, may I turn back to you and remember that you
have got everything handled.

Though I may not understand your timing, I trust your heart
and your plans. I trust you. Fill my heart with your peaceful
presence and steady my nerves as I remember how big
and capable you are. You will not fail me, and you will not
abandon your purposes in my life.

Are you comparing your life with others,
or resting in what God is doing for you?

Persevere

Keep yourselves in the love of God, waiting for the mercy of our Lord Jesus Christ that leads to eternal life.

JUDE 1:21 ESV

Perseverance is not something to be overlooked in our walk with the Lord. God's loyal love meets us in every moment, and we need never fear going without it. He gives strength for our weakness and offers joy for our mourning. But when we are in the depths of pain, it is not always easy to actively receive what God offers in the same manner we would in times of thriving. Instead, he comes close and wraps us up in his comfort. He carries us when we have no strength to move on our own.

As we wait for the promised fulfillment of all things being made new in Christ, let us rest in his presence. Let us press on in faith even if that looks like stagnancy to the outside eye. Only God knows our hearts, and only he can judge them. We know his voice, for he is our shepherd; as we wait, we are never alone.

Lord Jesus Christ, as I wait on your return, I know that I have everything I need in your Spirit. Keep me steady as my heart trembles. I won't stop holding on to your loyal love.

Await the mercy of our Lord Jesus Christ, who will bring you eternal life. In this way, you will keep yourselves safe in God's love.

JUDE 1:21 NLT

Merciful Lord, your presence with me in this life fuels the hope I have for eternity. Your love is my shelter, the place where I am hidden. Keep me safe and secure in your mercy, for I trust in you. When I can offer nothing but the tenacity to hope, will you flood me with courage? Remind me of your faithful Word and the promises that you have made. You never go back on your Word, so I need never worry about being ashamed about your promises.

You are the steady rock, and the firm foundation, of my life. You keep me in your perfect peace, and all I need to do is surrender. I am yours, Lord; I am yours! Light up the eyes of my heart with your revelation-knowledge. Show me your ways, and I will walk in them. May your mercy meet me every single time I turn to you.

How has perseverance played into your walk with the Lord?

Look to Him

Be of good courage,
And He shall strengthen your heart,
All you who hope in the LORD.

PSALM 31:24 NKJV

Today is a new day, and a new opportunity, to look to the Lord. What questions do you have? What hopes are rising in your heart? What disappointments can't you shake? Lay them all before him and invite him to speak into the details. Sometimes, God is just waiting for the invitation of our attention to share his wisdom and perspective.

After you have poured out your heart, look to him. Wait for him to speak. Ask him what is on his mind. Chances are, the words of life that you are looking for are on the other side of that question. He does not speak in riddles, confusing our hearts. When we seek him, he gives us clarity for our uncertainty. Trust him; his living Word will always line up with the Scriptures. Do you dare ask him what he is thinking about?

Lord, my heart needs your gracious strength. You are my hope, and you have been. I want to know what is on your heart today. Will you share it with me?

Be strong and take heart,
all you who hope in the LORD.

PSALM 31:24 NIV

Gracious God, you are the hope of my heart. You always offer strength for my weakness. Fear and doubt fall away in your presence, and you enlighten my understanding with your Word. Speak to me again; I can't get enough of your voice. I can hardly comprehend your kindness. You never cease to be tender with me. Even in correction, you are so kind! In your firmness, you still fully love and accept me.

It is unbelievable how you never cease to offer me your mercy. I've never known that kind of love. There are no limits, no reservations, no bounds. It is more than I can imagine and always overflowing from your benevolent heart. I take hope in you again this evening as I sit and wait for you. Increase my awareness of your already present, never-ending love. Breathe your peace into my thoughts and bring every anxiety to rest. I look to you.

When was the last time you asked God what was on his mind?

Giver of Life

*"You gave me life and showed me kindness,
and in your providence watched over my spirit."*

JOB 10:12 NIV

As the originator of our lives, our Creator God does not stop showing us kindness as we look to him. He knows us better than we could ever understand ourselves. There may be many mysteries to our humanity, but God sees everything clearly. In his kindness, he meets us where we're at with the mercy of his heart.

He leads us patiently, knowing that we are hesitant to trust him fully. Still, we get to choose him over and over again. He tenderly reveals his pure love to us as we look to him. He reveals the wonders of his affection as we align our lives in his truth. He watches over us like the Good Shepherd he is. We can trust the giver of life with our lives.

Creator, I offer you what you gave to me—my very life! I trust you to guide me into your goodness. You lovingly reach me through the resistance of my hurt heart and lead me into vibrant life in you.

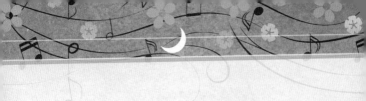

*"You gave me life and showed me your unfailing love.
My life was preserved by your care."*

JOB 10:12 NLT

Good Shepherd, I am so grateful for your careful leadership
in my life. You lead me beside the still waters of your peace,
and your mercy refreshes my heart. I trust your wisdom,
Lord, for you are good. I won't stop seeking you, for you have
brought me joy more times than I can count. You preserve my
life with your defense. No one can take away what you give.
My hope is secure, for it rests in the everlasting kingdom of
your reign.

I will not forget the kindnesses you have shown me already
in my life, and I won't stop expecting your overwhelming
goodness to meet me as I continue to walk this road with
you. Renew my courage as you remind me of your nearness.
Refresh my perspective as you share your own with me. I
depend on you more than I rely on myself. I fail and fall many
times, but you never do, and you never will.

How has God showed you his kindness?

Victorious Life

Be supernaturally infused with strength through your life-union with the Lord Jesus. Stand victorious with the force of his explosive power flowing in and through you.

EPHESIANS 6:10 TPT

With the Spirit of God as our constant companion and support, we have the power of the living God with us. The same power that resurrected Christ from the grave is the power we have alive in us through the Holy Spirit. There is supernatural strength for our natural weakness. There is overwhelming love to cover all our mistakes.

When we partner with the power of God, we experience the victory of his life within us. Let us press into knowing this victorious life that Christ has called us to. What does it look like to willingly connect with the grave-busting power of God within us? Surely wherever there is lack in our lives, God's abundance will overwhelm it. Let us learn what it looks like to walk through life as an overcomer.

Victorious One, I come alive in your life in me. Teach me to walk in your powerful ways. May I not be satisfied with just getting by; I want to know your explosive power.

*Be strong in the Lord
and in his great power.*

EPHESIANS 6:10 NCV

Lord, you see my strengths and weaknesses so very clearly.
I'm grateful that you never require perfection from me. I
would fail more often than not. But strength is not found in
perfection; your strength is made perfect in my weakness.
In those places, you show off your own power. What I could
never do on my own, you do for me.

What a wonderful father you are! I rely on your power in my
life, especially in the places that look like they are severely
lacking. You are more than sufficient. You will provide
for my every need, and you will make every crooked path
straight. I won't stop following you, because I know that
you have the best plans, the best solutions, and the best way
out—every time. I trust you to work miracles of mercy in the
impossibilities of my story. Nothing is impossible for you! My
courage is you, Lord. It is your presence in my life. You are my
greatest hope, and my even better reality.

How can you stand strong in God's power?

Freedom Is Mine

The Lord is the Spirit,
and where the Spirit of the Lord is,
there is freedom.

2 CORINTHIANS 3:17 NIV

The freedom that Paul speaks of here is the kind of liberty that comes with the unhindered connection we get in relationship with God through Christ. There is nothing that keeps us from his love; not even the greatest distance can come between us. We reflect the glory of God in our lives in ever-increasing measure as we fellowship with the Spirit.

What a wonderful and mysterious exchange—our attention for his transformative power in our lives. There is no greater liberty than the one we already have in relationship with God. Since God does not put anything between us, let us throw off the things that hinder us. He has already overcome every hindrance with his powerful love.

Spirit of the Lord, I submit my heart to yours, and I lay down everything that would keep me from true freedom in you. Your compassion is my covering, and there is nothing that it misses. Since you are with me, I have everything I need to live in the liberty of your love.

The Lord is the Spirit;
and where the Spirit of the Lord is,
there is liberty.

2 Corinthians 3:17 NKJV

Yahweh, you have set me free from sin and shame, and I can run unrestricted in your love. I am more grateful than I can express. You do not hold back even a droplet of mercy, and you don't require anything of me but my surrender. And why would I resist? Your mercy has led me into the abundance of your kindness. I don't want to live outside of it.

Spirit of God, continue to lead me in your love as long as I draw breath in this fragile frame of mine. You are faithful, and you are just. I have no reason to fear, for you are with me. You are my strong and mighty tower; in your presence I am safe and sound. In your fields of opportunity, there is more than enough for abundance of vibrant and thriving life. Why would I limit myself in your love when you never do? I run free in your grace.

How has God's Spirit brought you greater freedom?

Be Open

Whoever conceals his transgressions will not prosper,
but he who confesses and forsakes them will obtain mercy.

PROVERBS 28:13 ESV

Shame thrives in the shadows, but it has no power in the light of truth. Whatever we hide for fear of being found out will one day be brought to light. Instead of concealing our disobedience, what would it look like to let God's light shine on it? He already knows us through and through. He is kind and trustworthy, and he leads us in repentance that closes the distance that we put in our relationship with him.

There is power in the confession of sin. There is freedom in forsaking worn-out ways that keep us cycling in shame. Let today be the day we open our hearts to God's wisdom, truth, and love in the hidden areas of our hearts and lives. His ways are better than any we could advocate for on our own, and he is trustworthy.

Merciful Father, I open my heart to you again today. I don't want to keep anything hidden from you. Meet me now in your love and shine the light on the shadows. I welcome you to do it.

Whoever conceals their sins does not prosper,
but the one who confesses and renounces them finds mercy.

PROVERBS 28:13 NIV

Lord, though there is some resistance in my heart toward full surrender, I will not stop your love from flooding my life. I want you to have access to every area—nothing hidden. The allure of secrets is losing its luster. I'd rather be fully known and be open with you and those I love. I do not want to cover any shame. You have offered me true freedom, and that's the kind of life I want! I recognize that your kingdom ways are full of wisdom, light, and life. There is joy, peace, and love in your presence. I want all that you have to give.

I offer everything that keeps me from running in fullness of joy this evening. I gladly receive your grace, which empowers me in your vibrant life. Thank you for restoration, redemption, and reconciliation. What a wonderful, kind, patient, and merciful father you are! No secret sin can compare to the goodness you offer.

Is there any secret sin you have been hiding?

Compassionate Heart

"Show mercy and compassion for others, just as your heavenly Father overflows with mercy and compassion for all."

LUKE 6:36 TPT

It is not enough to receive God's compassion in our lives. The Scriptures say that the world will know we are followers of Christ by our love for one another. Compassion should be a natural response of the redeemed. And where it is not freely flowing, we still get to choose to extend mercy!

We reflect God's nature in the transformation of our lives. When we offer others understanding in place of judgment, and kindness in place of disdain, we reflect the love that God offers us. The great news is that there is always more for us to fill up on. When we run dry and find it difficult to offer mercy, we can always first go to God, the giver of love, and receive what we need. We will then have a resource to give out of. There really is no excuse for lovers of God to not love people, as well.

Compassionate One, may I never withhold kindness when it is mine to give. Keep my heart rooted in your love, that I may give out of the overflow of your mercy in my life.

*"You must be compassionate,
just as your Father is compassionate."*

LUKE 6:36 NLT

Merciful Father, I know that compassion is not mine to hold back from others. Your love is not reserved for those who willingly accept it; it is also shown to those who never will. In the same way, mercy is mine to give because it is what I have received. When I am tempted to give a cold response to someone I dislike, remind me that your love has no conditions.

May my heart stay pure in your love. I know that your Word says that I should not judge or condemn unless I want both in return. You know me, Lord! You know my humanity. And yet, your grace is enough to empower me to choose kindness when I would otherwise choose judgment. May I remember that I am accountable to you, Lord. Your love is stronger than death, and it can certainly break through my fear. I give you permission to lead me back in your love whenever I start to get stuck in my own offense. Your mercy is bigger!

What place does compassion have in your life?

Law of Love

*"Do to others what you want them to do to you. This is the
meaning of the law of Moses and the teaching of the prophets."*

MATTHEW 7:12 NCV

When we treat others with the same respect and kindness
we desire to receive, we are reflecting the law of God's love.
In everything, when we extend mercy, we reveal that we
are becoming like the merciful one we worship. Instead of
getting caught up in details that don't matter in the end, let's
be sure to keep first things first.

God's merciful love is the standard by which we are to live
our lives. The path to God's kingdom isn't narrow because it
is difficult to find, but rather because not many will choose to
walk the way of laid-down love. When we choose his way, we
will find the life that we seek. Our leader is humble, but he is
beautiful in all he does. Let us follow the leadership of Jesus.

Lord of my life, thank you for your love that sets the standard.
Your ways are better than the world's, and your thoughts are
wiser than the intellect of earthly sages. I will follow you, and
I will offer others the same love you freely give to all.

"In everything you do, be careful to treat others in the same way you'd want them to treat you, for that is the essence of all the teachings of the Law and the Prophets."

MATTHEW 7:12 TPT

Father of love, may I never fall into the trap of thinking that judgment instead of mercy is godly. You alone are judge, and only you can dole out just rulings. Instead of fixating on what others do or their possible responses to my actions, I will offer the same kind of love and understanding that I desire to receive, whether or not I get it from them in return. May I carefully choose my responses to others, with kindness as my go-to.

As I follow your path of love, I know that there is no better way. Mercy is your nature, requiring patience along the way. Though not easy, your ways are best. They lead to life—everlasting life! I will follow you, Lord, for you are trustworthy and your Word will never fail. Your love is the highest way.

How does God's law of love influence your decisions?

Invitation

He said, "Come." And when Peter had come down out of the boat,
he walked on the water to go to Jesus.

MATTHEW 14:29 NKJV

Jesus' invitation to Peter in this verse is actually a response to a request that Peter had made. The disciples saw Jesus walking on the water toward them, but they did not recognize him. Jesus called out to them to not be afraid, for it was just him. Peter tested him, saying "Lord, if it is You, command me to come to You on the water" (verse 28). Jesus' response was to say, "Come."

Then Peter's faith was tested as he stepped out of the boat onto the water. With his eyes on Jesus, he walked on the water! It was only when he got distracted by the winds and fear began to take over that he began to sink. Jesus questioned Peter's doubt, revealing that if he had stayed strong in faith, he never would have sunk at all. Let this be our reminder to keep our eyes fixed on Jesus when we step out in faith.

Jesus, thank you for your invitation. When I step out in faith, may I keep looking at you, my life source and powerful Savior. May I not get distracted by the swirling winds around me; you are everything I need.

"Yes, come," Jesus said. So Peter went over the side of the boat and walked on the water toward Jesus.

MATTHEW 14:29 NLT

Savior, may I never hesitate when your invitation to step out in faith comes. May I remember that the most important thing to do is keep my attention focused on you, the one who set the sun, moon, and stars in their places. You are the giver of life, and you can do all things. Nothing is impossible for you.

Far be it from me to let the winds of testing distract me with fear. Oh, Lord, you know how often this happens. But thank you for new mercies. You do not stop helping your people when they cry out to you for help. I want to mature in my faith, standing strong because it all depends on you. Keep my heart rooted in your overwhelming love. I want to walk on the waters where you are, but more than that, I want to be completely confident in who you are and who you say I am.

Are your eyes fixed on the author of your faith?

Closer

One who has unreliable friends soon comes to ruin,
but there is a friend who sticks closer than a brother.

PROVERBS 18:24 NIV

When we bind together with others in purpose and vision in different areas of life, the character of a person speaks more loudly than their promises. In business ventures, a convincing salesman will likely close many sales, but if he is not consistent in the follow-through, it will come back to bite him later. In relationships, an unreliable friend leads to destruction of trust.

Though no one is perfect, there are character traits to look for in a friend, partner, or lover that will stand the test of time. Humility (the ability to repair broken connections) and consistency (the ability to follow through on one's word) are important in building trust in any kind of relationship. Above it all, God is always consistent, for he is perfect in loyal love.

Constant One, thank you for your unchanging, perfect nature. I know that your Word is reliable; what you say, you will do. I rest in the confidence of your unfailing love. You will never let me down.

Some friendships don't last for long,
but there is one loving friend who is joined to your heart
closer than any other!

PROVERBS 18:24 TPT

Jesus, my loving friend, there truly is no one else like you in all the world. Only you are perfect in love, representing yourself in the best possible way through your perfect track record. You fulfill every promise you make even though it may take longer than we anticipate. Your mercy motivates everything you do. You are the best friend I will ever know; you never leave me or forsake me.

Even when I go off on my own way, whenever I call on you, you are there to help me. You don't let me flounder in my failures when I call on your name. You lift me up out of the miry clay of my circumstances and set my feet on the solid foundation of your kindness. You are my deliverer, and you are my Savior. No one else can claim such a thing! You hear every request and see to the depths of my heart. You know me fully—through and through, and yet, you love me unceasingly. I could sing your praises forever just based off this truth. Thank you!

Do you trust God's consistency?

Filled with Kindness

The LORD is righteous in everything he does;
he is filled with kindness.

PSALM 145:17 NLT

When you consider God's work in the world, and when you look at his mercy in your own life, what conclusions can you make about his character? Do you look at the destruction going on around you—the wars and rumors of wars—and think that God is a punisher? Or do you look at the rebuilding happening, the justice and mercy of new beginnings, and see his fingerprints in those things?

Surely God is bigger than you can imagine, and there is mystery in the greatness and scope of his reach. But what we believe about God's nature and his motivations matters. It is the lens we see him through. The Word is clear that God is righteous and kind. He is full of love and mercy, and he is just and true. Look for the marks of his undeniable nature around you, and you will find him.

Righteous God, I know that your truth stands above every other law of the land. Your wonderful ways are not spiteful, nor do they exclude anyone who would come to you. Give me eyes to see your kindness today.

*You are fair and righteous in everything you do,
and your love is wrapped into all your works.*

PSALM 145:17 TPT

Holy One, everything you do is by the standards of your
perfect mercy and justice. Only you can judge a person's
heart, and I lay down my own desire to do it. It is not my place
to monitor another's choices; rather, you have called me to
offer love and extend mercy. My choices are the only ones I
can control, and I submit even those to you.

I want to walk in the light of your truth all the days of my life.
Keep me aligned in your kindness, and let your loyal love
be the constant thread that weaves every part of my story
together in your redemption plan. You are better than any
human, certainly seeing more clearly than I can. I surrender
my weakness to your strength. Show me the kindness of your
heart in a fresh way now as I look to you. You are wonderful—
more wonderful than I could ever deserve!

How have you witnessed God's kindness in your life?

Have Mercy

Answer me when I pray to you,
my God who does what is right.
Make things easier for me when I am in trouble.
Have mercy on me and hear my prayer.

PSALM 4:1 NCV

When you are weary from the race of this life, where do you turn for rest? When the demands of your current circumstances seem never-ending, let alone satisfied, how do you find peace? God, your God, promises never to abandon you. He is with you in the trials and through every storm of life. Turn your mind to him today and ask him for the help that you need! He will ease the heavy load you have been carrying.

Let him do the heavy lifting! He hears you each time you talk to him. He doesn't ever miss a word; you are not overlooked. You already have his attention. Pour out your heart to him again and find the relief you crave in his presence.

Merciful Father, how quickly I seem to forget that you really do love me completely. I offer you all that I've been wrestling with, and I welcome your ready help today. Have mercy on me again.

Answer me when I call to you,
my righteous God.
Give me relief from my distress;
have mercy on me and hear my prayer.

PSALM 4:1 NIV

Righteous God, you are the one I call to over and over again.
In times of need and in moments of rejoicing, you are the one
I turn to. Lift the heaviness of the burdens that I have been
brought low by. Give me your joy in their place. I know that
only true peace and rest is found in you, and I'm certain that I
can know it here and now in this very moment.

If you would meet me with the tangible goodness of your
presence, as you have done before, I will breathe deep sighs
of relief. Have mercy on me again; I know you will! You have
not failed me, sustaining Lord. I know you haven't given up
on me, and I won't give up on reaching out to you. Refresh me
in the peace of your presence, and may I rest sweetly in the
comforting atmosphere of your love.

How do you need God to meet you today?

My Protection

The name of the Lord is blessed and lifted high!
For his marvelous miracle of mercy protected me
when I was overwhelmed by my enemies.

PSALM 31:21 TPT

Even when we are surrounded by chaos and we cannot see a way out of it, God is with us. He protects us and keeps us close in his lavish love. He will not let us be overtaken by the circumstances that threaten to swallow us whole. We will overcome them all through the blood of the Lamb. He is our defender and our mighty helper. God has a plan when we ours have completely derailed.

Let us rest in the confidence of God's faithfulness today. He is worthy of our trust, for he is better than we can imagine him to be. He is reliable, consistent, and merciful. Let's place all our hope in him once more. He will do what no one else can; he will make a way where there seems to be none. All we need to do is trust and follow where he leads.

Mighty Protector, I run into the shelter of your name. You have been my Savior, and you will always be a ready help whenever I need it. I rely on your unfailing nature to see me through every unknown. I trust you!

Blessed be the Lord,
for he has wondrously shown his steadfast love to me
when I was beset as a city under siege.

PSALM 31:21 NRSV

Lord, I bless your name! You have been so wonderful to me. Over and over again, you show me your mercy as you work out your redemption story. My life is sown into the fabric of your kindness and restoration. You astound me with the works of your goodness in my life. Even in circumstances that looked impossibly grim, you shone your glory light and brought beauty out of the ashes. Who else can do such a thing? Only you, God.

I'm so grateful for your consistent and reliable compassion that leads me out of despair into a bright new dawn. You are my saving grace, and you are my living hope. I will not stop thanking you for all you have done. And you are not finished with me yet. Thank you for protecting me even when I did not understand that it was what you were doing. Your ways are so much better than mine; thank you for always leading me in love.

How has God protected you?

Pressing On

You need to persevere so that when you have done the will of God, you will receive what he has promised.

HEBREWS 10:36 NIV

In different seasons of life, perseverance may look different on the outside. When we have many different responsibilities to juggle, perseverance may look like believing that God is with us in it all, trusting him to take care of the details we miss. In times of deep pain and suffering, it may look like allowing God to sit with us in our sorrow and comfort us with his love. Perseverance is an active thing, but it is more an inner heart posture and choice than it is a measurable action.

Keep going and don't give up. In the little and the big things, remember that God is your help, and he will fulfill every promise he has made. He is faithful, and he will see us through every season of the soul. Let us stay submitted to his mercy through it all, choosing his ways over our own preferences. His grace is our strength.

God, my promise keeper, help me to stay lined in your love with every choice I make. I will keep believing that you are who you say you are. I will continue to live my life according to your truth and your incredible mercy. Today, I choose to keep pressing on in you.

You need the strength of endurance to reveal the poetry of God's will and then you receive the promise in full.

HEBREWS 10:36 TPT

Great God, you are the one who sets things into place and into motion, and I trust that, no matter the twists and turns in the journey, that everything will find its fulfillment in you, in the end. You have proven faithful throughout the ages, and you have shown your faithfulness to me. When I think about how you have done so much more than I thought to ask you for, my heart grows in gratitude.

Give me the endurance I need through your grace, to keep pressing on in faith. May I not give up believing in your goodness, for you never change. When the winds shift in my life and the storms rush in, may I press myself further into your peace and not let myself be swept away by the chaos of confusion. Keep me safe and guard my heart, for it is yours. As I press into you, make me aware of how very close you already are, and what thoughtful care you are taking of me. I love you!

What does "pressing on" look like in your current situation?

Not Finished Yet

There is hope for a tree, if it is cut down, that it will sprout again, and that its tender shoots will not cease.

JOB 14:7 NKJV

In the ebbs and flows of life, God is faithful through it all. He does not leave us when our worlds come crashing down around us. Even in destruction, God is more than able. His restoration work is more beautiful and thoughtful than we can imagine. His redemption is more powerful than the grave.

Whatever our losses, God will not let a single one of them go to waste in his hand. He will weave his wonderful mercy through every detail of our stories into the larger story of his redemption plan. As this verse in Job reminds us, if there is hope for a tree to sprout again after it has been cut down, how much more for us? It is not a vain thing to hope; it is courageous. Take heart today! God is not done with us yet.

Restorer, I trust you to do more than I can imagine with the ashes of my loss. You are marvelous in mercy. You are abundant in grace. I set my hope on you—the author and the finisher of my faith.

Even a tree has more hope!
If it is cut down, it will sprout again
and grow new branches.

JOB 14:7 NLT

Redeemer, thank you for the loving reminder of tenacious hope. Even a tree, after it is cut down, has hope for new life. My ultimate hope is in eternal life with you. But until I cross over that shore into the ocean of everlasting life, I know that here, in this life, you are not finished working your miracles of restoration and redemption. Your mercy has not run dry, and your faithfulness has not run out. Thank you for your limitless love. There is no end to the hope I have in you, for your wonderful love has no end.

I rest tonight in the confidence of your work in my life. I don't need to know how it is all going to play out; I trust your compassionate character to do a better job of rebuilding from the ruins than I ever could on my own. When I struggle to let go of the way things were, teach me to surrender in my grief to your overwhelmingly sweet love. You care, and I trust you.

How can you lift your eyes from loss to hope today?

Never Alone

The eye of the LORD is on those who fear him,
on those who hope in his steadfast love.

PSALM 33:18 ESV

The Scriptures declare that "the fear of the Lord is the beginning of wisdom" (Prov. 9:10). How do we 'fear' God? It is not a sense of dread, but of honor and respect. It is to rightly understand that God is worthy of our awe, and that he is far more powerful than we could ever imagine being.

God gives life and can take it away. He is just and true, and it is only his role to dole out judgment. We can fear God and hope in his unfailing love at the same time. God leads us to understanding, and he imparts his wisdom to those who look for it. God's eyes are on those who regard him. Let us look to him, our Creator and sustainer of life. He is with us.

Yahweh, as I look to you today, may I be filled with the understanding of your greatness. You are the only true and wise God. You are holy! You are my God, and my hope is in your steadfast love.

The eyes of the Lord are upon
even the weakest worshipers who love him—
those who wait in hope and expectation
for the strong, steady love of God.

PSALM 33:18 TPT

Lord, you have my worship today. Even my weakest worship, you accept and delight in. I can hardly comprehend how generous you are with your love, but I am so very grateful to receive it. You are my hope and my expectation. I know that without you, I would be lost. But you have set me on the firm foundation of your mercy-love that is stronger than anything else. It is the steady rock that my life is built upon.

Lord, in my weakness and in my strength, I offer you all that I am. There is no one else who loves the way that you do–so completely. You love me to life over and over again in your presence. I can hardly believe the great gift of your mercy that never ends. Thank you for loving me so well. Thank you!

What does your weak worship look like?

So Good

LORD, answer me because your love is so good.
Because of your great kindness, turn to me.

PSALM 69:16 NCV

Have you known the inexpressible sweetness of God's tangible love in your life? Think about the best day you have ever had. What was it that brought you such joy? What about it was wonderful? Now, think about the love of God. It is patient, kind, peace-loving, full of joy, and always flowing outward. This love is not dependent on circumstance or recipient; it is always pure, always abundant, and always life-giving.

Today, may you know the confidence of being met by God's overwhelming affection, no matter what your circumstances say. With this love as your strength, you can face anything, for you are not alone in it. Let God's kindness lead you to his truth. He is so very good!

Good God, thank you for your unwavering love that meets me in every moment with the same intensity. You, who are never lacking in love, will always give freely from your heart of mercy. Please, turn to me in kindness once more.

Answer me, O Lᴏʀᴅ, for Your lovingkindness is good;
According to the greatness of Your compassion, turn to me.

Pꜱᴀʟᴍ 69:16 ɴʀꜱᴠ

Compassionate One, answer me as I pour out my heart before you once again. I invite you into every detail of my life. There's nothing I leave out, nothing left hidden. I know that you see it all, anyway! Will you meet me with the purity of your lovingkindness and revive my weary heart in the strength of your grace?

I depend on you, God, for there is no one else who loves the way that you do. You are so free and ready with your mercy. You are consistently kind. You are full of compassion when I mess up. You are the strength of my life, Lord! Strengthen me once again, according to your mercy. Do not leave me waiting too long. Even so, I will wait on you. You are faithful, and I know you will come through for me again. You are worth every moment I offer you—and so much more.

How has the goodness of God's love met you recently?

Hemmed In

The LORD is near to all who call on him,
yes, to all who call on him in truth.

PSALM 145:18 NLT

When you feel hemmed in by the circumstances of your life, pressed in by your troubles, know that God is close at hand. Call on him, wait on him, and you will discover that he is already nearer than you know. Do not be overwhelmed by your troubles, for the Lord is a help to those who call on his name.

This is a forever-truth; you are not ever on your own. There is no need to worry when God is your rescuer. Though you may not be able to see a way out of your trials, God always provides a way. Trust him, lean on him, and let his wisdom and love guide you. He won't let you down.

Lord, I call on you in my day of trouble. Even the small worries and details, you take care of. I rely on your peace to flood my system and for your love to lead me. You are my help, and you are my hope. All my life long, it will remain true. You are my strong and mighty tower of refuge.

You draw near to those who call out to you,
listening closely, especially when their hearts are true.

PSALM 145:18 TPT

Great God, whenever I call out to you, I trust that you will
answer me. You listen to every word that I say even reading
the thoughts that never make it past my lips. You know me
through and through. And you love me! What a wonderful
truth. I will gladly love you in return, for you are my hope and
my joy. Meet me now and answer the cries of my heart. Even
the small questions, you do not overlook.

Will you see past the circle I am talking in and answer the
true nature of my questions? You see right to the root of my
thoughts. You are wise, and your words are clear. Speak your
living Word to me now and revive my heart with the vibrancy
of your love. My heart is yours, so mold it with the purifying
fires of your mercy. I know that you are gentle and kind. I
trust you!

How have you sensed God's nearness?

Give Thanks

Give thanks to the Lord, for He is good!
For His mercy endures forever.

1 Chronicles 16:34 NKJV

There is always something to be thankful for, though dark nights inevitably set in. What remains true in the black of night? What kind of goodness is present in darkness? May you never be so discouraged by your circumstances that you are unable to see where God's kindness is still present.

Before you begin your day, take a few moments to find five specific things you are grateful for. They can be little or big things. Is there love in your life? The reliability of a true friend? A pet that brings you joy? When you begin to look for these things, you may be surprised at how much good there truly is in your life. Give thanks, for God is good! His mercy endures forever.

Merciful God, thank you for the blessings of your goodness in my life. You never fail in faithfully reaching out in love. Thank you for your mercy breaks through the darkness with glimmers of glory. I'm so thankful!

Give thanks to the LORD, for he is good!
His faithful love endures forever.

1 CHRONICLES 16:34 NLT

Lord, I give thanks to you this evening for your wonderful love that completely covers my life. I am never without your powerful mercy. What a wonderful and humbling thought! And what an even more gracious reality. As I wind down from a busy day, I give you all the leftover questions and cares that I've picked up along the way. I know that in you is rest. I offer you the heavy, burdensome things and take the light yoke of your peace. I lay down my need for immediate answers for things that will wait until tomorrow.

I want to rest in the calm of your presence. I know that your love is overflowing; it is always more than enough to abundantly cover all my losses and weakness. You are so much greater than the best people on this planet. It is my delight to know you, and it is my honor to be known by you.

What are you thankful for today?

Gracious God

*In Your great mercy You did not
utterly consume them nor forsake them;
For You are God, gracious and merciful.*

NEHEMIAH 9:31 NKJV

Do you feel as if God has left you? Is it difficult to sense where he is in your life? Today, ask him for a fresh look at his presence with you. His mercies are promised new every morning. There is no moment like now, no day like today to begin anew.

Can you leave the disappointments of yesterday aside even just for a few moments? He answers all those who call on him. He is full of abundant mercy that never runs out. He has not grown impatient with you, no matter what you have done or haven't done. He knows you better than you know yourself, and he loves you through and through. Look to him again.

Gracious God, meet me with your overwhelming love again today. I need a fresh encounter with your grace. I long to know what you are doing and what is on your heart today. Speak, Lord, for I am listening. Be gracious to me.

In your great mercy, you did not
destroy them completely or abandon them forever.
What a gracious and merciful God you are!

NEHEMIAH 9:31 NLT

Merciful One, thank you for your mercy that meets me in new ways every moment. It is not stale, and it does not grow old. Where my understanding has flattened, you shine your revelation-light and make it new again. You revive my heart in hope as you speak your living Word over my life. What a wonderful father you are! What a loyal friend!

You are God, and you call me your friend. I just cannot get over that. Thank you for bringing me into your kingdom by the power of your love. I recognize that it was never about me or what I could offer you. You just wanted my love; and what's more, you know how my heart needs yours. You are the fulfillment of everything I long for. You. Not your promises, not your gifts, not anything superfluous. It is you. It always has been and always will be. Thank you!

How has God's generous nature
transformed your understanding of him?

Mandate

Bear one another's burdens,
and thereby fulfill the law of Christ.

GALATIANS 6:2 NASB

We were not created to live isolated lives. We were never meant to function fully on our own. We may excel in some areas, but we lack in others. We were always meant to function in family—in community—so that we can strengthen and support each other, and so that we can lean on and receive help from others. It is the give and take of relationship.

There are times of life when we cannot escape our overwhelming need. Whether it is financial, emotional, spiritual, or physical; it is inevitable. In grief, for instance, we need the solidarity and support of others. In suffering, we often require the help of those who are not debilitated by sorrow. Let us not be ashamed of our great need, but instead reach out to others when we need it. And may we be quick to lift the burdens of others when it is in our capability to do so.

Christ, I follow the example you set and offer my life as a living sacrifice to you. I choose to love you when I help carry the burdens of others. And when I am the recipient, you teach me more about leaning on your love. Thank you for creating us for community.

*Love empowers us to fulfill the law of the Anointed One
as we carry each other's troubles.*

GALATIANS 6:2 TPT

Anointed One, the law of your love is the most important value to set my life to. When I am weary in expressing mercy, fill me up with your kindness once more, that I may have it to offer others. And when I am suffering under the weight of my own burdens, may I be quick to receive the help of those who offer it. Thank you for setting me in your family, and for giving me perspective of tangible love. May your compassion compel me to help others when I am able. And when there is a question of convenience, may I count the cost of surrender to your love that is worth it all. May I be kind in action, not just in speech.

Let my life reflect yours, Lord! When I am weak, then I am made strong in your grace. When I choose to extend the same kindness to others as I have received, there is power in it. Your love advocates for the defenseless and fights for the powerless. It leaves no one out, and it does not ever overlook the needy. Transform me continually into your loving image as I align my choices with your kingdom values.

How has helping to carry another's burden affected you?

Trust Him

*"You have also given me the shield of Your salvation;
your gentleness has made me great."*

2 SAMUEL 22:36 NKJV

When we struggle to make sense of the chaos in our lives and in the world around us, it is good practice to go to God's Word for guidance and encouragement. He has the words of life and wisdom that we need. His Word is the bread that feeds and nourishes our souls. May we read with our eyes enlightened by the Spirit and his words piercing our hearts with his truth.

We can clearly see God's consistent character throughout the pages of Scripture. His mercy is undeniable. His love, who can argue? He gives chance after chance to his people, and he always extends kindness when they turn to him. He is so very gracious with us. We can trust him to continue to be.

Savior, as I look into your Word today, pierce my heart with your truth. Let your living presence move within me as I meditate on your unfailing love and wonderful nature. Transform my mind with your kingdom values today.

"You have given me your shield of victory;
your help has made me great."

2 SAMUEL 22:36 NLT

Victorious One, I offer you my life again. You can have my
thoughts, my days, my ways. I submit them all to you in love.
I know that your ways are better than mine. They are full of
your wisdom and clarity, bringing light to the path ahead.
When I align myself with your higher law of truth, I find that
your grace is all the strength I need. You give me mercy to
uphold me, and you cover me with the peace of your presence
for every step I take. In you, I find the greatness I long for.

Anything I could ever achieve on my own pales in comparison
to the triumph of your love in my life. You have broken the
power of the world's systems with your blood. In you, I have
found abundant life. I am free in your mercy, for you have
broken the weight of sin's curse over me. Thank you, Jesus!

How has God's help made a difference in your life?

Tended

He heals the brokenhearted
and bandages their wounds.

PSALM 147:3 NLT

We cannot help but feel the sting of heartbreak in life, and pain is a familiar companion of loss. Let's not pretend that any of us escapes this sort of suffering! But there is good news. God tends to the wounds of our hearts and souls with expert care and healing power. He binds up our injuries with the salve of his love. He dresses our wounds with the balm of his mercy. He attentively takes care of us when we have no hope of healing on our own.

When we are wounded, let us remember that it does not make us broken; it does not make us less-than. Even so, God meets us with the power of his resurrection life and makes us whole in him.

Healer, only you know the depths of my heartache. You clearly see what even I have tuned out and shoved away. I receive your love as my healing salve. Come minister to the wounded parts of my heart and make me whole as only you can!

He heals the wounds
of every shattered heart.

PSALM 147:3 TPT

Holy One, you alone are the healer of my heart. You take the pieces that have been shattered, and you make me whole again. What you do, no one can undo. Your restoration power is more thorough than anyone can fully recognize. You don't miss a detail, and you won't leave a part of my heart untouched by your unfailing love. Heal me. As you meet me with the mercy of your presence right now; heal me!

You are such an attentive caretaker. You are a skilled healer. You are the master restorer. You are the Redeemer. You are my hope, and all my hope is in you. I have known your healing power in my life, but I need more of it now. I know you won't turn me away, so here I am before you. I have given you my heart; it is in your keeping already. Love me to life in ways I never dreamed you could and may your restoration work bring revived joy and hope to my life and to my future.

Have you known God's healing in heartbreak?

Learning to Rest

For God alone, O my soul, wait in silence,
for my hope is from him.

PSALM 62:5 ESV

When was the last time you took a week, or even a day, to truly rest? Where you stepped away from the demands of the everyday to simply do what brings you joy? There is purpose in rest; even God did it. After he created the world, he took the seventh day to enjoy what he made, without feeling the need to create anything more.

It is important that we learn how to incorporate real rest into our lives. There can even be whole seasons that are set apart for this purpose. Will we fight the urge to do more when doing less will actually bring more perspective? What could we miss if we are just rushing along into the next thing because we are uncomfortable with waiting in the stillness? There is so much purpose and beauty in the in-between. Let's make room to get comfortable in the still, waiting spaces in life!

God, teach me how to really rest in you. Sow your peace into my soul as I learn that waiting is not wasted time. I know that you have a plan and a purpose, and there is no hurry in your heart.

I am standing in absolute stillness,
silent before the one I love,
waiting as long as it takes for him to rescue me.
Only God is my Savior, and he will not fail me.

PSALM 62:5 TPT

God my Savior, thank you for your consistent presence in my life. You fill me with the oil of your love, and it soothes my weary heart. As I learn to lean into the uncomfortable spaces of waiting and stillness, do a miracle in my heart and teach me how to enjoy these times. I don't want to keep rushing from one thing to the next and completely miss what you had for me. I know that you know best, so teach me to live with rhythms of your rest worked into my life.

I am your humble and willing student. Though waiting is not my preference, I know there is treasure to be found there. Keep me close in your love. Draw me back to your heart when anxiety begins to demand I do something. I trust you more than I trust myself. I know you will not fail me.

How can you make space for stillness today?

Daybreak Is Coming

Do it again! Those Yahweh has set free
will return to Zion and come celebrating with songs of joy!
They will be crowned with never-ending joy!
Gladness and joy will overwhelm them;
despair and depression will disappear!

ISAIAH 51:11 TPT

Every night comes to an end, and every night season also draws to a close. With what? The shining dawn of a new day. The light will break through the darkness that shrouded you, and you will clearly see what has been hidden from your view. The heavy sadness will lift; despair will not remain. There is joy in the newness of a fresh moment where God's mercy-light breaks through.

Let hope arise today with the rising of the sun in the sky. Look around. Can you see that God is with you? He has been with you all along. He is faithful, and he has never left you for even a moment.

Yahweh, you are the hope that sets me free over and over again. I am full of joy, recognizing your constant presence in my life. You are better than I could ever give you credit for. Thank you for being so faithful to me.

Those who have been ransomed by the LORD will return.
They will enter Jerusalem singing,
crowned with everlasting joy.
Sorrow and mourning will disappear,
and they will be filled with joy and gladness.

ISAIAH 51:11 NLT

Lord, I know that everlasting joy is mine in your eternal kingdom. True freedom and joy I get in glimpses now, but I will know them fully when I am living in the fullness of your glory kingdom. Though I long for that day, I see the goodness of your mercy working out in my life here and now. You are working your miracles of restoration and redemption in beautiful ways in my life. You lead me in joy, giving it in exchange for my mourning. You have filled me with gladness, for your presence has never left me.

What delight is mine! As you open my eyes to the thread of your kindness in my story, I cannot help but be filled with awe at your love. You are more wonderful than I knew, and still more wonderful even than I can now comprehend. Keep doing what you do and love me to life.

Where in your life can you see the light
of God's glory breaking through?

How Long

How long must I worry and feel sad in my heart all day?
How long will my enemy win over me?

PSALM 13:2 NCV

In suffering seasons, it can be disheartening when we don't see the end. Even when we can't understand what God is doing, he is with us. He is constantly working on our behalf, for he is our good and faithful Father. We can trust that he is just as good in our times of prolonged pain as he is in our times of celebration.

Continue to connect with him, inviting him into the process with you. He has not abandoned you. Give him your worry again; he can handle it. Do not hold back from him. Let him meet you in the midst of your pain. He will never turn you away.

My God, when I have no strength to pretend that I'm ok when I'm not, meet me with your kindness. Lift the weight of my worries. I depend on you! Remind me of your power and do a miracle in my life again. Without you, I have no hope.

How much longer must I cling to this constant grief?
I've endured this shaking of my soul.
So how much longer will my enemy have the upper hand?
It's been long enough!

PSALM 13:2 TPT

God my strength, in the shaking of my life, I have been brought to my own end. I have nothing more to give; no strength of my own to stand on. I need you, Lord! Lift me from the mire of the heavy situations that don't seem to be changing at all. Give me grace to empower me to live in the light of your truth.

I would have given up if I didn't hope for your rescue. You have been my help before, and I am trusting that you will do it again. Break through the darkness of my suffering with your radiant light of hope. Shine on me, and I will live. Lift my heavy burdens, so that I can remember how to dance with joy once again. Thank you for knowing me well, and for meeting me with gentleness. I depend on your loyal love to get me through!

Is there a prolonged worry that
you can give to God again today?

Only One

God is the only Lawmaker and Judge.
He is the only One who can save and destroy.
So it is not right for you to judge your neighbor.

JAMES 4:12 NCV

As God's children, we must be careful how we live. Not as those who are wise in their own eyes, but as humble servants of the Lord's kingdom. This kingdom is known by mercy, love, and hope. Who of us, when we judge our neighbors, are exemplifying God's kingdom? Simple answer: we are not. Only God can rightly judge a person's heart and motives. Only he can save and destroy.

Can we let him have this role, without feeling the need to monitor or control another's choices? The thing that we are called to do, above all else, is love—the benefit of the doubt, extending mercy and kindness even in the face of ridicule, kind of love. God can handle the rest.

Just God, you alone know the true state of our hearts. I trust that you can handle the role of judge, and I can then focus on what you gave me to focus on: loving my neighbor as myself. Thank you for this reminder.

There is only one true Lawgiver and Judge,
the One who has the power to save and destroy—
so who do you think you are to judge your neighbor?

JAMES 4:12 TPT

Mighty God, I know that with you is all power to create and to destroy. You are Savior, and you are also the Righteous Judge. I lay down all my offenses before you, and I ask for your mercy to flood my awareness now. It is not my place to render judgment on those around me.

Forgive me for my pride, and for the log I overlook in my own eye to jump on the splinter in my neighbor's. Soften my heart in your love, that I may have a well of compassion to offer others. Keep me from getting so stuck in my own opinions that I refuse to look, with compassion and empathy, at others' lives in the same measure I expect. Your law of love is the standard that keeps my life in check with your merciful heart. I submit again to you, for your wisdom is full of clarity and understanding.

Do you believe that God is the only rightful judge?

Spirit Power

The Spirit of the LORD will rest on Him,
The spirit of wisdom and understanding,
The spirit of counsel and strength,
The spirit of knowledge and the fear of the LORD.

ISAIAH 11:2 NASB

There is absolutely nothing that we could ever need that is not found in the abundant provision of God. The Spirit of the Lord has been given to all those who believe. When we offer our lives in humble surrender to God, through Jesus, we have unhindered connection to him through the Spirit's life within us.

He is the Spirit of wisdom and understanding, giving us revelation to understand his kingdom ways. He is the Spirit of counsel and strength, empowering us in faith to believe that God is who he is revealed to be. He is the Spirit of knowledge and the fear of the Lord. He is all that we need, and more.

Holy Spirit, I'm so grateful for your presence and fellowship in my life. You lead me into joy, you set me free in your love, and you minister to me in more ways than I can count. What a beautiful treasure you are to me!

The Spirit of Yahweh will rest upon him,
the Spirit of Extraordinary Wisdom,
the Spirit of Perfect Understanding
the Spirit of Wise Strategy,
the Spirit of Mighty Power,
the Spirit of Revelation,
and the Spirit of the Fear of Yahweh.

ISAIAH 11:2 TPT

Spirit of wisdom, I rely on you to illuminate the truth of God to me. You lead me in perfect understanding as you reveal the wonders of God's marvelous mercy. When I press into knowing you more, I have found that there is sweet fruit in your presence. There is overflowing joy found in you. There is peace that subdues even the hardest heart. There is patience that endures whatever may be going on around. There is kindness that is backed up by action.

In you, there is bountiful goodness, overcoming faith, gentleness of heart, and Spirit-strength. The fellowship of your Spirit is my source of life. You radiate glory and joy from the inside out, and I am forever changed by you. Thank you for all that you are, all that you do, and all that I have yet to discover in you.

How has God's Spirit empowered your life?

Governed by Grace

Sin will not conquer you, for God already has!
You are not governed by law
but governed by the reign of the grace of God.

ROMANS 6:14 TPT

Are there any areas of your life where you feel trapped? Do you keep doing something that you know you should not? In our weakness, God's strength is made perfect. There is nothing in our lives outside of the power of his great and glorious love. The blood of Jesus is the covering that makes us clean and sets us free.

Paul reminds us that we ought not to keep sinning to test the lengths of God's grace (though we could never reach the end). Sin is not our master—Jesus is! Let us not give in to the lie that there is anything in our lives that God cannot handle and that cannot be overcome by the power of God's grace that strengthens us. Do not forget that reaching out to others for help is also an act of grace.

My God, you are the ruler of my heart. I have given you access to my whole life, and it is laid out before you like an open book. Let your grace empower me to change today—for my freedom, for your glory, and for good.

Sin shall no longer be your master,
because you are not under the law,
but under grace.

ROMANS 6:14 NIV

Gracious God, I yield my heart to you this evening. Where there is sin in my life, I know that your grace is bigger. Your mercy has plucked me out of the endless cycles of sin and shame. I am free in you. Lord, I submit every area that needs your grace, and I declare that you are Lord over my life. You are Lord over my mind. You are Lord over my heart. Everything I have, everything I am, is yours.

You have broken the power of sin and death, and you have brought me into life. I will not keep persisting in things that I know I should not do, for your grace empowers me to a better life in freedom. All of my wrongs have been covered by your love, and I am washed clean. I align my life to your kingdom ways, and I walk in the power of your resurrection life. You are my delight, Lord, and pure pleasure is found in you. You are the one I serve.

Are you living under the power of God's grace?

Medicine for the Heart

A joyful, cheerful heart brings healing to both body and soul.
But the one whose heart is crushed struggles with sickness
and depression.

PROVERBS 17:22 TPT

God's Word says that the joy of the Lord is our strength. It is deeper than the happiness of fortune, and it is full of God's pure delight and pleasure. When we are grieving, the greatest relief seems to come in moments of pure laughter and joy. The juxtaposition of the lightness of joy and the depth of pain make it that much more poignant.

Whatever we are facing today, the joy of the Lord is available to us. It brings healing and refreshment to our souls. No matter how long it has been since we have felt it, God's joy is near. Has your heart been crushed by struggles for too long? Ask the Lord for a fresh filling of his joy!

Joyful Father, thank you for never withholding any good thing from your children. Meet me with your joy today and fill my heart with the relief that your presence brings. Heal my heart in your pleasure.

A joyful heart is good medicine,
but a crushed spirit dries up the bones.

PROVERBS 17:22 ESV

Good God, thank you for your consistent compassion in my life. Whenever I turn to you, there you are with loyal love to wrap me up. I cannot begin to express the depths of my gratitude. When my heart was crushed under the weight of struggles and suffering, you lifted the heaviness with your pure delight. Your joy is unlike anything I've experienced in this world. It lifts me up and makes me feel like I can take on anything. You are the healing to my bones, the soothing balm to my wounds, and my great and mighty strength.

As I consider this evening how much you have done for me, I am undone in your presence. And you do not save and then enslave. You set me free in your joy, so I can dance like a child. The laughter that falls from my lips is a reflection of the joy that you have over me. What a wonderful father you are!!

What brings you joy even in hard times?

He Can Take It

Cast all your anxiety on him
because he cares for you.

1 PETER 5:7 NRSV

Are you in the practice of using anxiety to fuel your productivity? Are you so used to the worries that crop up throughout your day that you just keep going in spite of them, letting them be the background track to your life? Let this be the reminder that you don't have to carry those yourself.

Your stresses need not be your motivators. Give them to God today, asking him for his grace, peace, and love in return. He is always close, always ready to help, always there. His love for you is so much greater than you can imagine. He doesn't love you because of what you can do or offer him; he loves you because he loves you! Give him the heavy things today, and rest in his faithful mercy.

Merciful God, thank you for the reminder that I need not carry the luggage of my anxiety around. I give it to you, Lord; would you remove the weighty burden from my hands? I want to rest in the confidence of your faithful love as I move about my day today. Thank you!

*Pour out all your worries and stress upon him
and leave them there,
for he always tenderly cares for you.*

1 Peter 5:7 TPT

Faithful Father, who else is there like you? Your tender care
of my life, my emotions, and my very being is so thoughtful.
You have no hidden agenda in your love. You love me, and I
am revived in you. Thank you for lifting the heaviness of my
worries when I bring them to you. Keep me in perfect peace as
I continue to bring you every anxiety and stress that pops up.
You are my great reward, my living hope, and my holy help.

I cannot stop thanking you for all that you do for me! Your
freedom is unlike any other, and you never change in
unrelenting affection. Even when you correct me, you are
so kind. You are patient in your approach, and your tender
mercy brings strength and clarity to my soul. I have never
known a love like yours that loves me through and through.
Thank you, thank you, thank you!

Have you been holding anything back from God?

Help Is Right Here

From the depths of despair, O Lord,
I call for your help.

PSALM 130:1 NLT

When you have reached the end of your resources, and all you can do is hold on for dear life, call out to the Lord. He is always near, and he will help you. You can depend on his faithful saving grace. Do you feel as if you have already asked for too much from the Lord? There is no such thing. Search through the psalms and you will find themes of celebration and themes of desperation.

Never hold back from him, for he never holds back from you. Give him all your worries, your utter defeat, and the reins of your life. He is more than able to deliver you, no matter how often you find yourself crying out for his help. Let him be your champion Savior. He never fails!

Lord my God, I call out to you from where I am today. Meet me with the overwhelming peace of your presence and lift me out of the pit of my despair with your strong arm of mercy. You are my hope!

LORD, I am in great trouble,
so I call out to you.

PSALM 130:1 NCV

Yahweh, you are my mighty deliverer. You are my saving grace. You are the one I rely on, both in my times of need and the calmer seasons of life. When I am in trouble, I won't hold back from calling out to you. I turn to you over and over again. You are consistent in kindness and never changing in resurrection power. Revive my hope as you turn the tide of my battles. I cling to you; hide me in the crook of your arm and do what only you can do.

You never leave me, and I never need worry about having to fix anything on my own. You are my wise counselor, my holy help, and my shepherd. All that I need is found in you. Everything! You are close to those who call on your name. Holy Spirit, fill me with the confidence of your presence and remind me of your lavish love. Strengthen my spirit with your Word of life. You are good.

Can you recall a time when God's help
changed your trajectory?

Radiant Hope

*The Lord alone is our radiant hope
and we trust in him with all our hearts.
His wrap-around presence will strengthen us.*

PSALM 33:22 TPT

What are your hopes rooted in? Are they in checking off
the dreams that you have for your life? Are they in getting
to the next stage, whatever that may be? Or is your ultimate
hope in the Lord? It is no small thing to hope in him. He is
our brilliant confidence. When we trust him with our whole
hearts, it is based on his unfailing character.

He will never go back on his Word, and he will not let us
down in loyal love. He continually meets us where we are at,
filling us with mercy-strength to lift us from the ashes of
despair. His wrap-around presence is our constant covering.
We need never go without it. May we confidently follow him,
journeying through this life on his path of peace and love.
He knows what he is doing, and we can fully trust in his
goodness.

Good God, you are my confident expectation. Everything I'm
counting on in life is based on you being true to your Word.
You never change, and you never will! I trust you with my
whole heart.

Let your steadfast love, O LORD, be upon us,
even as we hope in you.

PSALM 33:22 NRSV

Lord, let your unwavering love cover me now. Do not let
it lift from my life. When my hope is waning, I will check
where it is placed. When it is dependent on anything but your
faithfulness, may I always give it back to you. Your unfailing
and unchanging nature is the guarantee of all that you speak.
Your Spirit is my constant and faithful support, offering the
goodness of your presence. Your promises are sure; you will
fulfill each one according to your Word.

Lord, may I never be tricked into thinking that your gifts
are better than your friendship. Knowing you and being
known by you is the greatest exchange. The Scriptures
say that you give joy for mourning, beauty for ashes, and a
garment of praise for a spirit of despair. Your love covers all
my weaknesses and brings down my defenses. I am safe and
secure in your presence. You are my holy hope, and there will
never be another that compares with you.

Is there something in your life that needs renewed hope?

Love Pours In

Hope does not put us to shame, because God's love has been poured into our hearts through the Holy Spirit who has been given to us.

ROMANS 5:5 ESV

The invitation of God's love is always open. It is like a flowing fountain, full of the purest waters to refresh our souls. Have you been filled with this love lately? Every time we turn to the Lord, he is moving toward us in living love. The Holy Spirit pours the oil of mercy-kindness into us, and it seeps into every cell of our beings.

When was the last time you experienced the refreshing cleansing of this love, the tangible goodness of his presence? We do not need to rely on our minds; God meets us as we are, flooding our senses with the purity of his peace. Let us take this moment to invite a fresh portion, turning our attention to God with us here and now.

Holy Spirit, I'm so grateful for your ministry and presence with me. You fill me with pure love, and my heart comes alive in you. Thank you!

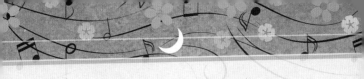

*This hope will never disappoint us,
because God has poured out his love to fill our hearts.
He gave us his love through the Holy Spirit,
whom God has given to us.*

ROMANS 5:5 NCV

Spirit of the Lord, meet me with the purity of your presence now. I'm so grateful that there is no limit to how much fellowship I can have with you. You always meet me with a fresh portion of love, and your mercies are new every moment. I will not hold myself back from coming to you as often as I think of it.

You don't require a ton of time and space; you meet me where I'm at, and you flood me with grace and strength. Even when I am working, or with others, your presence comes like a flood. I'm so very thankful for communion, for unhindered relationship. Thank you, God, for your Spirit. Fill me afresh, bringing new understanding with your wisdom. Shine the light of your glory on my mind and let me see from your perfect perspective. You astound me with your vast love!

Is your heart filled with God's love?

Limitless Love

Your mercy, LORD, extends to the heavens,
Your faithfulness reaches to the skies.

PSALM 36:5 NASB

There are no limits to God's love. He cannot be kept inside the small boxes of our experiences and expectations. He is so much greater! God's love reaches to the ends of the earth, beyond the galaxies' reach, and into eternity. It is the power that holds us to together. It sets God's promises into motion and fulfills his Word with faithful devotion.

Where we have lowered God's greatness to fit into the mold of our understanding, may we see him as the barrier-busting good God he is. His kindness cannot be measured. He is able to go beyond our knowledge of him, into the great unknown, and weave every detail of our lives together with the thread of his strong mercy. He is so much greater than we could ever give him credit for. Let's praise him today!

Kind God, how great you are! May my understanding be broadened today as you reveal new facets to your lovingkindness. There is nothing in this world better than you.

O Lord, your mercy-seat love is limitless,
reaching higher than the highest heavens.
Your great faithfulness is infinite,
stretching over the whole earth.

PSALM 36:5 TPT

Merciful Father, far be it from me to limit your love when you never do. You are lavish in kindness, and your mercy is more powerful than what I have yet witnessed. Thank you for glimpses of your goodness in my life. I have seen you work miracles of mercy as only you can. And yet, it is just a small taste of your glory. You are infinitely better than I can ever comprehend. I'm longing for the day when I stand in the fullness of your glory, face-to-face. Then I will understand, in a way that I cannot now, how wonderfully large your love really is.

In the meantime, give me revelations of your goodness that convince me that you cannot be contained by logic or reason. You are not limited by the worldviews or systems of humankind. You are so much greater. Show me your glory, Lord, and I will bow in awe of you once again.

How has God's love broken out of the box
of your expectations?

Set Free

"If you abide in My word,
you are My disciples indeed.
And you shall know the truth,
and the truth shall make you free."

JOHN 8:31-32 NKJV

If we want to truly walk in the freedom that Jesus offers, we need to stay in line with his Word. What did Jesus teach in his ministry? How did he instruct his disciples to live? What example did he make with his life? What did he promise for those who follow him?

The truth will always set us free. It does not bind us. When we surrender to God, we actually experience the liberty of his love that completely covers all our own insufficiencies. As we follow his ways, we will find the life he offers us is vibrant and so very worth it. Let us remember what Jesus promoted in his life, ministry, and Word. There we will find the truth that liberates us.

Jesus, you are the way, the truth, and the life. I come to the Father through you, and I experience the freedom of your Spirit's fellowship. Thank you for abundant life in you.

*"When you continue to embrace all that I teach,
you prove that you are my true followers.
For if you embrace the truth,
it will release more freedom into your lives."*

JOHN 8:31-32 TPT

Christ, I will continue to embrace what you taught your disciples, as displayed in Scripture. Thank you for being the living Word; you are still alive, still speaking in line with your Word, and still moving in mighty power in the earth. When I begin to lose the wonder of your living truth, remind me of your present power and support through the fellowship of your Spirit.

As I meditate on your Word, I find courage to follow along the pathways of your peace and love. Your ways are always better than the world's ways. Yours lead to truth and freedom, while the world's lead to cycles of consumption that are never satisfied. I choose you, Lord! Today, and every day, you are the leader of my life. When you speak, may my heart always listen. Your words of life change me from the inside out.

How has God's truth liberated your life?

Lasting Appeal

The world and its desires pass away,
but whoever does the will of God lives forever.

1 JOHN 2:17 NIV

How we live our lives matters. When we choose to live with love as our banner, choosing compassion in place of judgment, it makes a lasting mark that we may not even realize the true value of. When we live to satisfy our whims and desires, feeding our own bellies while ignoring the hungry around us, we will never find the contentment we seek.

Let us instead live with Jesus as our leader and example. He will lead us into everlasting life. The troubles we face here are temporary, and they will soon pass away. When we stand in the fullness of God's glory, we will not regret choosing his ways over our own. Everything else will fade away in his radiant presence.

Almighty God, thank you for the perspective shift of the importance of following your pure desires instead of my shifting whims. I know that it will be worth it, no matter the cost here and now, to follow you. Lead me on in your love.

This world and its desires are in the process of passing away,
but those who love to do the will of God live forever.

1 JOHN 2:17 TPT

Loving Father, I know that the desires of this world will not
last forever. Your will and ways prove true into eternity. May
I choose wisely and well, aligning my life with your living
Word. Keep my heart pure in your love, and teach me how
I should live, according to your Scriptures. I want to leave
an impact on future generations, not just on my own little
corner of life. Give me your greater vision and perspective,
that I might not be short-sighted.
I want to build with you an eternal impact.

Thank you for your Spirit of wisdom that reveals the
mysteries of your heart. I know that your kindness does
not change, and I am asking for a fresh visitation of your
goodness. You are so very faithful, and you always will be.
Lead me on in your everlasting ways, as you do for all of your
loyal lovers.

What is your life building toward?

Until the End

*"Teach them to obey everything that I have taught you,
and I will be with you always, even until the end of this age."*

MATTHEW 28:20 NCV

This passage is found at the end of the Great Commission,
where Jesus instructs his followers to go and make disciples
of all nations and baptize them in the name of the Father,
Son, and Spirit. Jesus' promise that he will be with his
followers always—literally all the days—is as much our
promise as his modern-day followers as it was for the
disciples he was speaking to directly.

He is with us! He will help and empower us to do everything
that he has called us to do. We don't lean on our own
understanding; rather, we follow the wisdom of his teachings
and obey him with our lifestyles. As we teach others about the
wonders of his love, we partner with his eternal purposes.

Jesus, thank you for your Word that is as true to my life as it
was to the people you lived with, walked with, and taught.
I'm so grateful for your Spirit and presence that is with me
wherever I go. With you, I can do all things!

> *"Teach them to faithfully follow*
> *all that I have commanded you.*
> *And never forget that I am with you every day,*
> *even to the completion of this age."*
>
> MATTHEW 28:20 TPT

Faithful One, I willingly follow your loving lead in my life.
You are full of perfect peace, pure love, and incomparable
wisdom. Why would I look for a better way when there is
none? As I share the ways that your love has changed me with
those around me, I trust that you will work a miracle of mercy
as only you can do in other's lives and hearts.

May I never skimp on your truth, but partnering with your
Spirit, may I boldly be able to give an account of my faith
for all who ask. There is nothing to be ashamed of in your
kindness; it is life itself. It is vibrant joy and hope. Encourage
me with your presence and embolden me with your Spirit's
life in mine. Thank you for grace that accompanies,
strengthens, and fuels my faith.

Do you believe that God will help you follow him?

Through Everything

Even if my father and mother abandon me,
the LORD will hold me close.

PSALM 27:10 NLT

Even in the midst of terrible loss, when those we love choose to leave us, God himself never will. Though we long to be held close by those we care for, the Lord will hold us closer than they ever could. Whether we have that companionship or not, God is near. His love is perfect, and it will revive hope, heal our hearts, and shine brighter and purer than any other love.

God never abandons his children—not for any reason! We can rest assured that he will always be there for us. He is a faithful and tender parent. He is full of so much affection and kindness, patience and gentleness! Though our earthly parents, friends, siblings, and lovers will all fail us in some way, God is perfect in all his ways.

Perfect Father, there is no one else like you. No one loves the way you do, so completely and full of pure kindness. Thank you for loving me well and drawing me close. Do it again, Lord.

My father and mother abandoned me.
I'm like an orphan!
But you took me in and made me yours.

PSALM 27:10 TPT

Faithful One, even when those I love and trust choose to walk away from me, I know that you never will. Keep me from projecting my own disappointments in human relationships onto your unblemished character. Your track record is perfect in love. You don't abandon your own. Never, ever. You have welcomed me into your family, and you have prepared a place for me at your table. You say that no one else can take my place in your kingdom; there is room for everyone.

Thank you for your loyal mercy that reaches out in my distress and sorrow. Draw me close in tender love when I am disillusioned in life. You are so much better than any other. I lay down my unmet expectations in life and love and ask that you would meet me with the abundance of your glorious affection. You are so rich in love, and you'll never run out.

How has God's nearness comforted you?

Endless Grace

Grace to you and peace from God our Father and the Lord Jesus Christ. I thank my God always concerning you for the grace of God which was given you in Christ Jesus.

1 CORINTHIANS 1:3-4 NASB

There is always fresh grace to meet us where we are. Today, there is a wealth of it in God's presence to strengthen you for whatever lies ahead of you throughout your day. Will you take a moment and fill up on his mercy? Ask God to give you strategies for the problems you can't solve. Ask him for his heavenly wisdom. Ask for the energy to deal with the exhausting people and situations you cannot avoid.

Let his affection for you flood your heart and overflow into your relationships. Those who have been given much have much to offer. There is no need to rely on your own strength and resources when God is your endless and ready help.

Gracious God, thank you for the reminder that I am not alone in anything. Instead of just coasting on cruise control, I yield my heart to yours today. Fill me with the goodness of your presence and pour out into every area of my life.

*May joyous grace and endless peace be yours continually from our
Father God and from our Lord Jesus, the Anointed One!*

1 CORINTHIANS 1:3-4 TPT

Father God, your peace that quiets chaos is the peace that
I long for—the peace I need. Meet me again as I look to you
this evening. Fill me with the joy of your presence. When you
shine your revelation-light on my mind, my understanding
of your wonderful nature expands. I cannot get enough of
you! You are so much kinder than I naturally am, and your
patience never runs out.

As I follow you, may my life transform into your likeness.
There is no better aim in life than to become more like you.
May your love be the banner that is lifted over my life. May
your mercy, peace, and joy be markers of your magnificent
life in mine. Thank you for fulfilling every need, satisfying
every deep desire, and for being the source of everything I
require in every moment. There is nothing your love has not
already accomplished for your glory and for my salvation.

How has God's grace strengthened your life?

Wonderful Wisdom

The wisdom from above is first pure, then peaceable, gentle, open to reason, full of mercy and good fruits, impartial and sincere.

JAMES 3:17 ESV

How many of us, when looking for advice, go to God's Word for guidance? And how often do we want the clear "do this thing" or "do that" answer? There are often no blanket answers, but his wisdom is large enough to direct us, full of grace that allows us to choose in line with his characteristics.

We can clearly see the elements that describe godly wisdom laid out in this passage from Scripture. If the wisdom we are following is pure, peace-promoting, gentle, open to reason, full of mercy-kindness and the good fruit of the Spirit, unbiased, and sincere, then it is God's wisdom! This is an amazing way to measure the kind of advice we are heeding in life. Let us take these keys into consideration and use them. And when we are offering wisdom, let us use the same gauge.

Wise One, thank you for the direction you give. Thank you for the fruit of your Spirit and wisdom that are clear indicators of a life submitted to you. Open my understanding, so that I may follow in the ways of your wisdom more and more.

The wisdom from above is always pure, filled with peace, considerate and teachable. It is filled with love and never displays prejudice or hypocrisy in any form.

JAMES 3:17 TPT

Almighty God, I look to your wisdom for guiding principles in this life. I know that your Spirit's presence in my life is a help in every area. Give me your discernment as I make decisions. I want to be aligned with your purposes and ways, not the world's. I know that your wisdom is full of love, and it does not exclude based on preferences. There is no hypocrisy in you, and I want to be full of the same kind of sincerity you demonstrate.

Though I am not perfect, I am perfected in your love. As I continually surrender my heart, my mind, and my life to you, I know that I will demonstrate the same kindness that you do. Where there is discord in my heart and life, sow seeds of peace. Where there is pride, I will humbly allow teaching by others. Thank you for your pure wisdom that sets the bar of what is right far above our actions; it includes our hearts and motivations.

What kind of wisdom are you allowing to guide you?

My Life's Song

My loving God, the harp in my heart will praise you.
Your faithful heart toward us will be the theme of my song.
Melodies and music will rise to you, the Holy One of Israel.

PSALM 71:22 TPT

Do you ever wake up with a song in your head? When that happens, it tends to stick for the day, right? What if the song we wake up singing is a reflection of our heart's fellowship with the Spirit? Then again, it could just be something that our minds remembered in sleep.

Is there a theme of God's character that you just cannot shake? Does one of his attributes hit more deeply and consistently than others? Whatever we love about God is a great place to start in praise. It's an easy access point to adoration. As you spend some time in reflection and prayer, why not incorporate a song that you love to sing?

Faithful One, I love to sing about your character. You have been so wonderful to me, and the melody of my grateful heart cannot help but spill forth. You are so good!

With the lute I will praise You—
And Your faithfulness, O my God!
To You I will sing with the harp,
O Holy One of Israel.

PSALM 71:22 NKJV

Holy One, you are worthy of every bit of worship I could ever offer you. You are worthy of my songs, and you are worthy of my time. You are worthy of my attention, and you are worthy of my life. You are worthy of it all. May I never stop singing about your faithfulness, for who else is as loyal in love as you are? You are too wonderful for words to express. You are too glorious for a melody to capture your beauty. And yet, I will try!

When words fall short, I will offer you my wordless worship. As I glorify you, will you meet me with the power of your presence? You are full of everything I could ever want. In you is all the joy, peace, and love I am looking for. I adore you!

What is your favorite song to sing to the Lord?

Joyful Freedom

I prayed to the LORD, and he answered me.
He freed me from all my fears.

PSALM 34:4 NLT

What fears have kept you from the freedom you once walked in? Are there anxieties that have overtaken your conscious thoughts? Will they just not leave? Take a moment now and pray to God. He hears you, he listens, and he answers. Pour out your heart to him; write it out if that is easier, or simply talk to God about it.

Don't hold back a thing. He does not simply hear you, waiting for you to finish so that he can say what he will. He cares about you. He listens to your heart, to all the things you want to share with him. He gladly participates, for he loves relating to you. When he speaks his truth, he will set you free. Hear his response and let him lift the burdens from your shoulders.

Victorious One, I will not hold back from you today. I offer you the specifics of worries and things that I have not been able to get off my mind. Will you respond with your Word of truth? Set me free from my fear.

Listen to my testimony: I cried to God in my distress
and he answered me. He freed me from all my fears!

PSALM 34:4 TPT

Great God, I cannot forget what you have done for me. When I cried out to you in my despair, you answered me. You freed me from fears I didn't even know I was believing. Thank you for your truth that sets my heart free. I am full of joy, for you are my rescuer and my ever-present help at all times. There is no shame that can remain when you shine your glory-light on me.

Thank you, Lord. Thank you! I will not stop looking to you, for you are better with each glance. You are beautiful in all your wonderful ways. With my life joined to yours, there is an open avenue that joy flows in from. Why would I fear when you are my God?

What answers to prayer have left you
with radiant joy as a response?

At All Times

May the Lord of peace himself give you peace at all times and in every way. The Lord be with all of you.

2 Thessalonians 3:16 NIV

There is clearly an invitation from the Lord of peace to experience his overwhelming peace in every circumstance, in every way, at all times. He is already with those of us who have yielded our lives to him. There is nothing that can separate us from his love.

Are there any areas that we don't think to ask for God to enter in with us? He is more than able, more than sufficient, more than willing to help us in every way. Let the fullness of God's presence guide, influence, and empower us to know his overwhelming shalom in our lives. This is where we find our well-being, wholeness, and restoration in his victory.

Lord, you are my present and perfect peace. Calm every chaotic thought and cycle in the overwhelming peace of your presence. In you, I am restored. I am made whole in the flood of your mercy.

May the Lord himself, the Lord of peace, pour into you his peace in every circumstance and in every possible way. The Lord's tangible presence be with you all

2 THESSALONIANS 3:16 TPT

Lord of peace, you are my plentiful portion in every single moment. As long as it is called the present, your abundance is mine. I submit my heart to your own, and let your loving redemption work out in my life. I trust your perfect love to lead me even when I cannot comprehend the wisdom of your ways. I trust you. I choose you. You have already chosen me as your own; why would I turn away? Why would I look for my own way, when yours leads to the vibrant and abundant life of your kingdom?

Spirit, come close in your tangible presence and love me to life again in your restorative mercy. Your nearness brings me incomparable joy and comfort. You always know what I need; encourage my soul. I am yours, Lord; there is no better communion than yours.

How do you experience God's peace?

My Defense

I will sing of Your power;
Yes, I will sing aloud of Your mercy in the morning;
For You have been my defense
And refuge in the day of my trouble.

PSALM 59:16 NKJV

Let us stir up the remembrance of God's wonderful works in our lives. His miracles of mercy do not leave one of his children untouched. He is our strong and mighty defense, our keeper and protector. How has his love kept us secure? Surely, there is a testimony in every life submitted to God's great care over us.

Let us look to his Word and over our own histories. Let us remember the stories of loved ones who have walked his path of love and seen the wonders of his provision along the way. Let us look to the stones of remembrance and let our hearts come alive in the awe of his faithfulness once again. Today is the day we are given; let us sing his praises, giving thanks, for he has been so faithful to us.

Powerful God, when I consider the ways that you have been faithful in the lives of your loved ones, I cannot help but grow in hope and courage for how you will continue to be loyal in love. Thank you for your faithfulness.

Your strength shall be my song of joy.
At each and every sunrise, my lyrics of your love will fill the air!
For you have been my glory-fortress,
a stronghold in my day of distress.

PSALM 59:16 TPT

Glorious One, I will not hold back my gratitude from you this evening. Your strength has been my own; I can see it so clearly! Where there was once hesitation in my heart, I now feel complete confidence in your Word. I know that I will not escape your miracles of mercy. You will continue the work that you started in my life, as well as in the lives of those who look to you. There is no reason to fear the unknown.

Every time I remember how you have come through for me, it causes my faith to grow a bit more. It is more than wishful thinking. Your tangible love and mercy have powerfully changed my life, and I know they will continue their work in me! You are so wonderful! How could I but love and adore you? Let your name be lifted high in my life.

How have you seen God's faithfulness in your life?

Ancient Path

Be mindful of your mercy, O Lord,
and of your steadfast love,
for they have been from of old.

PSALM 25:6 NRSV

The story of God's mercy is as old as time itself. Humanity has never been without it. His love is more ancient than the ruins of abandoned and forgotten cities. This same love will continue until this present earthly age passes away and we are brought into the eternal kingdom of his glory.

When we ask God to be mindful of his mercy, and to recall his loyal love, it is more a reminder to our hearts of his unchanging nature than anything else. He could not forget his love. It motivates everything he does! When we walk the path of his laid-down love, we join with those have gone before and those who will follow after. It is an ancient and proven path.

Merciful Lord, I know that you do not need to be reminded of your unfailing love; but I do. As I walk the path of your peace, submitted to your law of love, may I remember that many have gone before and overcome their fears. You are a faithful companion.

Give me grace, Lord! Always look at me
through your eyes of love—
your forgiving eyes of mercy and compassion.

PSALM 25:6 TPT

Compassionate One, thank you for your mercy that covers the failures of my youth. You have thrown the sins of my immaturity into the sea of forgetfulness, and I am covered in your redemption love. I ask for your grace to refresh my heart now as I enter fellowship with you. I don't simply want to talk to you. I want to know the give and take of real relationship. Look at me with your eyes of love and remember how you care for me as a loving parent cares for their beloved child.

I am yours, Father. You have been so good to me. I must know you more, now. I want to know what you are thinking at this moment. What are you up to?

How has God's mercy affected how you relate to him?

New Levels

He who sits on the throne said,
"Behold, I am making all things new."
And He said, "Write, for these words are faithful and true."

REVELATION 21:5 NASB

God is masterful in his restoration work, and he is incomparable in his redemption power. He takes the ashes of our defeat and tends to it until it is a garden of his glory. He is so wonderful in his ways! From moment to moment, there is always something new happening. When we look at creation, we can catch glimpses of this truth. No wave of the ocean looks the same; no snowflake is identical to another. Nature is full of similar and yet distinct particles.

Similarly, God did not create a blueprint for humans, but rather made us a unique expression of his own image. He is always up to something new in our lives. What a glorious God! He is endlessly creative, and each moment we can find a new facet to his goodness.

Creator, it is almost too wonderful to comprehend how infinitely inventive you are. You are the ultimate problem solver, for you see it all so clearly. Show me what you are doing in a new way today!

He who was seated on the throne said,
"Behold, I am making all things new."
Also he said, "Write this down,
for these words are trustworthy and true."

REVELATION 21:5 ESV

Trustworthy God, you are high and lifted up on your heavenly throne. And yet your Spirit is alive and moving in the earth, and in my very life. I am so grateful for your mercy that restores my life. You are always working, always doing something, always. Open my eyes to see what you are up to. Instead of being discouraged by the change in the world, give me eyes to see where your peace, mercy, and love are being promoted.

May I be an agent of this same kind of change, partnering with your kingdom values on earth as they are in heaven. Thank you for the fresh air of hope on the breeze of your Spirit wind that blows through the caverns of my soul. What encouragement I find in your active work in my life. Thank you!

Do you recognize areas where God is doing a new thing?

Encouragement for Today

Everything that was written in the past was written to teach us.
The Scriptures give us patience and encouragement
so that we can have hope.

ROMANS 15:4 NCV

When we meditate on God's Word, we will know the encouragement of his faithful love written out in its pages. The Scriptures instruct us in his wisdom, and they show us the values of his kingdom. If we want to know what God is like, let us look to his Word. If we want to know how to please him, his living Word will show us how. There is clear instruction to lead us to a living relationship with the Creator of all we see.

The Scriptures are not meant to stand on their own as a manual for living, but to lead us to God's greater law of love through the mercy-love and fellowship of his Spirit. He doesn't simply want followers; he wants friends who will know his heart and bear his likeness.

Living Word, teach me through the wisdom of your Scripture. When I read your Word and see how your faithfulness played out in your own timing and ways, it encourages me to hope in your timing rather than my own. Sow patience and encouragement into my heart.

Whatever was written beforehand is meant to instruct us in how to live. The Scriptures impart to us encouragement and inspiration so that we can live in hope and endure all things.

ROMANS 15:4 TPT

Holy One, may my heart be encouraged by your wise instructions to seek the ways of your kingdom. As it is in heaven, may it be on earth. May I be a promoter of your peace, full of joy, thanksgiving, and praise. May I be constantly inspired by your living Word that consistently leads me back to mercy-kindness and compassion as a way of life.

Whatever comes, whatever challenges I may face, I know that with your Spirit as my strength, source, and supply, I have all I need. I can still live a thriving from the inside kind of life, no matter the troubles I wade through. You are faithful and true, and I choose to follow you through valleys up to the mountaintops, and through all kinds of terrain between the two. I trust you more with each passing breath. You are my living hope.

How does God's Word encourage you to hope?

Spirit Help

LORD, you know the hopes of the helpless.
Surely you will hear their cries and comfort them.

PSALM 10:17 NLT

Look into your heart this morning and observe how you feel. What are your hopes? Do you feel strong in them, or are you battling weariness and heaviness? Whatever the case, take a deep breath and invite the Spirit to move into the depths of your heart. He is the lifter of our burdens and our radiant joy. In his presence is fullness. There is nothing you need to do to enter his gates today but to open your heart to him.

Let him breathe hope into the caverns of your soul. Let him light up the shadows that have hidden disappointments. Let him minister healing to your wounds. He is such a good and faithful comforter! He always hears the cries of his people. Do not hesitate in his presence today; he is full of delight and affection for you.

Loving Lord, you know my deepest hopes; I know you do not overlook them. I open my heart to you today; you are welcome into every part of it. Minister to me in your kindness and restore me in your mercy.

Lord, you know and understand all the hopes of the humble
and will hear their cries and comfort their hearts,
helping them all!

PSALM 10:17 TPT

Comforter, you are quick to reach out in lovingkindness to those who call out to you. I won't stop myself from calling on your name, for you are faithful and you comfort me with your nearness. There is nothing that your mercy cannot make completely whole in you. Reach to the recesses of my heart and flood every space with your radiant glory. Let what was dead come alive in you. Disappointed hopes, broken dreams; they are yours. Will you heal the parts of me that have been shattered by heartbreak? Only you can do it.

Thank you for your tangible presence that loves me to life, restores my hopes and completely fills my soul with radiant joy. You are my faithful help, and I won't stop singing your praises. Do what only you can do in my life, raising dry bones and breathing life into skeletons. I know that I will see your resurrection power at work!

How do you experience the comfort of God's Spirit?

Over and Over

Our fathers who were delivered from Egypt
didn't fully understand your wonders,
and they took you for granted.
Over and over you showed them such tender love and mercy!

PSALM 106:7 TPT

Our understanding of God can never diminish his wonderful and glorious love. He loves because he loves! There are no hidden motives or contingencies. Though we may take his mercy for granted, he still pours it out over and over again. He always gives generously even when we prove our inconsistency in belief.

Today, let's throw down our defenses and our disappointment in ourselves and welcome the tender love and mercy of God. He won't fail to pour it out as many times as he sees fit. He is abundant in lovingkindness, and that will never change. Instead of writing it off, or disqualifying ourselves because of our pasts, let's welcome his wonderful compassion toward us with open hearts of wonder and surrender.

Father, you are so incredibly generous with your love. I cannot comprehend how you could pour it out so freely to those who forget so quickly. May my heart be woven into yours, with gratitude as my heart's response to your mercy. Thank you!

Our ancestors in Egypt
did not learn from your miracles.
They did not remember all your kindnesses,
so they turned against you at the Red Sea.

PSALM 106:7 NCV

Merciful God, your love is incomparable; there is no human equivalent to the purity, generosity, and endless kindness of your heart. Even when we dismiss your mercy, forgetting how wonderful you have been, you still show us love again. It is almost too much to take in! Thank you for loving me so completely, and for choosing to do it over and over again. When I don't deserve forgiveness, there you are with open arms to welcome me back in and to restore relationship as if nothing had interrupted it in the first place.

May I build a practice of remembrance in my life, so that my heart softens in the great ocean of your compassion toward me. I am undone at your marvelous kindness. Thank you seems insufficient, and yet it's all that comes to mind. Thank you. Thank you for your miraculous love. Thank you!

Are you resistant or open-hearted to God's love in your life?

Unimaginable Power

He will take our weak mortal bodies and change them into glorious bodies like his own, using the same power with which he will bring everything under his control.

PHILIPPIANS 3:21 NLT

Let us not forget the incredible power that God has. Surely, we have caught glimpses of it as we have walked the path of surrender with him. What we have seen is but a glimmer of the overwhelming glory of his resurrection life. When Jesus returns, he will transform us into his likeness forever. The weakness we now know will be gone forever. There will be no more hurt, no more suffering, and no more death.

The same power that he will use to subdue nations and all creation will change our reality forever. What a glorious hope we have to look forward to in that day. Whatever we experience now is temporary, but his glory is eternal.

Glorious God, I cannot wait for the day when all wrong is made right and when our weak and decaying bodies are revived and transformed in your everlasting life. Keep my heart sown into the hope of your victorious and vibrant life that you will share with all those who believe.

Who will transform our humble bodies and transfigure us into the identical likeness of his glorified body. And using his matchless power, he continually subdues everything to himself.

PHILIPPIANS 3:21 TPT

Victorious King, thank you for the reminder of your resurrection life and power that disarms every other stronghold. May I walk in the confidence of your matchless power. I look forward to the coming age of your kingdom reign, where I will dwell with you in glory. This humble body of mine will be transformed into a glorious and eternal form.

It is difficult to imagine what this will be like, but oh how my heart hopes! Would you give me a glimpse of this greater glory as I spend time in your presence this evening? As Moses prayed in the desert, so do I tonight: show me your glory. You are faithful, and all who hope in you will not wear the shame of disappointment, but the radiance of joy in the fulfillment of your promises. Thank you for a wonderful hope!

Does thinking about eternity fill you with dread or hope?

Vulnerability

For Christ's sake, I delight in weaknesses, in insults,
in hardships, in persecutions, in difficulties.
For when I am weak, then I am strong.

2 CORINTHIANS 12:10 NIV

Paul was making a point in his letter to the Corinthians that no matter what we face in this life, we should count it all as joy. In everything, we can know God more. In suffering, we can know deeper fellowship with Jesus, for he suffered as well. Whatever we are facing, we never do it alone. Jesus knew what weakness felt like in his humanity. As his body gave way on the cross, he knew what suffering felt like.

Do we trust that in our deepest pain, Jesus understands us? Not simply because he is God, but also because he lived the life of a man. When we are weak, God's grace is our strength. Let us not despise the testing of our faith; instead, let us press into the fellowship of our Savior and help in every trouble.

Jesus Christ, may I never forget that you know what humanity is like. You limited yourself to the human experience, and yet you overcame it all by the power of your love, mingled with the sacrifice of your blood. I will delight in everything that leads me closer to you.

*I'm not defeated by my weakness but delighted! For when I feel my
weakness and endure mistreatment—when I'm surrounded with
troubles on every side and face persecution because of my love for
Christ—I am made yet stronger. For my weakness becomes a portal
to God's power.*

2 CORINTHIANS 12:10 TPT

Wonderful Savior, let the testing of the trials in this life lead
me into deeper fellowship with you. You are full of kindness
in every moment, and you meet me with your compassion
at every turn. When I have no strength left of my own, you
have an abundance that I am filled with by your grace. I will
not despise the things that cause me to run to you for help,
for there I find your overwhelming love that lifts me out of
despair.

When I am mistreated, I will not throw blame around; rather,
I will lean closer into your heart. There I find encouragement
and refreshment for my soul. You remind me of who I am and
who you are. You will not let me be crushed, and even in the
pressing, you are good.

How has your weakness caused you to lean on God?

Reliability Matters

"The one who is faithful in a very little thing is also faithful in much; and the one who is unrighteous in a very little thing is also unrighteous in much."

LUKE 16:10 NASB

In the ups and downs of life, may we remember that consistency is key. It's okay to get sidetracked; it happens to us all. There is mercy to restore us. But let's not forget that how we live affects not only us, but also those whose lives we touch. Can our loved ones rely on our word? Do we follow through with what we say we are going to do?

Let us take stock of the areas of strength we have but let us also look at how we can grow in areas that lack consistency. Perhaps we need to build better boundaries in our lives so that when we say yes to something, we have the capacity to meet that. Maybe we need to consider how much we are putting on our plates. How can we build a better foundation of faithfulness in our lives?

Faithful One, thank you for grace that strengthens me and your wisdom that brings clarity to areas I couldn't see before. Help me to know what needs repair in my relationships, and which areas of life I need to be more mindful of, so that I can be a person of my word.

> *"The one who manages the little he has been given with faithfulness and integrity will be promoted and trusted with greater responsibilities. But those who cheat with the little they have been given will not be considered trustworthy to receive more."*
>
> LUKE 16:10 TPT

Trustworthy God, I know that you see the small compliances as clearly as you do the large ones. May I never overlook the small things that require consistency. I want to be a person of integrity who is known for keeping their word. Help me to be wise in what I say yes to and what I can let go of and not take on as my responsibility.

No one has an endless capacity, except for you. I will not despise my humanity, but I am learning to lean on your wisdom to guide my choices. Keep me close in your mercy that instructs me. Let your grace cover my imperfections and lead me to repentance and restoration with others when necessary. Keep my heart humble, that no small thing would look too insignificant when it requires my attention. I know there's no shortcut to integrity; I have only to manage the little I have well until I am given more.

Are you a reliable person?

Not A Surprise

Do not be surprised at the fiery ordeal among you, which comes upon you for your testing, as though something strange were happening to you; but to the degree that you share the sufferings of Christ, keep on rejoicing, so that at the revelation of His glory you may also rejoice and be overjoyed.

1 PETER 4:12–13 NASB

None of us can escape the inevitable suffering that happens with the human experience. We will know loss, grief, and pain. We will know disappointment and hardship. This is no mystery; Jesus never promised us an easy life. And yet, he has called us overcomers, that we can know his incomparable joy even in the midst of our suffering.

When we allow ourselves to grow as we lean into the Lord and his support, we will come out of the other side of our grief with humility and gratitude.

Loving Lord, keep my heart tuned to your mercy, especially in times of anguish. I know that I cannot outrun pain, but even in the depths of it, your overwhelming love is stronger still. Keep me close in kindness and be my comforter in sorrow.

Don't be surprised at the fiery trials you are going through, as if something strange were happening to you. Instead, be very glad— for these trials make you partners with Christ in his suffering, so that you will have the wonderful joy of seeing his glory when it is revealed to all the world.

1 Peter 4:12–13 NLT

Compassionate Christ, may I never take for granted the smooth sailing times in life. And when storms come, and my world shifts, may I not be surprised by it. I know that you are with me, and that is the most important truth I can cling to. There is nothing I experience that is outside the realm of your understanding or of your redemption power.

I give you all the worries that overtake my mind in the face of the unknown. I cast my cares upon you. I tether my heart to you in hope and trust. You are my peace in the storm, my constant in the shifts of life, and my strong and mighty refuge. I trust you, Lord. Keep my heart calm, even in suffering, as I let your love minister to me in every season of the soul.

How do you react to suffering in life?

Humble Heart

He poured water into the basin,
and began washing the disciples' feet
and wiping them with the towel
which He had tied around Himself.

JOHN 13:5 NASB

In the days of Jesus, foot washing was not a ceremonial act. Rather, it was a necessary routine. After traveling dusty roads throughout the day, one's feet would be filthy. It was normally a servant's responsibility to wash feet. When Jesus chose to wash his followers' feet, it was no small act. He was humbly cleaning the dirt from them, doing the work of a servant.

They knew Jesus as their leader and teacher, and in times of revelation, as the Lord himself. Some of them resisted this act of humility at first, feeling that it was beneath Jesus to do so. When he was finished, he instructed his disciples to do the same for others, reminding them that no servant is greater than the master. How can we serve God and others in humility?

Humble Jesus, thank you for the example of love that you have set for all your followers. I am not too good to do what you have shown me to do. I am not above a single act of humble mercy. What you do, what you instruct, I too, will do.

*He poured water into a basin and began to wash his disciples' feet,
drying them with the towel that was wrapped around him.*

JOHN 13:5 NIV

Servant of all, you are the greatest example of living love.
Forgive me for the times when I have stuck in places of pride
instead of laying them down and humbly serving those whom
you have called me to love. You do not withhold mercy from
anyone, and far be it from me to assert that right.

I have received so much grace; therefore, I have so much
grace to give! Fill me with the knowledge of your loving
wisdom that prefers others over my comfort. You are the
ultimate model of humble leadership. As I recognize how
little I know, I submit my heart to what you reveal through
your living Word. I am yours, Lord—your humble servant.
Thank you for choosing me and for loving me so completely.
Where you go, I will follow. What you do, I will try to do. Give
me grace to empower me to live in the overcoming strength of
your mercy.

How does the humility of Jesus
affect your own approach to people?

Sharpened

As iron sharpens iron,
so a friend sharpens a friend.

PROVERBS 27:17 NLT

When we live our lives in community, we cannot escape the refining that happens in the overlap of our lives with one another. In family, do we not experience the range of human emotions? We are meant to learn from each other and to spur one another on in faith. But it is not always easy. Hard truths can lead us to restoration of relationship, or they can cause offense.

How we treat one another will go a long way in how much trust is present. The greater the trust, the safer the space to heal and to grow. There is great encouragement in the sharpening of our lives, in the context of loving relationship. May we be people who build each other up instead of cutting each other down. Our love is what sets us apart from those who are not in Christ. May we always remember to stay clothed in love.

Great God, would you fill me with your fresh mercy today? As I relate to those in my life today, may I be covered in the oil of your love. When I am tempted to take offense, may I instead extend mercy. You are so rich in love!

*It takes a grinding wheel to sharpen a blade,
and so one person sharpens the character of another.*

PROVERBS 27:17 TPT

Father, thank you for the sharpening of friendship. I don't want to grow lazy in love, thinking I have got it all figured out. As I interact with others, there is always an opportunity for growth. May my character continue to refine to your image. Keep me from getting stuck in my preferences and specific worldview. May I see from other's points of view with the eyes of compassion. May I offer kindness when I really want to disconnect and walk away. Cover my mind in truth, and may your love be the fuel for my choices.

Thank you for the grace of being able to practice instead of the expectation of perfection. There is so much room in your love to get things wrong and grow from experience. May I allow the same space in relationship with others—for them, and for me. Your ways are righteous, and I will follow them instead of the proud path that leads to isolation.

How have you been sharpened in your relationships?

Untold Secrets

"Call to me and I will answer you,
and will tell you great and hidden things
that you have not known."

JEREMIAH 33:3 NRSV

When was the last time you called on the Lord just to hear what was on his heart? How about the last time you turned to him simply to know him more? There is nothing wrong with coming to him in our need. In fact, it is necessary. He will always answer us. But most deep relationships are not just built on the hard times. They grow in the sharing of different contexts—of joys, of vulnerable moments, and in the ordinary.

What if today you asked God to meet you with his untold wisdom, just to hear what is on his heart? Give him space to show you what he will and let him move your heart in wonder. There is always more to discover in him.

Wonderful One, I give you space here and now to speak what you want to. What is on your mind and heart? What are you wanting to share with me? I am open and listening.

> *"Ask me and I will tell you remarkable secrets*
> *you do not know about things to come."*

JEREMIAH 33:3 NLT

Wise God, thank you for inviting open dialogue with you at all times. I want to know what's hidden in your heart. I long to know the secrets of your wisdom. Will you share your heart with me? Let me see a new perspective that up until now I didn't know existed. You are so full of grace, compassion, and mercy. You're full of glory-light that reveals who you are. As I look to you, I know that I am being transformed by your glory.

When I get too caught up in the details of my own story, will you give me eyes to see outside of myself? I want to see what you are doing in the world. I want to know what you have stored up for the future. I want to know you more, Lord! You are more beautiful than anything I've ever known, and I must know you more.

What revelations have expanded your understanding of God?

Everything Is Covered

They shall neither hunger nor thirst,
Neither heat nor sun shall strike them;
For He who has mercy on them will lead them,
Even by the springs of water He will guide them.

ISAIAH 49:10 NKJV

When God led his people into the desert, out of their captivity in Egypt, it was with signs and wonders. When we look throughout the Scriptures, we can see God's faithfulness in his tending of his people. He provided food and shelter, had unending mercy on them, and they had all they needed.

Will he not also take care of us? We are his children, and he will not let us starve. He will always provide what we need, for it is his name at stake. He is a good father, giving out of the generosity of his abundant heart of love. There is no reason to fear how our needs will get met. He will provide a way; he always does.

Gracious Father, thank you for the reminder of your faithful provision. I will not let worry shake the confidence I have in you. You are better than the best parent. I trust your provision, and more than that, I trust your heart.

They will never be hungry or thirsty.
Neither scorching sun nor desert wind will hurt them,
for he, the Loving One, will guide them
and lead them to restful, renewing streams of water.

ISAIAH 49:10 TPT

Loving One, lead me in your mercy-kindness. When I don't know which way to turn, I will trust in your guiding wisdom to direct me. As I journey along the path of this life, you will always provide for my needs. When I start to question your goodness, redirect my vision to your faithful love that never lifts from my life.

I have set my compass to the north star of your love. You are my guiding light, and I will follow you. Refresh me in the streams of your living water when I am weary. Lead me to the still waters of your restorative peace. You are faithful, God. I know it to be true. Fill my heart with hope again as I see the clear marks of your mercy in my life. You are so good!

Do you trust that God will take care of you?

Saturated

Let every activity of your lives and every word that comes from your lips be drenched with the beauty of our Lord Jesus, the Anointed One. And bring your constant praise to God the Father because of what Christ has done for you!

COLOSSIANS 3:17 TPT

Though different seasons of life will bring out different sides of us, there is a through-line that never changes. With our lives submitted to the Lord, we can always align with his loyal love. The beauty of his life in ours is seen in the companionship of the Spirit.

May our words and deeds reflect the loveliness of Jesus. Where our lives do not reflect him, there is no shame, but there is an opportunity to readjust and invite his mercy. There is so much grace! Even in repentance, we experience the beauty of his redemptive power in our lives. May we not grow weary in the glorious goodness of his life-changing love.

Anointed One, I welcome your truth and love to permeate every area of my life. May I become more and more like you as I submit my life to you over and over again. You are worth every surrender.

Whatever you do, in word or deed,
do everything in the name of the Lord Jesus,
giving thanks to God the Father through him.

COLOSSIANS 3:17 ESV

Lord Jesus, thank you for your overwhelming mercy in my life. It saturates every part, and I am continually being made new in your resurrection life and power. Let my words and actions align with your love. Where they do not, I humbly surrender my own rights and pride to the kindness of your heart. Keep me humble in your love, that I may never assert my own rights over another's.

Your love sets the captives free, and it makes the weak strong. You are my overwhelmingly great reward! There will never be a better love than the love I know in you. You accept me, convincing me that I belong in your family. When you speak, my heart comes alive. When you move, I am moved. In the light of your life, I am being transformed. You can have every part of my life!

How thoroughly is your life submitted to Christ?

Led to Life

*Godly grief produces a repentance that leads to salvation
and brings no regret, but worldly grief produces death.*

2 CORINTHIANS 7:10 NRSV

In repentance, we are restored in relationship, and the guilt
of our sins is left behind. It is good to feel remorse over
sin, for that is what leads us to the kindness of God's offer
of mercy. Repentance is an act of repairing a tear in our
connection with God. He gladly covers every sin with his
lovingkindness. There is no regret in the wholeness we find
in him.

When we are led by the sorrow of the world, there is no end
to the cycle of shame. We may have relief for a moment,
but shame keeps us captive to fear and ultimately leads to
death. The better way is clear. Let us find freedom in God's
salvation.

Merciful King, thank you for leading me to you in kindness
time and again. I choose to lay down my sin. I want out of
the cycles of sin and shame. Set me free in the liberty of your
great love.

God designed us to feel remorse over sin in order to produce repentance that leads to victory. This leaves us with no regrets. But the sorrow of the world works death.

2 Corinthians 7:10 TPT

Wise One, thank you for godly remorse that alerts me to the disruption in connection with you. Your kindness leads me back to your heart, and as I lay down the pride of going my own way, you restore the fullness of our relationship. There is victory in your love that sets me free from the claims of sin and death. Thank you for liberating me!

I have no regrets living in the great sea of your mercy, sailing with your wind directing my life. Keep my heart humble and soft in your tender love. May I never resist the pull of your compassion. As long as I journey on this side of eternity, be my guiding wind and the gauge that my life is perpetually set to. Your wisdom is my compass. My life is yours, Lord.

How has godly grief led you differently than worldly grief?

From Birth

From birth I have relied on you;
you brought me forth from my mother's womb.
I will ever praise you.

PSALM 71:6 NIV

It does not matter how long we have been consciously following the Lord. For some of us, this may have been a very early decision—for others, much later in life. Life itself is a gift from God. When we were babies, we were helpless. We relied on our parents and caregivers to give us what we needed. And, in the same way, we rely on the Creator's provision.

If we look at our lives through the lens of God's kindness, we will recognize that he was working in our stories before we even knew to look for him. As we remember how he has kept us, delivered us, and redeemed us, may praise rise from our hearts to his today.

Father of love, in you I have my being. You are the one who imagined me in the first place. I would not be here without you. You are my creator, my source, and my sustainer. Thank you for breathing life into me, both physically and spiritually! I am so grateful to be yours!

It was you who supported me from the day I was born,
loving me, helping me through my life's journey.
You've made me into a miracle;
no wonder I trust you and praise you forever!

PSALM 71:6 TPT

Mighty Protector, I will praise you, for I am fearfully and wonderfully made. You have created me in your image, and I bear your likeness simply because of the way that you made me. It seems too good to be true! I delight in your love, and I come alive in your affectionate gaze. You have done miracles in my life, doing what no other could do.

I will trust you, Lord, for you have proven faithful. You are my success, and the only reason I rise in any capacity. I am not looking to promote myself in life, but you lift me up in your time and in your way, and I cannot deny your mysterious and wonderful favor. I will praise you forever, for you always make a way for me.

Can you see God's hand on your life
even back to the beginning?

Spirit Thoughts

To set the mind on the flesh is death,
but to set the mind on the Spirit is life and peace.

ROMANS 8:6 ESV

What are you focused on most these days? It is a good practice to be mindful of your thought patterns. Where they are overly focused on the things of this world, there will be signs of exhaustion, striving, and negativity. Where there is encouragement, life, and peace, those are signs of Spirit thoughts and focus.

There is always something to look forward to in the Lord. Always more love, more mercy, and more to discover in his wisdom. There is encouragement in his living words. Let today be the opportunity that we take on the mind of Christ, as 1 Corinthians 2:16 says, aligning with his ways and motives.

Spirit, I set my mind on you today. Fill my thoughts with your living Word. Encourage me in life and peace as I rely on your wisdom. Keep my eyes set on you when I am tempted to overly focus on the minute details of my troubles. You bring relief!

The mind-set of the flesh is death,
but the mind-set controlled by the Spirit finds life and peace.

ROMANS 8:6 TPT

Lord, you are the ultimate encourager. There is so much life and peace to be found in your presence. When I am burdened down by the worries of life, I turn them over to you. I don't want to be weighed down by jumping to unnecessary conclusions. Instead of playing out countless scenarios and possibilities, I choose to trust your leadership in my life. I rest in your wisdom, letting your mercy guide me.

There is peace for the restless heart in you, and I long to know that peace so fully that, whenever it is interrupted, it takes but a moment to turn back to you. As I meditate on your Word, my thoughts are trained to look for your righteousness, love, and mercy in this world. May I continually surrender my thoughts to you. With you is life. With you is peace. With you is all I long for, and so much more.

How often do you consider the trajectory of your thoughts?

Always Known

I will be glad and rejoice in Your mercy,
For You have considered my trouble;
You have known my soul in adversities.

PSALM 31:7 NKJV

There is no situation in this life that can ever disqualify us from experiencing the immense mercy of our God and King. Whatever suffering, whatever trouble, whatever wandering way we have taken, he is as full of loyal love for us as he ever was or will be. The generosity of his kindness cannot be overstated. We can never convince him out of his compassion toward us. Even if we were to go astray, his love would not change.

Let us run into his open arms instead of staying at a distance for fear of rejection. He won't ever turn us away. He has known us in our triumphs and in our failures, and his love remains unwavering. How could we not rejoice in his goodness? He is too wonderful for words!

Merciful Father, your love is astounding. It moves me with its generosity. I cannot imagine how you love so freely; and yet, it's indicative of who you are. You are my good and faithful Father. You know me through and through. Thank you!

In mercy you have seen my troubles and you have cared for me;
even during this crisis in my soul I will be radiant with joy,
filled with praise for your love and mercy.

PSALM 31:7 TPT

Loving God, I don't even know where to begin to thank you
for your incomparable love. It is the life source of my hope,
my joy, and my peace. You are so much more than I could ever
deserve, and yet you call me your own. My soul is radiant with
joy, for you care for me so completely. Your mercy has met
me in my deepest pain and in my greatest trials. How could I
stay away from you? Your kindness is sweeter than the golden
honeycomb. Your love is richer than the most decadent
chocolate I have ever tasted.

You are life. You are peace. You are everything I have ever
wanted, and everything I didn't even know I needed. You
are more than enough, full of beauty and glory. You shine
brighter than the sun, and your love completely eclipses the
pull of lesser things. You are so much better than I could ever
thank you for. I am undone in the presence of your pure love
in my life.

Have you experienced joy in the midst of adversity?

Abundant Provision

*May mercy, peace, and love
be yours in abundance.*

JUDE 1:2 NRSV

In the endless ocean of God's love, there is always more for you. More to receive, more to strengthen, more to enlighten the eyes of your heart. There is so much more than you could ever imagine asking for. In the abundance of God's heart, there is mercy for you today. It is a fresh portion. There is plentiful peace for you.

Is your heart anxious? Are you unsettled about things going on in the world or in your life? Let the peace of God that passes understanding fill your mind and heart today. There is more than enough to calm every chaotic storm. The Scriptures remind us that God will keep those who look to him in perfect peace. Put your trust in him again; there is more than enough for all you need in the storehouses of his goodness.

Generous Father, thank you for the abundance of your love that pours out in ever-increasing measure into my life. I look to you for all that I need today.

May God give you more and more
mercy, peace, and love.

JUDE 1:2 NLT

Kind God, you are so full of abundant mercy. Thank you for never withholding your generous kindness from me when I ask for it. You give me grace that sustains me in every moment. You offer wisdom that speaks to the issues I am facing, and you direct me in the ways I should go. When I ask for more of you, more of you is what I get. Thank you for your profuse peace that fills my heart with steady focus. As I look to you, I am not disappointed. You are so much more wonderful than I anticipate at every single turn. Thank you for your persistent presence that never leaves me.

I press into know you more this evening. I want to know your thoughts and see from your perspective. May my dreams be filled with the revelations of your truth and goodness. You are my exceedingly great reward, and you are with me every step of the journey of this life. Thank you!

What do you need more of today?

Wholeness in Him

May the God who gives us his peace and wholeness be with you all.
Yes, Lord, so let it be!

ROMANS 15:33 TPT

When we submit our lives to God, he does not just make them better. He brings us healing, restoring us with the thread of his mercy. He is the fullness who brings us wholeness. We are made complete in the overwhelming goodness of his love. He is not at war with us; he is the peace giver. He restores in kindness and makes us one with him.

We have the liberty of his love that leads us into unity with his Spirit. We have unhindered access to him at all times through Jesus. We have been redeemed from the cycles of sin and shame that were our death sentence. He has made us alive in him, and no one can ever take that life away from us!

Prince of Peace, thank you for bringing me into close relationship with you. What I could never do, you have already done; you have covered me with the purity of your love and saved me from the curse of sin. Thank you for freedom in you! I could never thank you enough.

May God, who gives us his peace,
be with you all. Amen.

ROMANS 15:33 NLT

Great God, you are my peace, no matter the climate of the times. You are my wholeness, for you have brought me into the fullness of loving relationship with you. Thank you for your mercy that lifts me out of the ashes of my despair. You are my holy help at all times. You are my constant comfort when the winds of the world tear down my defenses. You are my strong and mighty shelter, unmoving in faithful love. You are my loyal friend, my gentle father, and my mighty deliverer.

You are everything I could ever dream of, and so much more than I need. You are the source of my life, and I will trust you through it all. I know you are with me. What courage and strength that is to me—that my God is with me. Thank you. Revive my heart when it wanes with worry and redirect my gaze to where you are working in restoration and resurrection power.

Are there any areas of your life
that need God's restoration power?

Life Forever

That faith and that knowledge come from the hope for life forever,
which God promised to us before time began.

TITUS 1:2 NCV

In Jesus, there is living hope. The Spirit of God has been given us to prove the power of God's Word in the world. He is our constant help, and the one who brings revelation-light to our minds and understanding. He is the harbinger of God's faithfulness and of his persistent presence with us. He is the source of our faith, and the encourager of bold trust.

Before time began, God planned for his people to live with him forever. He still promises this to us, through the ministry and saving power of Jesus' redemptive sacrifice. This life, and its temporal pleasures and pain, pales in comparison to the abundant and radiant hope we have for eternal life. Eternal life, without hidden shame or sin to separate our understanding of God, is the confident expectation of the lovers of God.

God, you are my living hope. Where there is doubt, I still choose to trust in your unfailing love and promise for eternal life. You always exceed my expectations with the reality of your overwhelming love. I trust that you will continue to do so.

This truth gives them confidence that they have eternal life, which God—who does not lie—promised them before the world began.

TITUS 1:2 NLT

Perfect Father, it is your truth that I align my life to. Jesus, I believe that you are the way, the truth, and the life. In you is found the fullness of every hope and longing. I believe that what I hope for is but a glimpse of the greater, glorious reality of the wonders of who you truly are. Give me greater revelation of your goodness as I set my eyes on you. Fill my heart with the hope of beautiful things to come in your presence. I have tasted and seen that you are good, but I know that there is so much more that I have not yet understood.

Living in open connection with you, surrendered to your will and ways, I know that I need not fear what tomorrow will bring. You are all that I need, and everything I yearn for is found in the fullness of your wonderful mercy-love. May you always be my great confidence, for I have nothing that lasts apart from you.

Are you confident that you will live forever with God?

Continual Surrender

By the help of your God, return;
Observe mercy and justice,
And wait on your God continually.

HOSEA 12:6 NKJV

It is never too late to build a life on the foundation of God's mercy. Whether you have been following him for decades or for days, each moment is a new opportunity to rely on his love. His ways are better than our own. His wisdom is purer than the logic of the world's systems. God is more reliable than the sunrise.

When we learn to wait on him, we are better for it. Instead of rushing ahead in our own strength to accomplish what we think is best, let us surrender our plans to him. As we move forward, when we know him well, we will know when to pause, when to redirect, and when to keep pushing through. Above all, may we know him well. May we love him well, being merciful and promoting justice and peace with our lives. We will not be disappointed when he is our constant help and guide.

God, I surrender my attention, my plans, and my heart to you again today. I trust that your ways are wiser than my own. Fill me with your peace and your love, both as I wait on you and when I walk with you. Thank you!

You must return to your God;
maintain love and justice,
and wait for your God always.

HOSEA 12:6 NIV

Merciful One, I return to you again now. Whenever I begin to stray on my own way, will you call me back? Will you redirect my gaze to see where I am going and where you are already? I know that your ways are just, and you always give mercy freely to all. If I am not extending kindness to my neighbor, I know that there is some redirection of my heart that needs to happen. In your love, fill me with greater understanding of your mercy. I wait on you when I don't know what to do. And I will wait on you when I think I know.

May my ears be quick to listen to your voice. Redirect my attention when I am overly focused on things that don't promote life. You are full of peace, and you are the one who wields perfect justice. I look to you now, and I will look to you whenever I think of it. I know you are worth it! Meet me with the wonders of your living love again.

How often do you turn to God in daily life?

I Am Covered

You bless the righteous, O LORD;
you cover them with favor as with a shield.

PSALM 5:12 NRSV

Where is the energy of your focus these days? Where is your emotional energy going? What are you spending your time on? Whose wisdom are you relying on? As you take stock of these things, remember that God is your covering. He is your shield. He has chosen you as his own beloved child. He has promised abundant and vibrant life in him. How does your life align with these truths? God blesses the righteous, and he covers them with his generous kindness and delight.

The fruit of your life will surely indicate who you are serving. Are love, mercy, peace, and joy evident in your relationships? Is there safety to be seen and known? Remember, our blamelessness is not found in our ability to be perfect. It is found in submission to Jesus, who is our righteousness. He is our covering.

Lord God, thank you for giving me good standing with you. It is not by anything I could ever earn, but through grace alone. As I submit my heart and will to you again, will you fill my life with the fruit of your Spirit's work in me? Thank you!

Lord, how wonderfully you bless the righteous.
Your favor wraps around each one and covers them
under your canopy of kindness and joy.

PSALM 5:12 TPT

Wonderful Lord, thank you for the rich blessings you pour out on your children. There is nothing I could do to win your favor. You just love me! I am undone in the overwhelming goodness of this truth. Your mercy is unlike any love I've ever seen on this earth. You wrap your delight around me and love me to life over and over again. You restore what no one else can. You bring hope to the barren areas of my life, and I see your restoration working out in my heart. Thank you!

I am living under the banner of your kindness and your irresistible joy. How could I but give you back everything you have offered me? You can have my life. You can have it all. There is nothing that can compare to the awe-inspiring abundance of your favor. I am so incredibly grateful to know you and to be known, loved, and accepted by you.

Have you been trying to earn God's favor or joyfully living from a place of belonging?

Renewed Strength

"You were tired out by the length of your road,
Yet you did not say, 'It is hopeless.'
You found renewed strength,
Therefore you did not faint."

ISAIAH 57:10 NASB

There are times in life when we cannot meet the overwhelming demands of family, work, and life, in general. We cannot escape the sting of grief that limits our capabilities. We can't outrun the pain of health struggles. But there is a better way to cope than just running until we can't go any longer. We are not meant to push ourselves so hard that we end up completely depleted.

God is full of grace, and it is our strength. Let us find the rest we long for in the presence of our constant help and comfort. There is peace always available. There is mercy to cover what we cannot. There is power for miraculous transformation. Let us press into the abundant provision of God. Let us lay down our defenses, submit our weak offerings, and partner with the one who overcame death itself. There is joy, life, and peace in generous measure, no matter what we are facing.

Gracious God, I give up trying to meet endless needs. That's not my job. Keep me close in your mercy and fill me with the strength of your grace and the resolve of your love. Thank you for abundant provision every day.

> *"You grew weary in your search,*
> *but you never gave up.*
> *Desire gave you renewed strength,*
> *and you did not grow weary."*

ISAIAH 57:10 NLT

Merciful One, I will not give up looking for you. I won't stop searching my life for the evidence of your presence. You say that you will never abandon those who look to you. Thank you for the promise of your presence. Thank you for the strength of your grace that is made perfect in my weakness. You are my hope, Lord, and my hope will not be dashed. When I am too tired to keep going, I lay back in the arms of your loving embrace. You fill me with love, and you revive my heart.

Teach me to live with rhythms of rest so that I will not wear out. Your pace is different from the world's, and I'm taking my cues from you. I will live in the wisdom of your ways. Lead me, and I will follow, for I know that you are good. You are encouragement to my soul, and you are the radiant light I look to.

Are you on the road to burnout?

Tenacity

Remember to stay alert and hold firmly to all that you believe.
Be mighty and full of courage.

1 CORINTHIANS 16:13 TPT

When we are bombarded by differing opinions through media, society, and through forms of social connection, how can we remain strong in faith? Let us remember the defining characteristics of God's kingdom. Where mercy reigns, justice is the Lord's, and peace is a lifestyle. Let us not mindlessly consume what is put out there for us, but instead fill our minds with the Word of God.

When we focus on who God is, who he says we are, and his guiding wisdom, we will have the boldness that we need to stay strong in courageous love. We are not meant to be tossed by the shifting winds and opinions of this world but anchored by the truth of God's mercy.

Wise God, thank you for the reminder to stay alert in this life. Help me to see from your perspective when I am limited in my thinking. Fill me with courage as you strengthen my heart with your living hope.

Be on your guard;
stand firm in the faith;
be courageous; be strong.

1 CORINTHIANS 16:13 NIV

Living Word, you are my hope, my strength, and my firm foundation. You offer the wisdom of your Word that guides me in the ways of your life. Keep me on the path of peace when the world is shouting for me to fight my neighbors. May my life be lined in your mercy, that I may extend kindness to those I would otherwise judge. I don't want to be fooled into thinking that my ways are the right ways. Yours are. And there is so much room in your love to be different.

I will stand on the bedrock of your loving-kindness. I will not let fear fuel my opinions. You are full of righteous truth for all who look to you. I am looking to you, Lord. Keep me strong in the humility of a life of submission to your heart. I know that strength in spirit may look different from the world's definition of power. May I be full of faith, aligned in your love, and courageous in offering mercy.

How mindful are you of what you
are taking in from the world?

Fullness of Life

You make known to me the path of life;
in your presence there is fullness of joy;
at your right hand are pleasures forevermore.

PSALM 16:11 ESV

We are not meant to simply get by in life. Even in suffering, we can know the overwhelming goodness of God's comfort and presence. There is fullness of joy in fellowship with the Spirit of God. There are endless pleasures to be found in the kingdom of our great God and King.

He has made known the path of life; he has not hidden it from our sight. When we follow the path of love that Jesus outlined with his life, his message, and his death and resurrection, we find the abundance of living hope that walks with us. May we never settle for less than God has for us! Let us press into his presence, for he is with us. There, we will find renewed strength, courage, peace, and joy for every step of our journey.

Joyful King, I am overwhelmed by your goodness! You are full of delight, and the compassion of your heart is overflowing in my life. Thank you for loving me, choosing me, and filling me with your presence.

You will show me the way of life,
granting me the joy of your presence
and the pleasures of living with you forever.

PSALM 16:11 NLT

Great God, show me the way of life, and I will walk in it. Fill me with the joy of your presence, and I will never be without gratitude. There is so much pleasure in this relationship. You have poured out abundant mercy, and it has changed my life—and still continues to. Your living Word is working out miracles of restoration and redemption in ways that are too wonderful to fathom. You are better than anyone could ever fully portray, and you are my God.

I'm so grateful for your presence in my life. I'm overwhelmed by the consistency of your kindness toward me. May my life be filled with the fingerprints of your nature, flowing out to touch the lives of all I come into contact with. I choose your ways, Lord, above my own. I humbly surrender to your love. Keep me close here.

How has the fullness of God changed your life?

Timing

For every matter there is a time and judgment,
Though the misery of man increases greatly.

ECCLESIASTES 8:6 NKJV

When we grow tired of waiting on God's promises to be fulfilled, how do we stay lined in his love? God can handle our frustrations and our questions, so we can freely give them to him. In the end, doesn't it always come down to trust? Will we choose to trust that God is as faithful as we hope him to be? Will we rest in his all-knowing and powerful ways?

We may think we know what is best for our lives, but the truth is that God sees much more clearly than we ever could. He sees every detail of our lives and the effects of the choices of others. We cannot control an outcome, but God will always use what is there to bring restoration and redemption. He never fails, and he never will. Let's continue to place all our bets on him.

Great God, though I may grow tired of waiting, I know that your ways are perfect. You have not missed a detail, and you will do what you have said you will when the time is right. May my heart grow in trust of your character as you continue to faithfully come through for your people.

There is a right time and a right way for everything,
yet people often have many troubles.

Ecclesiastes 8:6 NCV

Holy One, I trust your perfect timing even when it conflicts
with my preferences. May my heart stay soft and humble
in your love, not rushing ahead to judgments that I am not
equipped to make. May I be quick to forgive, extending
kindness and the benefit of the doubt to those I would rather
shut down and out of my life. As I put up boundaries to
protect my peace, I will not let walls of offense be raised with
them. May I be patient, and trust that you will not forget a
single promise you have made.

I love you, and I trust you. You are endlessly good. I will
follow your example as long as I live, and I will reject the fear
and judgments of those who try to keep you small. You are
greater than any of us could boast you to be. Have your way,
Lord, and draw me closer in love every step of the way.

Do you trust that God's timing is perfect?

Justice

The Lord waits to be gracious to you,
and therefore he exalts himself to show mercy to you.
or the Lord is a God of justice;
blessed are all those who wait for him.

ISAIAH 30:18 ESV

God is full of endless mercy, but he is also the God of justice. Let us not forget that it is his duty to judge people's hearts, motivations, and lives. It is not our job, and it never will be. We may advocate for the defenseless, and we may seek justice for the helpless. We must be people who are marked by his mercy—not simply in the receiving, but in our lifestyles. If we are not merciful, how will we receive mercy?

May God help us see the difference between fighting for and fighting against. We fight for justice, peace, and mercy. Let us not confuse condemning wicked systems with judging and condemning people to hell. The Lord is just, and he is perfect in all of his ways. Let us look to him as the ultimate defender, advocate, and judge.

God of justice, you alone can rightly judge the heart of a person. When I am tempted to condemn a person's life, would you remind me of your mercy that is gracious and patient? May I stay rooted in your love, above all else.

The LORD must wait for you to come to him
so he can show you his love and compassion.
For the Lord is a faithful God.
Blessed are those who wait for his help.

ISAIAH 30:18 NLT

Lord, you are so patient in love, and you long to show your mercy to all. Far be it from me to rush your justice. You have not called me to apathy, for that is the opposite of love. You have called me to mercifully advocate kindness to all. May I follow your loving and long-suffering example.

Fill me with your peace, that I may have peace to offer. Fill me with your joy, that I may have joy to give. I entwine my heart in you, for you are my courageous hope and the fulfillment of everything I long for. Without you, I would waste away. But in you, I am revived over and over again in the abundance of your love. Thank you!

Do you believe that God's justice is enough?

Worn Down

Lord, have mercy, because I am in misery.
My eyes are weak from so much crying,
and my whole being is tired from grief.

PSALM 31:9 NCV

The mercy of God is more than sufficient for every season of the soul. When we are filled with the joy of celebration, and when we are brought low in times of overwhelming grief, his love meets us with the same generosity of his heart. It is not a failure to suffer, and it is not unspiritual to struggle. God accepts us as we are at all times. He welcomes us with kindness and covers us in his compassion. We are never without it.

When we feel confident about his affection and when we question his tenderness, he is the same giving God. He never stops loving us, so let's not keep ourselves from coming to him over and over again.

Merciful God, I come to you today an open heart. You see so clearly what is weighing me down. Would you be the lifter of my head? Comfort me, Lord, for you are my only hope.

O Lord, help me again!
Keep showing me such mercy.
For I am in anguish, always in tears,
and I'm worn out with weeping.
I'm becoming old because of grief;
my health is broken.

PSALM 31:9 TPT

Kind Father, when I cannot stop crying, you are there to wrap your comfort around me. You soothe my soul with the calming peace of your presence. Heal me, Lord, and I will be whole. Lift my burdens, and I will have joy again. Do what only you can do and minister to the depths of my pain. Restore my shattered hopes and broken dreams in your redemptive power. Put me back together in your love, that I may know the incomparable kindness of your resurrection life in mine.

I trust you, Lord. You are full of mercy all the time. You are overflowing in peace that surpasses my understanding. I stand under the waterfall of your grace today. Refresh me and revive my heart once again. You are the one I look to, for no one else can heal me the way that I know you can and do.

When you are worn down by grief, how do you cope?

Overflowing Mercy

The Living Expression became a man and lived among us! And we gazed upon the splendor of his glory, the glory of the One and Only who came from the Father overflowing with tender mercy and truth!

JOHN 1:14 TPT

If we struggle to pin down God's mercy in living examples, we have the perfect life to look to. Jesus was not just an exemplary human; he was and is the Son of God. If we want to know what the loving-kindness of God looks like, looking at the life and ministry of Jesus is the right place to start.

May we never fall into the trap of thinking that we can exaggerate the mercy of God. His grace cannot be overstated. It is generous, as we see through the ministry of Christ. Father, Son, and Holy Spirit are unified in purpose and in character. What one is, the others also are. The Godhead is always overflowing with mercy toward us. May we openly receive the love of our great God, letting it change our lives.

Lord God, may I never be so bold to think that I have a full grasp of your infinite wisdom. I lean into your love, knowing that it is what I need in every moment. Fill me afresh and transform my life with the miracles of your mercy.

The Word became flesh and made his dwelling among us.
We have seen his glory, the glory of the one and only Son,
who came from the Father, full of grace and truth.

JOHN 1:14 NIV

Living Word, thank you for making your dwelling among us, and for making a way to know you in spirit and in truth. There is no better way than you. There is no richer life than the life I find in you. I have caught glimpses of your glory, and it leaves me longing for more revelation. I want that fullness!

Keep me close to your heart as I follow your loving lead in this life. You who are full of grace and truth, you are my wonderful hope. The beauty of Jesus is unlike any other—full of pure love, mercy, and truth. You are the living expression of God, and you are the one I fix my eyes on. Show me your ways, show me your power, and show me your glory. You are wonderful, and I will not stop looking to you.

What has God's presence taught you about his mercy?

Transformed

Let no one deceive himself. If anyone among you seems to be wise in this age, let him become a fool that he may become wise.

1 CORINTHIANS 3:18 NKJV

We become more and more like the things we spend our time focusing on. The thoughts of our mind are not to be overlooked. Where is our attention most of the time? The things that we focus on are the same things that will change us. In relationship, this is also true. Who do we spend most of our time with? What kind of people are they? Whether we acknowledge it or not, the people we are around will affect us, for better or worse.

Let us be purposeful in our relationships and in our thinking. Let us be purposeful with our time and our lives. If we want to know God more and become more like him, we must spend time with him as well. Let today be a day filled with intention, purpose, and open connection with the Lord.

Spirit of the Lord, I look to you now. Meet me with the overwhelming peace of your presence and transform me into your likeness as I turn my attention to you over and over again.

Why fool yourself and live under an illusion? Make no mistake about it, if anyone thinks he is wise by the world's standards, he will be made wiser by being a fool for God!

1 CORINTHIANS 3:18 TPT

God, I know your wisdom is so much better than the logic of the world. I won't hold myself back from you this evening. Shine your revelation-light in my mind and show me the beauty of your goodness. I don't want to go my own way, living in the limits of my understanding. I yield my heart to yours, and I submit my mind to your wonderful wisdom.

Lead me, and I will follow. Show me your great love, and I will pour my love on you in return. Transform me into the likeness of your Son as I meditate on your truth. Thank you for the overcoming power of your love in my life. Thank you for choice and for agency—that I get to decide how I will live. Living in the light of your overwhelming love makes that choice much clearer. There is no one else like you in all the world. Even if I look like a fool to the world, I will still choose you.

How are you being transformed in thought and deed?

Seeds Sown

*Those who sow in tears
shall reap with shouts of joy.*

PSALM 126:5 ESV

In life, we will encounter seasons of deep sorrow, times when we cannot pull ourselves from the depths of grief that we must wade through. But Jesus is our constant help. The Spirit of God is our close comforter and faithful friend. He lifts us up when we are bowed low, and he soothes our aching hearts with his nearness. We cannot run from the angst of heartache, though we may wish to. Instead, let us welcome God into the process with us. God promises that those who sow in tears will reap with shouts of joy.

What we cannot understand in the depths of our pain is that the tears we shed are watering the seeds of our healing and our hope. When the seeds mature and break ground, we will be overjoyed with the fruit that is produced. With deep gratitude, we will see that nothing is wasted in God's hands.

Faithful One, thank you for being with me in every single season of the soul. When I am overcome with sadness, you are near. When I am full of joy, you are just as close. May I remain close to your heart, that I may know the confidence of your presence beyond the understanding of my mind.

*Those who sow their tears as seeds
will reap a harvest with joyful shouts of glee.*

PSALM 126:5 TPT

Wonderful God, thank you for the freedom to express the myriad of my emotions without hesitation about how you will receive me. You are amazing in kindness, faithful in patience, and always, always overflowing in loving affection. I won't stay away from you. When I am filled with the heartbreak of grief, will you hold me close? As I weep, I know that you will not let a single tear go to waste. You are the God of restoration, redemption, and reconciliation. What you are doing, no one can stop. Do your wonderful work in me even when I cannot fathom what it could be.

You are consistently better than I imagine you to be. You are weaving the beautiful thread of your mercy through every facet of my life. You don't miss a thing. Though I only see in part now, I know that one day I will see clearly. When I am in the fullness of your presence, you will make the mysteries as plain as day, and reveal the whole picture that I cannot contain in my understanding now. Even so, Lord, give me a glimpse of you this evening.

How has God's joy transformed your seasons of sadness?

Out of My Hands

We can make our plans,
but the LORD determines our steps.

PROVERBS 16:9 NLT

There are so many dreams and plans that we can make for our lives, and there is nothing wrong with that. We were created to envision our futures and to work toward goals. We were, after all, created in the image of the ultimate Creator. We dream of what we can build with our lives. Hopefully, we are not overly focused on what we can consume, but on what we can offer the world to make it a more peaceful, loving place.

In any case, whatever path we are taking in this life, may we keep an open heart with trust in the Lord as an anchor for our souls. Our plans will not always work. Our hopes may not materialize the way that we envision. But that does not mean that we have utterly failed. Let us trust in the Lord more than we trust in ourselves. He never wavers in love, and he always knows what he is doing. When we are at a loss, he is not. We can be confident in this: God will fulfill every promise and plan that he has made. Let's follow him even when our own plans fall apart.

Lord, thank you for your leadership in my life. I will follow you, growing in trust and in connection with you. You are wiser than I am, and I trust you.

Within your heart you can make plans for your future,
but the Lord chooses the steps you take to get there.

PROVERBS 16:9 TPT

Faithful Father, I am so grateful for your infinite wisdom that sees everything with clarity. There are no mysteries to you. You are able to see all options clearly, and you lead your people faithfully. Even when I start to wander off on my own way, you lead me back in your lovingkindness.

I will hold more tightly to you than I do to the plans of my heart. You know my longings, and there is little I can do to fulfill them outside of myself. I will continue to walk in faith, trusting that your hand will guide me along the way. Give me the grace and vision to build a life instead of just letting it happen to me. Thank you for the ability to choose, and the greater ability to trust you when I cannot understand. I will do what I know to do, and in the unknown, I will let faith guide me. I know that I can depend on you, for you never fail. I will praise you along the journey, for I get to know you more every step of the way.

Do you trust God to guide you in his goodness?

Lean on Others

Confess your sins to each other and pray for each other so that you may be healed. The earnest prayer of a righteous person has great power and produces wonderful results.

JAMES 5:16 NLT

There is power in community, and there is strength in family. We are not meant to journey through this life alone. There are definitely times that we might feel lonely. We are created for relationship—not just with God, but with one another. Do you have close fellowship with others who are following the Lord? Do you have people who will pray for and with you?

If not, there is an invitation here to find fellowship with other believers. We will find our faith being strengthened in the ability to share with, rely on, and encourage one another in life. Ecclesiastes 4:12 says that though a person standing on their own can be easily attacked and overtaken, they can conquer when they stand together, for a "triple-braided cord is not easily broken." We are stronger together.

Mighty God, thank you for the reminder today of the importance of fellowship with other believers. I am grateful that you set us in family and do not require us to do anything alone. You are so wise.

Confess and acknowledge how you have offended one another and then pray for one another to be instantly healed, for tremendous power is released through the passionate, heartfelt prayer of a godly believer!

JAMES 5:16 TPT

Good Father, may I never take for granted the goodness found in fellowship with your people. There is power in confession, for there is an opportunity for restoration and healing. There is so much strength in standing in solidarity with one another in prayer. When I don't know what else to do, there is always prayer. And it is powerful and effective. May I never forget that!

This evening, I am lifting up the needs of those I love and of those who are heavy on my heart and mind. Move in powerful ways in the lives of those you love, Lord. Do not hesitate to move in power, for our need is eclipsed by your great abundance. Teach me to lean into your Spirit even more as I constantly offer up prayers for those around me as I see needs. And may I never withhold my support from those I can help, any time I am able to meet a need. Make me more like you, and even more so as I live in the context of community.

Who can you reach out to today for confession, encouragement, or prayer?

Lasting Peace

"Peace I leave with you; my peace I give to you. I do not give to you as the world gives. Do not let your hearts be troubled, and do not let them be afraid."

JOHN 14:27 NRSV

What is troubling your heart today? Is there a worry that you have been unable to shake on your own? Take this opportunity today to invite God's peace into your being. He will settle your uneasy heart with the calming clarity of his presence. Whatever your concerns, you can be confident in the everlasting love of your faithful Father. He has not changed his mind from his mercy-kindness. He is just, and he will do all that he has set out to do—in your life and in the greater world.

He is not weary. He is not tired. Rely on his strength and be encouraged by his peace, which can never be upset by the state of the world. He gives freely from his generous heart. Let his peace cover you. Put all your trust in him, for he is constant and reliable.

Prince of Peace, you are my holy hope. I open my heart, my arms, and my life to you once again. Come and fill me with the perfect peace of your presence, and let every fear settle in the brilliance of your lavish love.

"I leave the gift of peace with you—my peace. Not the kind of fragile peace given by the world, but my perfect peace. Don't yield to fear or be troubled in your hearts—instead, be courageous!"

JOHN 14:27 NKJV

God, thank you for the gift of your perfect peace. It is better than the harmony of the world that lasts for a moment and then is upset by conflicting interests. Your peace is not fragile but incredibly strong and constant. It is dependent on your character, not on the current state of affairs in the world. It is my plentiful portion at every moment, in every storm surge and in every bright and clear day.

You give me confidence as you flood my awareness with the clarity of your peace that calms the chaos and confusion of the world's shifting winds and ways. I take courage in your persistent presence that covers me. I will boldly keep following you on your path of love, promoting your lasting peace every step of the way.

How have you known God's peace in adversity?

A Way Prepared

"Build up, build up, prepare the road!
Remove the obstacles out of the way of my people."

ISAIAH 57:14 NIV

There is an open road to heaven's gates laid out before us. The courts of our great God and King are welcoming and accessible to all who will enter in. His Word says that he offers peace to those who are far from him and peace to those who are near (Isaiah 57:19). Jesus made it clear through his life and through the ministry of his Word that all who want to come to the Father must come to him first.

Through Jesus, we are able to enter into unhindered connection with the Father of glory. There are no hoops to jump through, no moving targets to master in order to know God. In submission to God, through faith in Jesus, and in the aligning of our lives with his loyal love, we find ourselves at home in him, with no obstacles to separate us from God.

Jesus Christ, thank you for leading the way to the Father. Thank you for redeeming me out of the bonds of sin and death and leading me into life everlasting. There are no more obstacles to overcome to know you.

> *"Let the people return to me.*
> *Build! Build up the road, clear the way, and get it ready!*
> *Remove every obstacle from their path."*
>
> Isaiah 57:14 TPT

Father, I return to you. I do it over and over again as I realize my wandering ways. Thank you so much for your grace that empowers me to know you. Thank you for mercy that covers the error of my ways. You are greater than any pride I have in myself. You are better than the greatest teachers I have known. I can hardly imagine that you never hold my sin against me. You are magnanimous in kindness, always seeking restoration of relationship. There is nothing more that need ever be done.

I submit myself to you again, Lord. You are so worthy of my attention, my humility, and my very life. As I walk in the path of your surrendered love, would you remove the obstacles from my life that may keep others from knowing you through it? In the end, I know that the fruit of your Spirit is all that matters. As I live for you, may my life be filled with evidence of your life in mine.

Is there anything that has kept you from unhindered
relationship with the Lord?

Patience

The Lord is not slow about His promise, as some count slowness, but is patient toward you, not wishing for any to perish but for all to come to repentance.

2 PETER 3:9 NASB

Though we see through the lens of our preferences and timelines, God's ways are bigger than our understanding. When things aren't going as we planned, and when progress isn't as quick as we had hoped, what then? Do we give up and go on our way, or do we understand that patience is a part of the progression and should be a practice? Time will pass either way; will we trust God's timing and wisdom, or will we insist on quick fixes and turnarounds that won't truly fulfill?

Lasting change and transformation require patience in the process. God has not changed his mind about his mercy. Are we as convinced of his faithful love, or are we easily talked out of his goodness? He is patient with us, so let's learn to patiently wait on him.

Lord, I realize that your timing takes things into consideration that are not in my ability to comprehend. Teach me to practice patience as I lean into your presence that never leaves. Thank you for grace that helps me.

*Contrary to man's perspective, the Lord is not late with his promise
to return, as some measure lateness. But rather, his "delay" simply
reveals his loving patience toward you, because he does not want
any to perish but all to come to repentance.*

2 PETER 3:9 TPT

Merciful God, as I meditate on your constant faithfulness,
will you expand my understanding of your wonderful
kindness? Thank you for patience that does not want anyone
to miss out on the saving power of your mercy. As I come to
know your love in deeper ways through the experience of
fellowship with you through the valleys and the mountaintops
of life, may I grow in more confident trust of your timing and
your ways.

You are so good, God. I can clearly see your kindness on display
in my life. Your tender affection lightens the load as you lift
every worry from my shoulders. I rest in the confidence of your
faithful love that sees everything clearly. You will not fail us.
You are my freedom and my joy, and I will keep pressing into
knowing you more.

What place does patience have in your life?

God's Terms

*It depends not on human will or exertion,
but on God, who has mercy.*

ROMANS 9:16 ESV

It is such a beautiful and marvelous mystery, the mercy-kindness of God. We have been saved through faith, and brought into the kingdom of God's kindness, not by anything we offer, but because of his love that was poured out in his death. His resurrection power is our hope of everlasting life. It is not based on our actions. What a relief!

It doesn't matter how many times we mess up or fail; our mistakes are not weighed against our victories. They have been engulfed in the bottomless sea of God's mercy. He does not hold our sins against us. When we surrender our lives to him, we are forever changed by his fellowship. Let's take the pressure off of proving ourselves, and instead press into knowing and loving him, just as we are fully known, loved, and accepted by him.

Wonderful Savior, thank you for making a way to know you where before there was an impossible standard. As I follow you on your path of surrendered love, I find all the strength I need to know you more. You are my greatest reward; in fellowship with you, I find abundant life.

God's choice doesn't depend on how badly someone wants it or tries to earn it, but it depends on God's kindness and mercy.

ROMANS 9:16 TPT

Kind God, I am so grateful for your wonderful mercy. It is the lifeblood of my faith, and it is more than I could ever imagine or earn on my own. Reveal the lengths of your love in new ways to me today, that I may see an aspect to your incomparable character that I have not yet known. You never withhold your love from me; how could I ever thank you? You are the originator of my faith; even the seed that was planted in me was from you. Nothing I have been offered in you was ever dependent on my own goodness or ability. I will not let pride puff me up, leading me to think that I deserve your mercy more than another.

As you cover me in your compassion, I am compelled to extend the canopy of your compassion to others. What a gift! What a marvelous reality. I am more thankful than I could ever express. You are worthy of all I could ever offer you in return. Be glorified in me.

Are there any areas where you are trying
to prove yourself to God?

Taken Care Of

"People everywhere seem to worry about making a living, but your heavenly Father knows your every need and will take care of you."

LUKE 12:30 TPT

Throughout Scripture, there are numerous examples of God reminding his people that he is faithful and trustworthy. He tells his people over and over again to not be afraid but to be courageous. He reminds us that he is with us, and we never go into any circumstance alone. When Jesus gave his Sermon on the Mount, he gave many examples of how the Father provides for the birds of the air and the lilies of the field.

If in nature, all is provided, how much more will he provide for his people? He was making a case for people to trust God and to confidently follow him. God is our provider. He encourages us to lay aside every worry and care and to focus on him. In fact, he says that worry is wasted energy. How much energy have we been wasting when we could have been resting in trust?

God, my faithful provider, thank you for the reminder of your trustworthy character. You have more resources than the wealth of the entire world. Why would I worry when you are my provider? I will rest in your watchful care instead.

"These things dominate the thoughts of unbelievers all over the world, but your Father already knows your needs."

LUKE 12:30 NLT

Good Father, I am so thankful that I don't have to continually advocate for myself. You already see and know every need I have before I even realize it's there. You are attentive to my life, and you always know exactly what I require. Thank you for your faithful love that meets me with abundance and generosity, no matter my circumstances. There is no need for me to worry about a thing, for you have it all covered.

Lead me in the persistent peace of your presence and calm my heart with the confidence of your love. I will lay aside every anxiety and offer you every fear. Come in and expand my awareness and understanding of the grand scope of your mercy that doesn't miss a single detail. You are trustworthy; I have placed my life in your hands, and I won't try to take the reins back. You are more dependable than I can grasp, so I choose to trust you again and again.

What worries can you give to God today?

Strong in Joy

"Don't be sad, because the joy of the Lord
will make you strong."

NEHEMIAH 8:10 NCV

There is a place for sadness and a place for weeping. There is a time for it. But there is also a time to enter into the joy of the Lord. The people of Israel had gathered and were listening to the words of the Law being read. As they listened, many started weeping, for they were gaining understanding of the meaning behind the Book of the Law.

This is the response of people understanding the error of their ways; it is godly grief that leads to repentance. However, Nehemiah, the Levites, and Ezra encouraged the people to go and celebrate. Instead of wallowing in regret and sadness, they went and celebrated with great joy that they had heard and understood the Word of the Lord. This is a great reminder for us when we are convicted of sin. Sadness and regret are not a place to stay; we are to celebrate with thanksgiving the wonderful mercy of our Lord.

Lord, thank you for your forgiveness. Thank you for your mercy. I will not stay in the sadness of my wrongdoings, but I will rejoice today in the abundance of your mercy-kindness, for you have set me free to know you in spirit and in truth.

"Do not grieve, for the joy of the Lord is your strength."

Nehemiah 8:10 NIV

Great God, your joy is my strength. You make a feast and celebration out of the error of my ways. Whenever your people understand your heart and nature, you cause them to rejoice! May I sow into my life a rhythm of joy and celebration whenever I understand your love in a new way. Instead of wasting energy on regret, you draw me into the embrace of your unrelenting love that erases the shadows of my wicked ways.

You are so much better than any other love. Yours is not contingent upon anything I can ever do, say, or earn. You give freely to all who seek you. I listen with an open heart and mind today to your living Word of truth. Transform my heart in the glory of your goodness. You are marvelous. You are wonderful. How could I not celebrate the wonders of your kindness?

How have you experienced the strength of God's joy?

Consider It

*If you are truly wise, you'll learn from what I've told you.
It's time for you to consider these profound lessons of God's great
love and mercy.*

PSALM 107:43 TPT

There is wisdom to be found in humility. When we think we know everything we need to already, there is no room to grow in understanding. Are we leaning into the heart of God with hearts that are open to teaching, transformation, and reconsideration? Let us lead with modesty, for then we will be more moldable to God's great mercy.

When was the last time you changed your mind about something? If you are so set in your ways that you cannot see another point of view, you may find it difficult to relate to others and to God. Keep a humble heart before God and people, and you will learn from the faithfulness of the Lord.

Mighty God, I humble myself before you today. Teach me, and I will learn from you. Let me not join with those who are wise in their own eyes, but instead may my heart remain pure in seeking you and your kingdom.

Those who are wise will take all this to heart;
they will see in our history the faithful love of the LORD.

PSALM 107:43 NLT

Father, teach me your ways according to your wisdom. I want
to follow on your path of mercy-kindness that leads straight
to your kingdom. You have been so faithful to your people,
and I believe that you will continue to be. My life is tethered
to yours through Jesus, and I am free in the liberty of your
love. Thank you for your generous goodness. Thank you
for patience, and that you do not rush a thing. May I learn
how to slow down in your love and enjoy the communion of
fellowship with you, reveling in the peace of your presence.

I will not forget what you have already done for me, and I
know that you do not abandon your people or your promises.
You, who have been trustworthy from the beginning, are still
dependable today. May I grow in your wisdom as I continue to
grow in relationship with you. I am grateful to be yours.

How have you grown in wisdom?

Once Again

You will increase my honor,
and comfort me once again.

PSALM 71:21 NRSV

God is full of new mercies every morning. We have heard it time and again, have we not? Lamentations says that the faithful love of the Lord never ceases, and his mercies never come to an end. If God's mercies are new with the dawning of a new day, let us remember that each day is a new opportunity to turn to the Lord. It is a fresh chance to receive from the outpouring of his love.

This present moment is all that we have. Will we waste it worrying about the next, or will we learn to let God meet us in every single one? With each breath, we are surrounded by his love. We are never without it, and we are never without him. May we turn our attention to God who meets us with everything we need in every moment. He is so generous.

Comforter, thank you for your presence in my life. I don't have to reach back into my memory to find you, and I don't need to lean into the future to grab hold of you. You are here right now. I'm so grateful!

*You will restore me to even greater honor
and comfort me once again.*

PSALM 71:21 NLT

Restorer, thank you for never giving up on me. Every moment is an opportunity to know you more. Would you reveal your kindness to me in a way that meets me where I'm at in this moment in my life? You always know better than I even know how to ask, making me feel so seen and loved.

Comforter, when I need solace, draw me into the embrace of your peace. Redeemer, when I need hope, open the eyes of my heart to see what you are doing. As long as I am living, you are not finished working your redemption power in my life. As long as I look to you, I will find everything my heart longs for. Keep doing what you do so well; love me to life in your presence and fill me with the strength of your grace that keeps me going. There is more than enough in you for a thriving and rich life. I love you!

Do you believe that God is not finished with you?

Every Morning

The Sovereign Lord has given me his words of wisdom,
so that I know how to comfort the weary.
Morning by morning he wakens me
and opens my understanding to his will.

ISAIAH 50:4 NLT

For those who seek the Lord and his wisdom, there is a wealth of insight to be found. He does not hide his knowledge from those who are looking for it. He is generous with his perception, and he gladly shares his understanding with his children. How hungry are we for his wisdom? Have we grown complacent in our understanding of who he is? Have we reached a point where the truth feels stale?

Then let us go after the Lord and search the Scripture for more of his revelation. Let us spend time fellowship with his Spirit through prayer and meditation, leaving him space to speak and move in our hearts. Jesus said that he is our Good Shepherd and that his sheep know his voice. Let us listen for his voice today.

Sovereign Lord, your wisdom is better than any other. You bring clarity to confusion and you calm chaos with the illumination of your living Word. Speak to me today, for I am listening.

The Lord Yahweh has equipped me
with the anointed, skillful tongue of a teacher—
to know how to speak a timely word to the weary.
Morning by morning, he awakens my heart.
He opens my ears to hear his voice, to be trained to teach.

ISAIAH 50:4 TPT

Yahweh, whatever it is I do in life, may I always be submitted to your heart, will, and ways. Your kingdom truth stands firm when the wisdom of the world fails. Fill me with your perfect love that drives every fear away. You are radiant in shining glory, and in the light of your presence, I gain understanding. Awaken my heart with your Words of Life and fill my thoughts with your instructions.

As I meditate on your Scriptures, I get to know your voice more and more. As I get to know the consistency of your character, my understanding enlarges, and I can more clearly spot you working in the world around me. You are my teacher, my guide, and my leader. May I always remain sensitive to your love that leads the way.

How has growing in relationship with the Lord
helped you make wiser decisions?

A Season

"Now is your time of grief,
but I will see you again and you will rejoice,
and no one will take away your joy."

JOHN 16:22 NIV

Though grief may hit us hard for a time, there will be joy in the dawning of God's forever kingdom. To be clear, we get to experience God's joy in the here and now. But our experiences may not always align. There is coming a day and an age where every wrong will be made right, and there will be no more crying, or sadness, or pain. Those things will be a memory when we are finally in the fullness of God's reigning kingdom in eternity.

Jesus' words to his disciples were to reassure them of the joy that would follow their deep grief. When Jesus resurrected from the dead and visited with them before he ascended to the Father forty days later, this promise was directly fulfilled. The joy in the realization that Jesus was who he said he was would forever change his followers' lives. Let us take hope in the ministry of the Holy Spirit with us, and in the promised return of Jesus to set things right once and for all.

Holy One, thank you for promises fulfilled and for the assurance of more. You are wonderful in all of your ways. Minister to me in my grief and be my holy hope.

"So will you also pass through a time of intense sorrow when I am taken from you, but you will see me again! And then your hearts will burst with joy, with no one being able to take it from you!"

JOHN 16:22 TPT

Resurrected One, you are the way, the truth, and the life. I come to the Father through you, and there is nothing keeping me from your heart. I'm so grateful for the open door of your love in my life. It has changed me, encouraged me, and spurred me on in faith. I know that when I go through times of deep grief that I have not reached the end. It will not be my undoing. And even when it feels as though I will fall apart in the fires of pain, your close comfort relieves the pressure.

You are my hope, my joy, and my present strength. Your companionship is more than I could ever ask for, and it is all I need to get through every season of the soul. Be close, Jesus, in the midst of my suffering, and lovingly lead me in your joy. I believe that I will see your goodness in the land of the living again!

How has the comfort of the Holy Spirit ministered to you?

More Than Able

*"I know that You can do all things,
And that no plan is impossible for You."*

JOB 42:2 NASB

What God sets out to do, he will accomplish. Though we cannot put his will on our timelines, he is always faithful. When we look through the Scriptures, we can see time after time of God fulfilling his Word. And he is still doing it. He is more than able to do all that we could ever imagine. In fact, he can do so much more than that. His purposes will stand firm forever, for he has already set in his heart what he will do. His mercy meets us in unending measure more than we can perceive. His kindness is the pull of our hearts to his.

Is there anything that you are unsure of? Is there something that God has spoken over your life that you just cannot see a possibility for? He is the God of the impossible, for all things are possible with him. Will you lean into his heart with trust today? Let him speak to the questions you have. He is good, faithful, true, and so very patient with us.

Good God, I will echo Job's prayer today. I know that you can do all things, and that no purpose of yours can be prevented. Thank you!

> *"I know that you can do anything,*
> *and no one can stop you."*

JOB 42:2 NLT

Loving Lord, no one can stop the purposes of your heart. I'm so grateful that you cannot be talked out of your lovingkindness. No one can dissuade you from pouring your mercy out on our lives. Even when I am caught up in the chaos of confusion, you are never distracted from your pure wisdom. You have everything handled in a way that I could never dream of. You are so much better than anyone I've ever known, and I trust that your faithfulness will continue to guide me into your goodness.

It doesn't matter what is going on around me; your loyal love will never change. Your peace is undisturbed. May I live in the overflow of your joy and delight. I want to always be found rooted in the confidence of your Word. You are my living hope and the foundation of my very life. I love you so much more than I can express, Lord! Thank you for calling me your own.

Do you trust God to do what you cannot?

Not Forgotten

"Can a woman forget the baby she nurses?
Can she feel no kindness for the child to which she gave birth?
Even if she could forget her children, I will not forget you."

ISAIAH 49:15 NCV

When we think of God, is it as some far-off, detached being that looks over our lives disinterestedly? Or do we think that he is a judge who is waiting for us to break our parole? There is a reason that he is referred to as a loving father. He is a perfect parent who cares for us with endless mercy-kindness. He does not forget us. It is not in his nature to do so, for he has created us and chosen us as his own.

What relief we find in his love. What belonging! There is nothing we could ever do to make him love us more or to make him love us less. Not a thing. He loves us thoroughly, purely, and without measure. Let us run into the light of his love today and come alive in the waves of his delight.

Kind Father, thank you for always welcoming me into your presence with mercy. I trust your heart more than anything else in this life. You have been faithful to me in love, and I know you always will be.

*"How could a loving mother forget her nursing child
and not deeply love the one she bore?
Even if a there is a mother who forgets her child,
I could never, no never, forget you."*

ISAIAH 49:15 TPT

Good God, I am undone in the mystery of your large, merciful love. Thank you for choosing me as your own, for lovingly knitting my person together in my mother's womb. You imagined me before I was made, and you created me in kindness. You said that you would never forget your children. I rest in that truth—that you see me, you know me, and you accept me. Thank you!

In areas where I have felt forgotten, will you reveal the fingerprints of your love on my life? I know that you will never abandon me; there's no chance that I'll have to get through any circumstance on my own. I could not begin to recount my gratefulness that I am never alone. Pour your love over me in a fresh wave and awaken my senses to your presence with me now. I love you.

How have you felt overlooked by the Lord?

Discernment

The wise see danger ahead and avoid it,
but fools keep going and get into trouble.

PROVERBS 27:12 NCV

What does it look like to be discerning? If we equate faith with blind belief, then we may dismiss the warnings of those who discern patterns and cycles as unbelief. But this is not what faith actually is. Our faith is rooted in the faithfulness of God. There is fruit to be found in this. There are patterns at work in this world that we can prepare for, knowing how to spot them.

We do not need to spiritually bypass real concerns, wishing away the negative sides of life. We can be prepared for inevitabilities and still rely fully on the Lord. We can look ahead and see how a relationship or job may fall apart because of the glaring red flags that are there now. We can avoid danger by dealing with the realities in the present. To be sure, there is so much grace and mercy to cover us. But there is also maturity in practicing discernment, and in being selective about our yeses.

Merciful One, thank you for your wisdom that guides me. Teach me to lean into discernment found in your Spirit, and in those who are naturally more able to see patterns and cycles. May I learn restraint in my choices, so that I can grow in this area.

A wise, shrewd person discerns the danger ahead
and prepares himself,
but the naïve simpleton never looks ahead
and suffers the consequences.

PROVERBS 27:12 TPT

Wise God, thank you for leading me in love. As I follow your ways, my understanding is opened in the light of your radiant nature. May I look ahead with eyes that perceive your truth. When I am making decisions, may I not simply look at what is true right now, but let me consider the fruit of obedience to your Word. You always see things more clearly than I ever will. May I trust your guidance even when I cannot put words to the reason why I feel led in the way you are leading.

I don't want to be simple in my understanding, blindly plowing into an unwise decision. May I learn from the wisdom of those that have walked longer with you, and may I trust you in them. I don't want to pretend not to see the realities when you have called me to consider them. Why deal with consequences of things not thought through when I could have planned for them in the beginning? In all things, may I stay close to you in love, not wavering in worry, but trusting your wisdom and guidance.

How does discernment instruct your decisions?

Growing

Let us stop going over the basic teachings about Christ again and again. Let us go on instead and become mature in our understanding. Surely we don't need to start again with the fundamental importance of repenting from evil deeds and placing our faith in God.

HEBREWS 6:1 NLT

How actively we engage the Lord and his teachings will affect how quickly we mature in our faith. As in nature, growth spurts will happen along the way, and there will be times where it looks as if growth may have slowed down. But there is so much more to learn in God's kingdom ways than we could ever master.

We will never stop developing in his wisdom as long as we live. There are foundational truths that we set our lives upon in him. Repentance and faith in Jesus are two of these truths. But once we have them, we do not need to keep going over them, for there is so much more that we can grow in understanding of. Let us become mature in our understanding, knowing that as we grow, there is greater freedom to be found.

Jesus, you are the source of my faith. I want to grow up in understanding, and I realize that means to keep following after you in surrender and in open connection through prayer. Thank you for teaching me who you are.

Now is the time for us to progress beyond the basic message of Christ and advance into perfection. The foundation has already been laid for us to build upon: turning away from our dead works to embrace faith in God.

HEBREWS 6:1 TPT

My God, thank you for the invitation to grow in the knowledge of your wonderful ways. As long as I am breathing, there is so much more to discover in you. Keep me from the pride of youth that believes it knows it all. I have only caught a glimpse of the lengths of your love. That's it! But it keeps me going back to you.

I never want to be without your Spirit's presence, guidance, and help in this life, and I never need to be. Thank you for your consistent nature revealed in the wisdom of your Word. Teach me, Lord, and I will continue to mature in faith. I don't want to just grow; I want to be healthy. May my faith flourish under your leadership. You are worthy of my whole life, and I trust that your love will never lead me astray.

In what ways has your faith matured?

Made New

Create in me a clean heart, O God,
and put a new and right spirit within me.

PSALM 51:10 NRSV

What a beautiful invitation this prayer is! "Create in me a clean heart, O God…" This request was David's prayer after his sin of adultery with Bathsheba was exposed. David was a man after God's own heart; the Scriptures declare this. And yet, when we look over his life, it is clear that he was far from perfect. His righteousness was built on his relationship with God, not on his own merit and deeds.

We love to talk about David's victories—the slaying of Goliath the giant, the conquering of Jerusalem, the plans for God's temple, etc. But we don't often spend much time on his failures. It is his response to these moral faults and shortcomings that teach us so clearly about God's mercy. Let us join with David, lay down the need to be perfect, and instead invite God to change us from the inside out with his kindness.

God, thank you for your mercy that covers my sin. You are so gracious in forgiveness. Create in me a clean heart and renew my spirit within me.

Create a new, clean heart within me.
Fill me with pure thoughts and holy desires,
ready to please you.

Psalm 51:10 TPT

Merciful Father, you are so rich in kindness to all. Thank you for David's example of repentance and restoration. You led him back to you with compassion. He clearly confessed all of his sin before you and Israel through this psalm. I ask for your guiding grace on my life, as it was with David. Fill me with pure thoughts and holy desires, Lord, for I want to please you above all else.

Every lesser love pales in comparison to the beauty of knowing you and being known by you. You have washed me clean in your mercy-love more times than I can count. And every time I am restored by your love, it is as if no time has passed at all, and nothing was lost. Only you can do that. You don't hold my sin against me. I don't know anyone else who can say the same. Thank you for your wonderful, overwhelming, purifying love.

What evidence do you see in your life
of God's purifying mercy?

Source

All things are of God, who has reconciled us to Himself through Jesus Christ, and has given us the ministry of reconciliation.

2 CORINTHIANS 5:18 NKJV

The work of reconciliation is ultimately God's. He birthed all of nature with his imagination and word. He created humans from the dust of the earth and formed their beings with his hands. He breathed his breath of life into them, and they woke up to life. We are created in his image, and he has been doing the work of resolution in relationship since it was first broken.

Through Christ, we have been brought into reunion with God. There is nothing that can keep us out of his courts when we come to him. We will not be turned away when Jesus is our path, our door, and our welcome. We who have been brought into alignment with his kingdom are also able to share this ministry of reunion with those who have not yet heard. Let us be like our perfect Father and reconcile in love whenever we have the chance.

Father of love, thank you for providing the way to reconcile with you once and for all through Jesus, your Son. I come to you freely, and freely I receive from your mercy. I won't keep this wonderful news of reconciliation to myself.

*God has made all things new, and reconciled us to himself,
and given us the ministry of reconciling others to God.*

2 CORINTHIANS 5:18 TPT

God, thank you for making all things new in you. What you
touch is restored, and you have your hand of mercy on my life.
Thank you for the restoration work you are doing. Thank you
for your redemption power that brings life to dry bones and
the ashes of broken dreams. Anything can resurrect in your
presence. You are able to do all things. There is no end to the
wonder-working power of your love as it moves in this world.

May I never forget the potency of your mercy. Every chance I
have, may I offer your love to those who have not yet heard of
its might. You are so quick in kindness, Lord. As I spend time
with you through prayer, fellowship, and your Word, I grow
in your kindness, as well. Continue to make all things new in
you. You are wonderful!

What power has reconciliation had in your life?

Good Food

> *"Don't work for the food that spoils. Work for the food that stays good always and gives eternal life. The Son of Man will give you this food, because on him God the Father has put his power."*
>
> JOHN 6:27 NCV

When Jesus was speaking to the crowd and encouraging them to work for the bread that comes down from heaven and gives life to the world, he was talking about coming to him. He makes this clear as the passage of Scripture progresses. What are we spending our lives on? Are we seeking approval from others? Are we looking for wealth and to satisfy our bellies with the pleasures of this world? Or are we looking to Jesus, building our lives upon his eternal kingdom values?

We have access to the Father of all creation, and we need never settle for anything less than the fullness of relationship with him. We come to the Father through Christ, the Son, and we experience the pleasure of knowing him through his Spirit who is with us. What a glorious and wonderful reality!

Son of Man, thank you for revealing the heart of the Father through your ministry on earth. You are glorious! I want to know you more than anything else. I may think I know better when I taste the pleasures of this world, but they never last. Your delight never ends!

"Why would you strive for food that is perishable and not be passionate to seek the food of eternal life, which never spoils? I, the Son of Man, am ready to give you what matters most, for God the Father has destined me for this purpose."

JOHN 6:27 TPT

Father God, I am so grateful for your reconciliation power in my life. You have brought me into the fullness of your eternal kingdom by the chain-breaking power of Jesus' sacrifice. Thank you for resurrection life that calls me from the grave, out of the dead ends of my sin, into your glorious life, full of abundance and provision. I will live for your everlasting love, for it is lasting, bringing new life out of the ashes and rubble of disappointment.

Your ways are so much better than my own. I don't want to struggle and strive for temporal, changing pleasures that may last for a short time, but are quickly replaced with something else to reach for. Your desires are pure, and you generously and gladly give freely out of the delight of your heart to your children. Why would I look for something lasting in the ways of the world which will never stand the test of time? I look to you, the author and finisher of my faith, for all that I need or long for, and my deepest desires.

What are you working to gain in this life?

Greater Understanding

> *Blessed is a person who finds wisdom,*
> *And one who obtains understanding.*

PROVERBS 3:13 NASB

The longer we live, the more we discover how little we already know. In the wealth of God's wisdom, there are keys to thriving in fellowship with him. Following his ways and Word requires trust. Do we believe that God is faithful? Do we believe that he is good? Do we believe that he is above all? Do we believe that he is who the Word says he is?

May we take the risk of spending our lives on him. Surely, he will come through with the reliable power of his mercy in our lives. If we have yet to find how good he is, let us place our bets on him. Let us give following his ways a try. May we take his wisdom to heart and let it change our lives. The world may look on and think that the path of love is a foolish one to take, but we will know the great reward of unrestrained fellowship with God if we choose to take it.

Great God, there is no one like you in wisdom. You see everything so clearly. I don't need to spend my energy speculating about the right way. I only need follow you. Thank you for guiding me and opening my understanding.

*Those who find true wisdom obtain the tools for understanding,
the proper way to live,
for they will have a fountain of blessing pouring into their lives.
To gain the riches of wisdom is far greater
than gaining the wealth of the world.*

PROVERBS 3:13 TPT

Wise One, thank you for the wisdom of your love that you freely share with all who look to you for understanding. You bring clarity to the confusion that clouds my mind. You shine your revelation-light on my thoughts, and you bring order to the swirling mess of questions and doubts. You make everything right in your presence. Fill my heart with your peace as I align my ways with your love. I know that obedience is a sign of trust, and Lord, I trust you.

I have tasted and seen the goodness of following you. I have experienced the all-surpassing kindness of your truth working out in my life. I want to know your ways better than I know my own. Yours is a path of mercy and love that looks different from the methods of man that seek to satisfy self above all else. I will spend my life seeking your higher wisdom and following the voice of your leadership. You are so good.

What kind of wisdom is informing your choices?

Not My Way

Going a little farther, he fell on the ground and prayed that, if it were possible, the hour might pass from him. And he said, "Abba, Father, all things are possible for you. Remove this cup from me. Yet not what I will, but what you will."

MARK 14:35–36 ESV

This passage is so important for us to take in. Even Jesus, the Son of Man and Son of God, did not want to do what he knew God the Father was asking him to do. The reward was clear, but the path of pain just as poignant. When we face suffering, it is human to want to avoid it. It is in our nature to want to escape misery when we see it coming. But in this life, we cannot escape the anguish of grief that will come our way.

May we follow Jesus' example and wrestle it out, if we must, with the Lord. Ultimately, may we come to the same place of surrender that Jesus did. "Yet not what I will, but what you will." The Father knows us well, and he promised that he would be with us in our suffering. We are never alone! Can we trust him even in the face of pain? He will use even our greatest pain to teach us about his love.

Father, you see the parts of my heart that are resisting change. I don't want to suffer, but I do trust you to love me, care for me, and guide me in the dark nights of my soul.

He walked a short distance away, and being overcome with grief, he threw himself facedown on the ground. He prayed that if it were possible, he would not have to experience this hour of suffering. He prayed, "Abba, my Father, all things are possible for you. Please— don't allow me to drink this cup of suffering! Yet what I want is not important, for I only desire to fulfill your plan for me."

MARK 14:35–36 TPT

Abba, thank you for the reminder of Jesus' humanity, and that it is not sinful to resist the pull of pain. But I will walk in surrender, trusting your love to lead me through the darkest hours of suffering. Your ways are better than my own. Knowing that I cannot escape pain in this life, I will trust you to comfort me and keep me close in your love. I put your plans above my own, confident that your mercy will never leave. You see more clearly than I ever could, and I trust your kind, unchanging character. In my grief, be near. In my sorrow, come close. Through it all, minister your healing presence. Be with me through it all! Thank you for your persistent presence that never leaves me.

Is there something you are resisting surrendering to God?

My Refuge

The LORD is good, a refuge in times of trouble.
He cares for those who trust in him.

NAHUM 1:7 NIV

What a wonderful meditation for our hearts today. "The Lord is good." His nature is untainted by hidden motives. He is pure in his goodness. He is full of lovingkindness and mercy for all who look to him. "The Lord is...a refuge in times of trouble." He is a place of sanctuary in our troubles. He protects us, keeping us safe from the arrows of the enemy. He is our shelter! "He cares for those who trust in him."

When we place our hopes in him, and believe that he is for us, we will never be disappointed. He takes tender care of those who trust him! What an amazing God he is. There is no one else like him in all the earth!

Great God, thank you for being a safe place in the midst of my troubles. You rush in close with your Spirit, awakening my soul to your nearness when I tremble with fear. You are my great courage, and I trust in you!

The Lord is good,
a strong refuge when trouble comes.
He is close to those who trust in him.

NAHUM 1:7 NLT

Lord, you are infinitely good. You never fail. When I try to imagine the lengths of your lovingkindness, I cannot even conceive of a portion of your mercy. You are so wonderful to your people, reaching out in loyal love at all times. I will not give up my hope in you. You have been faithful to me, and I believe that you will continue to be forever! Be close, Spirit. Be near in the times of my great rejoicing and closer than skin-to-skin in times of my trouble. Though others may comfort me in small, meaningful ways, your comfort reaches to the depths of my being—beyond where anyone else could venture.

Be my shelter in every storm, Lord, and close around me with the liquid kindness of your presence when I am being hemmed in by my circumstances. You are the barrier-busting God. All things are possible with you! I will not let fear steal my hope, for you are my strong and sure foundation!

How has God been a shelter for you in times of trouble?

Hidden in Love

You are my hiding place;
You shall preserve me from trouble;
You shall surround me with songs of deliverance.

PSALM 32:7 NKJV

How has God's love delivered you from fear? Have you known his overwhelming peace in the face of impossible odds? When you are at a loss for what to do, run into the refuge of his presence! He will not fail to cover you with his perfect peace and surround you with the delight of his affection. He is a faithful defender and advocate. His grace is more than enough to strengthen you.

Do you need courage today? Go to him. Do you need wisdom? He has plenty to alleviate your confusion! In relationship with him, you will find everything you need. Fellowship with his Spirit is not a right reserved for the super spiritual. It is the basic tenet of restoration of relationship with God! It is where you will find your healing, courage, and where transformative life occurs! Do not hold back, for he will never hold back his love from you.

Faithful One, thank you for your Spirit that both surrounds and fills me with everything I need for abundant spirit-life! I need never rely on my own strength and abilities, for you are more than able to do all that you have planned. I lean on you, God!

Lord, you are my secret hiding place,
protecting me from these troubles,
surrounding me with songs of gladness!
Your joyous shouts of rescue release my breakthrough.

PSALM 32:7 TPT

Lord, I run into the shelter of your presence every opportunity I get. When I am surrounded by people, even then I can retreat into the hiding place of your heart. As I reach out in love and eager desire, you answer me. You fill me with the courage of your love. You surround me with songs of joyous victory, for you are my holy hope. You are my deliverer. When you release me from the strongholds of suffering, I break through into your gloriously liberating delight!

Even when the world around me hasn't changed, you free me up from the inside, out. I know that it is only a matter of time before my circumstances reflect the power of your breakthrough. Thank you for keeping me close in your mercy-love. You are my protector, and I lean into your heart of love and find courage with every beat. I breathe in your pure love, and I am strengthened in my spirit! Thank you.

What does hiding in God's love look like
in your relationship with him?

Tower of Strength

The name of the LORD is a strong tower;
the righteous runs into it and is safe.

PROVERBS 18:10 NASB

Have you ever been so overwhelmed in life that you just don't know what to do, and you find yourself calling on the name of Jesus? The name of the Lord is a strong tower! Whether it simply helps us to remember that Jesus is with us, hears us, and is advocating on our behalf, or it is our desperate cry for his intervention, the result is the same!

We rest in the confidence of his help. He will surely come through for us, as he has countless times before. He never stops being loyal in love, and he promises to be with us through every trial and trouble. Call on the name of the Lord today and find rest in the safety of his powerful presence!

Jesus, I call out to you when I am at a loss! You are the name I call upon, for you are my God! You are my Savior, strength, and help. You are my rescuer!

The name of the Lord is a strong fortress;
the godly run to him and are safe.

PROVERBS 18:10 NLT

Lord, I run to you this evening. Meet me with the
overwhelming peace of your presence. Surround me with the
melodies of your deliverance. Remind me of your great power
at work in my life. Refresh my spirit and soul in the life of
your Spirit in me! You are powerful to save! You are mighty to
rescue! I will not be afraid of what tomorrow brings, or what
the next moments hold. You are my constant help. You are my
comfort, my song, and my strength.

You are everything I need! Jesus! You are my holy hope, and
I surrender every worry to your all-knowing wisdom. You
already know what time will bring and which path I will
choose. And you promise to never leave me for a moment.
I rest in that truth—that you are with me now and always.
You are my confidence, Lord. Your presence is my spirit's
lifeblood.

How has your faith in Jesus empowered your life?

My Caretaker

The LORD is all I need.
He takes care of me.
My share in life has been pleasant;
my part has been beautiful.

PSALM 16:5-6 NCV

There is a depth of riches to be found in fellowship with the Lord, our God. He truly is all we need. He is the source of every living thing, and he is the one who set the planets in motion and created all that we see. He gives freely from the abundance of his heavenly storehouses to all who look to him.

When we need strength, he is the one who infuses us with grace. When we need help, he is there with deliverance-power. When we are suffering, he is close with comfort. When we need provision, he makes a way. He is the same God who made manna rain down from heaven each morning for the sustenance of his people in the desert. He will not leave us or let us waste away. He is endlessly good, full of tenderness toward his children. He fills our lives with treasures of his goodness. He is wonderful!

Lord, thank you for taking such good care of me! I am so grateful to know you and to be loved by you. Open my eyes to see your goodness in a new way today. I long for more of you!

Lord, I have chosen you alone as my inheritance.
You are my prize, my pleasure, and my portion.
I leave my destiny and its timing in your hands.
Your pleasant path leads me to pleasant places.
I'm overwhelmed by the privileges
that come with following you,
for you have given me the best!

PSALM 16:5-6 TPT

Faithful One, you are my guiding light in this life. I have chosen to follow you and your wonderful ways. Though I may grow weary of humanity, I could never grow tired of you. Your goodness knows no end, and your mercy is new every morning! There is no stale air in your presence, for you are always moving. You lead me into the pleasant places of your presence, and I am renewed with your life-giving love again and again!

Even when I walk through dark valleys, you are with me. You are sowing seeds of sweet fruit in the soil of broken dreams. I know that with you is restoration and redemption power. Why would I look for a better life, when there is none to be found apart from you! I love you, Lord!

Can you pinpoint a time when God has taken care of you?

Leader of my Life

Whether you turn to the right or to the left,
your ears will hear a voice behind you, saying,
"This is the way; walk in it."

ISAIAH 30:21 NIV

Have you submitted your life, including your future, to the Lord? It is good to make plans and to build a future! How tuned to the voice of the Lord are you in your decision-making? When we walk with the Lord, we get to know the tone of his voice and we can recognize the indications of his leadership. When we are seeking the Lord in life, we will realize that there is so much grace in the journey! He is with us wherever we go, and those who look to him will be led to life.

May we trust his guidance and let his wisdom instruct what we choose for ourselves. May we keep our ears and eyes open to the possibilities of his goodness around us. There is often a deep knowing in our hearts, if we will tune into it. The Lord is the best and most gracious leader. He will not fail us!

Father, you are my loving leader. Thank you for speaking into my life in every area. I'm so grateful that even when the choice is clearly mine to make in freedom, you weigh in with your perfect wisdom. There is so much delight in following you!

When you turn to the right or turn to the left,
you will hear his voice behind you to guide you, saying,
"This is the right path; follow it."

ISAIAH 30:21 TPT

Faithful Father, I'm so grateful for your guidance in my life!
I'm also so very thankful for your consistent grace that covers
any missteps. I'm glad that you don't hold my failures against
me; everything is a teaching moment with you! When I begin
to wander off the path of your loving truth, would you guide
me back to the way of your mercy? You are faithfully with me,
and I can never thank you enough for that!

I trust that when I come to a fork in the road, you will be with
me, whatever way I choose. You never abandon me. But more
than that, I ask for wisdom and discernment to rightly weigh
the choices I make. You are infinite in wisdom and clarity,
and I rely on you to help me! Thank you for freedom in
relationship with you! Thank you for agency! I'm grateful that
as I grow in you, your principles become my lampposts along
the way. Keep leading me in love, Lord, and I will follow you!

How has God led you when you were at a turning point?

Whole in Him

"Those who love me will keep my word, and my Father will love them, and we will come to them and make our home with them."

JOHN 14:23 NRSV

When Jesus spoke this word to his disciples, he followed it by telling them that the Father would send the Holy Spirit to dwell with them. Part of the Spirit's work is to remind us of Jesus' words and to teach us. He is our advocate, our helper. When we are failing miserably at loving our neighbor, we have help. When we are losing confidence in our faith, there is one who advocates for us.

The Spirit of God is our strength, our loving leader, and truth-teller. He has everything we need. We don't ever need to rely on our own abilities even to love him. Let us learn to lean on God the Spirit whenever we waver. He is more than enough. He will strengthen our spirits in his mercy and remind us of forgotten truth. He will help us in whatever way we need.

Loving Lord, thank you for your Spirit that dwells with me. I am yours, and you are making me new in the regeneration of your Spirit life. Be at home in me, for I want nothing less than all of you.

> *"Loving me empowers you to obey my word.
> And my Father will love you so deeply that we will
> come to you and make you our dwelling place."*
>
> JOHN 14:23 TPT

Spirit of God, thank you for making your home in me. I cannot express the gratitude I feel for your leadership in my life. I love you more than I can say! Will you reveal to me again the overwhelming fullness of the Father's love? I cannot fully conceive of its intensity, but every time I get a new revelation of it, it sparks unrestrained awe and joy in my heart. I come alive in the kindness of your affection. I am humbled by your astute wisdom that guides me in goodness.

There is no other that can compare to you. The purity of your love seeps through my defenses and washes away any walls that I erect in self-protection and fear. You are better than anything I've known—always better. Thank you for strengthening me in your grace to choose your ways above my own. Continue to lead my life with the purity of your plans and purposes. You are so very good to me.

How has fellowship with the Spirit impacted your life?

Follow Through

The plans of the diligent lead surely to plenty,
But those of everyone who is hasty, surely to poverty.

PROVERBS 21:5 NKJV

How many of us make plans and then abandon them for a better one down the road? Though there is freedom to change our minds, may we not be led by fickle fancies, but by the steadfast wisdom of perseverance. That is not to say that there won't come a time when we change course. But when we do, may we do it with thought and consideration.

The Scriptures instruct us to persist. When we act in haste, not thinking through our choices, we run the risk of burning out on things that are not meant to last. May we grow in God's wisdom, letting the thoroughness of his discernment shape our choices. When we are persistent in well-laid plans, we will reap the reward with God's help.

Wise God, thank you for the reminder to think through the decisions and plans I make. Guide me in your gracious wisdom and bring clarity to what I should give my yeses to, that I may sustain perseverance in the follow-through.

*Brilliant ideas pay off and bring you prosperity,
but making hasty, impatient decisions
will only lead to financial loss.*

PROVERBS 21:5 TPT

All-knowing One, it is your wisdom that broadens my understanding. You see through the outer layers into the heart of a matter without even trying. Why would I rely on my own limited perspective, when your broad and perfect perception doesn't miss a thing? Instead of hastily moving ahead with preferences and choices, may I learn to lean on your understanding. I know that following your ways will pay off. Leaving behind my idealistic dreams that don't include you, I will look into your heart for your viewpoint.

You are welcome to instruct me, Lord. In fact, I depend on it! I don't want to find myself in situations where I wish I would have listened to that small voice that warned me against an easy 'yes.' As I grow in trusting your voice, I ask that you would help me to take that leap of faith even when it does not make logical sense in the moment. I trust that I will find relief, peace, and strength in following your nudges.

Does diligence play a part in your decision-making?

Architect

It is by faith we understand that the whole world was made by God's command so what we see was made by something that cannot be seen.

HEBREWS 11:3 NCV

When we look at the stars in the sky, and when we consider the magnitude of the seas and their depths, do we not respond with wonder? When we are too caught up in our own little lives and minds, a good way to get out of it is to get out into nature. God's handiwork is all around us.

May we never be so distracted by the scope of our problems that we fail to see the bigger picture all around us. God is in the details of the universe; we can find his fingerprints everywhere we look. The one who set the stars in their places and who created the vast expanse of the universe is the one who calls us each by name. What a glorious and humbling reality!

Creator God, thank you for the reminder of your workmanship all around me. When I consider the heights of the mountains and the mysteries of the deep sea, how could I not be in awe of your consideration of me? Thank you.

*Faith empowers us to see that the universe was created
and beautifully coordinated by the power of God's words!
He spoke and the invisible realm gave birth to all that is seen.*

HEBREWS 11:3 TPT

Great God, you are so much larger than my mind can comprehend. The extent of your mercy is far greater than my grasp of it. What a relief, that your loyal love is more than I can possibly contain. You are the one who planted the first seed of faith, and it is being watered in the soil of your faithful love. Your power is unmatched, and no one can undo what you have put in motion. I trust that you will continue to work out the purposes of your heart in the earth and in humankind.

You won't forget my little life, either. Whenever I begin to forget your greatness, may my attention be grabbed by the mysteries that are still unfolding in the world around me. There is so much that scientists are still discovering. There's so much we still don't know. But what I do know is that you are great, you are God, and you are good.

How does nature affect your relationship to the Creator?

Deep Springs

"Because of your father's God, who helps you,
because of the Almighty,
who blesses you with blessings of the skies above,
blessings of the deep springs below,
blessings of the breast and womb."

GENESIS 49:25 NIV

There is a depth of blessing found in the history of God's people. His mercy extends throughout every generation, back to the first. When Adam and Eve were thrown out of the garden, God began a lengthy and thorough plan of redemption. God's kindness can be found in every generation. His cord of love has never left his people, though the circumstances, trials, and triumphs may look different from age to age. He remains the same.

Let us look through the line of our heritage, whether it is a deep spiritual well or a new turn in our lineage. God is as faithful to us as he was to previous generations. May we never lose sight of God's goodness, as revealed through the lives of those who love and follow him.

God my hope, thank you for the perspective shift today. As I look through the ages, searching for your fingerprints of mercy, I know that I will find them. Show me how you were with previous generations, that I may be encouraged about where I am today.

> *"May the God of your father help you;*
> *may the Almighty bless you*
> *with the blessings of the heavens above,*
> *and blessings of the watery depths below,*
> *and blessings of the breasts and womb."*

GENESIS 49:25 NLT

God of the ages, you are the same God that the Israelites looked to in the desert. You are the same God who walked in the cool of the day with Adam and Eve. You are the same God who spoke to Moses in a burning bush, and who rescued David from the snare of the enemy. You are the God who shut the mouths of lions, who stood in a furnace and kept his followers from being burned up in the fire, and the God who put on flesh and bones and went to the cross.

You are the God of resurrection life; the one who heals, the one who restores, the one who makes all things new. You are my God. You are the one I follow. You are everything!

Where can you see the blessings of previous generations playing out in your life?

Rest in Hope

"You will have confidence, because there is hope;
you will be protected and take your rest in safety."

JOB 11:18 NRSV

When our hopes are rooted in the faithful love of God, they can never be stolen or shaken. What is built upon the foundation of God's mercy will last. Other hopes, whether based in our own abilities or in the promises of others, may shift, change, and be blown off in the winds of life. But God's faithfulness is unquestionable.

He is our firm foundation. He is our steady hope. He is the one who keeps us safe and secure in his mercy-tide. Even when everything seems to be falling apart on the outside, he renews our spirits on the inside. He is our joy, our strength, and our song. May we always sing his praises! He is our great confidence.

God of my hope, I place all my assurance in you. You have not failed your people yet, and you are not about to start now. Be my holy hope, growing deeper even in adversity. You are my shelter and my fortress; I take refuge in you.

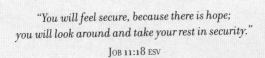

> *"You will feel secure, because there is hope;*
> *you will look around and take your rest in security."*
>
> JOB 11:18 ESV

Mighty God, you are my deliverer, my courage, and all that I rely on. You are my help when I can see no other way. You are my victory in the triumphs of life. You give peace in every season; no matter how tumultuous the times, I know the calm of your presence. Thank you!

I will take my rest in you tonight, as I lay every burden down at your feet again. You can have the things that I can't control, and you can have what I have been trying to manage on my own. Your ways are always better than my own, so I give up the right to have my own way. I trust your intentions more than any other. You are pure in motive, faithful in love, and you are the one I depend upon. Sing your songs of peace over my heart now, and may I sleep with the deep rest of one who is taken care of. You are my hope.

What is your deepest hope based on?

Forever Good

Jesus Christ is the same
yesterday, today, and forever.
HEBREWS 13:8 NCV

The message of Jesus is the same yesterday, today, and forever. He has not changed his mind, and God has not all of a sudden altered the trajectory of his great plan and purposes. We are not better in this day and age than in any other generation. What God required of his people then is what is required now.

The wonderful news is that God is with us. He is steadfast in loyal love, and his mercy is as plentiful as it has ever been. Let us not add anything to the message of Jesus in order to be sanctified. We are made holy by the sacrifice of Jesus. We are made alive and free in his resurrection power. There are no add-ons to his grace. It is always enough. May we be people of a pure mind, going after him as ones who are lovesick and totally convinced of his faithfulness. He is so worthy of our lives.

Jesus Christ, thank you for your pure and simple message of truth. May I not get distracted by tenets or lifestyles that do not matter in the end. May I wear your love as a cloak around me, and may I never take it off.

Jesus Christ is the same
yesterday and today and forever.

HEBREWS 13:8 NIV

Anointed One, you are worthy of my love today and always. You will never change. Who you are is who you have always been and who you will be forever. May I not be fooled into thinking that your mercy can run out. May I never be tricked into earning your love, certainly not after you have given it so freely.

Your faithfulness will never run dry. You are good. You are forever the way, the truth, and the life. There is no other path to the Father but through you. You have made a way where previously there was none. You have welcomed us into your eternal kingdom with open arms. What is yours, you give freely to those who look for you. You never leave us alone, and you never will. You are so much more wonderful than you can ever be given credit for. You are glorified and lifted up, and you are holy, Lord. Teach me your ways, and I will walk in them.

How does the unchanging nature of God affect your faith?

In the Meantime

It is not yet time for the message to come true,
but that time is coming soon; the message will come true.
It may seem like a long time, but be patient and wait for it,
because it will surely come; it will not be delayed.

HABAKKUK 3:2 NCV

When we are waiting on the fulfillment of God's promises in our lives, and in the world at large, it is important to maintain the right perspective. God's timing is not our own. Where we would be hasty, God is full of patience, waiting for all things to be properly aligned in his purposes. He is not slow in answering his promises. He is full of mercy, and he can see what we cannot. He is faithful. His character is unchanging.

Instead of being influenced by our circumstances, let's let our faith influence them. God's truth will always prevail, and he will not be made a liar. Practice patience and persistence. He is making a way, and when he says it is time, nothing will stop him.

Faithful One, thank you for acting in wisdom and mercy. I trust your ways even when I cannot understand them. I know that you do not grow weary, so I will lean your strength when my own wanes. You are worthy, you are true, and you will always come through.

*The revelation awaits an appointed time;
it speaks of the end and will not prove false.
Though it linger, wait for it;
it will certainly come and will not delay.*

HABAKKUK 3:2 NIV

God of truth, you are the living Word. What you speak, no one can refute. You are wiser than any other, and you are endlessly faithful. Though we await the fulfillment of your kingdom come to earth as it is in heaven once and for all, let us be filled with faith to confidently wait upon you.

In the meantime, thank you for your Spirit that ministers to us. I am overwhelmed by the goodness of your persistent presence in my life. I can see the deposits of your kindness all over my story. There isn't an area that you have left untouched by your mercy, and you are weaving the details of my life together with the unifying thread of your mercy. You are wonderful, and I trust you. Keep my heart anchored with hope, sinking into the ocean of your faithful love. You will not fail.

How can you practice patience in your perspective of life?

Pursue Peace

*Let us pursue the things which make for peace
and the things by which one may edify another.*

ROMANS 14:19 NKJV

When you look at the fruit of your life—how you spend your energy and time, what you promote in your relationships— what can be said of it? Are you continually caught in cycles of negativity, or are you producing fruit of peace? In God's kingdom, we are to be promoters of peace and love.

If you find yourself thinking "that's true, but…" It's time to call that into question. Can you ever show too much kindness to someone? Can you encourage another too much? If you find yourself trying to compensate for those things with a dose of 'reality,' then it may be time you consider what reality you are aligned with. Is it God's or the world's? It is never too late to offer mercy, the benefit of the doubt, and peace to those who need it. We need it, too.

Jesus, my giver of peace, forgive me for the ways that I have excused my lack of love for the truth. Your truth is always lined with love. May I be a promoter of peace instead of division. Thank you for this wake-up call.

*Make it your top priority to live a life of peace
with harmony in your relationships,
eagerly seeking to strengthen and encourage one another.*

ROMANS 14:19 TPT

Merciful Lord, from here on out, may it be my highest
priority to live as Paul encouraged—with peace and harmony
present in my relationships, eagerly looking to strengthen
and encourage others in you. In your family, we are called to
build one another up in love, not tear each other down in the
guise of truth. Your truth stands firm forever, and you are the
only wise judge. May I leave judgment to you and instead sow
seeds of peace in my relationships.

As far as I am able, may I extend the same kind of mercy I
have received so generously from you. When I am running low
on patience and understanding, may I see it for the warning
signal it is to spend time with you and fill up with love again.
When I am filled in your presence, I have plenty to give away
to others. Thank you, Lord, for abundance to draw from.

Are you pursuing things in this life
that promote peace or division?

Heavenly Citizens

We are citizens of heaven, where the Lord Jesus Christ lives.
And we are eagerly waiting for him to return as our Savior.

PHILIPPIANS 3:20 NLT

It is important to remember to whose kingdom we belong. As God's children, we belong to the kingdom of heaven, where the laws of the Lord reign supreme. Until Jesus returns and sets every wrong thing right, we are foreigners living in a strange land. The laws of this world are not the perfect laws of our God and King. We are sojourners in this short life, but we will find our forever home in the eternal kingdom of our God.

Until then, may we live according to his law of love as best we can on this earth. We eagerly await the fullness of his kingdom, but until then, we have his presence to strengthen, heal, and rescue us time and time again. He is our wisdom, our teacher, and our guide. We are not alone.

Lord Jesus, how I long for your return! I am expectant for your heavenly kingdom where all suffering will cease and only the glory-light of your presence will be needed to see everything clearly. Until then, keep teaching me your ways.

*We are a colony of heaven on earth as we cling tightly
to our life-giver, the Lord Jesus Christ.*

PHILIPPIANS 3:20 TPT

King of kings, I look to you as the ultimate example of loving leadership. I will follow your ways and your laws even throughout my journey in this life. I know that every sacrifice here will lead to reward in heaven. But the greatest reward is knowing you.

You set me free in the liberty of your law of love. Your wisdom never fails to separate the truth from lies. You are always full of clarity whenever I need it. Your perspective no one can match, for you see everything as clear as day! You are my life-giver, the source of my very being. Why would I try to wander my way through this life on my own when you have already agreed to lead me in love? Thank you for your family here on earth; may we love each other well and encourage one another until your return.

How does the kingdom of heaven affect
your choices here and now?

Submitted

You ought to say, "If the Lord wills,
we will live and also do this or that."

JAMES 4:15 NCV

In this passage of Scripture, James is warning the readers of this letter about being presumptuous with their future and plans. We are not promised tomorrow; therefore, if there is good that we can do today, we should do it. We should not proudly plan things far off in the future without being diligent with what we already have.

We do not know how much time we have, so when we plan, may we do it with the humility of this perspective. Whatever is in our power to do today, that should be our focus. Anything else must be humbly submitted to God, for it is in his hands either way.

Lord, thank you for your heavenly wisdom. Thank you for seeing things clearly at all times. Today, I offer you the work of my hands. I will do what I know to do, and I will do it as an offering to you. Everything else, I submit to your will.

You should say, "Our tomorrows are in the Lord's hands and if he is willing we will live life to its fullest and do this or that."

JAMES 4:15 TPT

Wise God, instead of focusing too far into the future and what you may be willing to grant me or not in this life, I offer you this moment. Meet me here with your tangible presence. Wrap around me like a warm blanket and pull me into the comfort of your love. Wipe away the disappointment from my brow and cover me in the glory-light of your compassion. I want you to be Lord over my every moment. As I fellowship with you in each one, you will lead me in love.

With my heart made whole in your mercy, I have kindness to offer others. Keep me from being too wise in my own eyes, and may modesty be woven into the fabric of my heart as I continually surrender my will to yours. Whatever comes, you will be good. You won't ever change. And knowing you and serving you is better than achieving great things on my own that will wither away.

Are you banking on your plans working out?

Eyes Open

We are approaching the end of all things, be intentional,
purposeful, and self-controlled so that you can be given to prayer.

1 PETER 4:7 TPT

There is wisdom in being sober minded about the times we
are living in. Sober minded doesn't mean overly serious, for
there is joy to be found in the presence of our God and King.
However, it requires living with intention, purpose, and self-
control. These are worthy things.

Let us build lifestyles of prayer. We have unrestricted access
to God the Father through Jesus through his Spirit. There is
not a moment where we cannot fully and openly communicate
with the Lord. May we learn to turn our attention to him as
often as we think of it. When a problem arises—pray. When
you are celebrating—rejoice and give thanks to God. When
you are down in the dumps—pour out your heart to God! In
all things, in all occasions, with eyes wide open, offer your
attention to God through constant communion.

Spirit, thank you for your presence with me. Tune my ears to
hear your voice and focus my eyes to see what you are doing.
I want to build a lifestyle of prayer and open communication
with you, not just at specific times. Thank you for faithfully
meeting me in every turn of my attention toward you.

The end of all things is near.
Therefore, be alert and of sober mind
so that you may pray.

1 PETER 4:7 NIV

Almighty God, I lift my eyes to you this evening, filled with
gratitude for your presence with me throughout this day. Keep
my mind clear in your truth, that I may be able to freely offer
you the prayers of my heart. Your love, oh Lord, is so very rich!
It fills me with reassurance and hope as I feel my burdens
being lifted once again. Thank you for the kindness of your
mercy that always flows so freely from your throne of grace.

I know that we are reaching the end; we are closer to it
than we've ever been. May I not take these days for granted;
keep me from wasting time. May I remember that you are
all that matters. I will continue to build my life around this
relationship—around you! You are worth it, and you will
always be. I believe that I will be grateful for the faith I cling to
now, when all is revealed in the light of your glory-kingdom.
You are full of light and life, and I come alive in you.

How can you build the practice of prayer into your daily life?

Even So

*"You meant evil against me; but God meant it for good,
in order to bring it about as it is this day,
to save many people alive."*

GENESIS 50:20 NKJV

When the trials of life seem too heavy to bear, remember that God is a God of restoration. What the enemy means for evil in our lives, God will use for good. Even from the most awful suffering under the hand of another, God can produce beauty. He does not let evil have the last word. He will not let loss be what defines us.

He is a God of overcoming love, and he will redeem that which seems gone forever. He is the God who makes a living army out of a valley of dry bones. He is the God who called to Lazarus to wake him from his death sleep. He is the God whose resurrection life broke the power of death once and for all. He will take every hardship and coax sweet fruit from the seeds that were sown in the dust of disappointment and watered with the tears of heartbreak. He is so much better than we can ever boast about him being.

Faithful One, may I not lose sight of your goodness even when I walk through the dark valley of despair. You never leave me alone, and you will lead me out with dancing; I know it. Please, don't let me go in the meantime. Minister healing and comfort as I trust in you.

> *"You intended to harm me,*
> *but God intended it all for good.*
> *He brought me to this position*
> *so I could save the lives of many people."*

GENESIS 50:20 NLT

Redeemer, thank you for your wonderful restoration power that works even in the most painfully barren situations. You never let anything have the last word over your mercy. It is your power at work in my life that turns my darkest hour into the most impactful and liberating portion of my story. You walk with me through the fires of this life, and you bring me out with a testimony of your faithfulness. Your love never leaves me alone. You are better than good news; your loyal love is the greatest news we could ever comprehend!

Expand my capacity to understand your lovingkindness. Deepen my gratitude as I watch you put together what was shattered by the world. Nothing is broken beyond repair; you breathe, and life is restored. You speak, and wounds are mended. You make me whole, and I come wholly alive in you. You are the goodness that every heart is searching for. It is you!

How have you seen God turn a terrible
situation around for your good?

Encouragement

Anxiety weighs down the human heart,
but a good word cheers it up.

PROVERBS 12:25 NRSV

When anxieties overwhelm our senses, what do we do? There are as many coping mechanisms as there are people in this world. When we are faced with the unknown, may we practice turning to Jesus. The more we do it, the more natural it will become. When we are filled with worry, we can take it all to God in prayer. He has plentiful, perfect peace to calm our anxious thoughts.

There is also so much power in an encouraging word from a friend. Good news can turn the tide of our angst. Instead of staying isolated in our anxiety, let us make time to talk to a good, trusted friend. Sometimes, an outside perspective is all we need.

Wise God, thank you for your promised peace that fills me as you remind me of your persistent presence that never leaves. Lift the load of my worry that I may diligently and delightfully do all that is mine to do today. As I share my life with others, may I be encouraged by what you are doing in their lives, as well.

Anxious fear brings depression,
but a life-giving word of encouragement
can do wonders to restore joy to the heart.

PROVERBS 12:25 TPT

God of my joy, I am so grateful for your love that never leaves me. You see the areas of life where worry and anxiety seeps in, almost incessantly at times. Will you fill me with the peace of your presence now, and give me eyes to see your faithful mercy at work around me? I need not jump into the unknowns of the future, for you already know everything that will happen, and every twist and turn in the road ahead of me. There are no mysteries to you.

May I be a person of peace and encouragement when others need it, just as my trusted friends and confidants are to me. There is so much joy in relationship; thank you for the community that you have set me in. Thank you for your love, above all. I am so very grateful. Turn my sadness into expectation as I fix my eyes on your faithfulness.

Where can you turn for encouragement today?

Qualified

It is not that we think we are qualified to do anything on our own.
Our qualification comes from God.

2 CORINTHIANS 3:5 NLT

Through the empowering presence of the Spirit of God, we are given strength to follow through on all that he has called us to. When Jesus commanded us to love our neighbors as we do ourselves, he did not say it lightly. It is not a suggestion, nor is it a requirement of being validated by God. God within us gives us the strength to love as he loves. His mercy covers our lives so that we have mercy to offer others.

What we do, we need never do in our own strength. God's grace empowers us to live lives that are worthy of his calling. Let us surrender our thoughts, our hearts, and our very lives to him. His leadership is what will guide us through the unknown into the light of his eternal glory, with peace and mercy as our resource and strength. It is God's compassion that changes us, and it is his love that leads us.

Great God, thank you for your mercy that is my constant connection to your presence. There is nothing I could do in a lifetime in my own strength that compares to what you can do in an instant with your power.

*We don't see ourselves as capable enough to do anything in
our own strength, for our true competence flows from God's
empowering presence.*

2 Corinthians 3:5 TPT

Mighty God, I lean on the grace that you give this evening.
Thank you for your compassion that covers my life, leading
me into restoration every time that I break connection with
you. You are wonderful in mercy, always covering the error of
my ways when I look to you. Though I cannot escape trouble
in this life, you are with me through it all. You redeem what
any other would say was lost forever.

I know the limits of my humanity, and I realize there is
so much that I cannot do on my own. I don't trust in my
own strength, but in yours. You are my holy help and my
confidence. You are all that I need, and everything I long for.
You are the ultimate treasure, and I will spend my life on you.
May I turn to you in every season, every moment, cultivating
the connection you so freely give in love.

How often do you lean on God's understanding
over your own?

Higher Thoughts

Set your minds on the things that are above,
not on the things that are on earth.

COLOSSIANS 3:2 NASB

When our minds are set on the things of this life, they will inevitably be overrun by the problems and shifting concerns of the world and its ways. There is no shortage of war, poverty, or strife in this current age. There is no escaping the pain of suffering that is happening around us. However, there is a greater reality at work.

When we set our thoughts on the kingdom of our great God, learning the principles and values of his ways over our own, we will see from the greater perspective of eternity. He is faithful and true in all he does, and he has not changed. Instead of getting caught up in the details of our lives today, perhaps we could practice perceiving heaven's reality. Let us look to him, and may we see the greater glory that awaits us in his everlasting kingdom.

King over all, I know that I only see in very small part, but you see the whole so very clearly. There is nothing hidden from your sight. I will set my mind upon your kingdom values and the wonder of your beautiful nature today. Thank you for glimpses of your eternal glory.

*Feast on all the treasures of the heavenly realm
and fill your thoughts with heavenly realities,
and not with the distractions of the natural realm.*

COLOSSIANS 3:2 TPT

Heavenly Father, your Word is like honey, sweet on the tongue. It is a refreshing break from the bitterness of this world. As I look to you today, flood my mind with the wonders of your kingdom's reality. Break open my understanding with the revelation-light of your living Word. There are so many distractions in this life, but your heart is full of pure love, peace, and joy that you freely pour out upon your people.

Why would I look for things that satisfy in this world when you are the only true satisfaction? Though temporary pleasures may soothe for a moment, there is no guilt in the pleasures of your kingdom realm. May I stay focused on you as you continually transform me into your likeness. I cannot help but want more of you when I taste your goodness. There is no bitter aftertaste with your gifts. You are pure in heart, in motive, and in all you do. I trust you more than any other.

What are your thoughts focused on these days?

Silent Support

*They sat on the ground with him for seven days and seven nights.
No one said a word to him because they saw how great
his suffering was.*

JOB 2:13 NIV

Have you ever been so overcome with grief that nothing anyone could say or offer made it better? Sometimes, there are no words to ease the deep sorrow we feel, for no one can truly understand our suffering, apart from God. In these times, it is the silent support of those who show up with love but without the need to offer empty platitudes that can truly make us feel seen and known.

Grief can be an isolating experience even when we are surrounded by those we love and who also love us. When those we are close to are suffering, may we be people who offer the support of filling needs without being prompted. And, when all else is done, may we sit with them in their grief, without the need to offer words of comfort that we are ill-equipped to give.

Comforter, thank you for your deep presence that meets me where no one else can. May I never forget what has ministered to me in my deep grief, and may I also offer it to others when they are in need.

They sat on the ground with him for seven days and nights.
No one said a word to Job, for they saw that his suffering
was too great for words.

JOB 2:13 NLT

Lord, your comfort is not a band-aid, but a healing oil that
seeps into the depths of my soul. You touch the parts of my
heart that are broken wide open under the pressure of deep
pain and sorrow. I'm so grateful that you do what no one
else can. Instead of offering words that seek to spiritually
bypass another's pain, may I learn to sit with them in their
grief. When there is suffering too great for words, there is
an invitation to put aside my discomfort and enter into the
pain with them. You are master restorer, and you are certainly
working your mercy's power in the lives of those submitted
to you.

When I am living in the peace of your promises, may I never
proudly look down upon those who are in seasons of undoing.
You are with them just as you are with me. You are faithful,
and you will never let them go. May I learn how to follow your
mercy into the discomfort of witnessing another person's
pain without feeling the need to fix it.

Have you ever known the comfort of silent solidarity?

Nothing Between

In all these things we are more than conquerors through Him who loved us. For I am persuaded that neither death nor life, nor angels nor principalities nor powers, nor things present nor things to come, nor height nor depth, nor any other created thing, shall be able to separate us from the love of God which is in Christ Jesus our Lord.

ROMANS 8:37–39 NKJV

Leading up to this Scripture, Paul describes how no troubles, pressures, and problems could ever come between those who Christ has declared to be his and his undying love. Jesus will never condemn those he has chosen. Again, let that sink in deeply today; in his love, Jesus will never condemn those who he is advocating for.

Though we may experience many trials and troubles in this life, nothing can ever separate us from God's love. There is nowhere we could run to where we could escape the reaches of his mercy-kindness. He is thorough in compassion, and his faithful love will not be deterred. Take hope today, for his love covers you through and through.

Christ Jesus, thank you for the overcoming power of your love in my life. There is nothing that your love will not overpower in my life as I continually submit to you. You are wonderful!

Despite all these things, overwhelming victory is ours through Christ, who loved us. And I am convinced that nothing can ever separate us from God's love. Neither death nor life, neither angels nor demons, neither our fears for today nor our worries about tomorrow—not even the powers of hell can separate us from God's love. No power in the sky above or in the earth below—indeed, nothing in all creation will ever be able to separate us from the love of God that is revealed in Christ Jesus our Lord.

ROMANS 8:37–39 NLT

Victorious Lord, what a glorious God you are! You poured out your love unto death, and you defeated the grave with your resurrection power. In your life, I have come alive. Nothing, nothing, nothing can separate me from your love. Let that truth go deep into my heart today as you expand my understanding in the revelation-light of your mercy.

Your nurturing nature takes care of me all the days of my life. You always welcome me in with lovingkindness. Your tender mercy meets me in every turn of my attention toward you. You melt my defenses in the warmth of your gaze. You shine on me, and I am undone in your presence. Thank you!

Do you believe that there is absolutely nothing that separates you from God's love?

Covered by Covenant

*I know that you will welcome me into your house,
for I am covered by your covenant of mercy and love.
So I come to your sanctuary with deepest awe
to bow in worship and adore you.*

PSALM 5:7 TPT

God's kingdom is one of mercy and love. It is the Father's welcome. Today, there is nothing standing in your way from entering his courts. Let love lead you in. Lay down your defenses. He is kind, holy, and infinitely wise. He has everything you need; everything you are looking for is found in him.

Will you let the wonder of your heart guide you into the light of his presence? There is more for you to discover in his love today. Worship him with adoration; you won't be able to help but do so when you catch a glimpse of his pure majesty. Turn to him, for he is already turned toward you with open arms.

Merciful King, I enter your courts with gratitude today. I humbly lay down my doubts and my hesitations. I want to see you as you are. I want to know you more. Thank you for the always-loving welcome you give.

*Because of your great love,
I can come into your Temple.
Because I fear and respect you,
I can worship in your holy Temple.*

PSALM 5:7 NCV

Holy One, it is because of your great love and mercy that I can confidently approach you. There are no checkpoints in your courts, for every curtain and veil that kept us from your holy presence has been torn. At all times, in all ways, you are with me. It is almost too much to comprehend! Language falls short when I try to come up with words to describe you. My words are not enough to express the great gratitude of my heart.

I honor you, Lord, for you have been, and will always be, faithful. You are pure in motive, your compassion great and long-lasting, from generation to generation. You are the ancient wisdom that we are all looking for, and you are the innovative leader that guides us in creative solutions. You are more than I can imagine, and all I'll ever need. I love you so!

Are you convinced of mercy's welcome over your life?

Priceless Treasure

How priceless is your unfailing love, O God!
People take refuge in the shadow of your wings.
They feast on the abundance of your house;
you give them drink from your river of delights.
For with you is the fountain of life;
in your light we see light.

PSALM 36:7-9 NIV

In God's light we see light. Does this seem too poetic to grasp? When we look to him, we can see from his perspective. He is the light of the world, and from his shining truth, we see truth. There is a never-ending abundance found in the storehouses of our God and King. His resources are unending. When we are in want, why would we turn somewhere else first, when he has more than enough to generously pour out in our lives?

May we always run to him first and run to him often. His love is the lifeblood running through our veins. He is our great hope and our deliverer. In him, all things will be made right. What he touches, he restores to life. May we not take for granted the wonderful generosity of his mercy in our lives.

God, you are my shelter, my resource of strength, and the keeper of my life. In you is everything I long for. I run into the abundance of your goodness today.

God, your love is so precious!
You protect people in the shadow of your wings.
They eat the rich food in your house,
and you let them drink from your river of pleasure.
You are the giver of life.
Your light lets us enjoy life.

PSALM 36:7-9 NCV

Giver of life, it is impossible to rightly thank you for all that you are. You are the source of my life, the giver of good gifts. You are the hope of my heart, and you are the light of my radiant joy! You keep me safe and secure in the refuge of your presence, and you take care of me all the days of my life. There is nothing that you withhold from those whose lives are hidden in you.

May I never wander away from the generosity of your heart, for it is what sustains me. You offer an abundance of joy, peace, and hope. Even when the winds of testing come, may my roots grow deeper in your love. You are the one I trust more than any other. I know you will not let me down.

How have you experienced the incomparable delight of God?

Delivered Again

The righteous person may have many troubles,
but the LORD delivers him from them all.

PSALM 34:19 NIV

No one's life can be rightly judged by the trials and troubles they face. Only the Lord is the righteous judge who can see into a person's heart. Do not let the circumstances of your life determine your faith in God, for God is faithful to all who look to him. Though you may have many troubles, the Lord will deliver you from them all.

Even in temptation, he always provides a way out that you may stand up under it. That's what his Word says. And even when you fall into sin, he is still your mighty deliverer. Sin and death do not have the final word on your life, for he has covered you in his mercy. Jesus has overcome every obstacle with his lavish love. His kindness covers your life, so continue to trust in him. He will not fail you.

Deliverer, thank you for your constant rescue in my life. You have done more than I could imagine, and certainly more than I have known to ask for. I look to you through every triumph and trouble, for you are faithful.

*Even when bad things happen to the good and godly ones,
the Lord will save them and not let them be defeated
by what they face.*

PSALM 34:19 TPT

Lord, I know that you don't let anything go to waste in your mercy. No circumstance or situation in this life can negate your goodness. You are constant in loyal love to all who look to you. When I begin to let the worries of what could be take root in my consciousness, I will offer them to you. You have not changed one bit! You are still faithful, you are still true, and you are still my mighty deliverer. When I am broken down by the pain of suffering, you are my close comfort, and the lifter of my head.

You will heal my broken heart and put together the shattered pieces of my hope. You will never fail me, and I rest upon that promise. You make whole what no human can. You restore what looks like a hopeless cause to others. You never tire of loving your children to life. Lead me, Lord, in your goodness. I will follow. Please, rescue me when I cannot see a way out of the troubles I face.

How confident are you of God's deliverance?

All Generations

*I will sing of the steadfast love of the LORD, forever;
with my mouth I will make known your faithfulness
to all generations.*

PSALM 89:1 NIV

There is a wealth of courage and encouragement to be found in the thread of God's faithful love throughout the ages. From generation to generation, he remains the same merciful King. The Lord cannot be convinced out of his love. It's impossible!

When we waver in belief, looking ahead at the daunting mountains we face, may we look back to see how God has faithfully delivered and led his people in mercy from the beginning until now. We have a living hope in the resurrection life and power of Jesus. He is the same God who shut the mouths of lions and who led his people into the promised land. Seek out the fingerprints of his kindness throughout previous generations, and you will be encouraged as you look forward with eyes of faith.

Faithful One, I look at your track record throughout history, and I can clearly see your love on display. May it bring courage to my soul as I continue to walk the road of this life. I am yours!

This forever-song I sing of the gentle love of God!
Young and old alike will hear about
your faithful, steadfast love—never failing!

PSALM 89:1 TPT

My God, I will sing about your goodness this evening. The song of my heart overflows to the melody on my lips. You are wonderful. You are glorious! You are full of love that never ends. Your everlasting kindness is my assurance and my strength. You do not leave even one of your loved ones behind. You are the God who leaves the ninety-nine who are on the path of life to rescue the one that has gone astray.

You are constant in compassion, and you are full of second chances. In fact, you don't put a limit on your mercy at all. It is never failing, never ending, and powerful to save. Why would I hide my joy when you are the pure delight of my life? You are too marvelous for words, though I won't stop declaring your goodness to all who will listen.

How have you recognized God's faithful love
in the lives of those who have gone before you?

Solid Ground

He lifted me out of the pit of despair,
out of the mud and the mire.
He set my feet on solid ground
and steadied me as I walked along.

PSALM 40:2 NLT

Can you pinpoint a time in your life where you were stuck and unable to move ahead on your own? How did God meet you there? How did he free you from the mess you were in? God is so faithful to us in his steadfast love. He does not pass us by when we cannot free ourselves. He does not abandon us even in the pits that we willingly go into.

He is the God who lifts us from the despair of our poor choices. He is the one who rescues us from the traps of the enemy. He is our loving leader, our constant help, and our merciful Savior. Are you walking on the firm foundation of his mercy? Will you let him guide you on the path of his laid-down love? He will steady you and be the arm that upholds you.

Savior, thank you for your love that reaches down into the depths of my despair and lifts me out of it. You are always dependable in mercy-kindness. I rely on you to lead me in this life.

He stooped down to lift me out of danger
from the desolate pit I was in,
out of the muddy mess I had fallen into.
Now he's lifted me up into a firm, secure place
and steadied me while I walk along his ascending path.

PSALM 40:2 TPT

Rescuer, I'm so grateful for your steady help in my life. No matter what I face, you are there with lovingkindness reaching out to me. When I am overcome by despair, you overcome it with your resurrection power. You lift me from the darkness of the grave, and you bring me out into the light of your glorious life. I walk in companionship with you, and you light up my world.

As long as I live, may my hand be found in yours. I know that your ways are wiser and purer than my own. I yield my heart, my soul, and my life to you. You are my radiant hope, Lord. Your love has steadied my heart, and you have given me visions of your greater goodness. How could I but follow you?

When was the last time God lifted you out of despair?

Shield around Me

You, O LORD, are a shield about me,
my glory, and the lifter of my head.

PSALM 3:3 ESV

The context of this psalm of David is that he wrote this when he was running for his life from his son, Absalom. He was in trouble, fearing for his very life. But David had a holy hope that was placed in God as Savior. He declared that the Lord was the shield that surrounded him and kept him safe. And we know this to be true. King David was saved, and his son defeated.

The Lord is with his people in every situation even when our lives are in danger. Let us have the same kind of holy hope that David exhibited in his life over and over again. The Lord is our shield, our strength, our glory, and the lifter of our heads.

God my shield, thank you for your help. I have given you my life, Lord, so I know that I am hidden in the shadow of your wing, tucked closely under your arm. I find rest here.

In the depths of my heart I truly know
that you, Yahweh, have become my Shield;
You take me and surround me with yourself.
Your glory covers me continually
You lift high my head when I bow low in shame.

PSALM 3:3 TPT

Yahweh, thank you for your constant presence that surrounds me. I am not alone—never alone. You are my help in times of trouble, you are my source of strength when I am weak, and you are the glory that continually covers my life. I will not trust in my own strength, or in the power of armies. I will trust in your mighty deliverance. I will trust in your merciful love. I will trust in you.

Lift my head when I am bowed low and restore the honor of my life when my character is brought into question. You are my hope, Lord. I have no other. Surround me again with the liquid love of your presence, that I may rest quietly in your confidence. Calm my heart with your love again.

Is your life hidden in Christ?

No One Else

*"No one is holy like the LORD!
There is no one besides you;
there is no Rock like our God."*

1 SAMUEL 2:2 NLT

Let us never forget God's goodness in our lives, and may we honor him whenever he comes through for us in faithfulness. This declaration is part of Hannah's prayer to the Lord after he gave her a son. She had prayed long and hard for a child, and after an encounter with Eli, the priest, she was given the answer to her prayer.

There truly is no one holy like the Lord. He is our rock, our deliverer, our loyal defender, and our God. He answers the prayers of his people. Pour out your heart to him, for he is reliable in mercy. Don't hold back your prayers from him, for he will answer the cries of his children. Do you not know that he sees you? He will surprise you with his goodness over and over again as you look to him.

Holy One, there is no one else like you in all the earth. Who else can we depend upon like you? You are faithful to your promises, and you are attentive to your people. Thank you!

"There is no one holy like the LORD;
there is no one besides you;
there is no Rock like our God."

1 SAMUEL 2:2 NIV

Lord, you are my rock; my life is built upon the foundation of your faithful love. There is no one else like you. You are always reaching out to me in mercy-kindness, lifting me from my despair with your present support and help. You fill my heart with joy, for you answer my prayers! I'm undone in the goodness of your glorious life in mine. No matter where I look, I see the marks of your mercy at work.

I'm overjoyed at what you have done, and I'm hopeful for what you will still do. You guide me through the terrain of this life with your faithful hand. You direct me with your gentle voice. Your wisdom is faultless. When you speak, I will listen. When you move, I will move with you. I will not stop telling people of your goodness, for you have transformed my life with your resurrection power.

What desperate prayers has God answered in your life?

Counseled by Wisdom

*"I will instruct you and teach you the way you should go;
I will counsel you with my eye upon you."*

PSALM 32:8 NRSV

When we are at a crossroads in life, what are the tools we use to decide which path to take? Do we rely on our own understanding and expectation of results, or do we take the time to seek godly counsel and wisdom? What role does God's Word play in our decisions? Let us not take for granted that we have the wisdom of the ages at our disposal.

Our God is full of discernment to share with us when we look to him. He is the most astute counsel we will ever know. Instead of leaning on our own perceptions, calculations, or passions of the heart, let us submit our ways to his. He will speak truth and life and give us the knowledge we need.

Wise God, you are full of pure insight and revelation. Why would I rely on my own limited scope of understanding when you are my counselor? I look to you, Lord. Direct me in your wisdom.

*I hear the Lord saying, "I will stay close to you,
instructing and guiding you along the pathway for your life.
I will advise you along the way
and lead you forth with my eyes as your guide."*

PSALM 32:8 TPT

Lord, stay close to me as I walk through this life. Instruct me in the way I should go, and I will listen. I know with you have the words of life, and I trust your merciful ways more than the temporary passions of my heart. Give me patience in the process, that I may be confident in your perception that takes all things into consideration.

I will not fear when you lead me into spaces I've never been before. Though I may have chosen a comfortable life on my own, I know that you have purpose in all you do. I gladly follow along with you, for your nature is beautiful and tested throughout time. There is no one better than you.

Does God's wisdom influence your decisions?

In Process

I'm fully convinced that the One who began this glorious work in you will faithfully continue the process of maturing you and will put his finishing touches to it until the unveiling of our Lord Jesus Christ!

PHILIPPIANS 1:6 TPT

In this journey of life, we are always in process. None of us have achieved the pinnacle of faith. We have not reached the highest mountaintop, for there are always higher heights to attain. Will we have the patience and persistence to trust that even when we are experiencing parts of our story that we may never have chosen for ourselves, God is faithfully growing us in his love?

Even the harshest climates produce life. Will we wither up in the changes of our lives, or will we burrow deeper into God's mercy? He is more than enough to sustain us. He will continue to be faithful, no matter what we do. Why not trust and partner with him in the process?

Jesus, my constant companion, I yield my heart to you again today. You are dependable in mercy, and you will never let anything in my life go to waste. Continue your wonderful work in me.

Being confident of this very thing, that He who has begun a good work in you will complete it until the day of Jesus Christ.

PHILIPPIANS 1:6 NKJV

Jesus, you are my everlasting hope and the joy of my life. I trust that what you have started to do in me, you will continue until your work is completed. Open my eyes to see what you are restoring and redeeming in my story. I want to understand how your love is weaving the pieces of my life together into a greater tapestry of your mercy. My greatest hope is the day of your return, where you will make all things right in you. What remains a mystery now, will be completely clear then.

You are my confidence, certainly not the limits of my own goodness. Though I fall and fail you a thousand times, you are right there to pick me back up again. Your extravagant love covers over my sin, and you make me wholly alive in you. I will not stop trusting you, Faithful One. You are my great assurance.

Do you trust that God is working
in the process of your growth?

Eternal Life

"For God so loved the world that he gave his one and only Son, that whoever believes in him shall not perish but have eternal life."

JOHN 3:16 NIV

Who of us has not heard of or read this verse multiple times over the course of our lives? It is the gospel summed up in a single statement. If this is our first time reading this, may the truth of it go down deep into our understanding. If it is the hundredth time we are meditating on this Scripture, may it come alive in the revelation-light of the Spirit within us.

God's love is so great that he sent his one beloved Son to show us the way to his kingdom. Faith in Jesus is the basis of our Christian faith. He is the way, the truth, and the life. No one comes to the Father except through him! He has given us eternal life—life that will never end—in the glory realm of his everlasting kingdom.

Everlasting God, thank you for salvation through your Son. You are my holy hope, and all my life is yours. May the whole earth hear, know, and understand that you are Lord over all.

"This is how much God loved the world—he gave his one and only, unique Son as a gift. So now everyone who believes in him will never perish but experience everlasting life."

JOHN 3:16 TPT

Eternal Father, what a beautiful gift you have offered us in the life, death, and resurrection of your Son. Jesus is the promised Messiah who paved the way to your presence. His death nullified the power of death and of separation from you. The veil that hung in the temple, separating the people (including the priests) from your presence, was torn when Jesus died. In his resurrection power, he called us all to overcoming life.

You are my master, not sin or death. You have overcome me with your wonderful love, and I get to know you in unhindered relationship because of the sacrifice of your Son. Thank you for the Spirit that works all these things out. Your Spirit's presence is the assurance of the things spoken of and of promises to come. You are beyond good; you are great!

Has your faith in Jesus produced assurance of salvation in your heart?

At a Loss

In the same way the Spirit also helps our weakness; for we do not know what to pray for as we should, but the Spirit Himself intercedes for us with groanings too deep for words.

ROMANS 8:26 NASB

The Spirit is our helper in all things. There is nothing that is out of his realm of expertise even the depths of our hearts. He sees it all so clearly. When we don't know how to pray, he is able to offer up intercession on our behalf.

Have you ever been so grieved that all you can do is cry? Have you ever tried to formulate words to pray but found that you had nothing to offer? What then? Have you ever been surprised by sounds that escape you in desperation? God is with you in all of it. He helps us in all of our weaknesses even in our weakness to pray.

Faithful God, thank you for your Spirit's presence and persistence in my life. I trust that you will help me whenever I need it, in whatever way you see fit. Thank you!

The Holy Spirit takes hold of us in our human frailty to empower us in our weakness. For example, at times we don't even know how to pray, or know the best things to ask for. But the Holy Spirit rises up within us to super-intercede on our behalf, pleading to God with emotional sighs too deep for words.

ROMANS 8:26 TPT

Holy Spirit, when I don't know what to pray, would you speak on my behalf? You already see the depths of my heart; you have that access. When I have nothing to say, no words to get out, the groanings of my own spirit communing with yours is all I can offer. You always know what I need before I realize what it is.

Rise up on my behalf, Lord. What a wonder, that even when I don't know how to pray to you, you step in and do it for me. There truly is nothing that I need rely on my own strength and understanding for. Nothing! Thank you.

When you are at a loss for what to say to God,
how has the Spirit stepped in for you?

Make It Clear

Don't hide yourself, Lord, when I come to find you.
You're the God of my salvation;
how can you reject your servant in anger?
You've been my only hope,
so don't forsake me now when I need you!

PSALM 27:9 TPT

God will never abandon his children. He says it time and time again in his Word. He will never leave us. When we look to the Lord for help, he will not deny it.

Have you given your life to the Lord? Are you depending on his strength to save you from circumstances out of your control? Rest in his unfailing love. He is faithful, and he always will be. Though you may feel as if you cannot sense God, he is closer than you realize. Ask him today to reveal himself to you. He will not let you down.

God my hope, I look to you today. Reveal yourself to me; open my eyes that I may see where you are already working in the details of my life. Show me just how close you are. I'm relying on you.

Do not hide Your face from me;
Do not turn Your servant away in anger;
You have been my help;
Do not leave me nor forsake me,
O God of my salvation.

PSALM 27:9 NKJV

God of my salvation, you are the one I depend upon in every stormy gale and on every sunny day. Though the winds of the world are constantly shifting, I know that you remain unchanging. Will you meet me again with your tangible grace and mercy? Enlighten the eyes of my heart to see you. I want to know you more.

You have been my help, and I need you to continue saving me. Do not hide yourself from me when I look for you. Open my understanding, that I may see how very near you already are. My life is built upon the premise of your faithfulness. My hopes rest on your unfailing nature. You are my saving grace, Lord. Calm my mind and heart in the perfect peace of your presence. I love you!

Have you ever felt like God was hiding himself,
only to find he was with you all along?

Overcome with Peace

"I have said these things to you,
that in me you may have peace.
In the world you will have tribulation.
But take heart; I have overcome the world."

JOHN 16:33 ESV

There is nothing that the sacrifice of Jesus left untouched. His power was made perfect in his resurrection, and there is nothing left to separate us from the love of God. He has given us his perfect peace—the peace that we have in relationship with God. This, no one can take away from us.

Though we may walk through many difficulties in this life, there is nothing that the power of Jesus' life in us, through his Spirit, has not already overcome. We are under the leadership of Christ, and what he says, goes. Let us take our cues and our courage from him. His living Word is active in this world and in our lives. He is doing a new thing. Let our hearts rest in his faithfulness as we journey with him in this life.

Jesus, my giver of peace, you are the one who settles my heart and gives clarity to my vision. When I look to you, everything else dims. You are my vision, you are my hope, and you are my overwhelming peace.

"Everything I've taught you is so that the peace which is in me will be in you and will give you great confidence as you rest in me. For in this unbelieving world you will experience trouble and sorrows, but you must be courageous, for I have conquered the world!"

JOHN 16:33 TPT

Faithful One, thank you for the reminder of your overcoming peace. Let it settle over me like a blanket now as I focus my attention on you. You are my great confidence. May I never forget it! What you lead me into, you will equip me for. There is nothing that is out of the realm of your powerful love.

You are the strength I need in every moment, and the wisdom that instructs me. You will show me what to do whenever I am unable to see the way on my own. Your insights are clearer than any I have attained on my own merit. Even when I am full of sorrow, your joy is an undercurrent, feeding the springs of my soul. I set my eyes on you again, Lord, for you are my great reward, and there is no one else like you!

How has God's peace affected your outlook on life?

A Better Gift

*"I am leaving you with a gift—peace of mind and heart.
And the peace I give is a gift the world cannot give.
So don't be troubled or afraid."*

JOHN 14:27 NLT

When Jesus rose from the dead, he spent forty days with his followers, encouraging and reassuring them. After that, he ascended to the right hand of the Father's throne in heaven. But he promised us that he would send a helper—the Spirit of God. He would be our comfort, our peace, and our strength.

He is the one who empowers us in all things, in every way. A blessed part of communion with God through his Spirit is the peace he gives that passes all understanding. No matter what is going on in the world around us, we have peace with God. No one else can offer such a thing! Look to him today and be strengthened by the Spirit's calming and clarifying presence. He is all you need.

Great God, thank you for offering us peace through fellowship with you, There is no greater gift than knowing you. Will you calm my heart and mind in the confidence of your nearness today?

"I leave the gift of peace with you—my peace. Not the kind of fragile peace given by the world, but my perfect peace. Don't yield to fear or be troubled in your hearts—instead, be courageous!"

JOHN 14:27 TPT

Holy Spirit, giver of peace, thank you for your perfect peace. When fear is closing in around me, may your peace settle and push back every anxiety. You are unchanging in merciful kindness, and I need never give into the fears of this world. Your higher law of love is the ruling force of my life. I follow along the pathways of your peace that lead straight to your kingdom.

Give me courage whenever I look to you. You are my confidence and my strength, the one who holds me together through it all. You are the one I look to when the shifting winds of change come. You are the one I rely on in the steady times, as well. You are everything! You are my holy hope, and I surrender to the wonders of your faithful love. Thank you for your constant presence, Spirit. Thank you.

Have you known the impact of God's perfect peace?

Steady Love

*Let your steadfast love become my comfort
according to your promise to your servant.*

PSALM 119:76 NRSV

When our lives seem to go off-track from what we once knew,
where do we look for reassurance? When our plans derail, are
we crushed in spirit, or do we have the confidence of knowing
one who knows better? When we are facing disappointments
and setbacks, the Lord is as near in loyal love as he ever was.

Let us look to him for the comfort our souls need. He is close!
No matter what you awoke to today, God's steadfast love has
not changed. He is still full of mercy, overflowing in peace,
and rich in joy. Invite him to meet you; he is the God of
fullness and abundance, not scarcity. Find your needs met in
his overwhelming love.

Constant One, thank you for the reminder of your love that
never changes in intensity. Fill my awareness with the purity
of your heart today. I depend on you in everything. Settle my
heart and encourage my spirit as I fellowship with yours. You
are so good.

May your unfailing love be my comfort,
according to your promise to your servant.

PSALM 119:76 NIV

Loving Lord, when my heart is confident in your love, I feel as if I could take on the entire world. When my heart is weighed down by worries, I feel hesitant to hope that you are as good as your Word proclaims. But! Your love remains consistent, no matter my confidence. May I never be so discouraged by my own lack of perfection that I project that onto you. You are consistent in kindness, and the power of your mercy knows no end.

Though I fail and fall, you never do. You pick me up with your strong right hand and lift me from the despair of my failures. You are so much better than any other partner, friend, or lover. You are better than the most attentive parent. Your love is purer, truer, and more glorious than any other. You are too wonderful to recount. Thank you for your faithful love that never leaves me. You have been so reliable, and you will never stop. Continue to be my comfort, my strength, and my song. I love you!

How has God's love comforted you?

All I Need

God will never give you the spirit of fear,
but the Holy Spirit who gives you mighty power,
love, and self-control.

2 TIMOTHY 1:7 TPT

When we are walking with the Lord, there are clear cues as to the fruit of God's Spirit in our lives. There are also keys for us to recognize what is not the work of the Lord in our lives. We know that God's Spirit is exhibited in love, in the power of his might, and in the ability to follow the Lord's ways over our own. The Spirit of God does not fill us with fear of man; rather, he fills us with confidence and boldness in his name.

There is nothing to fear when we stand on the rock of God's faithful love. There is no shame in proclaiming the goodness of God in our lives. He is wonderful; why would we keep that to ourselves for fear of how others may react? Let us proclaim his glorious ways, covered in the mercy of his heart and extending it to others.

Holy God, thank you for the grace of your presence in my life. When I have an opportunity to share about your goodness, may I not hesitate. And when I feel led in love to extend the kindness I have received, may I have the courage to do so.

God has not given us a spirit of fear,
but of power and of love and of a sound mind.

2 Timothy 1:7 NKJV

Father, thank you for the power of your Spirit. You did not see it fit to leave us without help. You sent your own Spirit to dwell with us and in us, to give us inner strength and to do your miracle work in this world. We need never rely on our own strength again. What you do, you do in mercy and with generosity.

When I start to feel the fear of man creeping into my consciousness, may I always turn it over to you. That is not what you offer. You offer power, love, and a sound mind. I can courageously rise out of the shadows of doubt and stand strong in the light of your truth and love because I have your help to do it. Fill me again, Lord, with the fresh outpouring of your mercy through your Spirit's life within. May it spring up like a geyser in my soul.

Where can you see the fruit of fellowship
with the Holy Spirit in your life?

Root System

*He will be strong, like a tree planted near water
that sends its roots by a stream.
It is not afraid when the days are hot;
its leaves are always green.
It does not worry in a year when no rain comes;
it always produces fruit.*

JEREMIAH 17:8 NCV

When our lives are rooted in the kingdom of God, there is plenty of growth that happens from the inside out. Our hearts, like a root system, go deep into the soil of God's love. There they draw upon the waters of his faithfulness. Even when there is not much fruit producing in our lives, it may be a time of exponential growth under the surface.

In the shifting seasons of life, there may be different markers of spiritual health in our lives. When we are grieving, we probably won't be carefree, for instance. But the fruit of God's Spirit at work within us will faithfully produce at the right time. In God's kingdom, there is never a drought. His kingdom is always full of abundant life. May we draw from his abundance at all times, through every season.

Father, thank you for welcoming me into your kingdom with open arms. May I be rooted and established in your love, growing deeper and stronger in your truth all the days of my life.

He shall be like a tree planted by the waters,
Which spreads out its roots by the river,
And will not fear when heat comes;
But its leaf will be green,
And will not be anxious in the year of drought,
Nor will cease from yielding fruit.

JEREMIAH 17:8 NKJV

Faithful One, I am so grateful for your goodness in my life. With my roots established in your mercy, there is more than enough room for them to grow and expand in you. You are the foundation of my life; may everything else flow out from this place. When I am discouraged by painful circumstances that cannot be avoided, will you remind me of your unfailing love that feeds my soul at all times? I am so thankful that there is always abundance available in you.

Though times of scarcity may come in life, you will provide for me through them all. You will be my generous Father, as you have always been. There is no fear of abandonment in you. There is no fear of failure. You will have your way, no matter what. Your life will always bear fruit in mine, for I am firmly planted in your kingdom.

From where do you draw your strength?

Covenant Promise

"My covenant I will not break,
Nor alter the word that has gone out of My lips."

PSALM 89:34 NKJV

God never changes. His unfailing love cannot be interrupted, not even for a moment. His promises are as good as his Word, and his Word will always be fulfilled. What he vows to do, he will do. In a world of empty promises, it is a practice of hope to believe that God is better. He is true, he is faithful, and he will never fail.

Are there promises that you can pinpoint in your own walk with him? What did he work out on your behalf? At times, you may have even forgotten, but he is still faithful to fulfill his Word. Take a moment and look through your history with him. What was something that he spoke over your life that you could not comprehend happening, and yet it did? Take courage from your experience and know that he is good, he is still working, and he will not leave you.

Faithful One, your Word is as good as done, In the waiting periods of promises, give my heart strength to persevere in faith. Thank you for faithfully fulfilling things I had forgotten about. You are so, so good!

*"How could I revoke my covenant of love that I promised David?
For I have given him my word, my holy, irrevocable word.
How could I lie to my loving servant David?"*

PSALM 89:34 TPT

Loving God, when I look through the Scriptures, your loyal love is on display for all to see. You never left your people, and you still haven't given up on them. You are our hope, our joy, and the one who works it all out in the end. Even when our faith wavers, you are still faithful.

Lord, continue to interrupt my life with your devoted love. When I am losing my way, unable to see your perfect plan unfolding, may I always tune into the gentle voice of your leadership. You never leave me alone. What a wonder! You are always close in mercy-kindness, redirecting me onto the best possible path for my journey. I look to you, Lord, for there is no other as good as you. You are full of truth, and the whole world will see it. You never lie. Thank you! I trust you, God. You are beautiful in all of your loving ways, coaxing beauty out of the messes that we make.

How confident are you in God's promises?

Abundant Goodness

*How abundant are the good things
that you have stored up for those who fear you,
that you bestow in the sight of all,
on those who take refuge in you.*

PSALM 31:19 NIV

Do you think that you have reached the end of God's kindness? Do you feel as though you have run out of second chances? May you take courage in the truth of God's Word today. May you know the greatness of his mercy as it meets you in a fresh way. Do not give up hope, for God is with you still. He is as full of lovingkindness in this moment as he was in your most courageous, triumphant period of life. You could never deplete his compassion, for it is endless.

Lay down your regret and shame at his feet today. Drink deeply of the goodness he offers. There are untold treasures stored up for you. Run into the shelter of his love again. Be restored by the rest and peace he offers in his perfect presence. Let your discouragement peel off and hope rise within your heart as you receive the fullness of his affection.

Good God, you are so merciful to me. Thank you for new opportunities to press into your generous love and to receive from the goodness of your heart. Fill me up, Lord, for you are my sustenance and every good thing I need,

Lord, how wonderful you are!
You have stored up so many good things for us,
like a treasure chest heaped up and spilling over with blessings—
all for those who honor and worship you!
Everybody knows what you can do
for those who turn and hide themselves in you.

PSALM 31:19 TPT

Wonderful Lord, who else can compare to you? There is no one in the earth who gives as freely, as generously, or as purely as you do. I am in awe of your goodness toward me. I am humbled by the great flow of your mercy-tide in my life. Open my eyes, that I may see what you have done and what you are doing. I want to give you all the credit for the goodness that you have placed in my life. Your works of mercy miracles are overwhelmingly kind.

Let the whole world know how good you are to those who come to you. Thank you for bringing me into your kingdom as a child as your own. You do not call me servant; you call me friend. You call me family. What a glorious mystery that is to me! That you would want to know me and have me know you in such an intimate way. I am undone by your love.

Where in your life have you experienced God's abundance?

On His Mind

*"See, I have written your name on my hand.
Jerusalem, I always think about your walls."*

ISAIAH 49:16 NCV

God is not some distant puppet master, interjecting his control tactics from time to time to keep us in line. No, he is a merciful Father, attentive to his children's needs. He is mindful of us. No one is excluded from this; he is aware of our deepest hopes and longings. He sees the reality of our circumstances, and he sees the way that he will work out his promises in our lives.

He is a tender caretaker, and he does not miss a detail. He is a faithful leader, and he will not lead us astray. He sees, knows, cares for us in ways that we cannot even comprehend. May we throw all our hopes on him, for he cherishes us.

Mindful One, thank you for seeing every detail of my life and for leading me through the twists and turns of it with faithful love. You are so attentive to me! I will not stop coming to you over and over again. You are the one I rely on in all things.

*"Can't you see? I have carved your name
on the palms of my hands!
Your walls are always my concern."*

ISAIAH 49:16 TPT

Wonderful Savior, you have not forgotten a single one of your followers. You have written our names upon your heart, and the scars of your hands bear the power of your love over each one. I am so grateful to be grafted into your family. You have welcomed me in with the open arms of a loving father and wrapped me up in your mercy.

What could have been held against me, you throw into the sea of forgetfulness. Your love washes over every sin, and you make me new and whole in you. Thank you for your tender care over my life. I submit every area to you, and I ask for your mercy to fill the details of my story. Bring it all together in your love, and may the bigger picture glorify your name. I see your kindness, Lord, and I cannot look away. Your love is better than life!

Do you trust that the Lord is aware of your life
and all its details?

Ready Help

God, hurry to help me, run to my rescue!
For you're my Savior and my only hope!

PSALM 38:22 TPT

Have you ever read through Psalms and thought, "Wow! David was in a lot of trouble in his life." The truth is that he had a wealth of human experiences. We tend to put heroes of faith on a pedestal, forgetting to account for the weakness of their humanity. David was far from perfect. But he was rescued by God time and time again.

Is this because he earned it? No. It is because he kept turning to the Lord, crying out to him as often as he was in need. He loved the Lord and built his life upon him. He messed up, repented, and gave thanks to the Lord—over and over again. He lived with relationship with God as his ultimate goal. He never stopped going to him, in times of celebration and in times of desperation. May we take his lead and always go to the Lord.

God, you are my help, so don't fail me when I cry out to you. Thank you for your faithful rescue in my life. You are my only hope!

Make haste to help me,
O Lord, my salvation!

PSALM 38:22 NRSV

Lord, when I am in trouble, hurry to my rescue. When darkness is setting in around me, be the light that overcomes it. You shine, and every shadow is lit up. O Lord, you have been my faithful salvation. Please, continue to be. I offer you the praise you are due in every season of the soul. Thank you for not looking for perfection from me, but for submission. I surrender my life to you over and over again. Only you know the best way to live, with purity, humility, and mercy. I want to be like you.

I know that you won't fail to answer me. You have been so kind, and I know that you still are! Show up in power and turn the mountains I face into anthills. May I step over them with the power of your Spirit. You are so faithful, and I will not stop calling out to you. I remember that you are closer than my breath. Even a whisper draws your full attention. Thank you!

How quick are you to call on God when you need help?

Chosen

You are a chosen generation, a royal priesthood, a holy nation, His own special people, that you may proclaim the praises of Him who called you out of darkness into His marvelous light.

1 PETER 2:9 NKJV

Though once we did not know the mercy-love of God, we have been brought into his glorious kingdom as children of the Most High. He has called us as his own—not to replace anyone else, but to enlarge his kingdom. May we know the identity we hold as beloved children, with the favor of God as our good and faithful Father. May we never cease to give him credit for his wonderful mercy in our lives. May we always declare his goodness, as long as our lungs have breath.

We have been grafted into his family, chosen to represent the King of love in the earth. May we live with the confidence of dearly loved daughters and sons, for that is what we are.

Great God, thank you for choosing me as your own. This is no ordinary, mundane thing! I am overwhelmed with gratitude, for you have called me from death to life, from darkness into your glorious light.

You are God's chosen treasure—priests who are kings, a spiritual "nation" set apart as God's devoted ones. He called you out of darkness to experience his marvelous light, and now he claims you as his very own. He did this so that you would broadcast his glorious wonders throughout the world

1 PETER 2:9 TPT

Lord Jehovah, I cannot begin to express the gratitude that overflows my heart when I think about your wonderful love toward me. You are so rich in mercy-kindness. Who else loves like you? You are the Creator of the universe, and yet you are mindful of me. You are the resurrection and the life, and you still think of me.

It is too much! And yet, I will gladly give you all the honor you are due. Your love is without blemish or hidden motive. You are pure in affection, and your love breaks through every one of my fears. Thank you. I won't stop surrendering to you as often as I remember to turn my attention to you. You are my great joy and the one who continually loves me to life.

Do you know the confidence of being God's chosen child?

Stick It Out

Blessed is the one who perseveres under trial because, having stood the test, that person will receive the crown of life that the Lord has promised to those who love him.

JAMES 1:12 NIV

There is a rich treasure to be found in the presence of God in our lives. He never wanes in lovingkindness. He does not withhold a single goodness from his storehouses of mercy from those who depend on him as their strength. May we never forget that perseverance is a part of our faith. When our lives turn on their heads, and we can't tell up from down, we have a steady anchor for our souls. Emmanuel—God with us— will never leave us on our own.

Let's keep going, no matter what happens, relying on his grace to strengthen us along the way. Let us draw from his mercy that overflows from his presence into our lives. He is near, he is for us, and he is not letting go. We can persist in confident assurance of his faithfulness.

Lord, thank you for your persistent presence in my life. Strengthen and encourage me when I am weak. I rely on you to help me keep going. I lean on your love today.

If your faith remains strong even while surrounded by life's difficulties, you will continue to experience the untold blessings of God! True happiness comes as you pass the test with faith, and receive the victorious crown of life promised to every lover of God!

JAMES 1:12 TPT

Father, as I journey through this life, may I never take my hand out of yours. You have been my loving leader, and I trust you to continue to guide me in your goodness. Though storms may come, your faithful love wraps around me like a cloak. You are my assurance. You are my hope. I will press on with your presence as my power. You are everything I need for every obstacle I face.

Sustain me when I waver, Lord, for I will not always stand strong. But even in my weakness, you are my steady strength. I want nothing more than to stand in your fullness when I have breathed my last breath in this decaying body. May I live for that day, with the vision of your glory as my guide. With you, I can do all things.

How has perseverance enriched your life?

Draw Near

I am praying to you because I know you will answer, O God.
Bend down and listen as I pray.

PSALM 17:6 NLT

What a wonderful, inexpressible reality it is that God hears us when we turn to him. He always does! When we don't know where else to turn, let us approach him. When we are at a loss for what to do, let's pray to him. He is faithful in love, and he will never turn away from us in our need.

He will not just hear us; he will answer us. Every time. He is that good. In fact, he is better than we can imagine. What a beautiful God he is. Let's not hold back a single thing from him today. There is an open line of communication here and now.

God, you are my God. You are my help in times of trouble, and you are my close comfort in times of sorrow. Though I can't seem to retain the enormity of your goodness, I keep coming back to you. You never fail. Answer my prayers in your mercy today.

You will answer me, God;
I know you always will,
like you always do as you listen
with love to my every prayer.

PSALM 17:6 TPT

God, you are such a good father. You always answer me when I cry out to you. I am overcome with emotion when I consider how good you are to me. Thank you! You never fail to show up when I need you in the power of your Spirit. You turn things around when I cannot see a way out. You shine your revelation-light and I understand what to do.

Thank you for your wisdom that brings clarity. Thank you for your kindness that wraps everything you do with the purity of your love. I can't begin to express the depths of my gratitude. It is more than words can rightly convey. But you see my heart, and you know its response. Thank you for deep calling to deep. You don't need my words. Thank you for fellowship, for knowing, and for deep peace.

How has confidence in God produced fruit in your life?

Move My Heart

Jesus, when He came out, saw a great multitude and was moved with compassion for them, because they were like sheep not having a shepherd. So He began to teach them many things.

MARK 6:34 NKJV

Jesus is the Good Shepherd. He leads us with tenderness, and he teaches us with the living understanding of his Word. He is moved with compassion toward his people. Will we not let him deepen our insights into his kingdom with his wonderful wisdom?

He gives us the wealth of his truth, and he teaches us with love so that we may follow in his footsteps into the great glory of his kingdom. He offers himself to all those who come to him. There is boundless mercy in his presence and unending revelations of goodness. Come to him with an open heart and let him feed you with the bread of his Word and the living water of his presence!

Good Shepherd, you lead me beside the still waters of your mercy and restore my soul. How compassionate you are. How wonderful! Teach me your ways, and I will follow.

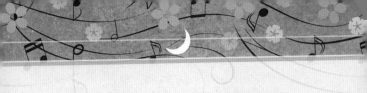

By the time Jesus came ashore, a massive crowd was waiting.
At the sight of them, his heart was filled with compassion,
because they seemed like wandering sheep who had no shepherd.
So he taught them many things.

MARK 6:34 TPT

Jesus, thank you for the leadership of your Spirit in my life.
Thank you for the mercy of your ways, for the kindness of your
heart, and for the wisdom of your guidance. May I be moved
in compassion, just as you were. As I live my life submitted to
your love, I will be transformed by it. There is no staying the
same in your kingdom. We are continually going from glory to
glory. As you mold me into your likeness, I become more like
you in mercy-kindness in my life.

May I stay humble in your love and throw pride aside
whenever I recognize its talons digging into my soul. Your
ways are better than my own, and I long to be led by your
compassion that moves me outside of my comfort zone into
the realm where your miracles happen. Give me courage and
give me wisdom. You are worthy of every act of submission
and surrender. You are worthy!

Have you ever felt the compassion of Jesus for others?

Here's My Heart

My child, give me your heart,
and let your eyes observe my ways.

PROVERBS 23:26 NRSV

What a wonderful God we serve! He is a good father, a faithful friend, and a close comfort and confidant. When was the last time you let go of what you thought you wanted in favor of the greater pull of God's heart? We can trust him with our dreams, plans, and futures. We can trust him with our present, for he is with us now. He is able to do more than we could ask or imagine in his goodness. He is more loving than we give him credit for. His mercy cannot be exaggerated.

Let's give him our whole hearts today and follow the loving lead of his kingdom ways. Every act of surrendered trust will be rewarded with his faithfulness. He cannot change from the loyalty of his love. Lean on him and find your strength. He will keep you whole and keep you safe.

Father, here's my heart. You can have it! I know that you will carefully tend to it. Heal what needs to be healed and restore what needs to be restored. Love me to life in your mercy again.

*My son, give me your heart
and embrace fully what I'm about to tell you.*

PROVERBS 23:26 TPT

Good God, you can have access to every part of my heart.
I know that I have already given you permission, but I
don't want to miss even the smallest bit of healing. I trust
you, Lord. You are faithful, and what you ask me to do, you
empower me to do. May your Spirit-strength infuse me with
everything I need to obey your Word.

I know that you are all about relationship and the give and
take within the bonds of this connection. Though I am still
learning your goodness, you already know me through and
through. You love me like no other can. The purity of your
affection is undeterred by my questions. You are not put
off by me in any way. Oh, how I love you! How I worship
you. Thank you for the overwhelming goodness of your
friendship. You are my God, and I will follow you, for this is
what I was made for.

Who holds your heart?

Save Me

He will care for the needy and neglected
when they cry to him for help.
The humble and helpless will know his kindness,
for with a father's compassion he will save their souls.

PSALM 72:12-13 TPT

One of the most beautiful pictures of God as father is in the parable of the prodigal son. If you need a refresher, Luke 15 contains this story. Jesus painted a picture of God as the patient and merciful father of a son who had gone off on his own and squandered away his inheritance. When he returned with nothing but his shame, the father ran out to meet him when he was still far off. He put his robe around him and welcomed him back with celebration and restoration.

Our Good Father is like this. He is there with a father's compassion to welcome us whenever we come to him. He is ready and willing to help us whenever we cry out. He never fails to show up in kindness.

Compassionate One, thank you for your wonderful kindness. It doesn't matter how many times I fall, you are there to lift me up and restore me. I am overcome with gratitude. Thank you!

He will deliver the needy who cry out,
the afflicted who have no one to help.
He will take pity on the weak and the needy
and save the needy from death.

PSALM 72:12-13 NIV

Faithful Father, you see so clearly the areas of my life that are in need of your intervention. I cannot pretend to have it all together. I am in deep need of your help. I know that you will answer me when I call out to you. It's what you do! I know that you will continue to show me mercy, for it is who you are.

Thank you for meeting me in the midst of my messes with your overwhelming grace. There is no situation that is too difficult for you. There is no problem that I get into that you cannot change with the sharp edge of your Spirit's power in my life. Thank you for your watchful care over me. I cannot begin to repay you, and you don't ask that I do. I want to know the depths of the riches of your kindness all the days of my life. May I never turn away from you. Keep me close in your love.

Have you known God's help in your helplessness?

Holy Helper

"The Helper, the Holy Spirit, whom the Father will send in My name, He will teach you all things, and remind you of all that I said to you."

JOHN 14:26 NASB

Our greatest teacher is the Holy Spirit. Does it seem strange to say such a thing? Jesus lived for a short time on this earth, and his ministry was only three of those years. He taught straight from the Father's heart. He gave us the keys to his kingdom, and he showed us the way to be restored to the Father. In Jesus, we have been brought into the kingdom of God's eternal reign.

But Jesus himself is the one who says that the Holy Spirit will teach us all things. Not some things. Not a select few things. All things. That makes the Holy Spirit our greatest teacher in this life. Do we live with this truth as our reality? As our confidence? He is the living Word, enlightening our understanding and leading us deeper into the realms of Jesus' mercy-kindness. He will never lead us astray, and he will never contradict what God has already made clear in his Word. Let us lean into his wisdom.

Holy Spirit, I'm so grateful for your leadership in my life. Teach me your kingdom ways, and how I ought to live in this present day and age. Show me how to align my life with the Father's heart. You are my guide.

"When the Father sends the Spirit of Holiness, the One like me who sets you free, he will teach you all things in my name. And he will inspire you to remember every word that I've told you."

JOHN 14:26 TPT

Father, thank you for sending the Holy Spirit as a holy helper to all who look to you. In your Spirit's presence, I am able to understand what I could never comprehend on my own. You teach me how to apply the words of Jesus to my life. Your wisdom instructs how to offer mercy when I would rather not. As I live surrendered to your leadership, I am led along the pathway of peace. You lead me in the way of laid-down love.

There is no better way to know you than through the fellowship of your Spirit. You make the Word of God come alive in my heart and mind. You move me in compassion, and I follow you outside the realm of my own limits. You are the strength I need in my weakness, the clarity I need in my confusion, and the joy I need in my disappointment. You set me free, and I am free indeed.

How has the Holy Spirit taught you God's ways?

Cheered On

*Since we are surrounded by so great a cloud of witnesses,
let us also lay aside every weight, and sin which clings so closely,
and let us run with endurance the race that is set before us.*

HEBREWS 12:1 ESV

Have you ever run a race? When you are training, it is one thing to persevere in preparation. Some days you may hit your mark, and others you may struggle to meet it. But there is nothing like the energy and thrill of a crowd to push you beyond your normal peak. Knowing that others are watching can cause one to gain a new burst of energy and focus. There is a finish line ahead!

In faith, too, there are times when we are pushing through with all we've got on the lonely stretches. But then we remember that there is a crowd of witnesses cheering us on. Let us throw off the things that hinder us and keep that pace. The finish line is not far off!

Great God, thank you for the reminder that there is strength to be found in the camaraderie of faithful followers in the race of life. I remember today that I am not doing this alone. Thank you for this reminder.

Since we are surrounded by such a great cloud of witnesses, let us throw off everything that hinders and the sin that so easily entangles. And let us run with perseverance the race marked out for us.

HEBREWS 12:1 NIV

Father, I will continue to follow the path that you have marked out for me in this life. I will not give up hope, for that would do me no good. Remind me of what's at stake here. Give me renewed focus and perseverance as I lean into your strength. When I am too weak to go on, come alongside of me and be the support that lifts me when I fall.

With you by my side, I will not fail. Though I may stumble, you will not let me wipe out. And when it feels as if the finish line will never come, will you give me a glimpse of the end? Will you encourage me through the cheering on of your witnesses—both those who have gone before and those running their own races? I know that you are faithful, and I depend on you. Thank you!

How does knowing that you walk a path that others have walked before encourage you in faith?

Big Picture

A thousand years in your sight
are like a day that has just gone by,
or like a watch in the night.

PSALM 90:4 NIV

In the great scheme of things, our lives are but a breath. They are like steam rising from parted lips on a cold morning, only to evaporate a second later. If our lives are so small, do they count for nothing in God's eternal kingdom? Certainly not. Should we live as though what we do doesn't matter in the long run? No way! The seeds of our faith will have eternal impact, though we may not be able to comprehend the effect.

God is faithful to fulfill his Word in every way. His timing is not our own, but it does not change that he is eternally faithful. He will always do what he says he will. In our lives, this truth is just as steadfast. Let's trust him above all else, and live our little lives according to his wisdom, for we will not be disappointed if we do.

Eternal One, what a wonderful mystery that you are mindful of me even though my life is a tiny breath to you. I am undone in the tidal wave of your love. I am like a grain of sand tossed in its midst.

One thousand years pass before your eyes
like yesterday that quickly faded away,
like a night's sleep soon forgotten.

PSALM 90:4 TPT

Everlasting Father, thank you for the perspective of your
eternal nature. I needed to be reminded how large you
are. You are unending! There is no beginning and no end
to you. Who is your creator? Who made you? You are from
everlasting, and you will be to everlasting. I am honored to be
yours. Though you may take longer than I would like to fulfill
some promises, your wisdom is unmatched. I see only a very
small speck of what you do, and I trust that your ways are
better than my own.

Keep my heart tethered to yours in loyal trust. You are worthy
of every bit of trust I could ever give you. You are better than
a thousand devoted lovers, and you are more wonderful than
the treasures of all the earth. What you give, no one can take
away. And what you take away, no one can get back. You are
the Redeemer, the restorer and unifier of all things. You are
my holy hope, and my life is built upon you.

Do you trust that God's timing
does not nullify his faithfulness?

He Won't Forget

God is not unjust to forget your work and labor of love which you have shown toward His name, in that you have ministered to the saints, and do minister.

HEBREWS 6:10 NKJV

God sees all that we do for him. He remembers every act of surrender, and he accounts for every extension of mercy and compassion toward others. Though acts of kindness may be overlooked by others, he does not forget a single one. Whatever we do in love has eternal effects. We won't know the extent of them until we stand in the glory-realm of our great God and King.

Let us continue to live lives of surrender to the one who sees it all. His opinion of us is the only one that truly matters. Let us not give up doing the good that he has called us to.

All-knowing One, may I never grow weary of living for your audience, and yours alone. It does not matter what accolades I receive or don't receive on this side of things. Faithful obedience to your love is all that matters.

God, the Faithful One, is not unfair. How can he forget the work you have done for him? He remembers the love you demonstrate as you continually serve his beloved ones for the glory of his name.

<small>HEBREWS 6:10 TPT</small>

Faithful One, you are just and righteous in all your ways. Your love is my constant strength and assurance. When I am discouraged by how life is unfolding, will you breathe your living Word of encouragement into my heart? I know that your ways are better than my own. I won't give up living in the overflow of your mercy. What I receive from you, I freely offer to others.

May my heart remain knit into yours; let the words of my mouth and the attitude of my heart reflect your love in every area of my life. I want to be obedient to your love more than I want recognition for my acts of service. I know that you see it all, anyway. You are worthy of my love, Lord. And you are worthy of all I could ever offer.

Whose acceptance are you living for?

Keep Asking

*"If in my name you ask me for anything,
I will do it."*

JOHN 14:14 NRSV

Directly before this, Jesus said that the works he did in his ministry, his disciples would also do—and even greater things. When we look at the ministry of Jesus, it was filled with miraculous signs and wonders. He promised that when we believe and follow in his ways, that we would also do these things.

What is the biggest, boldest prayer you've ever prayed? Let that be a starting point. May we never grow weary in asking God for the greater things he promised. May his signs, wonders, and miracles flow from us the way they did from Jesus' life, for the glory of his name and for the spreading of his fame. His Spirit is as living, active, and powerful as in the days of the early church. May we lift our faith to match his Word, not limit his Word according to what we've experienced.

God, you are a miracle worker. I know that you are powerful to save. You are also just as powerful to heal, deliver, and destroy the works of the enemy in our lives. Today, I will let bold faith move my prayers, for you are able to do even the impossible.

"Ask me for anything in my name,
and I will do it!"

JOHN 14:14 NLT

Great God, I am done asking for the bare minimum; you are a big God, with big plans and mercy-power that moves you to act on the behalf of your people. I lay down the limits of my faith, and welcome your Spirit's power to break through the mold that I have put you in. I know that you are better than my mind can conceive. You are healer, and you are the resurrection and the life. What you did in your ministry on this earth is but a taste of what you are still doing.

May I grow in boldness as I see you come through in miracle working power again and again. May my faith grow in proportion to your faithfulness. When I stop myself from praying the big prayers, will you remind me of your Word, which says that if we ask anything in your name, you will do it? You are that good. You are that powerful. You are that near. Thank you!

Is there something that you have hesitated
to keep asking God for?

Better Desire

They desire a better, that is, a heavenly country.
Therefore God is not ashamed to be called their God,
for He has prepared a city for them.

HEBREWS 11:16 NKJV

What is the driving force of your life? What is the vision you are moving toward? Do you have your eyes set on things that end in this life, or does your vision look beyond into eternity? What is seen with the naked eye is temporary, but what is unseen is eternal.

Today, will you adjust your perception to include the perspective of God's everlasting kingdom? May you trust the value of his kingdom ways over the world's ways. He is full of mercy to help you along the way. He gives grace to strengthen you. He pours his love over your life, and he will restore what you cannot make right in your own might. He is able, and he is with you. Lift your eyes to him today.

Holy One, you are the one I look to. I don't want to get distracted by the priorities of the world and its ways. May my whole life align in the mercy-tide of your kingdom. Living for you will always be worth it.

They couldn't turn back for their hearts were fixed
on what was far greater, that is, the heavenly realm!
So because of this God is not ashamed in any way to be called
their God, for he has prepared a heavenly city for them.

HEBREWS 11:16 TPT

Everlasting Father, as I build my life upon your love, you are renewing my strength with the endless flow of your grace and mercy. There is nothing I lack, for I have you. I fix my eyes on your forever kingdom that will never be overpowered.

While I walk the dust of this earth, sowing seeds of faith, you are the one I look to for every provision along the way. Even when I forget, you are near. When I get distracted, you lovingly redirect my gaze to your close presence. As I partner with you in this life, everything I do is made better because of your grace. In failure, you restore. In victory, you rejoice and bestow favor. You are too wonderful for words! I won't stop coming back to you. You are all that matters.

What is your heart fixed on?

Goodness in Store

"No eye has seen, no ear has heard, and no mind has imagined what God has prepared for those who love him."

1 CORINTHIANS 2:9 NLT

There is an endless treasure trove of wonders found in the great presence of our God and King. Directly after this quote from Isaiah, Paul goes on to say, "It was to us that God revealed these things by his Spirit. For his Spirit searches out everything and shows us God's deep secrets." (verse 10)

Though no eye has seen, no ear has heard, and no mind has imagined what God has prepared for those who love him, we have the Spirit who teaches us about these things. He gives us revelation-insights. He opens our understanding, that we might catch a glimpse of this greater glory. There is so much to discover in the wisdom of God through fellowship with the Spirit.

Spirit, thank you for revealing the mysteries of God to me through fellowship with you. Thank you for revelation-knowledge. Would you expose the glorious goodness of God to me in a fresh way today? I adore you!

*"Things which eye has not seen and ear has not heard,
And which have not entered the human heart,
All that God has prepared for those who love Him."*

1 CORINTHIANS 2:9 NASB

Wonderful One, there is no one like you in the whole world, nor will there ever be. You are full of wisdom, full of pure and loyal love, full of kindness, full of truth, full of joy. I could keep going on, but the wonders of your nature would never be rightly contained in my praise. You are so much better than I could ever give you credit for. And you love me! You love me completely, purifying my heart in your mercy.

Give me greater insight to the wonders of your unending love. You are beautiful. You are glorious. You are radiant. Show me your glory, Lord, that I might see, know, and understand how wonderful you truly are. I've caught a glimpse, and I want another. Spirit, reveal yourself to me again in this moment. I must know you more!

How confident are you of God's goodness?

Peace Here

"Glory to God in the highest,
and on earth peace among those with whom he is pleased!"

Luke 2:14 ESV

What a wonderful season to celebrate both the glory of God and the peace he offers. As we remember the glorious mystery of Jesus, the God-man who humbled himself to be born a helpless baby and raised in the limits of flesh and bones, may we also remember the great gift of peace with God.

There is no more striving for perfection according to the Law. Mercy's law has been perfected through the life, death, and resurrection of Jesus Christ. He is our holy hope. Let us lift our unrestrained worship to him today! Let us glorify his great and holy name, for he is our peace.

Mighty God, thank you for the gift of grace and for the peace that we now have with you through Jesus. Glory to your name. Glory in the highest! You are worthy of my adoration, my honor, and my very life. Thank you for reconciling us to yourself. I am humbled by your wonderful mercy.

"Glory to God in the highest,
And on earth peace, goodwill toward men!"

LUKE 2:14 NKJV

Wonderful Jesus, there is no sweeter name in all the earth.
Jesus! My hope, my salvation, and my resurrection life. You
have ushered us into the kingdom of our great God. You have
torn the veil that separated us from his presence. You are the
way, the truth, and the life, and there is no other way to the
Father. You bring us in with love to cover the errors of our
ways. You have washed me clean in the mercy-love of your
sacrifice. You are the only one who has the power to declare
my freedom, and you have made me free.

Your peace is unlike any other—unshakeable and perfect.
It drives out the incessant questions of my fear. It calms
the chaos of storms and raging people alike. Your peace is
plentiful. Surround me, fill me, and fully engulf me in it this
evening as I meditate on your goodness. You are wonderful.

How have you experienced the peace of God
in the worship you offer him?

Welcomed In

"Everything that the Father gives Me will come to Me,
and the one who comes to Me I certainly will not cast out."

JOHN 6:37 NASB

We have been welcomed in with open arms into God's great kingdom through Jesus. We come to him through faith, and he transforms us by the power of his Spirit in our lives. He will never turn us away when we come to him. Whatever your hesitations have been, leave them behind today and run into the arms of your loving God. He is already running toward you.

Let that sink in. He welcomes you with the undying affection of a father toward his children. He runs to meet you whenever you turn to him. There is nothing that could keep him from meeting you. His love compels him toward you, so run freely toward him without delay.

Jesus, I lay down all the things that have kept me from coming to you. I'm leaving them behind now and running into your presence. Meet me with the power of your mercy and encounter me with your love!

"Everyone my Father has given to me, they will come. And all who come to me, I will embrace and will never turn them away."

JOHN 6:37 TPT

Father, thank you for welcoming me back to you with restoration, celebration, and joy. You are the God of my belonging, the one who lifts me out of the disparity of my circumstances and makes me new. Your love is full and unwavering, and it covers over every mistake and error of judgment. You cover me with the robe of your righteousness, and you make it clear to everyone that I am yours.

When I find my home in you, there is no greater confidence of identity I could ever find. You are more than good, and you amaze me with your mercy at every turn of my heart toward you. Thank you for the overwhelming kindness of your heart, and for calling me your own. I want to spend my life knowing you more. You are so loving!

What is it like to know that Jesus welcomes you with love and acceptance?

An Open Book

All my longings lie open before you, Lord;
my sighing is not hidden from you.

PSALM 38:9 NIV

God sees everything that is hidden in our hearts. He sees our longings, both great and small, and he knows the state of our hope and our disappointment. He is a faithful God, but that does not mean that he does not meet us where we are in our weakness. When we are growing impatient and discouraged in the in-between of longing and fulfillment, how do we react to God? Do we let him into it, or do we keep him at a distance?

Surely, he is good. Surely, he is dependable. But even more surely, he is with us. He allows for the great depth and breadth of our humanity and every emotional expression. He is a safe place, and he will never use our vulnerability to wound us. We can trust him. May we experience the comfort of his presence today.

Lord, you see my longings. My heart is like an open book before you. Would you meet me in the vulnerability of this place and minister your powerful presence that imparts peace, belonging, comfort, and joy? You are my hope.

Lord, you know all my desires and deepest longings.
My tears are liquid words and you can read them all.

PSALM 38:9 TPT

Comforter, draw near to me again with the tangible peace of
your presence. I don't ever want to be without the confidence
of your nearness to me. I know that you store my tears, and
you read the prayers written in the depths of my weeping.
You are so much better than any coping mechanism I could
find. Rather than distract, you heal. Rather than coddle,
you confirm with words of truth. I love you more than I can
express, and I rely on you for any and every hope I have. You
are so gentle in your comfort, and yet you are the fiercest
defending lion when your loved ones are threatened.

I cling to you this evening. May I rest in your presence,
whether I am asleep or awake. Minister to the deepest parts
of my heart, and bring encouragement, strength, and holy
hope. I don't want to eke out a living in my own weakness any
longer. Be my overwhelming strength!

How has God met you in the place of deep longing?

Today

This is the day the LORD has made;
We will rejoice and be glad in it.

PSALM 118:24 NKJV

What a wonderful reminder from Psalms to embrace the present moment! Let us not be overcome with the regrets of yesterday or the worries of tomorrow. They are both out of our hands. Let's offer them to Jesus, who is with us now. His Spirit is our strength for this moment. Instead of dwelling in the past or jumping ahead into the unknowns of the future, may we slow down, and ground ourselves in this present moment.

This is the day the Lord has made. Let's rejoice and be glad in it! There is always something to be thankful for. May we count the ways turn our attention to the one who is with us. Fellowship is ours, here and now, with the Spirit of God.

Lord, thank you for today. Thank you for the breath in my lungs and for the new mercies of this very moment. Meet with me now with the power of your presence. Speak, for I am listening.

*This is the very day of the Lord that brings
gladness and joy, filling our hearts with glee.*

PSALM 118:24 TPT

Yahweh, I'm so grateful that you are present and constant in
lavish love in every moment. You are as full of kindness now
as you were this morning. You are as perfect in present peace
as you were when I was filled with the awareness of your
nearness. You are powerful, you are strong, and you are for
me. My heart fills with delight as I remember how wonderful
you are.

Refresh me again in the living waters of your mercy, and I
will breathe deep sighs of relief. Cover me in the kindness
of your compassion. Oh, but you already have! Thank you for
loving me so purely, so completely, and for restoring hope
in my heart. You are my great joy, and you will always be. I'm
thankful for this day, for your persistent presence, and for
each new moment that you meet me with the overwhelming
power of your peace and joy. I love you.

How can you give thanks today for what God has given you?

Highest Law

> *"'Love the Lord your God with all your heart,*
> *all your soul, all your strength, and all your mind.'*
> *Also, 'Love your neighbor as you love yourself.'"*
>
> LUKE 10:27 NCV

What does it look like to love the Lord your God with all your heart, all your soul, all your strength, and all your mind? We are each unique in our makeup and expression. This is a personal call to revival. It does not say that we must love the Lord in specific, rigid ways. This means that what it looks like for one person, will not necessarily look like it does for another. But it does require our whole beings.

How can we offer our bodies as living sacrifices of worship to our Creator-God? We turn to him in all things, forever building the relationship that he so freely has offered us. Let's give him the honor he's due. He is worthy!

Lord my God, I offer you my heart, my soul, my mind, and my strength as my worship. You can have access to it all. Teach me how to love like you do; I know that will happen most fluidly in relationship. Keep teaching me your ways.

> *"'You must love the Lord God with all your heart,*
> *all your passion, all your energy, and your every thought.*
> *And you must love your neighbor as well as you love yourself.'"*
>
> LUKE 10:27 TPT

Worthy One, I realize that submitting my thoughts, my energy, and all of my passion toward you means that you are the pinnacle of my life. You are my vision. Thank you for the grace of your Spirit that empowers me to live as you call me to. With everything I have, I will keep turning back to you over and over again. Open my understanding of your love as you reveal the lengths of your mercy every time I turn and return in surrender.

I'm so grateful that relationship with you is the standard. I'm not working anything off here. I'm working to know you more, and there is so much generosity in your affection. As I feed on the kindness of your presence, it is so much easier to extend kindness to others. Meet me and fill me again with the pure pleasure of your presence.

How does your life reflect these principles?

Abide

Let what you heard from the beginning abide in you.
If what you heard from the beginning abides in you,
then you will abide in the Son and in the Father.

1 JOHN 2:24 NRSV

In this passage of Scripture, John was warning against being led astray by "new" teachings that added to the Gospel of Jesus Christ. We have been given the Spirit, who affirms the truth of staying in close fellowship with Christ. He will never lead us beyond Christ to a 'higher' way because Jesus was, is, and will always be the way, the truth, and the life. If we abide in him, his truth abides in us.

There is a reason that relationship with God is so important. Trusting in the Spirit's wisdom to guide, instruct, and correct us, we get to know the ways in which God moves. We become accustomed to the tone of his voice, the fruit of his presence, and the clear indicators of his peace, love, mercy, and joy. We also become clearer about how he does not move—namely, in fear or shame. So, let us learn to abide in the truth of the simple Gospel, and not stray from his teachings.

Father, thank you for your truth that illuminates the shadows of doubt. I align my heart, mind, and life in your kingdom ways again. Lead me in truth, Spirit, for I am yours.

You must be sure to keep the message burning in your hearts;
that is, the message of life you heard from the beginning.
If you do, you will always be living in close fellowship
with the Son and with the Father.

1 JOHN 2:24 TPT

Word of God, thank you for the message of life that lives
within me. I am submitted to your ways above every other,
and it is your truth that brings me to the freedom of your
kingdom life within mine. Keep me close in fellowship with
the Son and Father through the communion of Spirit to spirit.
I want to walk in the ways of your mercy-truth that sees
everything clearly for what it is, and yet still offers grace for
transformation.

Lord, above all else, may my life be hidden in the great tide of
your kindness. The burning message of your love will never
lose its power in this world, and I pray that it never loses
its power in my life. Transform my life and likeness in the
radiance of your glory. I look to you every day, and I look to
you now.

How has the impact of the Gospel kept you close
to God in relationship?

Get Back Up

The godly may trip seven times, but they will get up again.
But one disaster is enough to overthrow the wicked.

PROVERBS 24:16 NLT

When we look at the 'greats' of the faith—Abraham, Moses, David, etc.—we often look at their triumphs. But they were not perfect people. They tripped many times in their faith and in their lives. But God's mercy met them time and time again when they turned to the Lord for help. It is the same for us today. God does not expect perfection from us. And when we fail and fall, we can never fall out of the reaches of his mercy.

Instead of wallowing in the shame of our defeat and mistakes, let's turn to the Lord and be restored in his lovingkindness. That's the destiny for those who believe and follow after him. Restoration is what we get. Redemption is what he does. Let's never give up, for he never gives up on us.

Great God, thank you for the endless chances of getting up again and walking on the path of your righteousness. I'm so relieved that you don't want perfection from me, but rather persistence and relationship. You can have it, Lord! You are so kind.

The righteous falls seven times and rises again,
but the wicked stumble in times of calamity.

PROVERBS 24:16 ESV

Merciful Father, thank you for restoring me in your kindness whenever I turn to you. It is not my own righteousness that qualifies me as your child, but your own. And yours is perfect and limitless. Jesus, it is through you that I have any relationship with God at all, and the fact that it is Spirit to spirit only deepens my awe. Thank you for your resurrection power that brings life out of death and breaks the chains of sin.

I am free in your love; I am free to make mistakes and be restored. I am free to do my best and have your strength in my weakness. I am free to run in the joy and peace of your presence. I am free! Thank you for so diligently caring for me. You are my rescue and my hope every time I fall. I never need to lean on my own strength or understanding, for yours is always accessible. Thank you.

How have you risen from failure in the past?

Yours

> *"Whatever you ask in prayer,*
> *believe that you have received it,*
> *and it will be yours."*
>
> MARK 11:24, ESV

Jesus did not make light of the fact that faith moves prayer into action. Right before this statement, Jesus said, "Truly, I say to you, whoever says to this mountain, 'Be taken up and thrown into the sea,' and does not doubt in his heart, but believes that what he says will come to pass, it will be done for him" (verse 23). There is tremendous power in the convictions of our hearts. When we pray with confidence, there is a response that happens even in nature itself.

Jesus demonstrated this as well, when he and his disciples were caught in a storm at sea. When his disciples awoke him because they feared that they would all die under the force of the storm, Jesus spoke to the winds and waves. "Peace, be still," he said, and the storm calmed. May we pray bolder prayers, full of confidence as we meditate on this amazing truth.

Jesus, may my heart have the confident assurance of pure faith in you as I pray bold prayers in line with my convictions. May my heart grow deeper in trust as I see your Word being fulfilled in my life.

*"I urge you to boldly believe for whatever you ask for in prayer—
believe that you have received it and it will be yours."*

MARK 11:24 TPT

Lord, you are the giver of my faith. The reason I have any
at all is that you placed it within me to begin with. May it
grow deeper, surer, and more confident as I follow in your
kingdom ways. I want to know you in spirit and in truth
more than I want anything else. I have tasted the fruit of your
faithfulness, and I long for more.

May I have bolder belief as I grow in wisdom and
understanding. May I develop stronger convictions as I see
how you faithfully come through for those who love and call
upon you. Through the fires of testing, may my faith shine
purer and brighter. You never let anything go to waste in your
hands, and even the circumstances that arouse questions
about your nature will somehow bring me closer to you
in truth. For the truth is that you never fail. Your mercy is
endless, and you are always faithful. I trust you!

How has your faith affected your prayer life?

Perfect Pattern

I want you to pattern your lives after me,
just as I pattern mine after Christ.

1 Corinthians 11:1 TPT

We are not left on our own to figure out how to live. The same principles that Jesus taught and modeled in his life and ministry are the same that we can apply to our lives. The wisdom of God through the ages still stands true today. Though the details of our lives may look different, the values of God's eternal kingdom still hold up.

They are not the same as the values of this world, for those are constantly shifting and redirecting us back to things that divide, promote self, and at the same time, self-protect. The standards of God's kingdom are found in peace, love, joy, unity, and mercy-kindness. When we align ourselves in these through Christ, we will reap the benefits of these fruits of the Spirit. When we promote these principles in our lives, we can have confidence that we are patterning our lives after the way, the truth, and the life.

Holy One, thank you that your kingdom ways are better than the ways of this world. I will pattern my life in the values of your love, following the example of Christ. Thank you for reminding me about what truly matters in life, and in what produces lasting fruit.

Imitate me, just as I also imitate Christ.

1 CORINTHIANS 11:1 NKJV

Great God, thank you for countless godly examples to follow in the lives of those who have submitted their wills to yours. Ultimately, we are all looking to imitate Christ and his lavish love. Thank you for the freedom to adopt practices that help to sharpen my faith and fellowship with your Spirit. Thank you for the humility of those who choose to walk the path of laid-down love, just as Jesus did. I am walking that path as well, and I know that you are worth it.

Will you give me new insights into how to develop deeper intimacy with you through this life? I want to know you more, and I know that much of that has to do with time and intention. My heart is yours, Lord. I will give you my attention, for you are the one who enlightens the eyes of my heart to understand your ways. You are so wonderful and so worthy of me patterning my life after yours.

How have you patterned your life after those who walk closely with the Lord?

Free from Guilt

There is now no condemnation at all
for those who are in Christ Jesus.

ROMANS 8:1 NASB

In Jesus, we are no longer limited by the weakness of our human nature. Sin is not our master, for Jesus has overcome every guilt and power that sin once held with the power of his sacrifice. His resurrection life has brought us fully alive in him. Death has no claim on our souls.

Once, we were compelled to pursue what only benefitted us, but now the Spirit that is alive within us motivates us to pursue the things that please God. We are in Christ, so there is no condemnation. We have been declared free from sin and death's reign and are alive in his love. May we live as those who have been liberated, no longer living in the guilt and shame of our past mistakes. We have been washed clean in the mercy of God, and we are white as snow.

Savior, thank you for calling me out of the darkness into your glorious light. You are the Redeemer of my soul, and in you I find fullness of life. May I forever leave behind the guilt of my sin and run into the great unknown with the confidence and liberty of belonging to you.

The case is closed. There remains no accusing voice of condemnation against those who are joined in life-union with Jesus, the Anointed One.

ROMANS 8:1 TPT

Anointed One, I am so thankful to be found in you. You have given me access to life that is abundant and free. In your mercy, I have been made new. What a beautiful reminder that you aren't finished with me yet. There is no voice that can condemn me, for you have already declared me innocent in the union of my life with yours. Thank you! Even endless thanks and praise would never be enough to express the true gratitude you deserve.

In areas where the lies of shame try to keep me bound up, would you break through with the power of your mercy? There is nothing hidden to you, and I don't want to be bound to any lies. You have already set me free, so may I walk in the confidence of your liberty in my life. You are so outrageously generous, God, and I'm so grateful to be yours.

Are you completely free of condemnation and shame?

Courageous

*"Have I not commanded you? Be strong and of good courage;
do not be afraid, nor be dismayed, for the LORD your God
is with you wherever you go."*

JOSHUA 1:9 NKJV

In the different seasons of life, we will face many challenges
and trials. We will not escape without suffering. We won't be
able to avoid pain. If we wanted to stay away from heartbreak,
we would have to insulate ourselves from love. And a life
without love is no life at all. An apathetic existence is empty
of meaning and devoid of the great expanse of emotions that
we were given to experience.

May we remember that love requires courage. Let us be
strong, for God is with us through it all. He is with us in
the ups and downs, twists and turns of life. He is with us
wherever we go, in whatever we experience. Take heart today!

Lord my God, thank you for being with me in everything, no
matter where I am. You are with me in the different stages
of life, and you never leave. Give me courage to love loudly
today.

"This is my command—be strong and courageous! Do not be afraid or discouraged. For the LORD your God is with you wherever you go."

JOSHUA 1:9 NLT

Yahweh, your presence is my strength. It is my courage, the reservoir that I draw from when I am thirsty, and it is my solid support. You are my solid support. No matter what the days bring, you are faithful. No matter the struggles I face, you are still strong in love. May courage rise within me whenever a new obstacle forms in my path. May I look to you quickly, before I do anything else. When I feel discouragement settling in, may a single glance to you dissipate the fog of disappointment.

You are ever so near, and you are full of wisdom. I know that you will not leave me to pick up the pieces of broken dreams and delayed longings on my own. I lean on you, God. And more than anything else, I breathe in the peace and confidence of your presence, and I take courage.

How does knowing God is with you give you courage today?

Growth

Grow in the grace and knowledge of our Lord and Savior Jesus Christ. To him be glory both now and forever! Amen.

2 PETER 3:18 NIV

Learning and growing in knowledge is a lifelong journey. Even Jesus grew in wisdom and stature, as the Word tells us. To develop and expand in wisdom is to be like Jesus. Let us never grow tired of the process of maturing in our faith. We don't ever truly "get there," for there is always more to discover in the unending lengths of God's mercy.

It is more than okay to admit that the things we have learned along the way have affected our understanding in ways that cause us to question the limiting beliefs we once took to heart. The truth of Jesus becomes clearer, and the extraneous religious preferences also do. May we not weary of the journey of outgrowing old philosophies and ideas and putting on the humble clothing of lifelong learners.

Jesus, thank you for your perfect example even in growing in wisdom and understanding. You are more than enough to settle every doubt, and the superfluous things lose their luster in your great mercy. Continue to teach me, for I want to follow in your ways.

*Continue to grow and increase in God's grace and intimacy with
our Lord and Savior, Jesus Christ. May he receive all the glory both
now and until the day eternity begins. Amen!*

2 PETER 3:18 TPT

Savior, you are worthy of all the glory I could ever give you.
You are worthy of the praises of every soul. As I grow in the
knowledge of your grace in my life, may I always offer the
gratitude of my overflowing heart. You are wonderful! You are
glorious in all your ways. You are kind, and good, and true.

As I grow closer to you in relationship, I can see the wonders
of your comfort, your peace, and your joy not only in my
understanding, but also in the response of my heart. You
heal what no one else can even touch. You restore what goes
unseen by others. You are our Redeemer, the rescuer and great
hope of every heart. I can't help but pour out my thanksgiving
to you, for you have made me new in your love, and you're still
doing it. Thank you!

How do you approach your faith as a lifelong pursuit?

Still Trust

When I am afraid,
I will put my trust in you.

PSALM 56:3 NLT

God knows us so well. He commands us to take courage and to not be afraid, but he is also patient with us in our humanity. He understands that we are limited in faith and trust, and still he offers us the fullness of his love over and over again. When we are afraid, let us put our trust in God. He has never changed. He is constant in loyal love, always extending mercy to us when we look to him.

He is the one true judge, able to decipher the motivations of every human heart and every worldly matter. He is a strong and mighty deliverer. He is the Alpha and Omega, the one true source of all life, and he is the King of kings. No one else compares to him. He exceeds all others in power, majesty, and authority. He is trustworthy. Call on him and put all your trust in him, for he is faithful.

Constant One, when I am afraid, I will put my trust in you. Bring my deep-seated fears to the surface today, that I may cast them before you. Give me your perfect peace, and I will rest in you.

In the day that I'm afraid,
I lay all my fears before you
and trust in you with all my heart.

PSALM 56:3 TPT

Faithful Father, there has never been another like you, and there never will be. You are so lavish in mercy-kindness. Thank you for delivering me from my fears. You give me the confidence of your presence, and my anxieties are put to rest. May my heart continually latch to yours in trust, especially when I encounter trials in this life. You are so faithfully loving toward me, and I am so thankful.

I want to walk in the assurance of your life within mine. I want to be more confident of your faithfulness than I am of anything else even more than the rising of the sun. Will you strip away the layers of self-defense and protection that I have built up over a lifetime? You are the one I rely on more than any other. You are my safe place, and my firm foundation. You are everything.

Is there a fear you can trust God with today?

Healed

*"Behold, I will bring to it health and healing,
and I will heal them and reveal to them
abundance of prosperity and security."*

JEREMIAH 33:6 ESV

Have you known God as your healer? Has he restored or made whole something that no one else could? He is constantly working in our lives to redeem and restore; this includes our souls, hearts, minds, and bodies. He is full of supernatural power to heal us, and he also sometimes offers us the wisdom of partnering with him in faith.

There are steps we can also take to seek healing. And God is in it all when it restores us and promotes our healing. May we not ignore the hunches that we have about taking steps toward greater wholeness in our lives when we have them. The Spirit often is speaking in whispers and in quiet knowing. He has given us intuition, and we can use it, knowing that he will help guide us into greater freedom in all he does.

Healer, I offer you the areas that I need your healing touch. Meet me with the power of your Spirit. Align my body, mind, and heart on earth as it is in heaven. Give me ears to hear your voice and understanding, that I may grow in partnership with you in my healing.

*"Nevertheless, I will bring health and healing to it;
I will heal my people and will let them enjoy
abundant peace and security."*

JEREMIAH 33:6 NIV

Good God, thank you for your restoration power at work in
the lives of your people. Thank you for your redemption,
which brings life and beauty out of the ashes of destruction
and suffering. You are powerful to save, and you are powerful
to create new things.

Breathe your peace and sense of security into my being. I
want to be so at home in your presence, that as soon as my
peace is interrupted, I look to you for answers. Your ways are
wonderful, and you are moving in my life even in ways I have
yet to see. Would you give me a glimpse of your healing power
and remind me of when you did what no one else could in my
life? You are so worthy of my surrender every moment, and so
I yield my heart again to your love. Be my peace, my strength,
and my joy.

Is there something you need healing for
or that God has recently healed in your life?

Mindset

Think about the things that are good and worthy of praise.
Think about the things that are true and honorable and right
and pure and beautiful and respected.

PHILIPPIANS 4:8 NCV

What we think about affects the quality of our lives. What we focus on will inevitably direct our actions. If our minds are constantly filled with worries, or if we are spending most of our time-consuming media, ideas from others, and so on, without space to have our own thoughts, then we may struggle to connect with God.

It is a good practice to take inventory of our thought-lives from time to time. In his letter to the Philippians, Paul encouraged them to think about things that reflect the kingdom of God in our lives. May we follow his advice and find the peace of God's presence in shifting our mindsets to things that honor him.

God of truth, I invite you into the thoughts of my mind. Bring clarity, peace, and truth. May I shift my thoughts toward your kingdom and your character, which is with me. Thank you.

*Keep your thoughts continually fixed on all that is authentic and
real, honorable and admirable, beautiful and respectful, pure
and holy, merciful and kind. And fasten your thoughts on every
glorious work of God, praising him always.*

PHILIPPIANS 4:8 TPT

Worthy One, I turn my thoughts to you now, and I welcome
you to rearrange old patterns of thinking into new pathways
as I continually turn my focus to you. There is so much
goodness to focus on, but when I get caught up in the
overwhelmingly bad news of the day, it can be almost too
much to turn around.

Instead of letting the world's noise dictate my thought-life,
I will make space for you to be my focus. May I grow ever
more sensitive to the things that I listen to, watch, or read
that promote anxiety, fear, and general thought-chaos. When
I find my mind going down a path that leads me away from
your goodness, may I redirect my attention toward you and
take the steps needed to shut down that mind-road. I choose
to focus on you and the ways of your kingdom, for there is
abundance of life found there.

What honorable, pure, kind, and authentic things
can you focus your thoughts on today?

Motivation

Every person's way is right in his own eyes,
But the LORD examines the hearts.

PROVERBS 21:2 NASB

Though we do the best we can with the information we are given, we still cannot know the full extent of the repercussions of our decisions. When we are making decisions, who are we looking to please? Ourselves? Or are we seeking to honor God and others through them? To be clear, there is so much grace in the heart of God for us.

But let us not abuse this grace by thinking we should do whatever we want to do, whenever we want to do it. If we truly want to know the freedom of God's love, then let's trust his heart and his wisdom. Let's yield our hearts and lives to him and let him lead us in his mercy, He is trustworthy, and we will find the fulfillment of all our longings in him. Remember, God is not looking simply at how we act around others; he is looking at our hearts, and he doesn't miss a thing.

Lord, purify my heart in your mercy-kindness, that my motivations may reflect your love. And when they don't, lead me and teach me, so that I may grow up in your wisdom. Thank you.

*You may think you're right all the time,
but God thoroughly examines our motives.*

PROVERBS 21:2 TPT

Wise God, you see the hidden motives of every heart even the ones we do not recognize in ourselves. Thank you for your mercy that leads me into your truth. I have lived long enough to understand how little I truly know. There is so much to learn from you. When I was young, I may have thought that I understood your ways. Now, I see as I grow in knowledge and experience that you are beyond comprehension.

You are constantly working in my life to bring about good. You are using the painful trials of this life to purify my heart and teach me to lean on your support. I know that you don't torment me, and you never will. You always move in love, grace, and peace. You hold me together when the world would tear me apart. You repair what loss has stolen. You are wonderful, and I will keep following you, for you are worthy.

What is the underlying motivation
for most of your decisions?

Blessing

"The Lord bless you and keep you;
the Lord make his face shine on you and be gracious to you;
the Lord turn his face toward you and give you peace."

NUMBERS 6:24-26 NIV

In the priestly blessing given from God to Moses, God instructed that Aaron and his sons should bless the Israelites in this way. It is a powerful declaration over their lives, and it is still powerful over ours. There is tremendous power in the words that we speak over one another. Proverbs 18:1 says, "The tongue has the power of life and death" (NIV). When we choose to bless others, we are offering the power of life. Also, when we receive a blessing from someone, it covers us with the same influence.

Take a moment and read this blessing again, and this time, receive it as one who is being blessed directly. When you have the opportunity today, choose to bless another in the name of the Lord. Use the power you have to spread life, not death.

Lord, thank you for the reminder of the power of my words in both my own and in others' lives. May I choose to bless and not to curse others. Keep me close in your love, that I may have more love to offer!

> *"May the LORD bless you and keep you.*
> *May the LORD show you his kindness*
> *and have mercy on you.*
> *May the LORD watch over you*
> *and give you peace."*
>
> NUMBERS 6:24-26 NCV

Yahweh, I am overwhelmed by the kindness of your love in my life. You keep me close to your heart as I walk through this life, leaning on you. You show me your kindness over and over again. You show me mercy as often as I turn to you. You are always extending the compassion of your affection to me. You continually watch over me and give me your peace. I am alive in the life that you have given! Thank you for never giving up on me.

May I offer the same kind of love that you offer me—so patient and kind—to others. Instead of reacting out of hurt and accusation, may I leave room for the benefit of the doubt. Whether or not another deserves my kindness in the moment, you always give it, so help me to bless those around me, especially those that I would rather not.

Who can you bless today?

Father's Help

Give us a Father's help when we face our enemies.
For to trust in any man is an empty hope.

PSALM 108:12 TPT

Where does your trust lie? Is it in your own abilities? Is it in the dependability of another? Or is it in God? Though we can find a dependable person in this life, we cannot find a match for our Good Father. He is not only reliable; he is all-powerful. He has defeated every enemy with his resurrection power that crushed the power of sin and death. Who else can claim such a thing?

Let us look to our Father for help whenever we need it. He is generous and strong, and no one can stand against him. Let him be our confidence, and not the feeble abilities of human strength. He will never fail to help us.

Father, thank you for your power that puts every person in their place. You are quick to save those who cry out to you. I know that I can rely on your help in this life. You are my hope.

Oh, please help us against our enemies,
for all human help is useless.

PSALM 108:12 NLT

Great God, turn the tide of my battles as I call out to you.
I am waiting on your intervention in my life, for there is
nothing I can do to help myself. Even now, I remember your
kindness. Draw near with the overwhelming love of your
heart. Wrap your presence around me like a shield that covers
me. Encourage me from the inside, out, and fill my heart with
courage to face every antagonist.

I know that you are with me. I know that you are for me. May
your mercy-kindness keep me steady in bold resolution as I
wait on your response. Be my help, Lord, for I have no other.
You are the one that I have put my hope and trust in, and I rely
on you. May this be yet another memorial of remembrance to
your great faithfulness in my life. I praise you, for you are not
through with me yet.

Do you trust in your Father's help more than any other?

No Comparison

*I consider that our present sufferings are not worth
comparing with the glory that will be revealed in us.*

ROMANS 8:18 NIV

Whatever you are going through on this side of heaven, know
that it will all be worth it. Suffering will not last forever. The
pain of separation and loss will one day be a memory. There is
nothing that you walk through alone in this life. Call on your
helper, the Holy Spirit, who will comfort, support, and guide
you. His wisdom will give you proper perspective when you
cannot see past the end of your nose. He will minister to you
in healing, and you will know the purity of God's love in his
presence.

What you do not understand now, you will comprehend fully
someday. When you are face-to-face with your Maker, all
of the present sufferings and trials will fade. Take heart!
Take courage and remember that God is with you now. He is
leading you into eternity.

Glorious One, would you give me a glimpse of your glory, that
I may take hope in the coming fullness of your kingdom?
I know that you are merciful. Be merciful to me and show
yourself. Thank you.

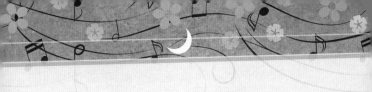

*What we suffer now is nothing compared
to the glory he will reveal to us later.*

ROMANS 8:18 NLT

Comforter, be near to me now in my suffering. The pain of this life and the troubles that I face are not skimmed over by you; you see them all. Will you minister to me with the close presence of your Spirit? Give me revelation-insights into your wonderful glory that is yet to be revealed in its fullness. Enlarge my capacity to understand just how large your love is. I want to know you more; I must know you more! May the confidence of my heart grow as you faithfully answer every cry for help and every whispered prayer.

You are so very wonderful in the ways that you minister to me. You are trustworthy, and I will not stop putting my hope in you. You are glorious, and one day, every question and doubt will forever dissipate in the light of your magnificence. Until that day, I will keep following you, for you are worth it.

How does looking ahead to eternity in God's kingdom help you to cope with your present circumstances?

Gift of God

*By grace you have been saved through faith;
and this is not of yourselves, it is the gift of God;
not a result of works, so that no one may boast.*

EPHESIANS 2:8–9 NASB

The grace of God cannot be overstated. His mercy cannot be exaggerated. It is by grace that we have been saved, through faith. And it all is a gift from God. Nothing we could ever do would be able to add to or take away from what Christ has already accomplished on the cross. We have not been saved and welcomed into God's kingdom by our own right. We do not earn our identity as his children. We have been offered the gift of eternal life, and it is the same offering he makes to all people.

May we never grow too proud of our religious lifestyles that we somehow think we are more deserving of God's love than another. His grace is long, and it is strong. It covers all our mistakes and levels the playing field among humankind. This is good, good news!

God, thank you for your great grace. I'm so thankful that there is nothing I need do to earn your love. You are that generous, and your love is that strong. May it influence how I interact with others, for you are worthy of every heart.

It was only through this wonderful grace that we believed in him. Nothing we did could ever earn this salvation, for it was the gracious gift from God that brought us to Christ! So no one will ever be able to boast, for salvation is never a reward for good works or human striving.

EPHESIANS 2:8–9 TPT

Gracious God, thank you for your wonderful grace in my life. What an enormously powerful gift. Help me to stop striving for your love, for I still see ways that I try to earn your favor. You have already said that I have it. Because you have made me your own, and called me into your family, I am fully accepted by you at all times. Even in my failures and when I fall, you lift me up and dust me off in your mercy once more.

Thank you for the beautiful gift of salvation. May it never lose its wonder! As I meditate on how generous your nature is, may I see the power of your grace working in the details of my life. May I always use the lens of compassion when I look at the lives of others. You are so amazing, Lord. You set the captives free and make us one in you.

How does salvation through grace
affect the way you approach others?

A Father's Compassion

As a father has compassion on his children,
so the LORD has compassion on those who fear him.

PSALM 103:13 NIV

When you consider God the Father and what he is like, what comes to mind? Do you know his compassion? Do you know his tender voice? He is so very patient with his children. He is so merciful. There is nothing that can stop his loyal love from reaching and covering his children at all times.

Are you afraid to come to the Father with your baggage today? Or do you know that he welcomes you with open arms and unhindered compassion? Whatever help you need, you have it in him. Whatever encouragement for your soul, it is found in him. Don't stay away, for you can never exhaust his love. It is flowing in fresh measure over you today.

Good Father, thank you for loving me so completely in every moment. I turn to you again, longing for a fresh filling of your mercy. Lift me up out of disappointment today. Speak your words of life; I am listening.

The same way a loving father feels toward his children—
that's but a sample of your tender feelings toward us,
your beloved children, who live in awe of you.

Psalm 103:13 TPT

Loving Father, you are the one who draws me in with kindness again and again. Your tenderness is like a warm fire on a cold night, and I can't stay away. You are so patient with me in mercy. I am in awe of who you are and what you've done. I know that you're not finished working things together in my life for my good and for your glory.

Keep drawing me closer in your perfect love. There's nowhere else I'd rather be found than in the ocean of your mercy-kindness. You are so good to me! Cover me tonight with the peace of your presence. Set in close and speak to my heart again. Your tender voice is calling me, and I'm turning to you. Your words of life are like food for my soul. I rest in your love again. Thank you.

How have you experienced the compassion of the Father?

Humble Love

Love is patient, love is kind.
It does not envy, it does not boast,
it is not proud.

1 CORINTHIANS 13:4 NIV

Choosing to walk in the path of Jesus' extensive love is the best choice we could ever make, but it is not an easy road. Love that is patient rejects the right to build walls of offense. Love that is kind requires choosing to act in mercy toward those who we may feel don't deserve it. Love that does not envy lays down the right to resent another for what they have that we do not. Love that does not boast does not leave room for us to overemphasize how kind we are to choose mercy. Love that is not proud means that we are choosing the humble path, letting our love speak for itself.

This love is pure and reflective of the heart of God. May he grant us the grace to walk in his footsteps.

Merciful God, your love is so different from the love of this world. I want to walk in your ways, but I need your help to do it. Teach me to follow your example in humble love. Thank you for grace along the way to strengthen, forgive, and redirect.

Love is large and incredibly patient. Love is gentle and consistently kind to all. It refuses to be jealous when blessing comes to someone else. Love does not brag about one's achievements nor inflate its own importance.

1 CORINTHIANS 13:4 TPT

God of compassion, your love is incomparable. When I am walking in pride, may you remind me how humble your mercy is. Instead of bragging about what I have to offer, may I remember that all I have is from you. You are the source of the kindness that fills my life.

Thank you for the reminder that your love is enough to fill, fuel, and spill out of my life. I need never rely on my own weak ability to extend mercy to others when it is your love that overflows. Your wonderful love is more than I can imagine earning. And you give it freely! You give it so selflessly, without a thought to what it costs you. May I be like you in love, giving the benefit of the doubt and not requiring anything in return. Your love is beautiful and pure.

Does your love align with Jesus' humble love?

Perfect Timing

*For everything there is a season,
and a time for every matter under heaven.*

ECCLESIASTES 3:1 NRSV

In this life, we will experience many different seasons, both physically and spiritually. It is helpful to recognize what season we are in. Ecclesiastes says that everything has a season. There is a season for celebration and a season for grieving. There is a time to laugh and a time to cry. There is a time to plant and a time to uproot.

When we expect to harvest in planting season, we will inevitably be disappointed. Let us be aware of the times, the seasons, and the signs of our current phases. And let us press into what God has for us here and now, in our current circumstances. He is always doing something.

Great God, you are over every season, every age, and every time period from the beginning until the end. Teach me to lean into your present goodness in my present season. I know that you are with me, and the marks of your mercy can be found right here and now.

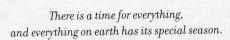

There is a time for everything,
and everything on earth has its special season.

ECCLESIASTES 3:1 NCV

Holy One, you stand far above the circumstances of my life. Whatever I face, you are with me, fighting for me to know your love. You are my mighty deliverer. You are my present help. You are my support, my guide, and my hope! I trust the timing of your perfect plans. You are wiser than any other, so why would I look for answers outside of you?

Give me your revelation-insights to help me see what you are already doing now. Give me vision to follow you, no matter the trials or troubles I face. Give me hope in my heart, as you lean in with your love and cover me with your kindness. You are the one I look to this evening. You are the one I look to my whole life long. You are faithful and true, and I will trust you. I trust you! You are so loyal in love. You are so plentiful in your persistent peace. Thank you.

What kind of season are you in right now?

Wonderful Counselor

A child has been born to us;
God has given a son to us.
He will be responsible for leading the people.
His name will be Wonderful Counselor,
Powerful God, Father Who Lives Forever,
Prince of Peace.

ISAIAH 9:6 NCV

Who is like the Lord our God? Who else would send his only Son to be the Kinsman-Redeemer of his people? Jesus, the Messiah and coming King, is the answer to our wandering ways. He is the anchor of our faith. He is the faithfulness of God, come in flesh and blood. He is the Savior of every soul. He is our great leader, our wonderful counselor, the all-powerful God, and the Prince of Peace. He is the Father who lives forever, for he and the Father are one.

As we meditate on the overwhelming goodness of Christ's coming, may awe and wonder rise within our hearts. He is worthy of our praise, now and forever.

Wonderful Counselor, thank you for coming to us in human form and for setting us free in your love. There is no one better than you. There is no love stronger than yours. I worship you!

A child has been born for us;
a son has been given to us.
The responsibility of complete dominion
will rest on his shoulders, and his name will be:
The Wonderful One! The Extraordinary Strategist!
The Mighty God! The Father of Eternity!
The Prince of Peace!

ISAIAH 9:6 TPT

Prince of Peace, when I think about the way you entered this world in humility, I can't help but be amazed by you. You are the King of kings and Lord of lords, and yet you saw it fit to humble yourself in humanity so that we might know God with us.

Everlasting Christ, you are worth all that we could ever offer you and more. The storehouses of treasure on this earth do not come close to your worth. You are the mighty God, our wonderful deliverer. You are our Savior, the hope of every nation. We find our being in you, our belonging in your eternal kingdom. You are full of glory, God, and I worship and adore you! My whole life is in your capable hands.

How has the glory of God's Son influenced your life?

Messiah

*"Today in the town of David a Savior has been born to you;
he is the Messiah, the Lord."*

LUKE 2:11 NIV

Today is the day that we celebrate the coming of our Lord
Jesus. He is Emmanuel—God with us. The Messiah that Israel
had been promised had finally come, born as a baby. Jesus
was not what Israel expected, though he was the Son of God.
He grew in stature and in wisdom throughout his life. He
experienced the full spectrum of the human experience; he
was a man acquainted with our suffering. He understands us
better than we know.

What a wonderful God we have! What a beautiful Savior we
serve. May we worship him with honor and reverence today
as we remember his first coming. He is worthy of all the
praise we could ever offer him.

Messiah, thank you for coming as a man and for leading us
to the Father. I look to your life today, and I remember the
wonderful gift of your life, your ministry, your death, and
resurrection. You are my Savior, and I love you.

"Today in Bethlehem a rescuer was born for you. He is the Lord Yahweh, the Messiah. You will recognize him by this miracle sign: You will find a baby wrapped in strips of cloth and lying in a feeding trough!"

LUKE 2:11 TPT

Emmanuel, you are the Lord, the rescuer of all people. You humbled yourself, leaving your throne in heaven to be born in a stable. You grew up in humble circumstances, the son of a carpenter. You grew in relationship with your heavenly Father throughout your life, as you matured in age and stage. You ministered to the lowly and broken and broke bread with outcasts.

You did not consider yourself too holy to spread your message of hope to any who would listen. Far be it from me to act proud when you were humble in all of your ways. The King of heaven set the highest example in laid-down love, so I will follow you. I will follow your ways. You are wonderful, King Jesus. I worship you!

How can you honor the Messiah in your life today?

Overflow

*"He who believes in Me, as the Scripture has said,
out of his heart will flow rivers of living water."*

JOHN 7:38 NKJV

Jesus is the way, the truth, and the life. He is the way to know the Father in spirit and in truth. He is the Messiah-King, and he is the giver of life. We are not expected to produce rivers of living water on our own—no. We look to Jesus, the author and perfecter of our faith, and he produces it within us. He makes fountains spring up within our inmost beings.

When our hearts are his, he will not let them remain dry, lacking, or yearning for what does not satisfy. He is our satisfaction. His love revives what no one else can even perceive. May we cast all our hopes on him. He is faithful, he is able, and he is with us, working his miracle wonders in our lives.

Christ the Lord, I believe that you are the Son of God. I believe that you are the only way to know God. Thank you for welcoming me into your kingdom and for reviving my heart in your living love.

> *"Believe in me so that rivers of living water will burst
> out from within you, flowing from your innermost being,
> just like the Scripture says!"*
>
> JOHN 7:38 TPT

Jesus, I believe in your wonderful love. I believe that you are the Son of God. I have been given your Spirit that confirms your power in my life. You make rivers of living water spring up from within, and there is life growing from the inside out. Thank you for your presence in my life that makes all things new. There is no dashed hope, no disappointment, no shame, no wound that is left untouched by the restoration and redemption power of your Spirit's life in mine.

Thank you! Where there has been dry ground in my heart, will you burst forth with the oil of your love again, seeping through every crack? Revive my weary soul in the confidence of your living love. Work your miracle power in my life. You are my holy hope, Jesus. You are it, and no other.

How has your belief in Jesus overflowed
from your heart and life?

Forgiveness

*"If you forgive those who sin against you,
your heavenly Father will forgive you.
But if you refuse to forgive others,
your Father will not forgive your sins."*

MATTHEW 6:14–15 NLT

Jesus was very practical in his advice to his followers. Though he often spoke in parables and stories, he also gave clear direction and application. When he taught about prayer and fasting, as we see in Matthew 6, he was clear about how to go about it. We should not showcase our holiness by praying for all to hear. It is, as we often see in his sermons, a heart issue. God sees our hearts, so we should not think that we can fool him by making displays of holiness when our hearts are full of pride.

After he taught his disciples to pray (what we know as the Lord's Prayer), he instructed them to forgive those who have wronged them. This remains true for us. Let us not overlook this important point. When we forgive others, God forgives us. We should never withhold forgiveness, for it will be to our own detriment, in more ways than one.

Merciful God, forgive me for my pride when I would rather let offenses build a wall around my heart than offer forgiveness. Help me, Lord, to choose forgiveness.

> *"When you pray, make sure you forgive the faults of others*
> *so that your Father in heaven will also forgive you.*
> *But if you withhold forgiveness from others,*
> *your Father withholds forgiveness from you."*
>
> MATTHEW 6:14–15 TPT

Loving Father, thank you for your abounding mercy in my life. May I never turn to another and refuse the same kindness that you have shown me. When I am tempted to withhold forgiveness from those who have wronged me, will you help me to see the bigger picture? Forgiveness does not mean that I allow them free reign in my life. It just means that I will no longer hold their sins against them.

When the hurt cuts deep, will your love go deeper still and knit my wounds together in the healing of your mercy? I must put on your love in all circumstances, for that is the higher way. I will let you be the judge, for that is your job and not mine. Above all else, I want your life to be glorified in mine. Spirit, help me to choose your love every day, letting go of offenses and seeking restoration and peace.

Is there someone you need to forgive today?

Great Confidence

The LORD will be your confidence,
And will keep your foot from being caught.

PROVERBS 3:26 NASB

When we align our lives in the ways of our great God and King, our confidence relies not on our own abilities and strength, but on his strength in us. He is strong and able to save us, over and over again. Do we need a reminder of his faithful rescue? Let us look at the lives of those who have followed him before us.

Look at David and how many times he cried out in his desperation for the Lord's help and deliverance. And didn't God do it? He is faithful, and he will always help those who depend on him. Let the Lord be our great confidence, above every other thing. He is powerful, he is willing, and he is reliable.

Lord, you are my great confidence. I put all my hope in your unfailing love as you guide me through the twists and turns of this life. You are my vision. Open my understanding even more today, that I may see how wonderful you are.

The LORD is your security.
He will keep your foot from being caught in a trap.

PROVERBS 3:26 NLT

Faithful One, you are my safe place. When the storms of life are raging, I run into the shelter of your love. Your presence sustains me. Your mercy uplifts me. Even when I end up in a different place in life than I had expected, your faithfulness is unmoved. You don't change your mind about me, and you never abandon me. I am surrounded by the peace of your persistent presence in my life. You are loyal to your loved ones. You are my God, you are my King, and you are my faithful Father.

I rely on you in every season of this life. I need you to be my close confidant and my loyal support. Keep me on the path of your love that leads to your everlasting kingdom. Keep me close to your heart of compassion and be my highest hope. You are the foundation that my life is built upon. I trust in you.

What is your greatest confidence in this life?

Making Things Right

After you suffer for a short time, God, who gives all grace, will make everything right. He will make you strong and support you and keep you from falling. He called you to share in his glory in Christ, a glory that will continue forever.

1 PETER 5:10 NCV

When seasons of suffering come, how is your faith affected? Do you feel as if you have been abandoned by God, or does his presence with you comfort you? Whatever you're feeling about it, can you recognize that God is as faithful as he has ever been? God promises to never leave or forsake us. He promises to always help us, rescue us, and strengthen us when we need it. He is our ever-present help in times of trouble. He is faithful to fulfill every promise he has ever made.

Though we are subject to the ways of this world while we walk this earth, his overcoming love brings power to our inner worlds and makes us overcomers. He will keep us from falling. God never promised us a life of ease on this side of things, but he did promise that he would be with us. And when he comes again, every wrong will be made right.

Gracious God, may I know your persistent presence with me in the hills and the valleys of this life. May I know your overwhelming love, for you are my strength and my support. I depend on you.

After your brief suffering, the God of all loving grace, who has called you to share in his eternal glory in Christ, will personally and powerfully restore you and make you stronger than ever. Yes, he will set you firmly in place and build you up.

1 PETER 5:10 TPT

God, thank you for the hope of eternal life with you. There will be no more pain in your unrestricted glory. There will be no more suffering. I remember that the suffering of this life is but a short time. The everlasting kingdom of your goodness will know no end. Thank you for that blessed hope, and thank you for your kindness in the meantime.

Draw near, God, as I draw near to you. I need your love to sustain, uphold, and carry me when I have no strength of my own. Set my feet on the rock of your salvation, that I may never be moved from you. Bring restoration to what the enemy has laid waste to in my life, and redeem what loss took from me. You are my only hope, and you are all I need.

Can you see the glory awaiting you beyond your suffering?

Wisdom's Instruction

*Teach us to number our days,
that we may gain a heart of wisdom.*

PSALM 90:12 NIV

There is so much wisdom to be found in relishing the present moment. When we learn to slow down and appreciate what we have, here and now, we cultivate an attitude of gratitude. When we are too busy rushing ahead or mindlessly checking off the to-do lists of today, we miss out on the agency of choice. We may miss the pleasure of the present.

May we learn to number our days, so that every moment becomes an opportunity to relish the joys of God's love and mercy in our lives. Let's not miss what he is doing already. Let's not rush through the stage that we're in right now. There is beauty here even in the messiness of life. There is wisdom in enjoying what we have while we have it, for we will never get today back again.

Wise God, thank you for the reminder of the importance of the present. Would you teach me to slow down and engage in my relationships in deeper ways today? I want to learn to enjoy what I have here and now. Thank you.

Help us to remember that our days are numbered,
and help us to interpret our lives correctly.
Set your wisdom deeply in our hearts
so that we may accept your correction.

PSALM 90:12 TPT

Lord, may I keep in mind that this life is limited. The opportunities to choose you, here and now, are numbered. Will you teach me to keep this perspective in mind? Lead me in your loving wisdom, that it may broaden my understanding of the brevity of this life. I want to be quick to turn to you, and even quicker to readjust when I feel your loving correction leading me in a different direction than I was headed.

You are trustworthy and kind. Your love is the fuel to my soul, and my hope rests in your faithfulness. May humility guard my heart and mind as I make decisions of where to go and what to do. May I never take for granted the time that I am given, and may I learn to appreciate the present. Thank you, Lord.

How does remembering the limited time
you have on this earth affect how you live?

A Fresh Start

*"I am doing a new thing;
now it springs forth, do you not perceive it?
I will make a way in the wilderness and rivers in the desert."*

ISAIAH 43:19 ESV

God is always doing something new. Is this hard to imagine? He is the God of innovation and creation. When we look at nature, we can see evidence of his endless creativity. No two snowflakes are exactly the same, and neither are two grains of sand. Every person on this planet who ever lived or will live is a unique expression of humanity. He does not do carbon copies.

In our lives, too, he often works in similar ways, and yet it is never exactly how he has moved before. He is original in his approach to every situation. Let's look to the new year, and the new opportunities ahead, with fresh eyes. He is doing a new thing. Can we perceive it? He will make a way where there has been no way. Selah.

Creator God, thank you for always working your love out in new ways on this earth and in my life. Give me eyes to see what you are doing. May hope rise from within my heart as I see hints of your coming glory.

> *"I am doing something brand new, something unheard of.*
> *Even now it sprouts and grows and matures.*
> *Don't you perceive it?*
> *I will make a way in the wilderness*
> *and open up flowing streams in the desert."*

ISAIAH 43:19 TPT

Great God, you are always up to something in this life. I need never worry about how your love applies to my life, for you are working out miracles of mercy. You lead me along the path of truth and life, and I find hidden treasures of your goodness along the way. Even the part of the path that leads through darkness is full of untold goodness. What is sown in tears is reaped with joy. Thank you!

I will continue to trust you and follow you, for you are faithful. I cannot fully comprehend the wonderful ways of your mercy-kindness, but I will spend my life leaning into you, nonetheless. As I walk along, deepen and broaden my understanding of your kingdom ways. You are wonderful, Lord, and my life is made whole in you. Continue to make a way for me where there was none before. I trust you!

What new thing can you sense God doing on the horizon?